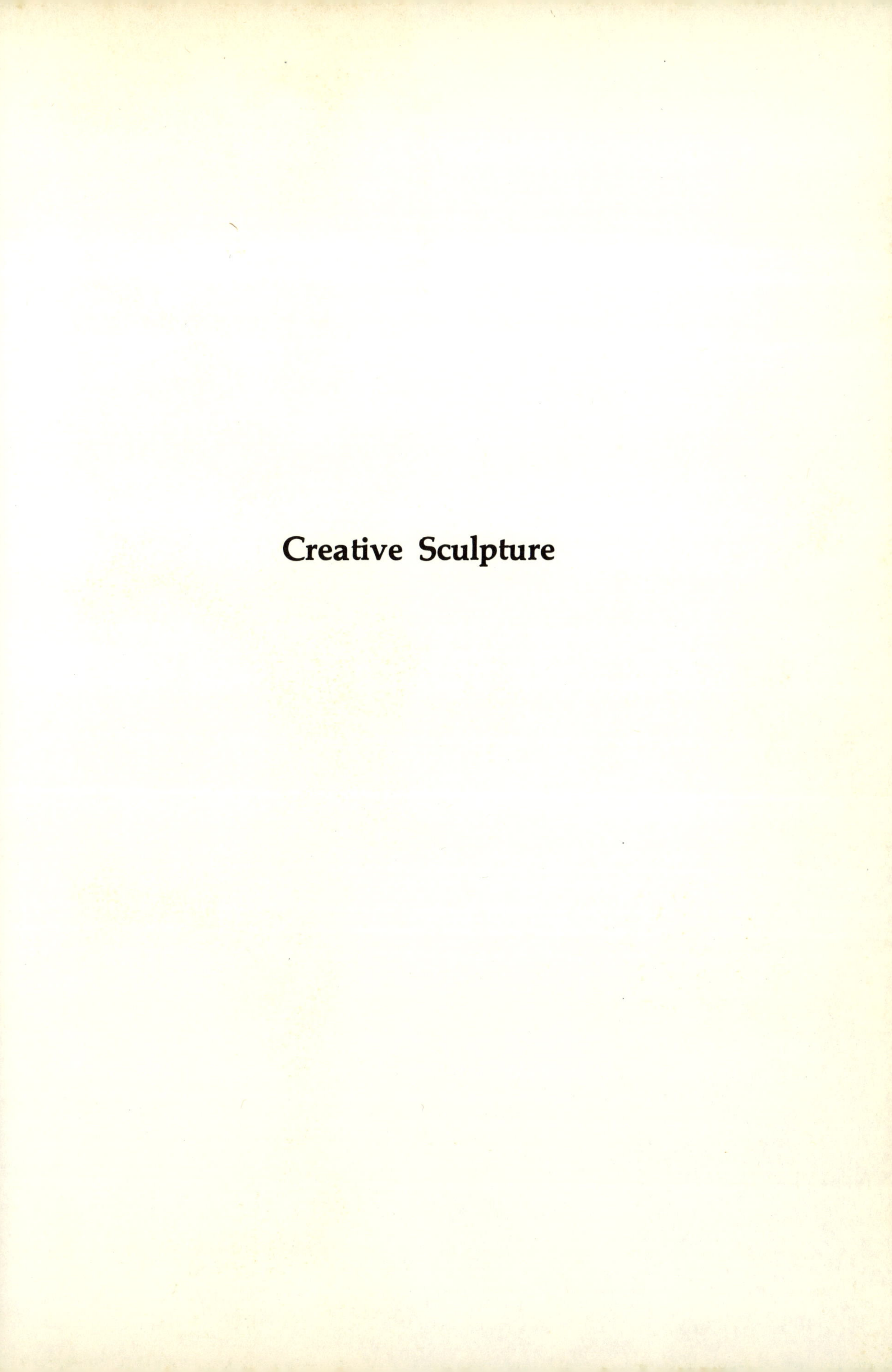

Creative Sculpture

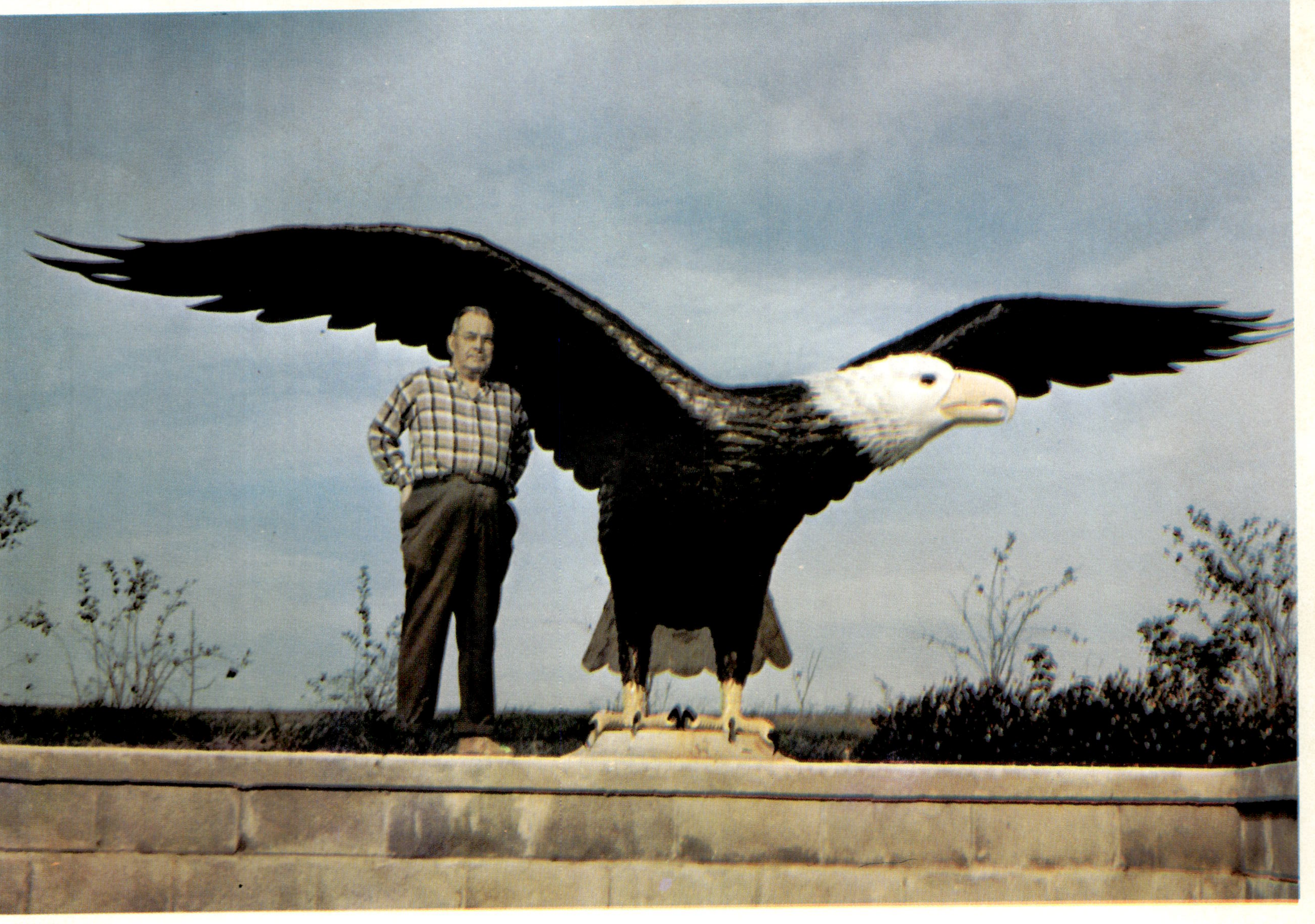

The author stands beside the Bald Eagle he fabricated of steel rods and sheet metal.
Photograph by Gra[illegible]

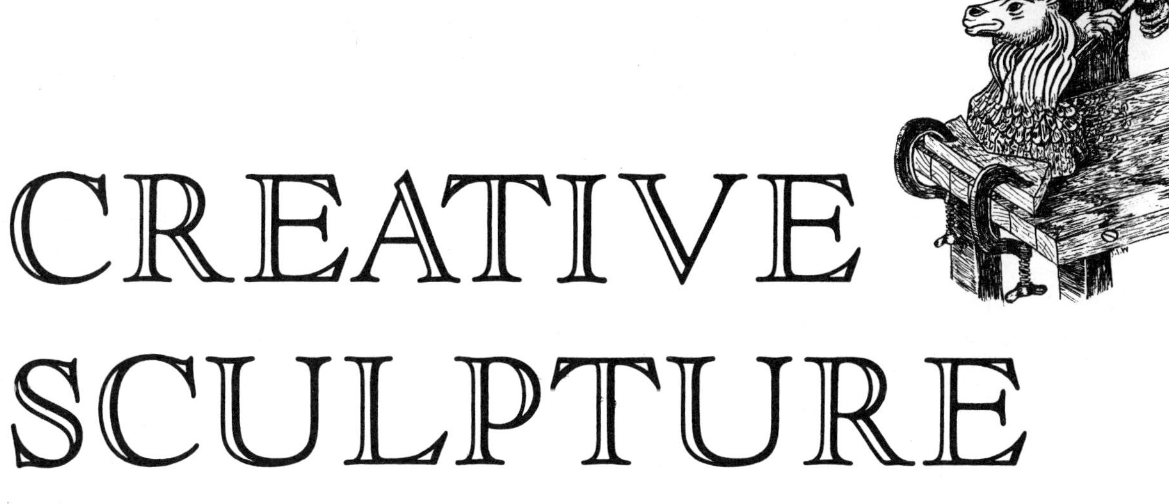

CREATIVE SCULPTURE

By

William I. Tawes

ILLUSTRATED

TIDEWATER PUBLISHERS / *Cambridge, Maryland*

1976

Library of Congress Cataloging in Publication Data

Tawes, William I
Creative sculpture.

Includes bibliographical references and index.
1. Sculpture–Technique. 2. Carving (Art industries) I. Title.
NB1170.T34 730 76–10862
ISBN 0–87033–219-8

Title page designed by G. William Kirschenhofer; printed and bound in the United States of America by Universal Lithographers, Inc., Cockeysville, Maryland and Optic Bindery, Glen Burnie, Maryland.

For Maria

Also by William I. Tawes

God, Man, Salt Water and the Eastern Shore

Creative Bird Carving

Contents

Acknowledgments

Many individuals have had a part in writing this book—some conspicuously, as Robert H. Burgess, Curator of Exhibits, The Mariners Museum, Newport News, Virginia. The chapter on *Figureheads* could not have been written without his kind assistance. He not only supplied all of the photographs, but was very helpful in other respects. Permission to use the Museum and his general enthusiastic support are deeply appreciated. His Assistant, H.C. Hancock, was carving a figurehead in the Museum at the time with the able assistance of Robert Brushwood, a professional artist. The pictures of the figurehead and the substance of the context concerning it are largely the work of Mr. Hancock. In this respect the Curators of both of the Academies, Army and Navy, were very cooperative in supplying me with the photographs I requested.

The editor of *Chip Chats* Magazine, Edward F. Gallenstein, was especially helpful in permitting me to reproduce any material I desired from his publication. His generosity is gratefully appreciated.

John Rood, the able sculptor in both wood and metal, became a martyr to his art while I was negotiating for his *Goin' Home* photograph. He died of cancer caused by the fumes from his torch. The pathos of the occasion prompted me to note his passing.

There were several writers who kindly permitted me to quote from their articles. Among them was A.G. Ivey, Director, News Bureau, University of North Carolina. His thoughts are reflected in the write-up on Carl Boettcher.

Alfred A. Knopf, Inc., kindly permitted me to use two photographs from their publication, *The First Civilizations,* by Jacquetta Hawkes.

Many sculptors from whom I requested photographs representative of their work responded favorably. Only a few ignored my request. Those who sent photographs of their work have been given special recognition in the text, and I hope greatly to their advantage. Their wonderful cooperation significantly contributed to the quality of the material which I have presented.

The lady of the Pond, Mrs. Frances Teal, should be given appropriate recognition for her story concerning her pet Canada Geese. She graciously loaned me the negatives for the pictures of Mickey and Minnie.

Harvey Z. Yellin, son of the metal-working genius, Samuel, invited me to visit his Museum in Philadelphia, where some of his father's work is exhibited. He allowed me to take many pictures, some of which are reproduced in the chapter on *Metal Sculpture.* My special thanks to the son of the poet in wrought iron for his cooperation. I hope my book will help to perpetuate the memory of his father who was probably the greatest metal sculptor of this century.

Ivan Bailey, who recently has won some fame as a metal sculptor, is a young enthusiastic artist. He sent me several photographs of his work and a brief account of his activities. His contributions are deeply appreciated.

Finally, I wish to express my appreciation for the help given me by all individuals who have not been specifically named in these paragraphs.

W.I.T.

Foreword

Creative Sculpture is intended as a sequel to *Creative Bird Carving.** The latter book was so successful that it exceeded the fondest hope of the author. It was written for beginners in the creative arts and directed specifically toward carving birds and painting them realistically. Many wildfowl carvers, now well known, have confessed that they had never carved a chip until they read *Creative Bird Carving.* Such heady, flattering remarks were the main inspirational drive and reason for attempting the present volume. None of it is theory (except as otherwise noted) but hard-earned "know-how" developed over the years. As far as the author is concerned, all of the material is original and many techniques have never been published before, to his knowledge. Such material certainly should be made available to artisans, craftsmen, and especially to all young artists climbing up the ladder of creativity, rung by rung. The text is an extension of the actual carving experiences of the author, including some editorial, philosophical padding to make more comfortable–it is hoped–the difficult technical procedures.

The assumption is made in the beginning that certain experiences beyond the beginner's stage have been a part of the reader's preparation. This does not mean, however, that inexperienced persons should be discouraged from reading the book. On the contrary, as discussed elsewhere, many individuals are unconscious of their powers and are as able to grasp technical instruction as well as others who have had years of carving experience. They require only the fanning of the spark of their creative talent to cause their latent abilities to burst into flame. But the book has been designed, primarily, for those who would like to have help beyond that given in *Creative Bird Carving,* and who desire to widen their field of activities; or challenge their abilities to perform on a higher level of creative effort.

Three distinct media have been presented for the reader to explore. In most instances interesting projects have been suggested to challenge his skills. Wood carving has been given the emphasis, but metal and cement have also been included to whet the appetite of those who hunger to express themselves in other media. Because of the growing popularity of metal sculpture, a chapter has been devoted entirely to this art. Stretching metal to artistic shapes is one of the oldest arts. It has been given a new dimension by the automotive industries with their huge presses several stories high. Fabrication of steel parts into real sculptural forms is also a comparatively new form of artistic expression, but the formation of images with nonferrous metals by this method is as old as history. Blacksmithing, which has always been considered a utilitarian craft, has now become an important art media. It also has a place in this book, featuring the work of two famous artists. Quite a

---

**Creative Bird Carving,* by William I. Tawes; 1969, Tidewater Publishers, Cambridge, Md.

wide range in which the artist may browse! Quite a challenge to creative effort!

Shaping cement or concrete into sculptural forms may become a distinctive art of the future. The surface of the possibilities has not yet been scratched. The artist has not taken over from the engineer in the creation of collossal works of concrete. The artist has yet to conceive and form such mammoth sculptures of concrete as the historic figures on Mt. Rushmore. But certainly the huge dams and other large concrete structures will eventually be turned into imposing sculptures of equal magnificence. Even seagoing boats are now made of cement. While the material is unsympathetic to sculptural design, it is a plastic which offers great possibilities to an ambitious skillful artist who thinks "big."

A simple functional sculptural creation is suggested for a start in this exciting field of activity. The Fish Pool should inspire the budding cement artist with the exciting possibilities of cement and concrete forms.

Finally, each chapter is started with a motivating discussion, informative, biographical or historical, and always interesting. The information has been carefully researched, or has been a part of the experience of the author. In most cases suggested projects accompanied by photographs of carvings related to the subject which have been created by able artists from all over the country. These photographs are a part of the motivating aims and should not only be informative concerning the work of others, but be an inspiration—an urge to get down in the shop and make the chips fly.

WILLIAM I. TAWES

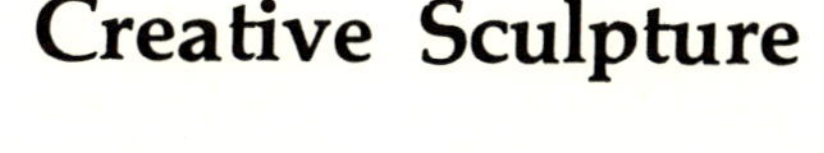

Creative Sculpture

Chapter 1

Appreciation and Enjoyment of Creative Art

The world is too much with us; late and soon
Getting and spending we lay waste our powers:
Little we see in nature that is ours;
We have given our hearts away, a sordid boon!
The sea that bares her bosom to the moon;
The winds that will be howling at all hours,
And are upgathered now like sleeping flowers;
For this, for everything, we are out of tune;
It moves us not. . . .

William Wordsworth

Due to some quirk of social inheritance or environmental influences, some individuals seem to be born with a keen sense of art appreciation. Others, for just as mysterious a reason, acquire the insight of appreciating works of art which they develop to admirable comprehension. For the rest of materialistic humanity, there is little hope of enjoying the blessings of creative art. During their early formative years they wasted their time and powers so far as art is concerned; they saw little in nature that was theirs. They gave their hearts away, a sordid boon! Now, when they are older, they give a creative masterpiece but a passing glance, thinking of other mundane things. They visit museums because it is the accepted routine of travelers, but they do so without interest and breathe a sigh of relief when the ordeal is over. Any artist can detect them while visiting his studio. He can discern these individuals while making a speech about his subject. These people simply cannot relate to his message and are either asleep or staring blankly into space. In the realms of art they are but stolid clods of unresponding earth.

When a magician pulls a rabbit from a hat he is demonstrating a magic art which represents no mean skill. There are few individuals who do not enjoy the show. His act is comparatively simple, however, performed in a few brief minutes on a stage, or in a drawing room, before a mystified, but not surprised audience. "Pulling" a rabbit from a solid log with mallet and chisel is quite another matter, but not without its aura of mystery to individuals of artistic temperaments, and they *are* surprised at the climactic results. The creative effort was one of imagination, manual dexterity, carving skills and abiding patience. Without any abracadabra the subject slowly, but surely escaped from its prison of wood cells, crisp and "alive," a joy to the sculptor and an object of beauty to the beholder.

In the field of art, as in all others, we find favor with that which we consciously or unconsciously like. We are impressed with creative work just in proportion to our acquired taste and powers of artistic evaluation. The faculty of imagination permits the experience of appreciating a creative effort by identifying ourselves, psychologically, with not only the work, but the artist himself. For, after all, a responsive chord must be touched because of a visual impact reflecting those experiences which have been a part of our lives. This does not mean that before an observer is "turned on" he must have had some carving experience of his own. On the contrary, comparatively few observers will have had any experience in this activity whatever, but they can *feel* form, beauty and artistic qualities, not only in concrete forms created by man, but in the whole realm of nature of which Wordsworth speaks. They feel a relationship with the artist, or with the creative forces of nature, as the case may be.

The whole carving is first perceived at a glance, a psychological Gestalt, the initial configurational impression. This initial impression is significant and not near as superficial as one may suppose. The emotional impact depends upon not only the insight of the observer, but the charismatic quality, beauty and subject appeal of the work itself. The more serious evaluation may come later, after the flood of admiration, even adoration, builds up to overflowing. Then a wing, an arm, a bundle of muscles, or a mass of hair may be separately and seriously appraised. Usually, with little exception, the first impression holds, so complete is the first conception. The details when studied apart should possess the aesthetic charm and skill of execution indicative of the intuitive and creating powers of the carver. The small masses will then logically fall in place, rounding out the full figure, recreating the visual image which was at first perceived, but with more studied evaluation. A silent approach is here implied, but the more demonstrative observers may shout an outburst of awe and wonder. Whether there is a mute expression of praise or of verbal, animated applause depends upon the personality of the observing individual. Whether the person's reaction is as audible as a waterfall, or as silent as a deep channeled stream, is irrelevant. In either case the joy and appreciation must be based upon a thorough understanding of artistic values, and a feeling for the aesthetic. When such an inclusive response is felt the carving has achieved its purpose and is as deserving of its place as much as the earth or sun, as Emerson would say.

To reiterate, the appreciation and enjoyment of creative art requires a preconditioning or preparation of the individual. For, as Malvina Hoffman says, "Understanding and appreciation of art will not come suddenly or even rapidly, but by gradual stages of self-education." She does not imply that a person must be formally trained, but rather by a conscious or unconscious means, learn more and more about the aesthetic values which embody good art. Even children, to some extent, possess this power of appreciation and some of them are uncanny in their insights. Instinctively, it seems, some individuals are blest with this faculty of aesthetic evaluation. Some are so sensitive that their understanding is comparable to that of a highly trained artist. In fact, most of our art critics are not creative artists themselves. This particular aspect of culture, therefore, may be either formally or informally acquired. It knows no particular strata of society, age, race, or creed. In fact, some of the more sincere, appreciative individuals are among the poor, while at the top of the social ladder are many callous persons who can discern little difference between an artistic creative work and a hole in the ground.

Imagination is in many ways, so far as this discussion is concerned, a vicarious experience of trying to fathom the artist's objective before chisel or brush was applied to the respective block or canvas. The flight of the imagination knows no bounds and may go far beyond the thinking of the artist concerned, and wonder in other related fields of introspection inspired by the theme of the work. Fantasy may even take over the thought processes and transport the dreamer into fairylands of origins and fate. Usually, however, as expressed above, introspection is more practical and the observer, with both feet on the ground, imagines the chips falling away from the log until the form is revealed in all of its nascent beauty. But, in all of these experiences the first requisite is a feeling for art—for beauty. It is the solid foundation upon which rests the enjoyment of any artistic creation.

Fantasy, the least obvious of all criteria set up for the enjoyment of art is a wild flight of the imagination in speculating certain aspects of a sculpture. For example, some 4,000 years ago Se'n-Wosret I, an early king of Egypt, commissioned a sculptor to carve his image in wood (Fig. 1). Standing erect upon a slab of cedar with a staff of authority in his left hand and an ankh in his right, the sculpture now reposes in the Metropolitan Museum of Art, New York City. It was discovered in the tomb of Imhotep and is of cedarwood. The dishpan-shaped crown signifies that he ruled lower Egypt. Had he a crown shaped like a bowling pin he would have been a king of the upper Kingdom. A combination of the two forms, as in the case of Horus, the son of the Egyptian trinity, would have been the supreme ruler of all Egypt. See what I mean? The mere name of the wooden statue led me to explain many features about it. Here are some more. The King appears to be young and handsome. His dress implies that he not only possessed the royal gift of power, but also of a charisma equaled to his regal authority, perhaps. As Egypt had no cedars, even at this early age, from what source did the sculptor receive his log? The tree probably grew in Lebanon and might even have been among the ancestors of those very cedars which King Hiram of Tyre sent to Israel by request of King Solomon to build the temple to Yahweh. Then by another quirk of fate, a certain tree from among all the others was destined to bear the likeness of Egypt's King; that it be preserved in Imhotep's dry tomb for thousands of years, long after all of the other trees of its generation—even the rafters in King Solomon's temple—had molded into dust.

Arousing oneself from the far-out world of fantasy and keeping at least one foot on the ground, who could imagine that a rough barked log of wood

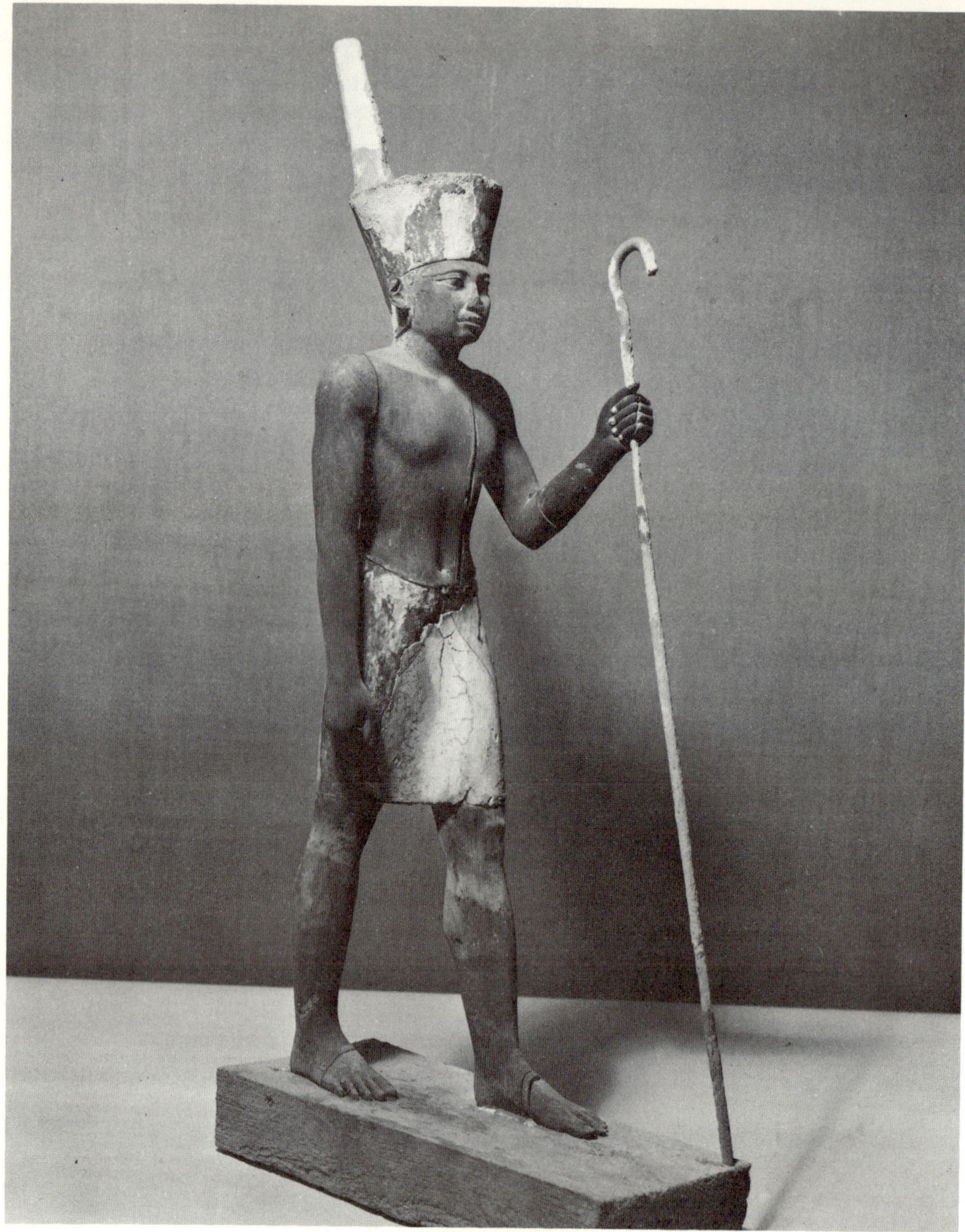

Fig. 1. Statuette: King Se'n-Wosret I, wearing the Crown of Lower Egypt; cedarwood, painted; from the tomb of Imhotep, Lisht. *Courtesy:* The Metropolitan Museum of Art, Museum excavations, 1913-14; Rogers Fund, supplemented by contribution of Edward S. Harkness.

could contain such a beautiful form! A form revealed after all of the unwanted wood had been chiseled away. Imagine the countless forms imprisoned in the trunks of all of the trees (or boulders of rock) in the whole wide world! This thought was borrowed from a young lad who visited my showroom. "Just imagine," he said, "of all the carvings hidden in a forest of trees!" The thought is breathtaking. Very few of these carvings escape to see the light of day. Michelangelo saw in a rejected boulder of marble the statue of King David. He chiseled him free and gave the world a sculptural masterpiece. Here is an outstanding example of the stone which builders rejected becoming the "head of the corner."

Imagine the image being set free by the chisel of the sculptor! After the rough form has been revealed, the carving begins to have meaning. Then the patient, knowing hands smooth out the planes to definite dimensions, proportion and form, making identification certain and complete. The symmetry and grace, whether expressed in static stillness or dynamic action, comes "alive"—becomes real. The figure born of the imagination has become a concrete form expressing the inspiration of the artist's dream.

What perceptive eye and skilled hands guided the chisels through the rough material to the "skin" of the form! Thousands of chips, every one cut unerringly to form the lines and planes of the various shapes—bent, curved, angular, concave, convex—to create the specific masses that together make the carving whole.

As indicated before, the skill of the artist will be appraised at first glance. If the appraisal is good the carver will most likely increase in stature among men and be judged as an individual part.

Why should one person have so much talent? The expression is trite, but often asked, and the answer is obvious: he earned his reward.

Aside from the initial impression, one may vicariously, in introspection, follow the carver as he chisels away the unwanted parts, or the painter as he blocks out his designs and fills in details. Such observational experiences may be uncommon, but they do become fringe benefits in the total emotional response.

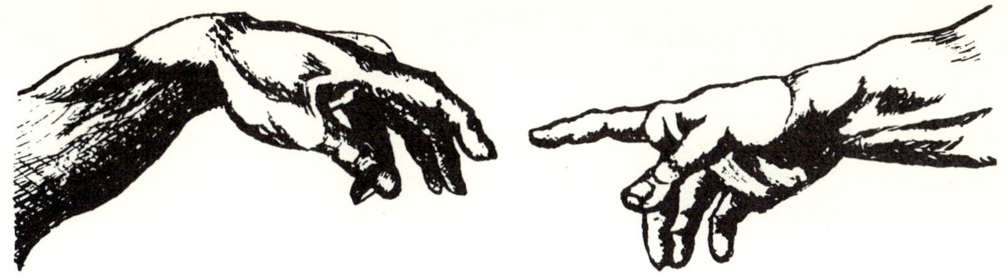

Hands after Michelangelo. *The Creation of Adam,* Sistine Chapel, Rome.

Chapter 2

Work with the Hands

> Though a little one, the master-word work looms large in meaning. It is the open sesame to every portal, the great equalizer in the world, the true philosopher's stone which transmutes the base metal of humanity into gold.
>
> Sir William Osler

> In the sweat of thy face shalt thou eat bread, till thou return unto the ground.
>
> Genesis 3:19

Nearly 200 years ago, Friedrich Fröebel, the great German educator who founded the kindergarten system, said, "Work with the hands builds character." Yet, despite the philosophical dictums of all the ages, man has instinctively disliked work and has exercised his intelligence to avoid it. This distaste accounted for the folklore of Genesis in the first place. The great physician was right and the curse of the garden has been man's greatest blessing. His aversion to work has spurred him to creative accomplishments and inventions, and his mind which was freed by the same curse has expanded his knowledge miraculously, and civilized him far beyond any other living creature. Instead of living in idle ignorance all the days of his life (or forever if by chance Adam had eaten of the Tree of Life) he has multiplied his blessings in the first instance and become a highly intelligent being in the second.

The curse of work bore heavily upon the profligate adventurers at Jamestown, whose main objective was searching for gold and precious stones. They had no intentions of raising crops or building houses. When starvation finally threatened to destroy them, Captain John Smith decreed that those who did not work would not eat. The leaders of the USSR reflecting upon the penury of their times decided, "Work is the duty of every able-bodied citizen, according to the principle: 'He who does not work, neither shall he eat.' "*

*Constitution of Union of Soviet Socialist Republic 1936, Article 12.

While it is quite difficult to imagine poetry coming from either the early colonist at Jamestown, or the prosaic destitution of Russia following the Revolution, the practical decree was, nonetheless, eloquent music, and is for all ages and all peoples of every clime. Combating hunger puts the people in tune with their environment, and gives impulse to their mental and spiritual faculties. Feeding the body, however, is only a means to an end; otherwise the individual is on a level with the beasts of the fields. While only a philosopher observes that man does not live by bread alone, the concomitants of work are so obvious as to be unnoticed and taken for granted. The very feelings of hunger whet the senses (especially found in the lower animals; a primitive instinct which man has not outlived) and awakens the subconscious mental and spiritual powers of survival and creative activity, to dance, to sing, write poetry and all other forms of symbolizing his feelings. The fact that many of the world's creative art masterpieces done in cold garrets is but concrete evidence of the gnawing pains of creativity in the face of poverty. Affluence would have aborted the urge in slothful sleep. Work is the fulcrum which balances the scales between hunger and creativity, the temperance ideal, the golden mean which feeds both the body and the soul. Blessed is he who earns his keep by the sweat of his face or the labor of his mind.

Our emancipation from drudgery and toil has had its ill effects upon society as well as its blessings. To those who cannot profit from the use of leisure time, freedom from work is a curse. Our labors have been further reduced by the many sophisticated gadgets allowing little opportunity, or necessity, to coordinate the mind with the body in a useful and worthy activity. Herein lies our greatest danger as a people. Indolence begets indolence and is easily acquired. It is habit-forming like a dangerous drug. The evil is already evident in the poverty of many, and our welfare rolls even extend to the third generation. Many of these unfortunate individuals do not intend to work again for their keep. They will not, along with some of the more affluent members of our society, unless some force, insistent beyond themselves, spurs them to seek work or perish. Unless this undesirable attitude is checked and eclipsed by a more worthy aim in life, these persons will probably not only lose their remaining vestiges of dignity, but descend to even lower levels of moral and spiritual decay, rotting away the very foundations of our government. A vigorous program of some description, not yet conceived by our social architects, to keep our people busy is imperative, not only for the welfare group, but for all our citizens who do not use their leisure time in worthy social activities. Many individuals have turned to golf or some other sport; others have chosen the arts in one form or another; all must find work for idle hands to do, or our way of life is in trouble. "The man," says Bernard Baruch, "who can master his time can master anything." Certainly the thought has been relatively true for the writer. Mary Tinsley in John Parris' book* when asked her secret of a long life (102 years) replied

---

**Mountain Bred*, by John Parris; Citizen-Times Publishing Co., Asheville, North Carolina.

that one must eat three square meals a day and work hard. She emphasized the thought that the hands must be kept busy. Nancy Rathbone of the same book speaks the same language with respects to health. Nancy is a tough old gal! She even now walks barefooted in the snow. Industry cannot be too strongly emphasized for all people if they desire to live life fully and remain in good health, mentally and physically. It is mainly through this magic power that they are most likely to succeed.

The mind of man cannot exist in a vacuum. Unless preoccupied in a desirable activity at all times an individual will retrogress, and be in danger of losing those noble virtues which have made him a little lower than the angels. For even though a person be as rich as Croesus and has not the will to work, he is poor; poor in those important aspects which make life worthwhile. He may sit in the seat of the mighty, but if he cannot administer to his own emotional needs, he is a weakling and doomed to spiritual failure. These individuals are really sick; they are not whole. Their last days are apt to be more miserable than their first, arriving at that period in life when "the best is yet to be" emotionally disturbed and destitute of any sound reason for living.

Our secondary schools have wisely included in their curricula shop courses and domestic science for their pupils. These inclusions were not made to teach a vocation. In fact, on the contrary, vocational training as an objective is not considered in these courses. The aim is strictly appreciation for the work of the world and an opportunity for the pupils to explore their talents through work with their own hands. There are other objectives, of course, but they do not concern us here. Another course has a similar aim for the creative arts. Guidance in the work of the world designed to inspire pupils to want to become a part of it is highly important. Boys and girls should be taught to work early in life while not engaged in school work. As the twig is bent the tree inclines, is trite, but so true! Many boys and girls profit from their secondary education but some, even at this tender age have resolved to evade work. They inhibit their minds to dislike it in any form. They have poor minds to begin with, usually, and they receive little or no encouragement at home to strive for a fuller life. They are numbered with the "dropouts." In many cases, they should be "kickouts" for they are a decided impediment to the learning of others. In many instances these unfortunate young people have become victims of their own erroneous thinking, or a way of life in their homes, or both of these aspects of their native and social inheritance. They are more to be pitied than censored!

In the middle forties the writer applied for a principalship in one of the more affluent communities in New Jersey. When the President of the Board of Education learned that he was a former shop teacher the President was no longer interested. He frankly admitted that the community was mostly made up of white-collar workers and business executives who commuted to the big city where they worked; they moved to the more rural community to enjoy a more cultural life.

"We do not want a vocational emphasis in our schools," he said. No wonder that secondary education has failed in so many places under such leadership. The President of the Board was a successful businessman himself, but the chances are he was denying his own children the invaluable experiences which led to his own success. He was ignorant of the aims of secondary education and the proper nurture of boys and girls. He did not believe in educating the whole child.

While it is true that man does not live by bread alone, it is also true that the spirit cannot survive without a physical body. They both must be properly integrated, one entity cooperating and supplementing the other. Work is the sesame which opens up the possibilities for a successful existence for both. Work provides bread and tends to control the emotional tides of sanity. The President of the Board was a pagan! His only concern was seeking wealth through mental activities alone, and on an academic highway which had no room for any other kind of traffic, especially physical labor.

The soul of a normal individual cries out for an opportunity to express itself in some form or other. These yearnings, while fundamentally religious (perhaps) cannot be ignored, and they cannot be satisfied by the church alone. In fact, this institution which has played such an important role in western civilization is apt to be very blunt toward the quest of a sensitive individual for spiritual truths. The teachings of its strange dogmas, so much like the mythology of old, are not inclined to encourage reverence towards physical creation in all of its myriads of forms. The very act of appreciating the work of the Almighty's hands is likely to be considered worldly—of the earth, earthy. In fact there is good scripture supporting such a view. Yet, it is only by the skillful efforts of the hands in fulfilling these creative attributes that man becomes most like God. Wealth, position and power are nothing if the individual is not at peace with his soul; if he cannot reach out and touch the divinity of the things about him; if he cannot come to grips with the elements of his environment. Creative efforts are hardly possible without spiritual yearnings coupled with physical activities to give them form. Also, experiencing the material benefits of life without spiritual fulfillment is equally frustrating, and makes for an unbalanced existence. Neither can exist in a healthy state alone, divorced one from the other. It is the effective integration of both the spiritual and material aspects of living that makes a whole individual. The President of the Board should have known these things; he should have been conscious of the fact that there is apt to be as much soul-stuff under the cap of a laborer as that which might exist under the silk hat of a business tycoon, or the mortarboard of an academic professor for that matter.

Significantly, the generation of children of the School Board President is the same as that of the young, misguided woman whose unworthy use of her leisure time and spiritual powers ended in the sordid surroundings of a dirty, damp basement of a hippie-joint. The account seems to indicate that her successful upper middle class parents were one in their thinking with the

President of the Board concerning the nurture of their children. As this piece is being written a similar case of a misguided young woman was reported in the Philadelphia papers. Coincidentally, this Italian girl was from the same community where the writer applied for a principalship. She had traveled to Philadelphia and shacked up at a deserted, boarded-up building with some black individuals. The next morning they all were found shot to death, gangland style, in the head. Drug users' paraphernalia was found in one of the rooms. This unfortunate woman had probably been fed on ashes at home and sought relief from boredom and emotional hunger from the lowest strata of human existence. This is the generation of adolescents from the middle and upper classes of society which are causing so much concern among the law enforcing officials and social workers. These young people have been undernourished by their parents in those things of the soul and they are wandering in a spiritual vacuum trying to escape reality, or boredom of their daily existence. They were conceived in idleness, born of indolence, and nurtured in the midst of a flowery bed of ease—a poisonous environment in which to rear children. Their hands were probably never soiled by honest work, nor did their brows know the luxury of salty sweat. Yet, these symbols of labor are so much a part of the history of the race that no sophisticated, educational, or social procedure can ignore them without paying a dear price. In our time the price is a hippie-joint, or a commune of sex and violence. A child effectively taught the values of work; to appreciate the labors of his own hands, and instilled with a concept of his duty and obligation to contribute to himself to promote the social weal, will have no time for psychedelic drugs. His time will be consumed in more satisfying activities which are healthful to both body and soul. The "drug" of creativity will expand his vision and glorify his whole life.

Early in life boys and girls should be taught to work and allowed to experience the "kick" of a job well done. This can be accomplished, for the writer has seen the elated spirits of a child mount up as on eagle's wings a thousand times. In recapitulation, the writer still remembers the thrill of picking up, for the first time, the long sheet lines of his father's skipjack and pulling in the wet tackle, hand over hand, while steadying the tiller with his body. Every person should have had the opportunity to experience these high crests in his growth curve and mature in memory of them. They should loom like buoys on a storm-tossed sea, and give reason and meaning to the dips or troughs which are just as much a part of living as life itself. Young people should know that life is not a straight line development, but an up-and-down progression, each crest, God willing, higher than the last. These thrills, however, should be in their time and place, and not those naturally reserved for later years. An individual should not gorge himself on the forbidden fruits of his age before he is thirty. If he has, he has become satiated already with living, leaving little opportunity for exciting experiences to spur him on in quest for a fuller life.

As this volume has been written for both adolescents and individuals of all age brackets, what has been said respecting young people is generally true of their elders. In normal living older persons, too, must have their rapturous moments. Their desire to be recognized is just as great as ever. The writer has seen their spirits mount up to fever heights with pride because of an outstanding achievement. He has seen them also wither and decay, the victims of boredom and idleness. There is no feeling quite as satisfying to older people as recognition and praise by some of their fellows. The thrill of being rewarded for a creative effort hardly knows any bounds, even if the intrinsic value is but the price of a colored ribbon. The comparative stature of an artist is apt to cause the skin of the most callous to rise in goose pimples. Fortunately, this emotional exaltation is within the reach of anyone who has the patience and stamina to carve and carve (to paint and paint, to write and write, or vigorously practice any of the creative arts or leisure time activities) until skill flows through the fingers with ease and confidence. For artistic skills are not inherited. Even those mentally dull in academics can achieve the joys and immortality which result from the creative work of their own hands.

The writer hopes that this discussion does not sound like a sermon. He certainly has no intentions to preach but to teach—to give meaning and reason for filling the leisure hours with profitable activities to make life more healthful and satisfying. The words have not been idly conceived for he has delved down in more than three-quarters of a century to bring them forth. He was not known outside of his own community until he retired from his work as an educator. He had never written a book, painted a picture, nor carved a bird. His own struggle with poverty, both of the creative spirit and physical want, were blessings in disguise. Whatever rewards he has achieved were the results of overcoming these handicaps with industry and courage. He has never considered himself exceptionally bright, but a garden variety of the species, so the development of this aspect of his personality should be an encouragement to all who read this book. Industry, the jewel of great price, works miracles, making the dull bright and the articulate even more erudite; all of this and more to the glory of the persevering.

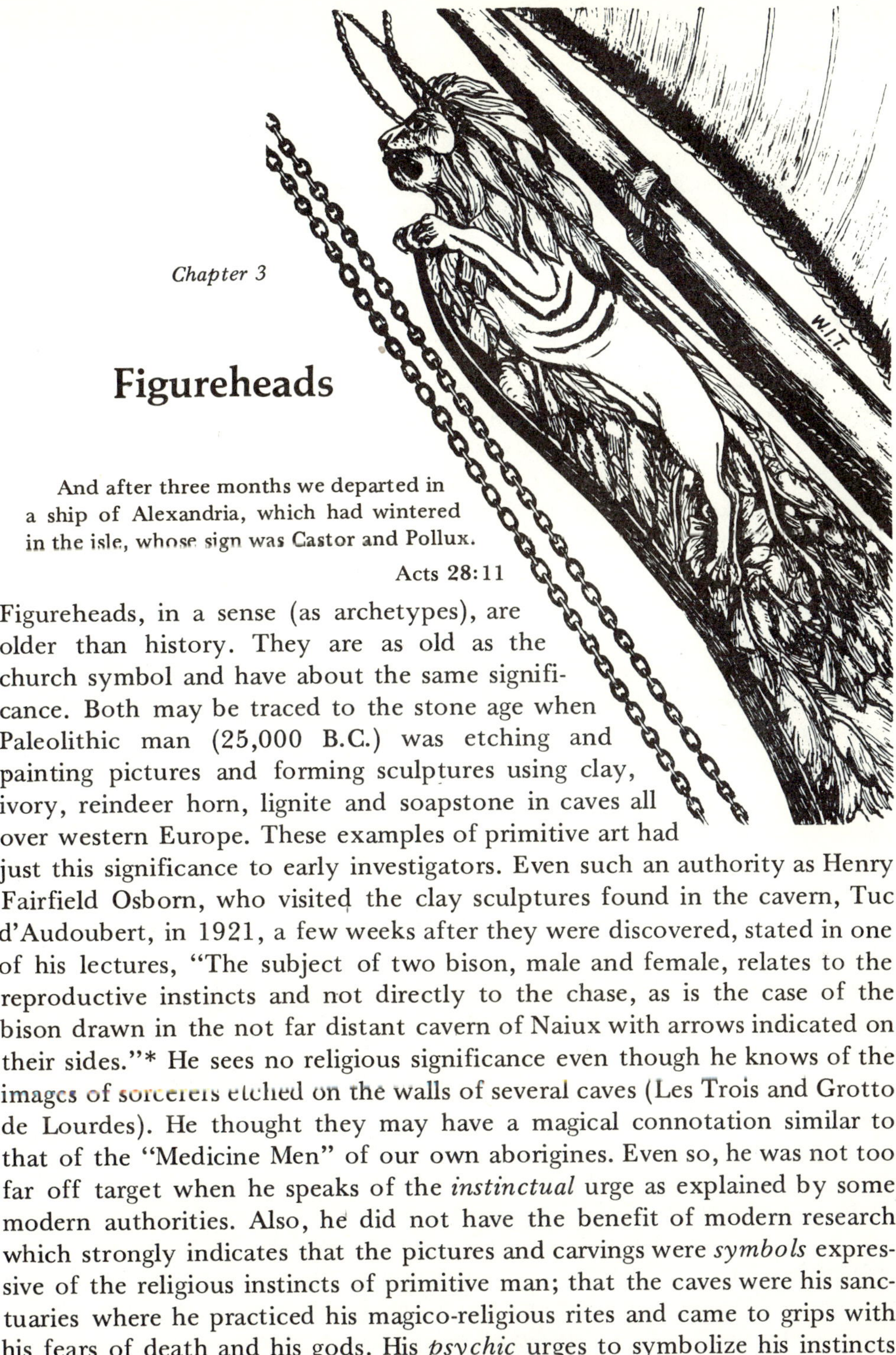

Chapter 3

Figureheads

And after three months we departed in a ship of Alexandria, which had wintered in the isle, whose sign was Castor and Pollux.

Acts 28:11

Figureheads, in a sense (as archetypes), are older than history. They are as old as the church symbol and have about the same significance. Both may be traced to the stone age when Paleolithic man (25,000 B.C.) was etching and painting pictures and forming sculptures using clay, ivory, reindeer horn, lignite and soapstone in caves all over western Europe. These examples of primitive art had just this significance to early investigators. Even such an authority as Henry Fairfield Osborn, who visited the clay sculptures found in the cavern, Tuc d'Audoubert, in 1921, a few weeks after they were discovered, stated in one of his lectures, "The subject of two bison, male and female, relates to the reproductive instincts and not directly to the chase, as is the case of the bison drawn in the not far distant cavern of Naiux with arrows indicated on their sides."* He sees no religious significance even though he knows of the images of sorcerers etched on the walls of several caves (Les Trois and Grotto de Lourdes). He thought they may have a magical connotation similar to that of the "Medicine Men" of our own aborigines. Even so, he was not too far off target when he speaks of the *instinctual* urge as explained by some modern authorities. Also, he did not have the benefit of modern research which strongly indicates that the pictures and carvings were *symbols* expressive of the religious instincts of primitive man; that the caves were his sanctuaries where he practiced his magico-religious rites and came to grips with his fears of death and his gods. His *psychic* urges to symbolize his instincts were probably the primary reasons which led to his civilization, rather than

---

**Man Rises to Parnassus*, by Henry Fairfield Osborn; Princeton University Press, Princeton, N.J., 1927, page 91.

the socio-economic factors formerly believed by anthropologists, sociologists and other pertinent authorities.

To arrive at this conclusion, the work of Carl Jung, one of the founding members of the psychological trinity, and Jacquetta Hawkes, author of *The First Great Civilizations,* have been the basic sources of reference. Carl Jung was the first person to conceive the *unconscious* mind as it is understood today; or the instinctual urges of which the individual is not conscious. Jung discovered what the artist already vaguely knew: man's instinctual urge to symbolize, to create legends, religion, and folklore. The cross, for example, has always represented man, and the idea of the symbol is probably as old as his capacity to think. It has not changed over the eons of time. In principle the paintings and sculptures found in the ancient caves have the same significance as Stonehenge, the temples on Mt. Olympus, figureheads, or the newly dedicated cathedral with its crucifix fetish. *The landsman took his god-symbols to the temple; the sailor affixed them to the prow of his ship.* The symbolic art of the caves is a part of man's animistic history, his creative psyche—and they are representative of the archetypes of his instinctual, religious nature.

"This primacy of the creative psyche has to be insisted upon at the outset because its obviousness appears to be so overwhelming that it is not to be seen. At the present time, when man's thinking has flowed into narrower and more consciously directed channels, many people are engaged in attempts to fit the whole glorious, unconfined, indefinable growth of civilization into various precise intellectually conceived shapes. There are the ecological, the economic-materialistic, the political, the social and moral shapes. The fact that these various explanatory forms often conflict is a reminder of their artificiality.

"That they are artificial does not mean that they are useless. It is only that in them the whole flow of life has been forced into various molds, just as the mud of the Valley of the Twin Rivers was forced into brick molds and hardened in the sun. Such blocks are good intellectual building material, but it must never be forgotten that it was the human mind, and above all the amazing energy of its image-making capacities that raised civilization and its greatest moments."*

As man's awareness of himself and his environment evolved so did his psychic unconscious being. Symbols of birds and animals no longer sufficed to express his religious feelings. Horus ceased to have the head of a falcon (although the bird was still perched upon his person). This transformation, this growth of concept, of conceiving the gods with human forms was not a sudden development, for vestiges of his beliefs in the divinity of animals still clung to his symbols for a thousand years, and are still evident in modern art and religious imagery. The angels have birds' wings and the Judeo-Christian

---

**The First Great Civilizations,* by Jacquetta Hawkes. Part I, pp. 3 and 4; Alfred Knopf, New York, 1973.

God, himself, is still represented by a dove. In time, however, man-gods took the place of animals as religious deities all over the civilized world.

When the maritime civilizations—especially the Egyptian, Phoenician, and later the Greek and Roman—developed their "navies" for war and commerce, their "pilots" took their god-images with them. They fastened them to the prows of their galleys and biremes. The stems of these vessels extended high above board and here in this conspicuous, forward location the skippers fitted their religious symbols to protect them and their crews from danger on the high seas; or as in the case of the Vikings, to strike terror in the hearts of their enemies and scare away their guardian spirits. The details of these Mediterranean figureheads are not known, but knowing something about their forms of worship gives us an inkling of what these figureheads might have been. We do know that the vessel in which St. Paul was a passenger on his way to Rome to face Caesar had the sign of Castor and Pollux on her bow. Castor and Pollux were the sons of Jupiter and Leda. They later became the guardian gods of sailors. The third sign of the zodiac, Gemini (Twins) was named after them. The sacred lotus leaf would surely be represented on Egyptian craft, and also the image, or symbol, of *Isis,* the patroness of mariners. She would or should have had an even more prominent place on the ships of Phoenicia and Greece as both of these nations were especially maritime and had embraced the ritual of the Egyptian goddess. In a true syncretic fashion the Virgin Mary later became the patron saint of sailors and was given the beautiful epithet *Stella Maris.* There have been figureheads of Venus, sometimes associated with the Virgin, but the image of the Mother, herself, appears to have been very rare as a carving for figureheads.

Even less is known of the imagery of oriental ships, but their shipmasters, too, took their god-images with them to sea. Such religious urges were probably universal because man's psychic nature differs little, if any, because of race or geographical location. These unconscious urges are universal and are not peculiar to any particular people.

Due to the custom of the Norsemen of burying their vessel along with their skipper when he died, the frightful dragon head terminating the high stemposts of their ships is familiar. Several of these old ships have been unearthed or drawn up from the sea, and can now be seen in some museums.

Millenniums of tradition, therefore, lay behind the seaman's religious feelings, superstition, and awe of figureheads. They symbolized the very spirit of the ship. Success or failure, good luck or misfortune, were mystically embodied in the image which the vessel carried on her prow. To lose or damage a figurehead was considered an evil omen. "It is enough to blanch the face of an old seaman to sail without a figurehead," confessed an old salt.* During a battle in 1794 the hat of the figurehead of *H.M.S.*

**American Folk Art in Wood, Metal, and Stone,* by Jean Lipman; Pantheon Books, Inc., 41 Washington Square, N.Y.

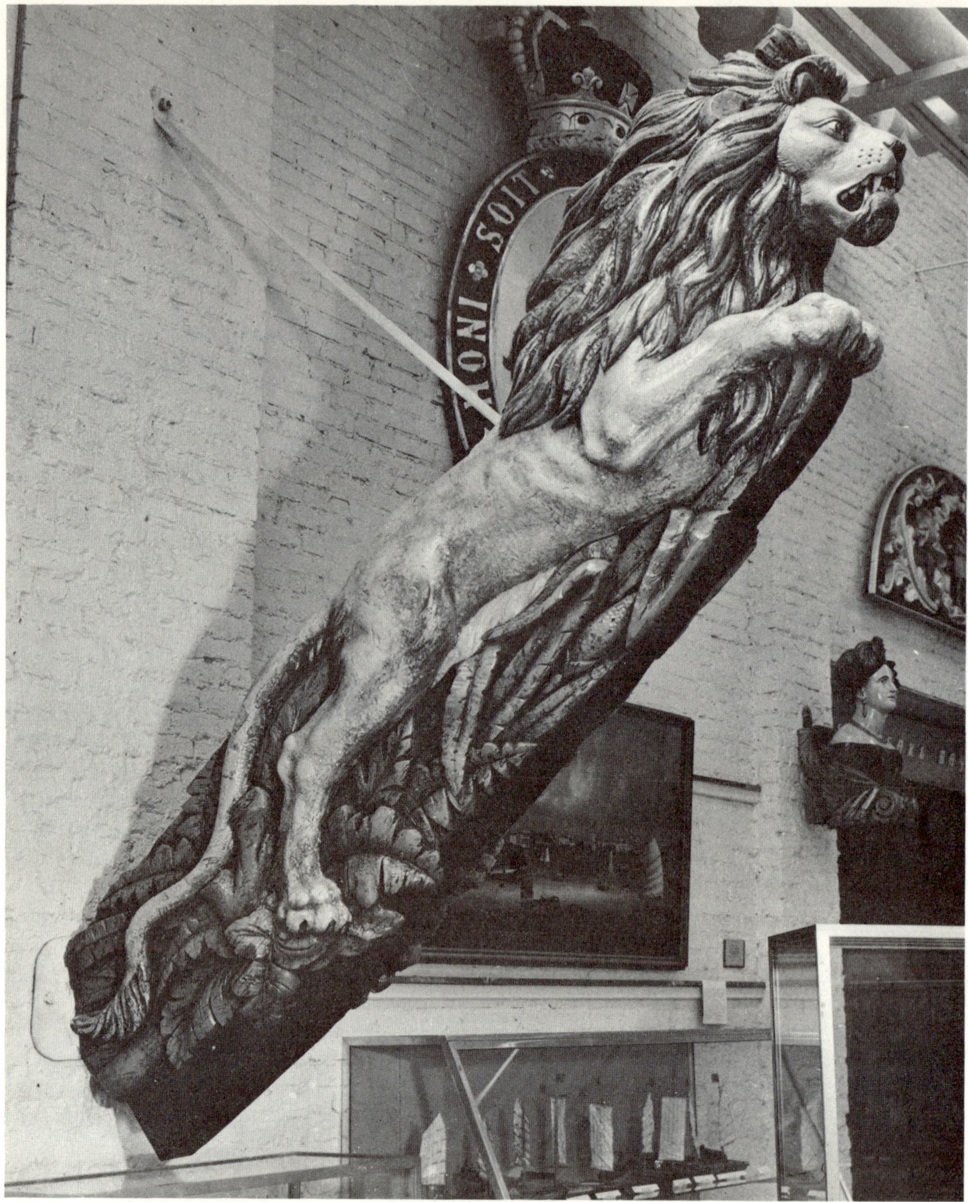

Fig. 1. Lion, Rampant. This figurehead graced the bow of the famous *Derwent,* a fully rigged, steel-hulled ship that had a long, active record as a sailing ship in the Australian trade. She was slower than most of the crack vessels, but more dependable and her cargo always arrived in first-class condition. For more than 40 years she led the big wool clippers, but finally had to bow before the vessels of steam.

As stated earlier, the "Lyon," both erect and rampant, was a favorite subject for figureheads at one time. This figurehead may have been carved during that period. It is an outstanding example of the ship-carver's art. *Courtesy:* The Mariners Museum, Newport News, Virginia.

Brunswick was shot off. Immediately some sailors rushed aft to request the captain to replace it with his own. The battle was not interrupted, but neither did the figurehead remain bareheaded.

A carved binnacle figure made in New York for the clipper ship *N.B. Palmer,* made but one trip to China for tea. The little sailor image was removed because the sailors claimed that the eyes of the figure moved at night and distracted their attention from the compass. Any soldier who has stood guard on the desert at night can appreciate the sailors' feelings. In the lonely vigil of the night strange things happen and are seen, for the imagination plays havoc with the senses. The figurehead of a ship is the combined imaginations of the centuries with religious superstition thrown in for good measure. So, it is not surprising that even up to the age of steam, and beyond, the figurehead symbolized the living spirit of the ship and sailors were unwilling to go to sea without it.

The art of ship carving in America began with the construction of the 30-ton pinnace *Virginia* at the mouth of the Kennebec River (1607). By the turn of the century the trade was well established, especially in New England. William Rush, John Bellamy, the Skillings, and many others became legends in their own lifetimes. John H. Bellamy maintained a private workshop in Portsmouth, facing Pepperell Cove. It was a meeting place for the intelligentsia of the nation. The Elliots of Harvard, William Dean Howells, Mark Twain, and other celebrities like Winslow Homer and Edwin Booth crossed wits in salty conversation.

In the beginning the image of a "Lyon" was the most popular figurehead. It was first carved in an upright position but was later changed to a rampant pose (Fig. 1). Probably this change was the result of the prow design of the ship. As if by an unseen hand the motif of an animal changed to mythological figures (Hercules dominated the bow of *Old Ironsides)* and finally to human forms of real life, a recapitulation of the evolution of religious imagery. By the early 1800's Indians were favorite subjects. The *U.S.S. Delaware III* carried on her bow the Indian warrier Tecumseh.* The remains of the old wooden image reposes in the Field House of the Naval Academy at Annapolis, Maryland (Fig. 2). The midshipmen of the class of 1891 had a bronze replica cast to replace the decaying wooden figure (Fig. 3). Tecumseh now stands on the campus in dignity and majesty, the god of 2.5 (passing grade) and the Middies toss pennies to him for good luck in their examinations. The first figurehead of the *Constitution* was a Hercules with the fasces of the U.S. Constitution. The figurehead was designed by William Rush, the famous sculptor of Philadelphia, and carved by one of the Skillings. The second figurehead was the image of Andrew Jackson and carved by Isaac Fowler. The third figurehead was also of Andrew Jackson, dressed in plain clothes, holding his hat and cane in one hand and the Constitution in the other. The figurehead was carved by Laban S. Bucher of Boston.

*The figurehead was of Tamanend. The Middies at the Naval Academy changed the name to Tecumseh.

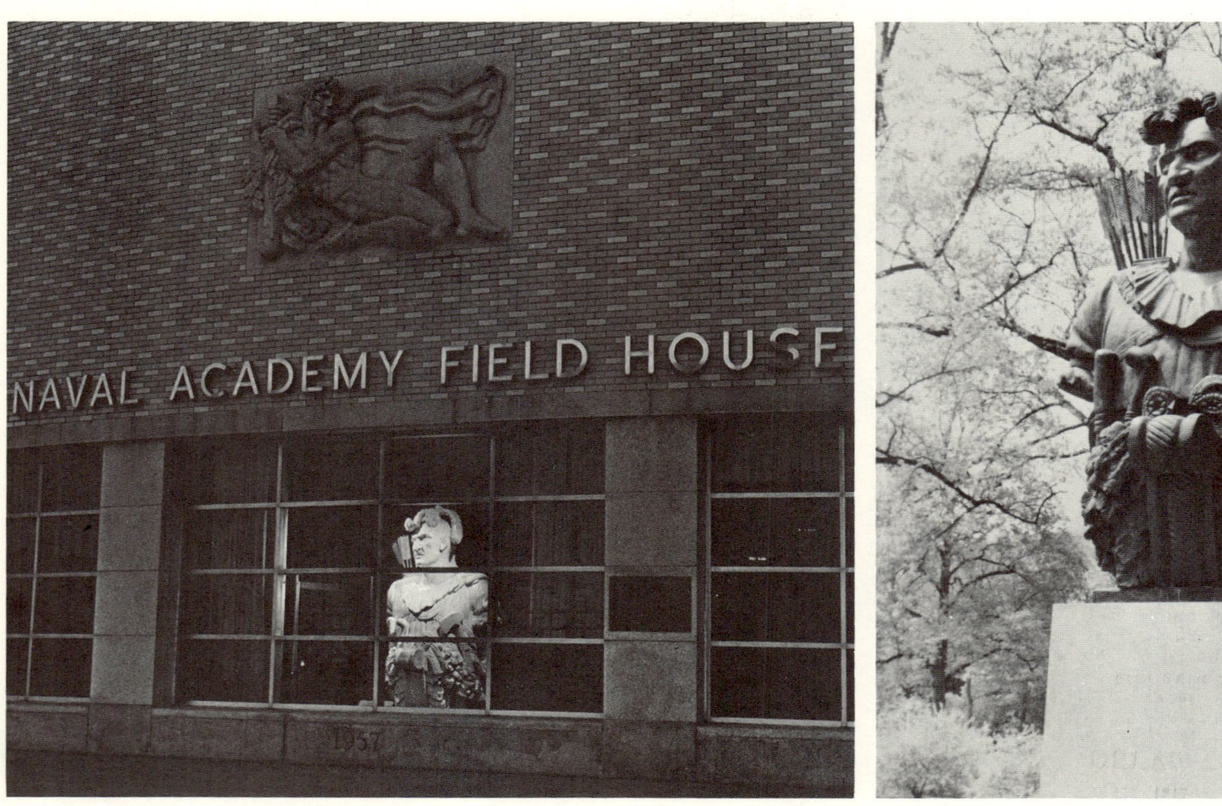

Fig. 2 (left). Figurehead Tecumseh (Tamanend) from the bow of the *U.S.S. Delaware III.* Artist, William Luke. (Note the carved plaque cemented in the wall above). *Courtesy:* U.S. Naval Academy Museum. Fig. 3 (right). Bronze replica of Tecumseh on the Naval Academy campus, Annapolis, Md.

The less famous sister ship to the *Constitution* was the *Constellation.* Her remains are now docked at Light Street in Baltimore Harbor. A billethead now serves as a bow ornament and the author has been unable to find any record of her ever having a figurehead. Nonetheless, she probably had at least one, for all of the ships of the line in the U.S. Navy were equipped with figureheads at that time. She was built to clear the seas of Barbary Coast pirates and it is difficult to imagine her going to sea "naked" without being rigged in proper battleship gear.

The exhibit of the *Constellation* at Baltimore sheds no light on this subject, or for that matter, hardly any other subject pertaining to the ship. The personnel are impolite and show little interest or sympathy for the visitor's quest for information. The visit is hardly worth the effort. The research of the writer indicates that the *Constellation* was repaired several times, and in one instance, the keel was lengthened 20 feet. The accounts are confusing and conflicting. It is doubtful if any timbers of the original ship remain.

All early ships were usually equipped with figureheads. Some whalers of New Bedford and Nantucket were notable exceptions. They were mostly owned by Quakers who not only thought the extra expense an extravagance, but perhaps an evil omen, or a form of idol worship. These shipmasters were too prosaic to comprehend the significance and romance of the tradition on one hand, and too frugal in their pecuniary dispositions on the other, to adorn their ships with figureheads. The story is told of a Quaker who purchased a whaler with the image of Rousseau on her bow. He cut the image loose and threw it overboard before arriving at New Bedford. He believed the carving not only a symbol of extravagance, but of evil intent. This Quaker thought that the likeness of one whom he thought was an atheist on the prow of his ship augured no good before heaven. Another Quaker objected to the figurehead of a woman on his whaler *Rebecca.* He might have felt like St. Chrysostom, the "golden mouthed," concerning women: "a necessary evil, a natural temptation, a desirable calamity, a domestic peril, a deadly fascination, and a painted ill." In any event, he dismantled the figure and buried it in the sand with an appropriate ceremony. Yet, the best figureheads were carved during this period and represent the apogee of the ship-carver's art.

Under such leadership as Donald McKay, the clipper ship became the thoroughbred of the sea designed to take over the rich China trade. Clipper ships were built larger and larger until, like the ancient dinosaurs, they overspecialized and became nearly extinct in a decade. But what a saga of the seas during the brief time of their existence! McKay's *Great Republic* was the largest wooden ship ever built and one of the last of the clipper line. She was 335 feet long and her masts were as tall as a 20-story building. An eagle's head, five feet long, served as the ship's figurehead. Unfortunately the *Great Republic* burned at her berth in New York Harbor before making her maiden voyage. She was rebuilt, but was so large that her owners had difficulty finding enough ladings to fill her holds. Then too, the China tea era was drawing to a close.

Clipper ships streamlined their figureheads due to the ship's slick design. Usually an eagle's head projecting from the upper end of the cutwater, just under the bowsprit (Fig. 4) served this purpose. The elaborate trailboards on either side retreating from the eagle's head (a billethead carving in Fig. 5) partly compensated for the lost work in carving comparatively simpler figureheads. The decreased emphasis in ship carvings created fewer demands for skilled ship carvers.

A more economical sailing craft succeeded the clipper ship, the schooner. It became the workhorse of coastwise shipping. These vessels were streamlined too, and with their fore-and-aft sails could probably sail a few points closer to the wind. The schooner might have several masts, but the majority

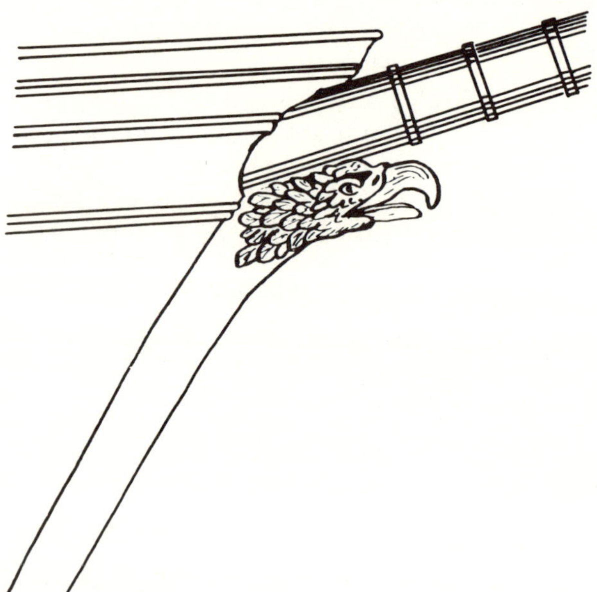

Fig. 4. Figurehead, clipper *Great Republic,* 1853, from plan of the vessel.

had but two or three. One seven-masted schooner was built, but apparently like the *Great Republic* was too large to pay profit to their owners. Their figureheads were usually an eagle's head also. These large ships were painted black usually and were quite common when the author followed the water.

When steam superseded sails and ships were made of steel, there was no functional use for the bowsprit. But tradition persists long after customs become obsolete and legends insignificant.

The City of New York, launched in 1888, was the proud queen of the Inman liners. She had three smokestacks and twin screws, but was also equipped with three tall masts for sail power, a bowsprit and elaborate trailboards terminating in a bust figurehead. Even so, the halcyon days of sails were over. The eagle of the figureheads "flew" to the center of the pilothouse. Ornate carvings decorated the wheelhouse and usually there were

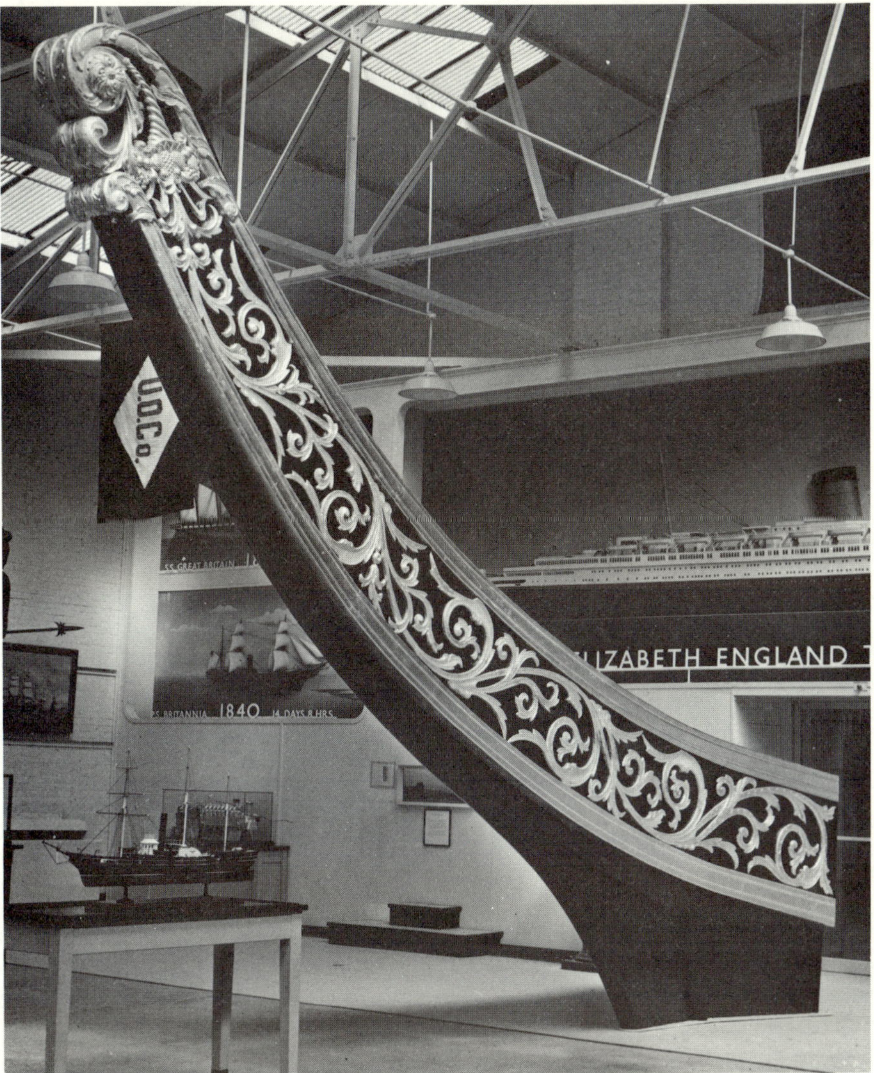

Fig. 5. Trailboard from the U.S.N. sloop *Hartford.* For persons unfamiliar with ship nomenclature, a trailboard is a decorative bow ornament situated just under the bowsprit and, in this instance, fastened to it by a bolt under the third scroll decoration. The other end probably extended well over the side of the sloop beyond the longhead. For a more simple illustration, refer to Fig. 6, a ketch bearing the name of the vessel carved on the trailboard. This is not unusual, but in more instances than not, the edges are embellished with gold-leaf carvings of a motif similar but simpler than the trailboard here illustrated.

The trailboard of the *Hartford* was in a very dilapidated condition when acquired by The Mariners Museum, but it was accurately restored by staff members with some outside help. The decorations are covered with gold leaf.

To give an idea of the size, the sloop *Hartford* was 225 x 44 x 18.6 feet. She displaced 1,800 tons and had a wooden screw. She was dismantled in 1957.

Courtesy: The Mariners Museum, Newport News, Virginia.

carvings in various places all over the ship. For a time, the navy persisted in bow and stern ornaments, but the die of the future had been cast. In 1908, all forms of decorations were removed from naval vessels and the white hulls were painted gray. The ship-carver's days were also over. The nostalgia of the seafarer is expressed in the following verse:

And there's many a story that could be told,
Of the fine figureheads that were chiselled of old.
On the dreary sands they crumble today,
From Terra del Fuego to Baffin Bay.
But the art is gone for the war ship of steel,
Is a barren stretch the length of her keel,
From her tier of guns to the waterline red,
With never a sign of a figurehead.

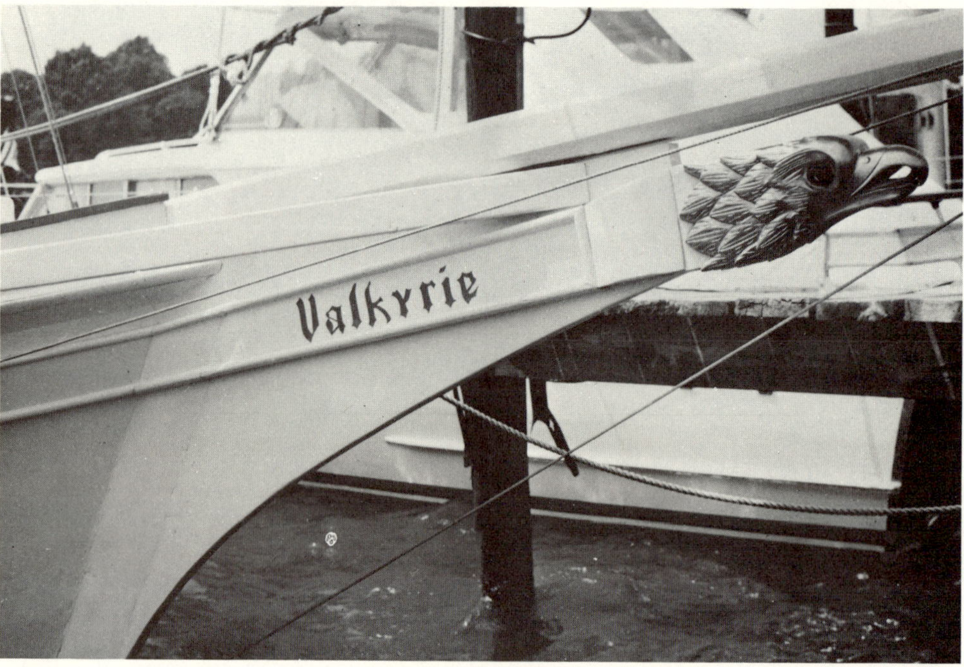

Fig. 6. Valkyrie was one of the warlike goddess-maidens of Norse mythology. The Valkyries rode on swift horses and were armed with spears, shields and helmets. Odin sent them to the battlefields to choose dead heroes for Valhalla. The name means "chooser of the slain." To lovers of Richard Wagner's music, the name may sound like a distant echo of his opera *Die Valkyre,* which is based on the theme.

Robert H. Burgess, who carved the figurehead and the owner of the ketch (shown at Warwick Yacht and Country Club, Newport News, Virginia) have modernized the theme and tamed it for peaceful pursuits.

The bard is mostly right. Of the hundreds of ship carvers who plied their trade in the shipyards along the Atlantic seaboard, only one carver (according to the records), Edward Bell Lovejoy, was actively engaged after 1850.

A new breed of carvers has now come upon the scene. Some of them have a yen to carve figureheads—and do. Occasionally an enthusiast for sailing ships breaks down and builds a Chesapeake Bay skipjack. Just a few years ago such an individual commissioned the author to carve him a figurehead and a pair of trailboards. The trailboards were made of white pine, carved with a vine motif around the edges and the name "Captain John" chiseled in five-inch letters. The eagle's head was carved of flowering cherry (Prunus Serrulata Kwanzan), probably the first and only figurehead ever made from this exotic wood.

Robert H. Burgess, curator of exhibits at The Mariners Museum, Newport News, Virginia, a skillful carver in his own right, recently carved an eagle's head for a Bay craft (Fig. 6). Any old salt would be proud to have this superb carving terminating his boat's longhead. Occasionally the National Wood-Carver's Association Magazine, *Chip Chats,* publishes articles concerning modern figurehead carvers. One such individual is Arlene Seitzinger of Portage, Indiana. The old ship carvers, even the best of them, could hardly do better (Figs. 7 and 8).

Probably the most ambitious and outstanding current attempt to carve a figurehead is being done at The Mariners Museum referred to above. It is of a Victorian woman of heroic size gracefully posed with her right arm relaxed by her side and the left hand holding a bouquet of flowers. The figurehead is being carved by C.H. Hancock, assistant curator of the Museum, and Robert Brushwood, a formally trained artist. Both men are proficient carvers, but Hancock modestly confesses that "Bob is the senior partner in the venture." The project was conceived to demonstrate the old ship-carver's art, which, as has already been noted, reached its peak in the middle 1800's. Carving demonstrations have been going on now for the past two years. The more-than-full-size "lady" is almost completed (Fig. 9), and any ship carver of the "old school" would be pleased to accept the work as his own, so far as technique and skill are concerned.

In attempting such an ambitious project considerable thought had to be given to research and design. Also, procurement of a suitable log from which to carve the figurehead could present some very tough problems. The research problems were partly solved by prior knowledge of figureheads by both of the carvers. The remaining information was close at hand in the adjoining library of maritime books and artifacts located all over the Museum. There are few museums which can boast of a better display of figureheads, model ships and rigging gear. Being a professional artist, Bob found little difficulty in arriving at a suitable design. Soon he had drawn the requisite number of full-size drawings to be superimposed on the smoothed planes of the prepared log.

The log had to be 30″ or more in diameter, comparatively clear and reasonably seasoned. Many an eyebrow was raised by dealers when asked if they could supply such a log. Finally, two logs were located, one of white

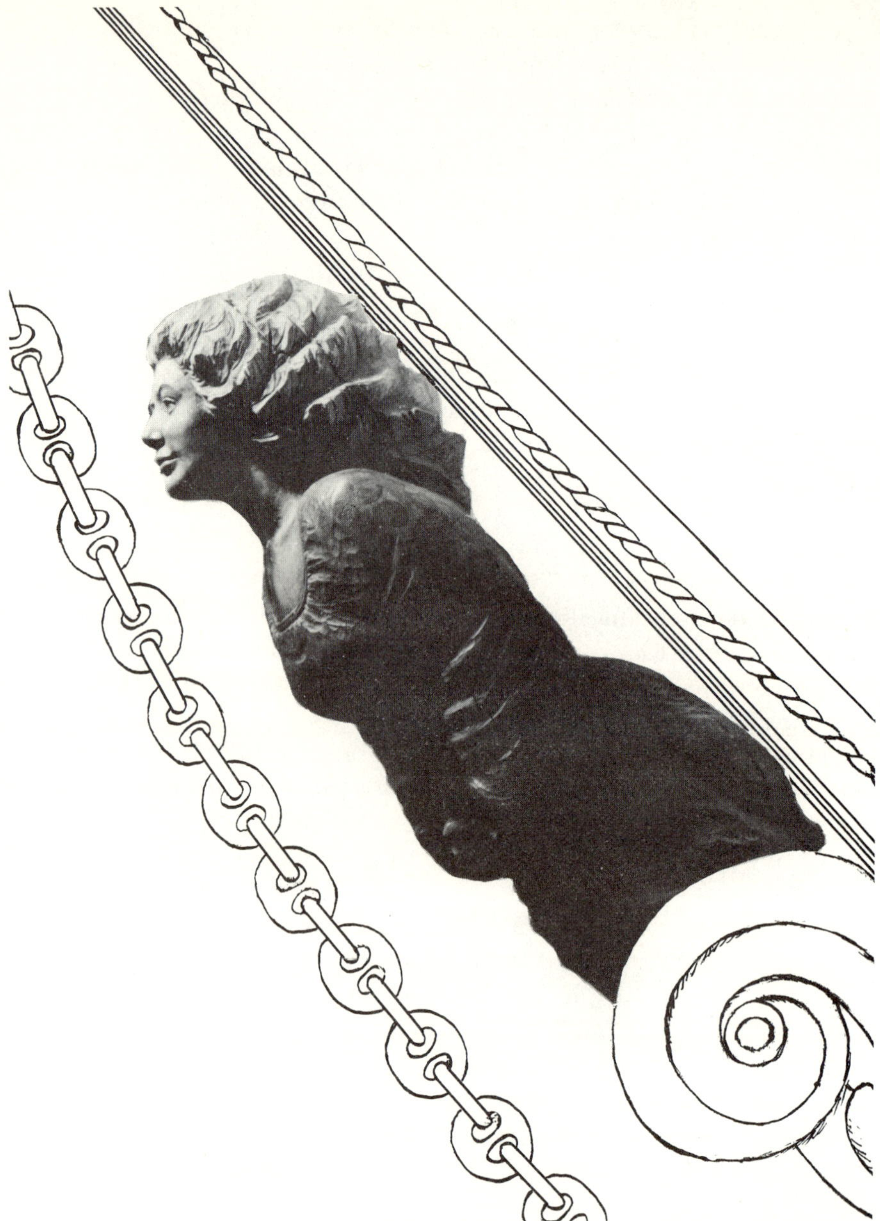

Fig. 7. Figurehead by Arlene Seitzinger. The motif is that of the square-rigger about the mid-1800's. These ships were equipped with sturdy bowsprits and long jib-booms. The figurehead was mounted under the bowsprit at the forward end of the cutwater. The author has mounted Mrs. Seitzinger's carving at the end of a billethead, a popular ornamental carving at the forward end of the cutwater on many later ships.

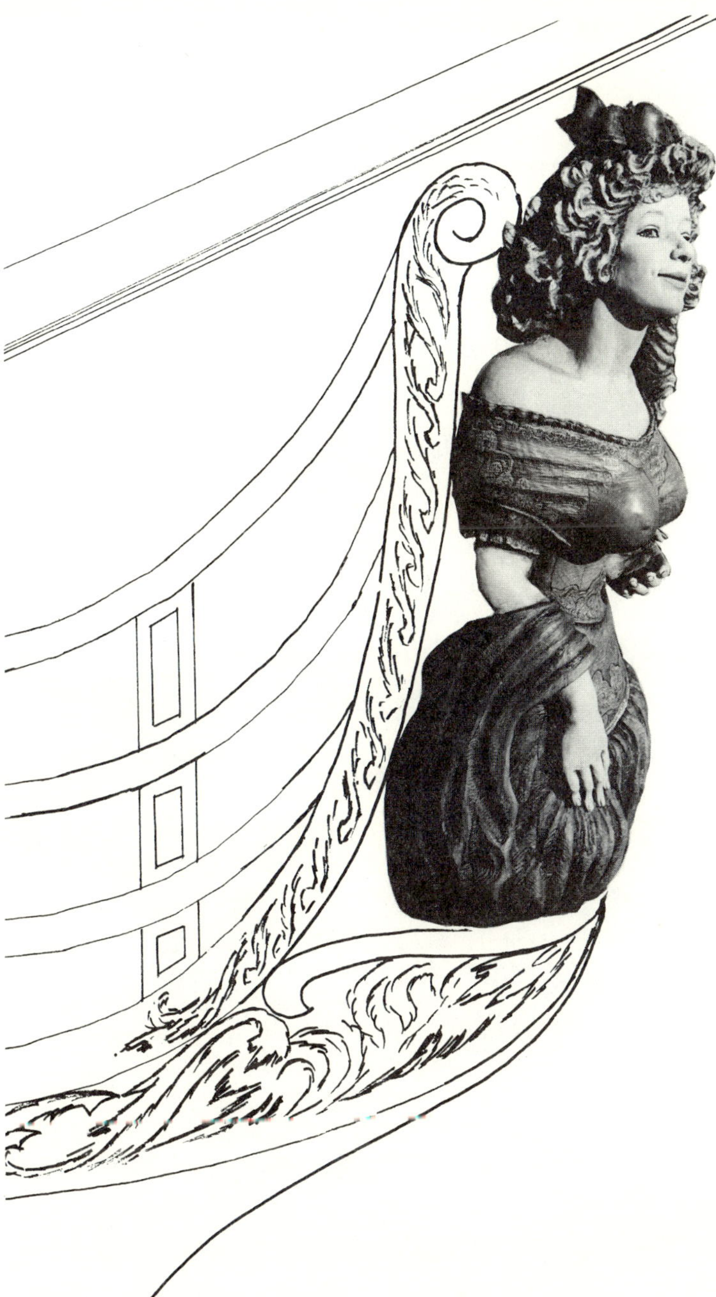

Fig. 8. Figurehead by Arlene Seitzinger. The penwork motif follows the bow design of a continental frigate of the 1770's. The ship carvers of the period favored large-breasted women. Mrs. Seitzinger has been influenced by this understandable urge.

oak and the other of cypress. The cypress log was chosen. It measured 7′ long, 32″ at the large end and 28″ at the other. The cost was $20.00 f.o.b. Now the fun began! Two adjacent sides were hewn flat and square with each other. A chain saw and axe were used for this operation (Fig. 10). The old ship carver would have used a ship-carver's adz, for he never knew the luxury of using power tools of any kind. Bob's designs were transferred to the smooth planes with a large felt pen (Fig. 11). Then transverse cuts were made 3″ apart on one side, being careful not to saw too close to the profile

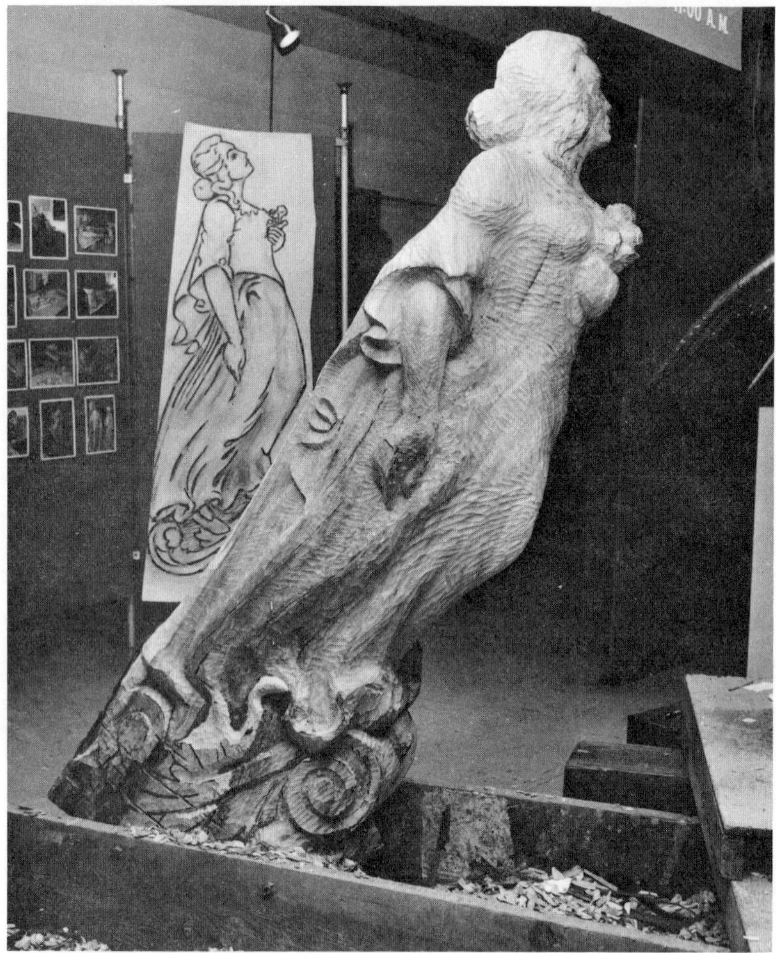

Fig. 9. Full-size figurehead being carved at The Mariners Museum.
Courtesy: The Mariners Museum, Newport News, Virginia.

lines on the adjacent side. The next operation was breaking loose the three-inch segments and smoothing the new surface with the axe and pneumatic chisel. After the new surface was tooled smooth the stencil was replaced and the design redrawn. The 3″ segments were cut on the adjacent side and the operation repeated.

"There is really no sensation which can quite compare to the satisfaction of this roughing-out stage of carving," states Hancock.

When the log had been roughed out in this fashion, the rounding-out process began. The carvers were now ready to put on their demonstrations. Before this stage had been reached they thought their modern procedures inconsistent with the old fashioned art. But now the old-fashioned methods of using chisel and mallet could be used in shaping the figure. So, the public was invited to observe the exciting work of carving down to the "skin." At

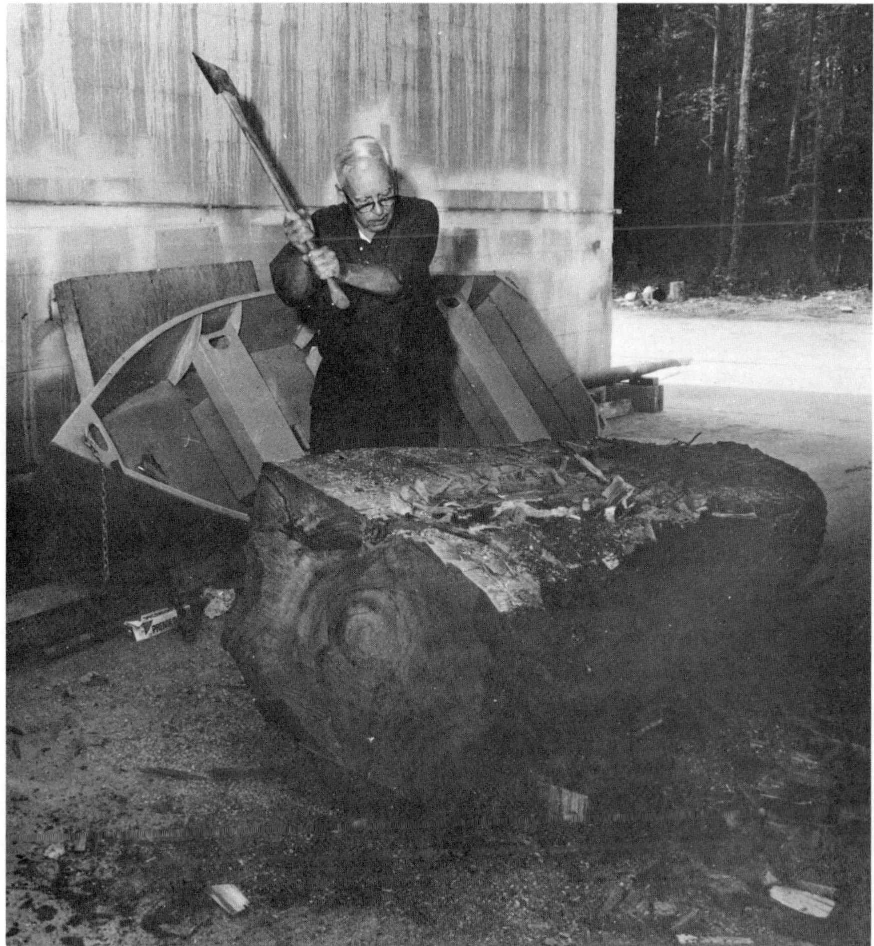

Fig. 10. Squaring the log with an axe. *Courtesy:* The Mariners Museum, Newport News, Virginia.

appointed intervals the carving proceeded before an interested audience. Figure 13 shows Hancock with chisel and mallet at work before a group of children and adults.

There are several suggestions Hancock makes that are followed by every experienced carver, but which should be repeated for emphasis. 1) When a

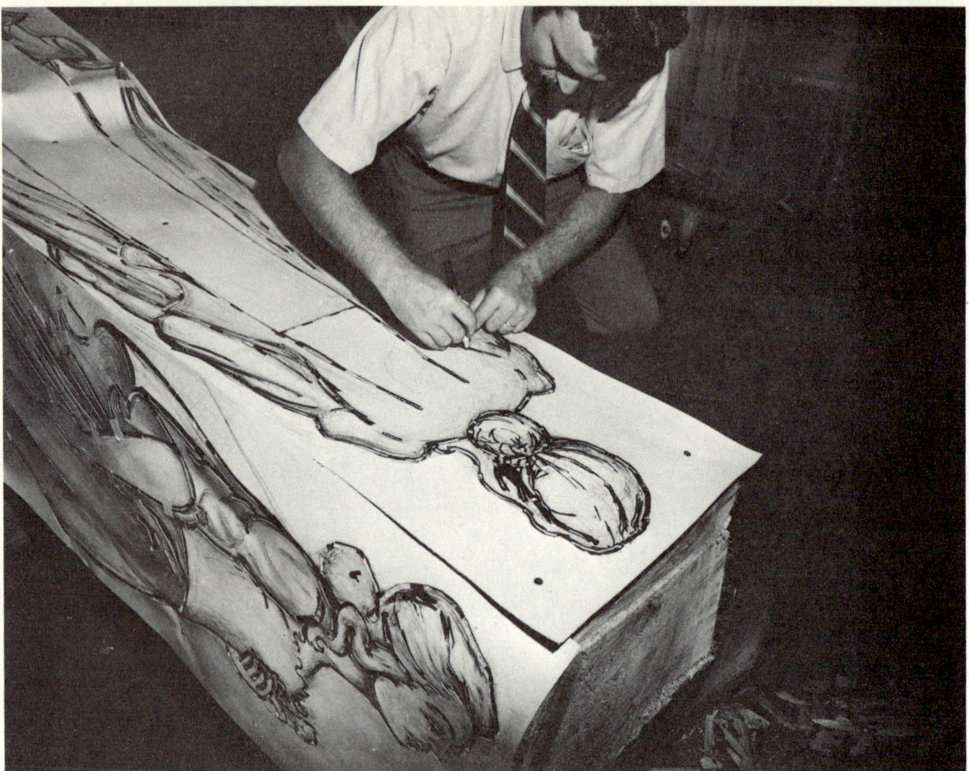

Fig. 11. Robert Brushwood stencils the design on the squared log. *Courtesy:* The Mariners Museum, Newport News, Virginia.

line is removed in the process of carving, replace it. 2) View the carving from all angles at appropriate intervals for guidance and correction. 3) Carve all over the figure to avoid distortion and achieve good proportion. Here are some other good suggestions for good measure. 4) Do not carve below the "skin"–it hurts. 5) Finally carve no "flying buttresses" to be later knocked off by accident. Flying buttresses detract from a sculpture according to some well known authorities. They prefer the static, "tight" compositions which indicate motion by indirection. The Hancock-Brushwood figurehead violates none of these orthodox rules. It is a fine piece of sculpture of a lady of exceptional beauty.

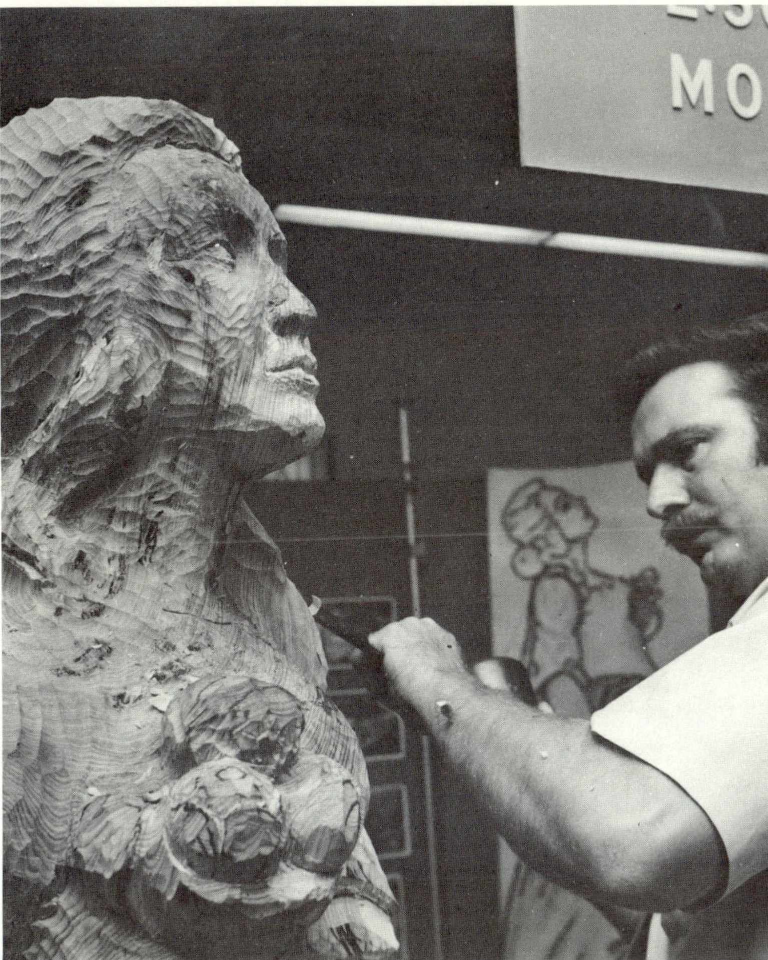

Fig. 12. Closeup of upper portion of figurehead during the early stages of carving. *Courtesy:* The Mariners Museum, Newport News, Virginia.

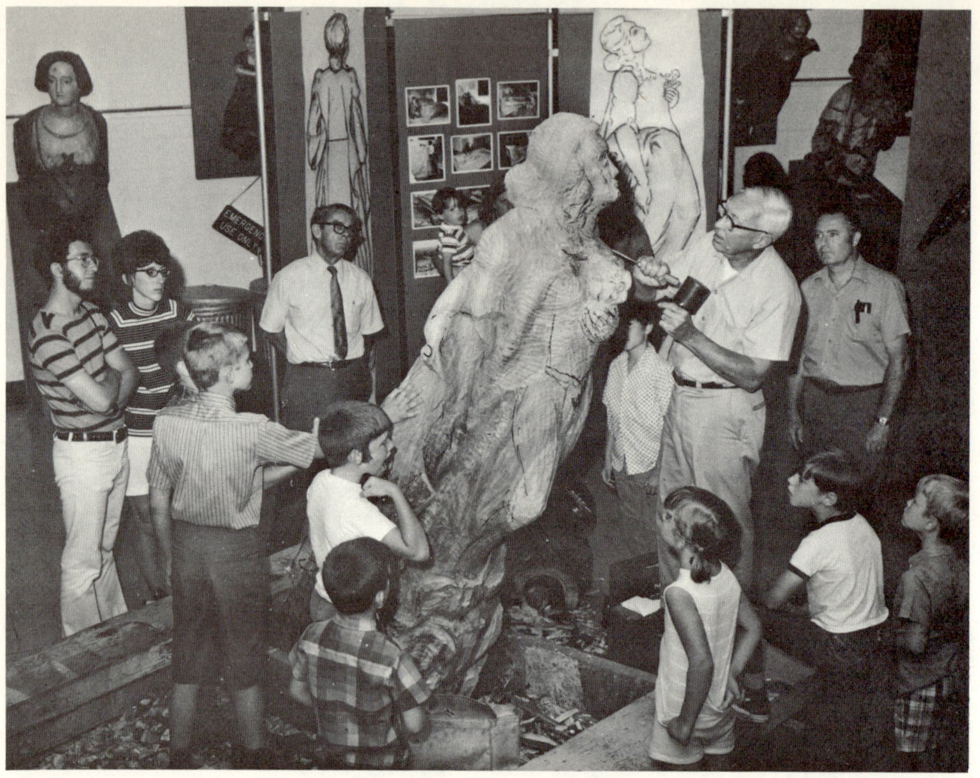

Fig. 13. C.H. Hancock carving figurehead at The Mariners Museum. *Courtesy:* The Mariners Museum, Newport News, Virginia.

The photographs (Figs. 14–26) show a selection of historical figureheads mounted in The Mariners Museum at Newport News, Virginia, and elsewhere.

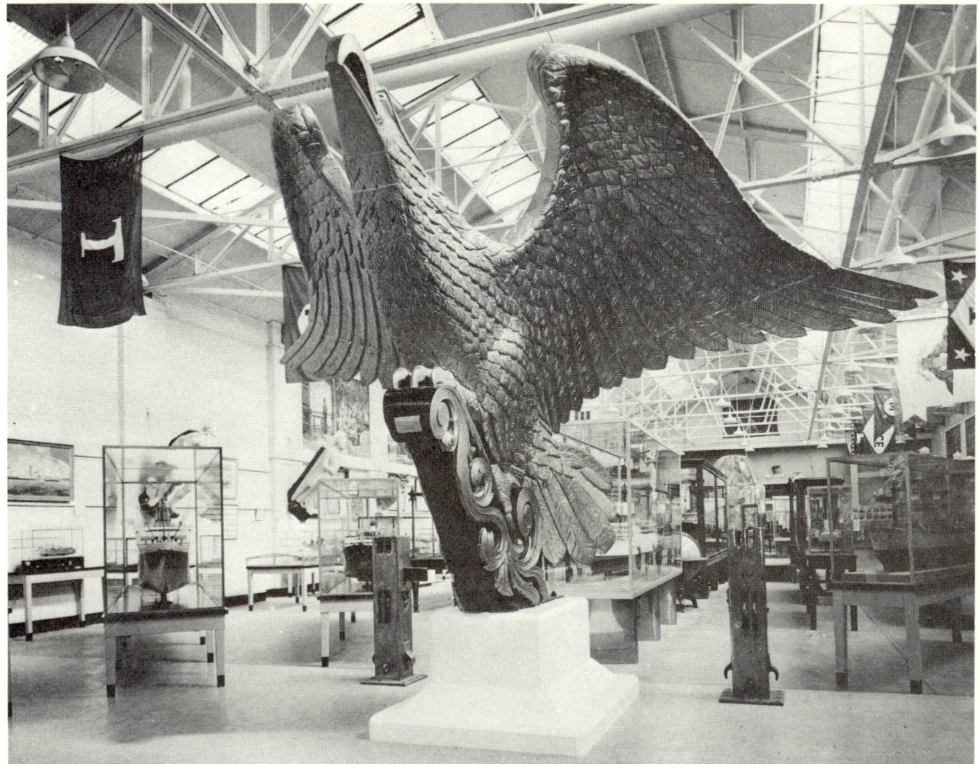

Fig. 14. Eagle figurehead from the *U.S.S. Lancaster* ("Bellamy's Eagle"). This heroic-sized eagle graces the entrance of The Mariners Museum. It is probably the largest figurehead ever carved. It has a wingspread of 18 feet, 8 inches, and weighs 3,200 pounds.

The figurehead was carved by John Haley Bellamy, one of the most famous ship carvers of his day. It was installed on the *U.S.S. Lancaster* while she was being reconditioned at the New Hampshire Navy Yard in the early 1880's. She was one of a group of steam frigates built by the U.S. Government, and among the first screw-propelled naval vessels.

The *U.S.S. Lancaster* was built at the Philadelphia Navy Yard in 1858. She displaced 3,250 tons, was 235 feet long, and had a beam of 46 feet. The old vessel finally became a training ship before she was broken up. *Courtesy:* The Mariners Museum, Newport News, Virginia.

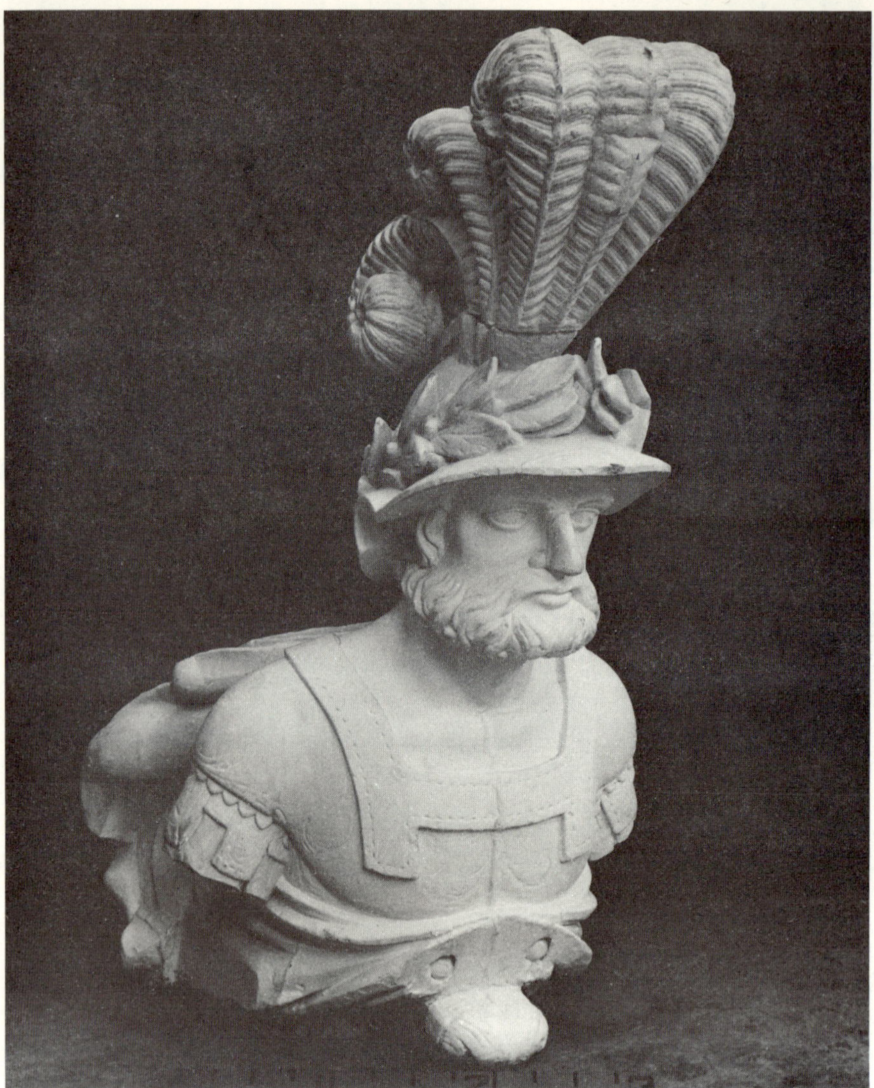

Fig. 15. Figurehead, *Formidable.* This bust type figurehead was from an 84-gun warship launched at Chatham, England, in 1825. After 1896 the *Formidable* was used as a training ship. She was broken up in 1906.

This flamboyant carving of an armored warrior, stolid in expression, was suitable for an English warship. He seems to say: "If you want a fight, let it begin here." The features are nicely carved, bold and clear, but the technique is more or less conventional or stylized. *Courtesy:* The Mariners Museum, Newport News, Virginia.

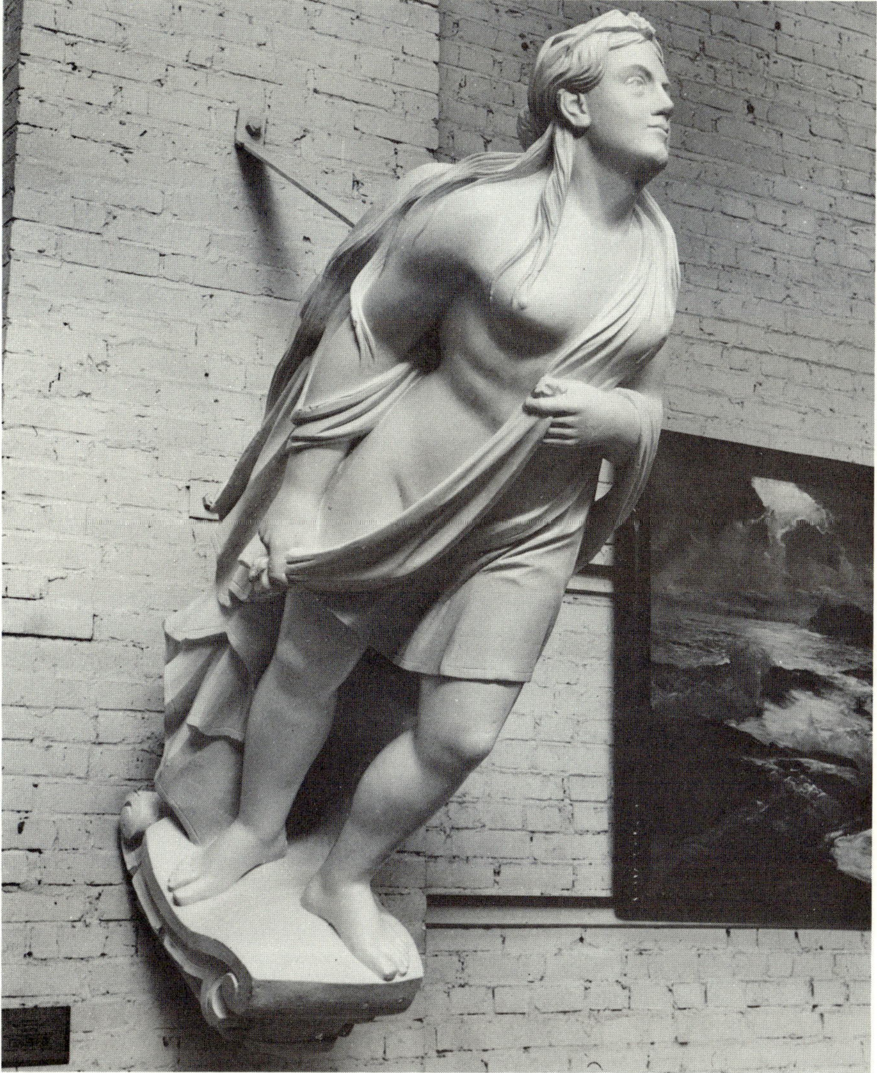

Fig. 16. Figurehead, *Galatea.* According to legend, Pygmalion prayed to Aphrodite to bring his sculpture, *Galatea,* to life. He had fallen in love with his own work! She heard his prayer, so the ivory statue of the maiden was brought to life. The ship carver who designed and carved the figurehead failed to use enough female hormones, for while it is skillfully carved, it is more masculine than feminine. But Pygmalion was a peculiar character himself and his statue might have been influenced by a father complex.

The clipper ship *Galatea* was built in Charleston, Massachusetts, in 1854. She was 182 x 36.6 x 23 feet, and displaced 939 tons. *Courtesy:* The Mariners Museum, Newport News, Virginia.

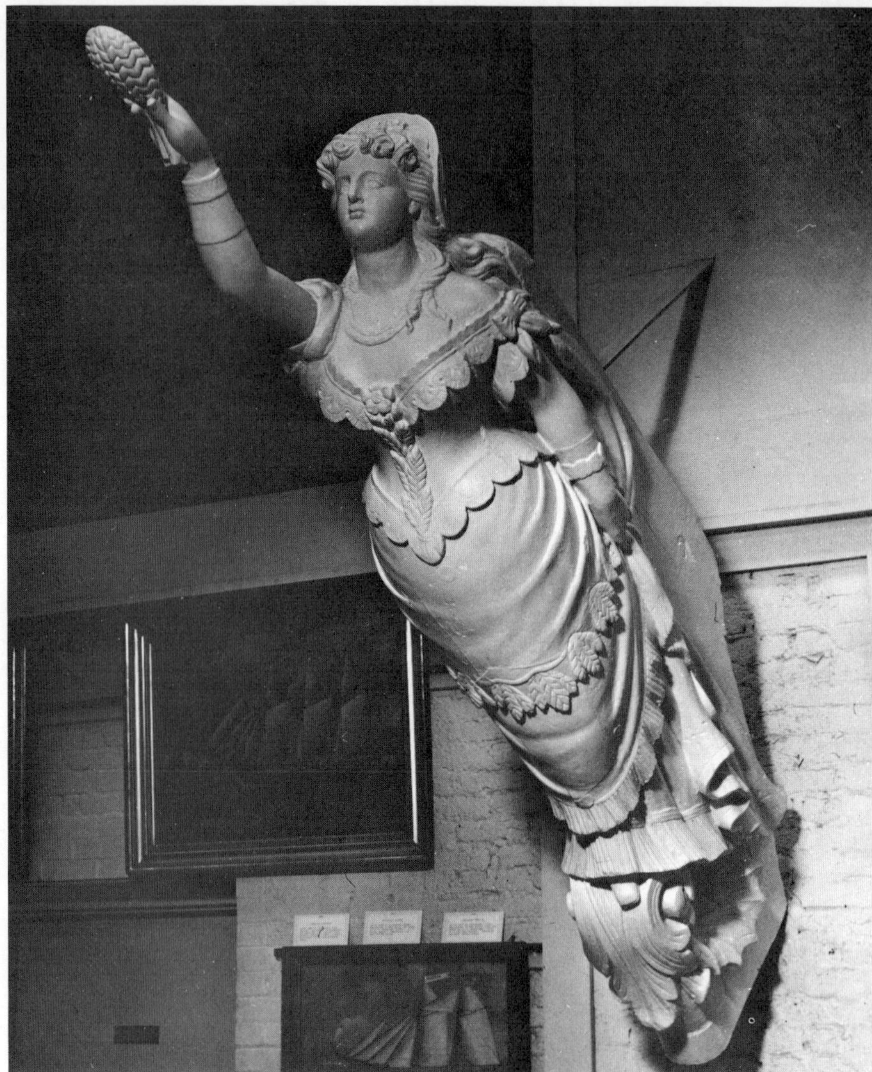

Fig. 17. Figurehead, *Belle of Oregon.* This exquisite carving is from the bark *Belle of Oregon,* built at Bath, Maine, in 1876. It was carved by Charles A.L. Sampson, a skillful ship carver who liked his women plump and fair. The figurehead measures 8 feet, 6 inches overall.

The *Belle of Oregon* was a merchant ship of 1,040 tons. She ended her days (as did many other proud vessels) in a menial capacity. Hopefully, the attractive lady was removed in the meantime, for it is difficult to visualize such a figurehead gracing the bow of a coal barge. *Courtesy:* The Mariners Museum, Newport News, Virginia.

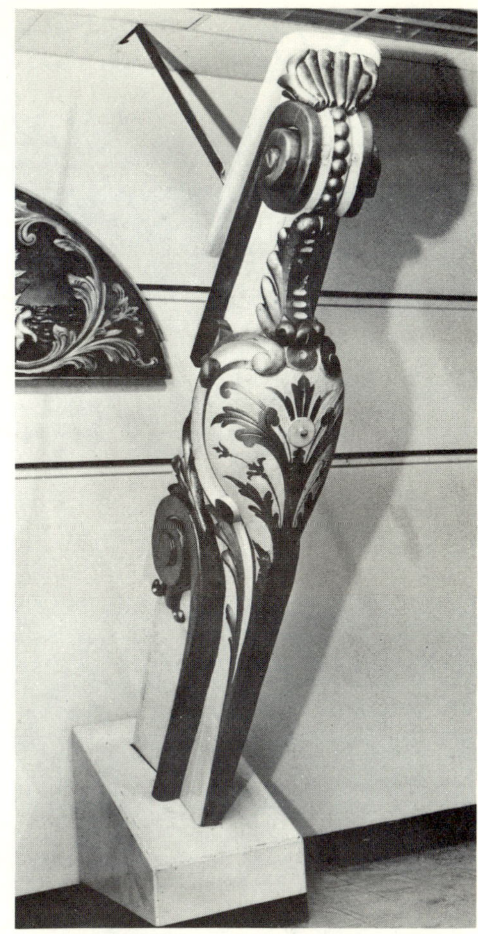

Fig. 18. Billethead from the ex-presidential yacht *Mayflower.* Sometimes a "billethead," a carved scroll ornamentation, was used for a bow decoration instead of a figurehead. The ex-presidential yacht *Mayflower* is an example.

The *Mayflower* was built at Clydebank, Scotland, in 1896. She measured 273 x 36 x 17.4 feet and displaced about 2,690 tons. Her first important mission was helping to block the harbor of Havana during the Spanish-American War. In 1902, Admiral Dewey used the vessel as his flagship. Three years later, President Theodore Roosevelt chose the *Mayflower* as the presidential yacht. For 35 years she carried United States' presidents and their cabinets on official cruises and vacations. Both Presidents Harding and Coolidge entertained in its spacious salon, but President Hoover thought the annual upkeep ($300,000) too expensive, so the *Mayflower* was laid up for sale.

In 1943, after several unfortunate incidents, the *Mayflower* was refitted and armed at a cost of more than $1,000,000 to join the fleet of destroyers in World War II. She was larger than most vessels of this class and was powered with two oil-burning engines developing 4,800 horsepower. In 1931, she was finally sold for junk for $7,666. In her heyday she was worth more than $430,000. *Courtesy:* The Mariners Museum, Newport News, Virginia.

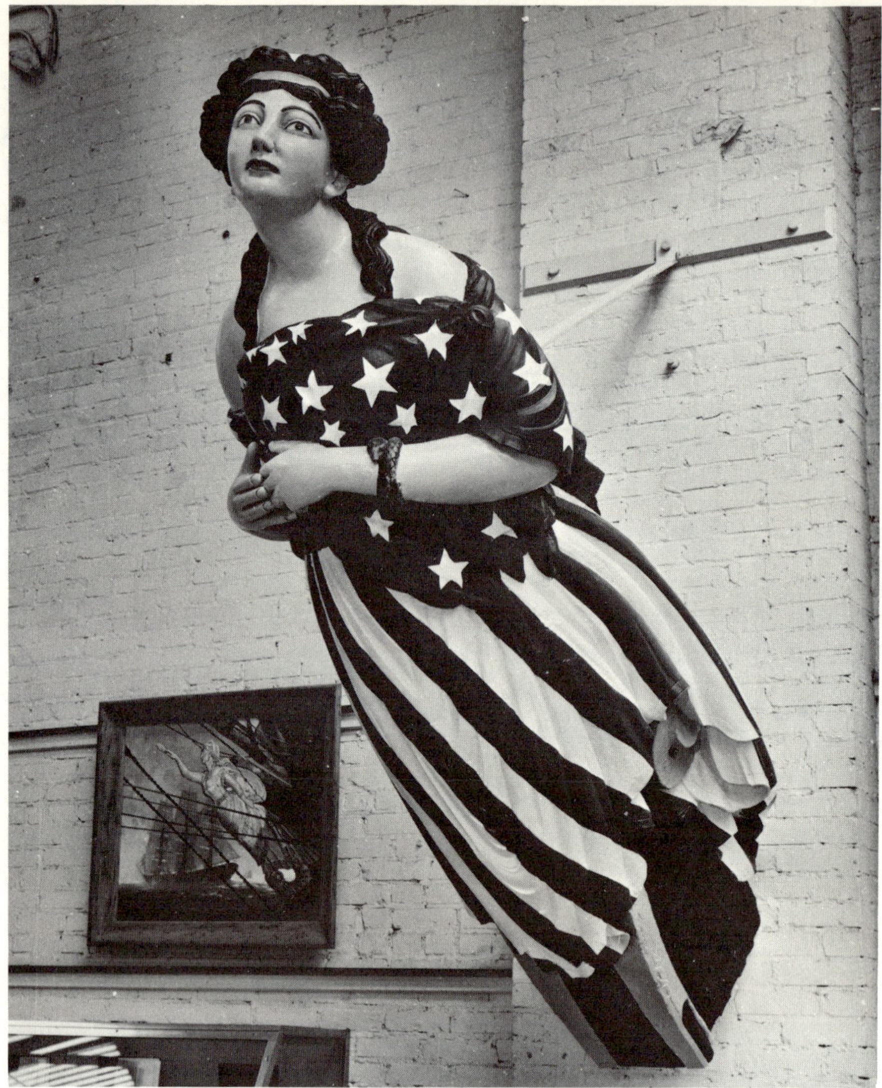

Fig. 19. Figurehead, *Flag Girl.* This beautiful figurehead graced the bow of the iron square-rigger, bark *Benmore,* built in 1870. She had two decks, was 242.0 x 39.2 x 23.6 feet, and displaced 1,460 tons. She sailed on her first cruise as the pride of the English Merchant Marine. Most of her history is clouded in mystery and folklore.

The figurehead probably was not an American carving. *Courtesy:* The Mariners Museum, Newport News, Virginia.

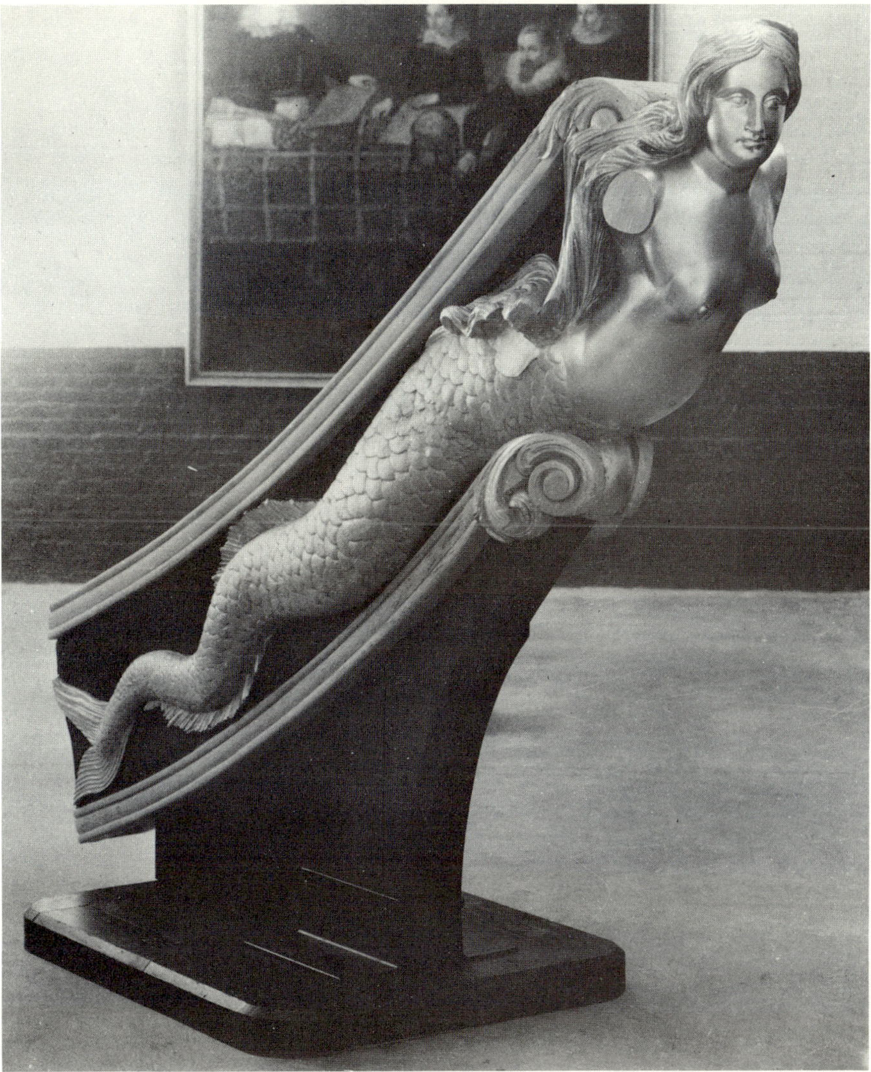

Fig. 20. Figurehead, *Mermaid.* The ship which carried this figurehead is unknown. It was presented to The Mariners Museum by Clifford W. Ashley and N.C. Wyeth in 1935. The photograph is reminiscent of Venus de Milo—she has lost her arms. These "flying buttresses" have been mentioned before, and here is a striking example to prove the point. The photograph indicates that the arms were originally carved, for a recess remains where the hands rested on the hair and hip. Farther down, the scales of the figurehead have been grazed, probably when the vessel came too close to a wharf or dock, knocking off the arms and damaging the "skin" of the mermaid. Abrasive tackle may have grazed the thighs.

This carving is another example of fine craftsmanship and it is an ideal subject for a sailing ship. *Courtesy:* The Mariners Museum, Newport News, Virginia.

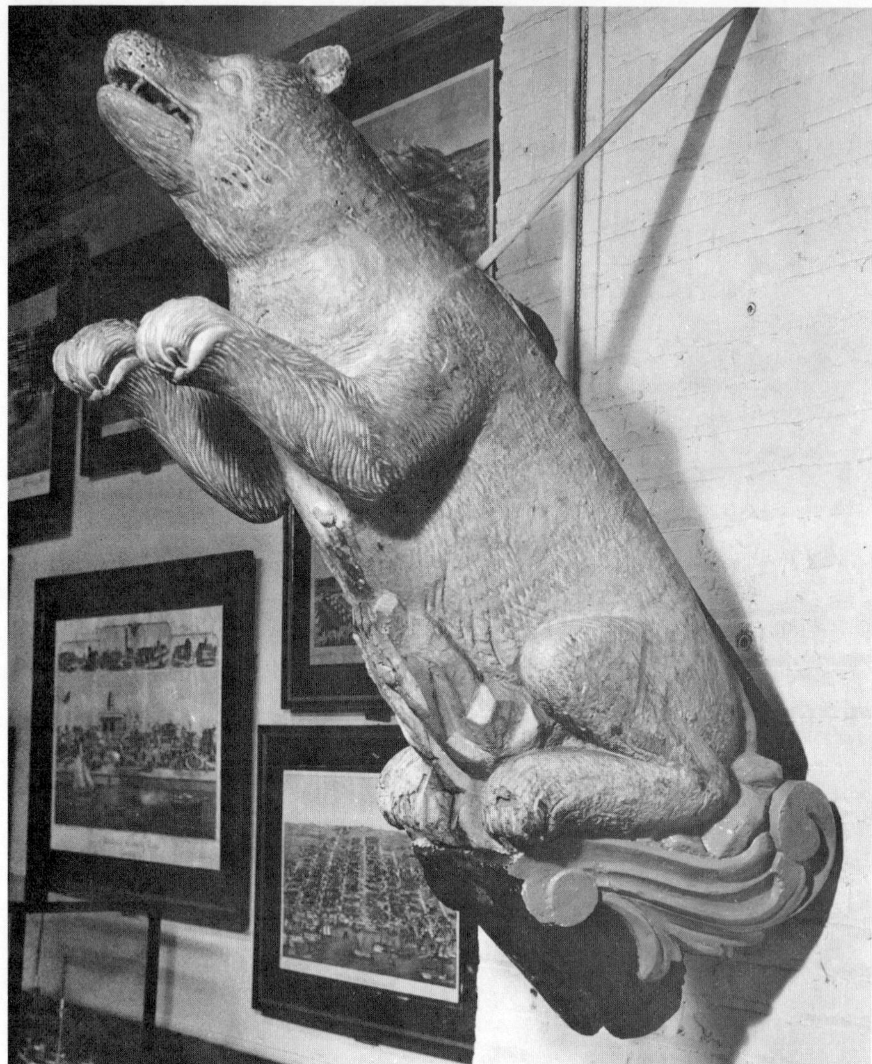

Fig. 21. Figurehead, *Bear.* This historic figurehead from a famous American ship was donated to The Mariners Museum by Rear-Admiral Richard E. Byrd, September 1935. It was the original figurehead of the barkentine-rigged ship, *Bear.* Sometime between 1935 and 1939, a second figurehead was carved, depicting only the head and neck of a polar bear. She carried this figurehead during the 1939-1941 expedition. Between 1941 and 1948 a third figurehead was carved, an almost exact copy of the first—a full-length polar bear. This figurehead still graces her bow.

The *Bear* was built in 1874 at Dundee, Scotland: length 200 feet; depth 18 feet, 2 inches; beam 32 feet. She was purchased from her owners by the U.S. Government on January 28, 1884 for $100,000 to be used in the Greeley R. Relief Expedition. Late in the same year she was transferred to the Revenue Cutter Service (now Coast Guard). *(Continued)*

(Continued)

The *Bear* was originally built for Arctic service, but the government further strengthened her by placing more frames, closer together, forward. Additional beams were placed between those already supporting the lower decks, and truss forms were put in extending from the bilge to the middle of the lower deck beams. Watertight bulkheads were installed both forward and aft. Her first northern assignment was to search for a crew of the whaling bark *Amethyst.* Until World War II, the *Bear's* history was a long succession of cruises in the Arctic. Her most famous rescue was for the relief of eight whaling ships trapped in the Arctic ice near Point Barrow in 1897. Nearly 500 whalers were aboard.

On May 3, 1929, the *Bear* was placed out of commission at Oakland, California. She was recalled to active duty by the Navy in 1933 and sent on the Byrd expedition to Little America. During World War II, the *Bear* was Navy manned and employed on the Greenland patrol. In 1956, there was a rumor that she would join the Newfoundland sealing fleet out of Halifax at the remarkable age of 84.

Courtesy: The Mariners Museum, Newport News, Virginia.

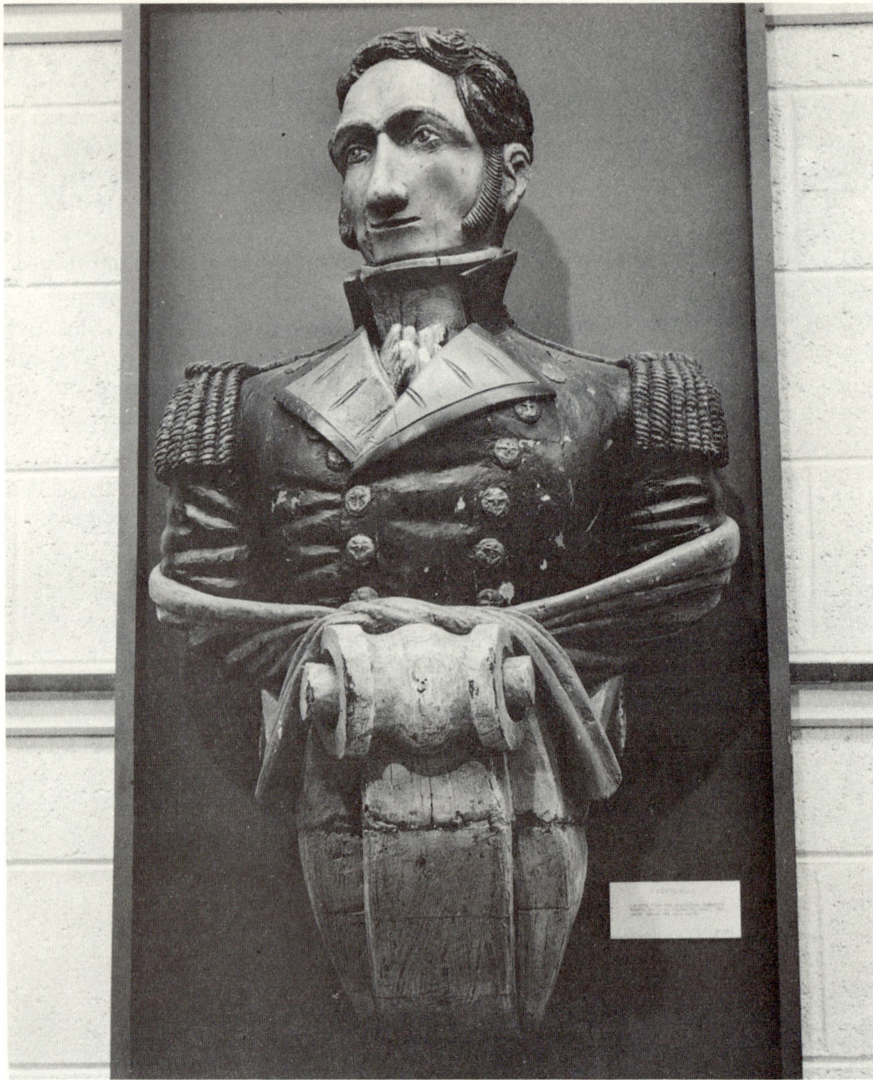

Fig. 22. Figurehead from the *Commodore Morris*. The *Commodore Morris* was a whaling ship of 355 tons. She was built in Falmouth, Massachusetts. After four whaling voyages out of Falmouth she made at least three more out of New Bedford.

This carving has some admirable features. The coat, eyes, and hair are good. The proportions are excellent, and the buttons on the coat have the anchor motif carved with patient care. The mouth is not skillfully carved. Note that the sideburns and the epaulets are archaically carved.

This photograph shows how the busts of men were mounted on the bow. *Courtesy:* The Mariners Museum, Newport News, Virginia.

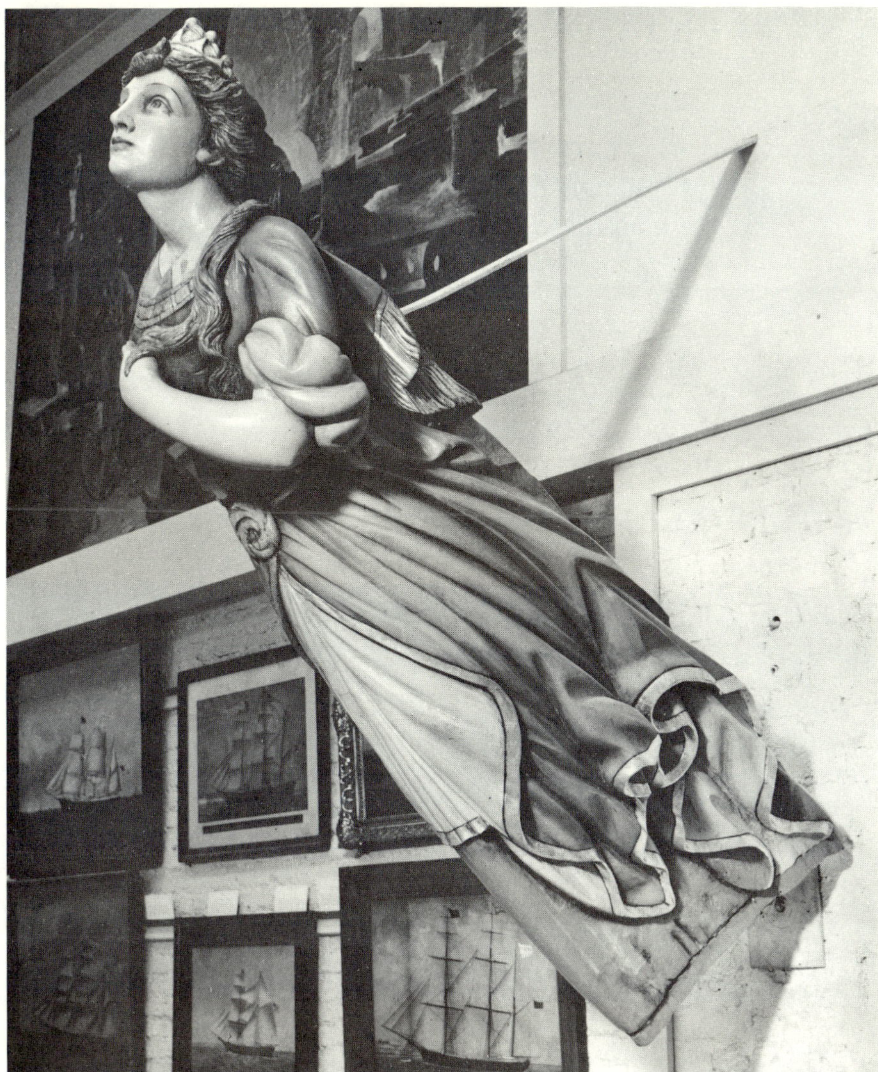

Fig. 23. Figurehead, *Calbuco*. The figurehead shown here might have originally been intended for a fascinating woman or an enchantress as the ship was built in Glasgow as a full-rigged ship, *Circe*. She had a number of owners. In 1924 she was bought by Jerman Oelckers of Puerto Montt, Chile, who gave her the name "*Calbuco.*"

The figurehead is a carving of a beautiful woman. The clothing is especially good; facial features are sharp and crisp—that is, the carving is bold and not "ragged." The hair is well done. The carver possessed skill comparable to the famous Skillings. *Courtesy:* The Mariners Museum, Newport News, Virginia.

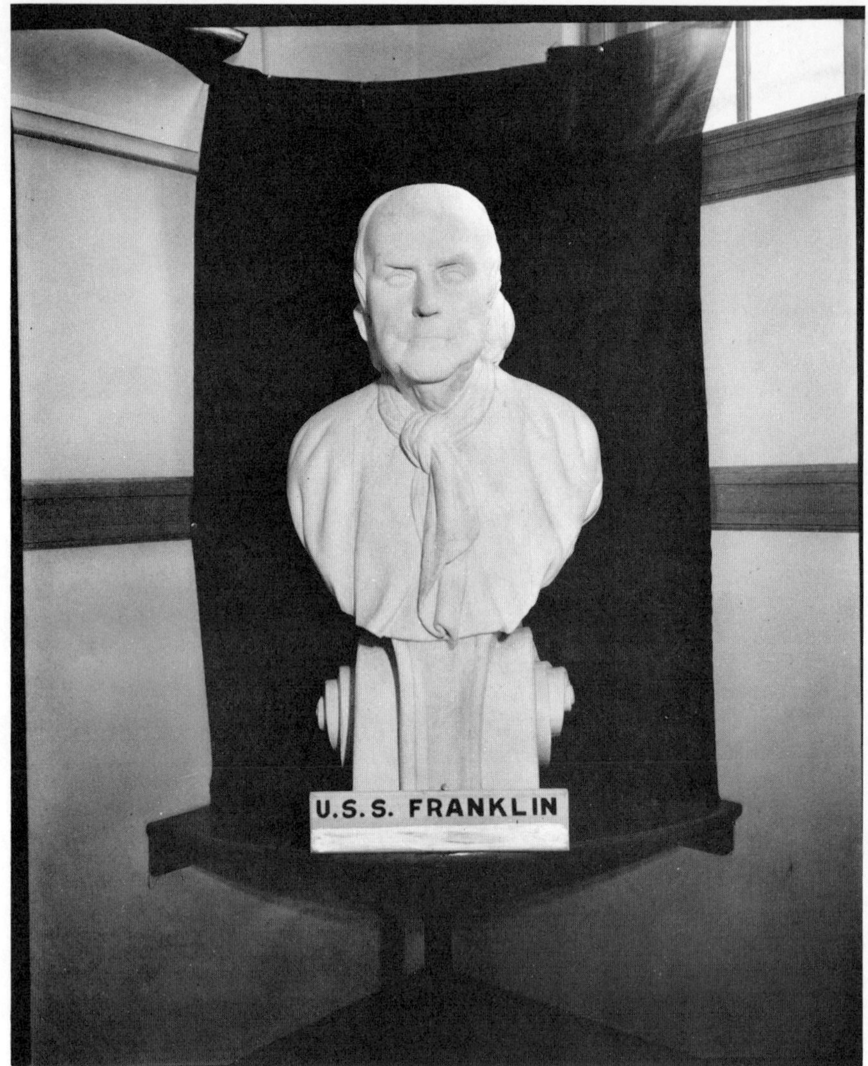

Fig. 24. Prior to the advent of ironclads, U.S. Naval ships carried figureheads of national leaders. The *U.S.S. Franklin* graced her bow with the portrait bust of Benjamin Franklin. The museum date on the photograph is 1815, probably the date of the sculpture. My notes have the dates 1766–1831. These dates would indicate two ships of the same name. The sculpture of Franklin was probably executed for the recommissioned ship.

The sculptor was William Rush of Philadelphia. Both of the dates, 1815 and 1831, correspond to the period in which the famous sculptor worked (the late 1700's and early 1800's).

William Rush, America's first native sculptor, began his career as a carver of ships' figureheads.

In 1794 William Rush was commissioned to design all heads of six frigates, four of which he carved himself. Benjamin Franklin was probably one of these.

The sculpture is mounted on a billethead. *Courtesy:* U.S. Naval Academy Museum.

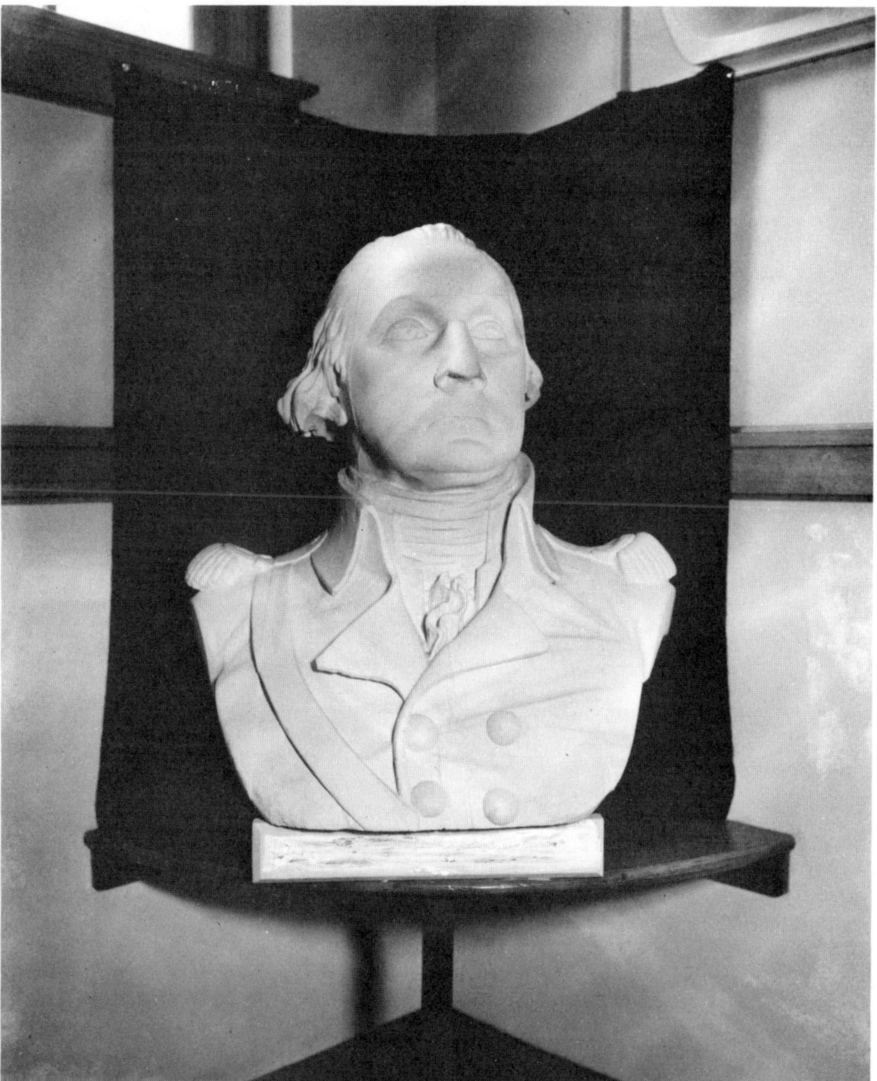

Fig. 25. Solomon Willard (1817) met William Rush in Philadelphia and executed the bust figurehead of the 74-gun ship *Washington.* This sculpture might have been one of the six which William Rush was commissioned to design. As he carved only four himself, there were two others he did not execute. The author believes the portrait bust of George Washington was one of those two. The bust is an excellent job, but lacks the superb skill of William Rush, one of the most famous sculptors of his day.

The busts of Franklin and Washington illustrate figureheads of the era when portraits of famous leaders were in vogue, just before the advent of the iron-clads. *Courtesy:* U.S. Naval Academy Museum.

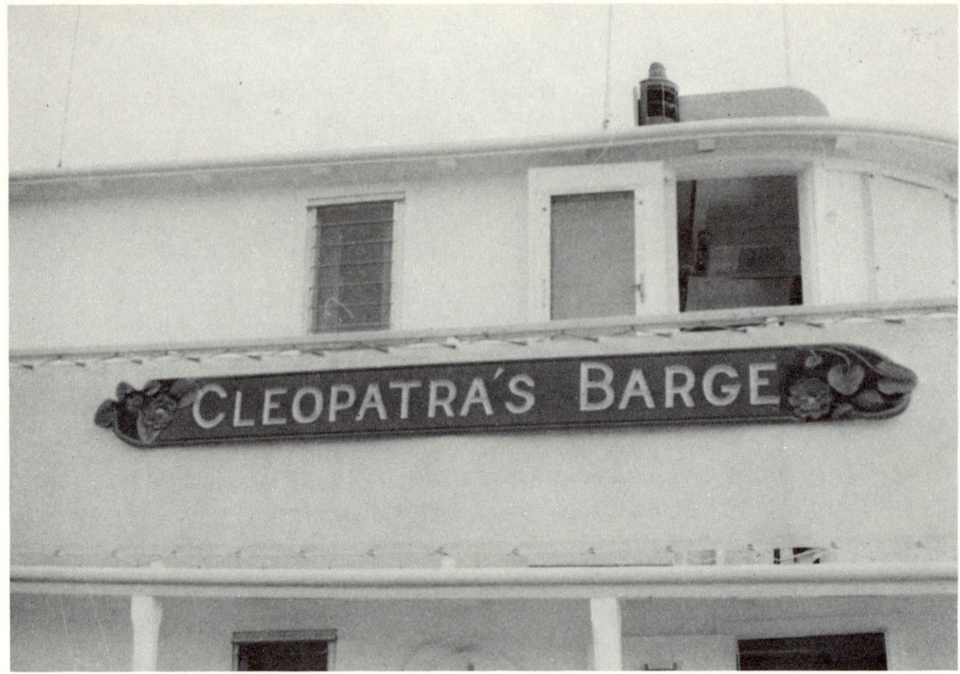

Fig. 26. Trailboards for Pierce Coady, Jr., Greenturtle Cay, Bahamas. The boards measured 12′ long, carved at each end with lotus leaves and flowers in color. Along the top and bottom sides a 1″ bead framed the 8″ gold leaf letters.

Cleopatra's Barge was built originally to serve as a "buy boat" to run oysters from the natural rocks to the oyster houses. Mr. Coady first used the boat after he purchased it to run freight. Finally, he converted the vessel to a floating home with all of the modern conveniences and appointments. When the author visited the barge expensive carpets covered the bottom, even rising up the side keelson. There were sleeping accommodations for several individuals.

"The trailboards brought out a lot of cameras as we sailed home through the inland waterway," observed Mr. Coady.

Chapter 4

The Canada Goose

PART 1

Mickey, Minnie, Moses and Tugboat

Mickey and Minnie knew no other life than that of the pond and the friendship of the kind lady who fed them. They were brother and sister and always maintained this close relationship. Each had developed a psychological mother-complex toward the lady of the pond and seemed delighted to be near her and eat from her hand. If they were swimming on the pond all required of the lady was to call their names and they would tread water to reach her quickly.

The skeins of geese which flew overhead in winter were interesting but they showed no desire to join them. Later in the fall many geese would splash down on the pond to rest, or perhaps glean the yard for grain the chickens had overlooked. Both Minnie and Mickey seemed unconcerned. Occasionally, the urge to fly did become obsessive, but their flight was short, never far from home. When in early spring the migrating geese became restless and began to fly north toward their Canadian fields and marshes, neither Mickey nor Minnie felt the urge to join them. Therefore, during the long hot summer months they were alone on the pond.

When autumn arrived and a bite was felt in the morning air, there was a stirring in their blood, for the hot, sticky days of summer were over. The first geese migrating from Canada would soon announce their arrival and the sky would be full of them. They were a welcome sight flying in long skeins across the bright orb of the moon.

One dark, cold wintry day a skein of geese flew low over the pond. On the tail end was a straggler that seemed indifferent to either following or maintaining the design of flight. He might have been tired, or a "maverick" that cared not a whoop about keeping in line. In any event he was not interested and did not care about the objective of the skein. He discovered the two geese on the pond swimming together leisurely and decided to drop down and join them. He splashed down near Minnie and paddled over to her. It was love at first sight. To Mickey's surprise and disgust the two swam off together, leaving him alone. Being a sociable bird he quickly followed them, but the visiting gander chased him away. He would have nothing to do with Mickey. Mickey, being less pugnacious, decided not to tangle with him. He hated being separated from Minnie, but if that was the way Minnie felt, he could do little about it. Mickey's docile spirit gave in to the attacks of the stranger, so he swam alone forlorn and deserted.

He began to sulk and take to the air more frequently, taking long flights with the migrating geese. Perhaps he would have stayed with them, for home was not home anymore. Then it happened! He heard a loud explosion and felt the pellets of the hunter's gun against his wing and breast. Fortunately, Mickey was not far from home and was flying high in the air. Instinctively he began to coast in the direction of the pond. He felt his strength being drained, but the safety of the pond was near. He managed to splash awkwardly on the surface, exhausted. Both Minnie and her suitor noticed Mickey's irregular, jerky flight and knew something was wrong. The visiting gander swam over to him and seemed to realize that Mickey was seriously hurt. He was no longer a rival to excite his jealous nature, but a fellow creature in trouble; more to be pitied than plagued.

The lady of the pond was looking through her window when Mickey splashed on the surface, and she realized that he was injured. She had heard the report of the gun and concluded that Mickey was the victim. Outside she called to him and he slowly paddled to her dragging his wounded wing. The lady examined Mickey's wing and knew he would never fly again. The flesh wounds in his breast were not serious, but she noted that the large bone of the wing had been shattered. First she strapped the wing in place, and then prepared a nest for Mickey on the sunny side of the house. Although concerned about Mickey's plight, she felt he would recover and adjust to his new way of life. Placing a bowl of fresh water nearby, she left him to recuperate.

The visiting gander, with such a keen interest in Minnie, became her mate. He made friends with Mickey and visited him every day. Minnie was always nearby and together they were a great comfort to the wounded goose.

For no particular reason the visiting gander was named "Moses" by the lady of the pond. Only in a few minor aspects did he resemble the deliverer of the Israelites from Egyptian bondage. He did deliver Minnie from a drab, routine life to one of great delight. Minnie was also confined to a nest for a short period each day. After she had laid four beautiful eggs, she decided to remain on the nest and keep them warm. She never left her nest except to take care of her physical needs. During these days Moses was alone on the pond except for a large number of visiting geese. Moses never cared much for them in the beginning; he cared even less for them now. But, even so, they were better company than none at all. So, when in early spring the long irregular skeins of geese began to migrate to their Canadian marshes and fields, he decided to remain and be with Minnie and Mickey. He visited Minnie every day and sat on the grass near her for hours at a time. On the way back to the pond, he would stop near Mickey's nest and pass the time of day. The rest of his leisure was spent swimming around the pond and making friends with the lady who fed him. Moses was enjoying his easy life. No more would he take the long fatiguing flights along the Atlantic flyway; no more would he fly so many miles before he slept. He had found his home and he did not intend to leave it.

When Minnie left her nest one morning, four little goslings trailed after her (Fig. 1). Her route to the pond passed by Mickey's nest. He became excited, and even though he did not feel equal to the task, he left his nest and followed after Minnie and her goslings (Fig. 2). Moses, discovering the return of the "natives," swam over to meet them. He seemed highly elated and

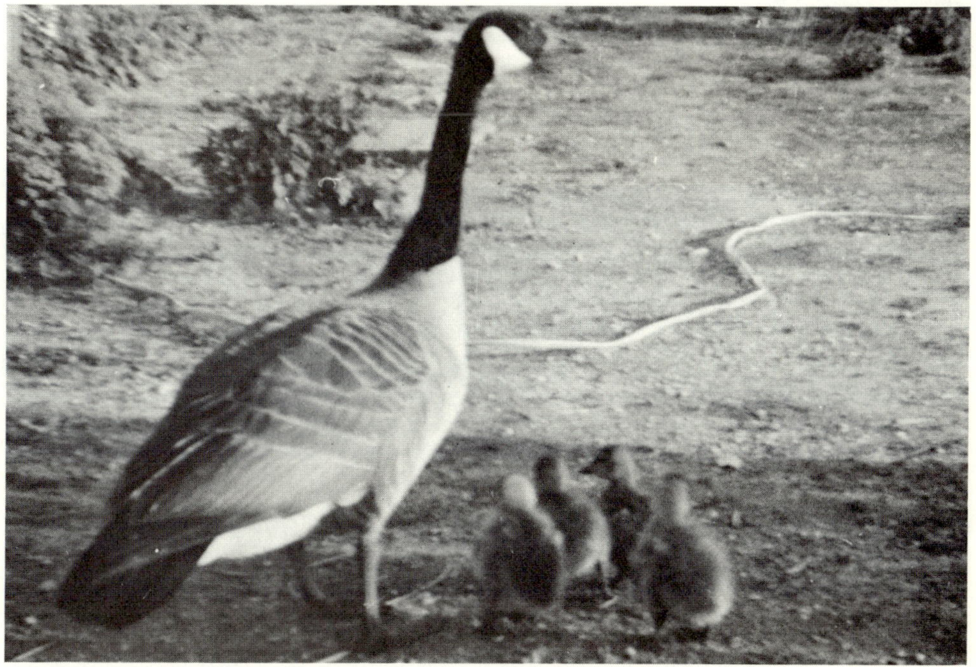

Fig. 1. Minnie and her goslings.

pleased with his new family. The lady, watching them through the window, thought she saw Moses wink his eye at Mickey. They all plunged into the water together and swam to the far side; the goslings in a single file behind, instinctively enjoying their new mode of transportation.

The barrel of grain now had to be filled more frequently. Five new mouths to feed made a great difference. But the geese believed in the magic of the barrel which was never empty but always full and running over. The summer went by without incident. Then the air changed to autumn again and the bite in the air heralded the long skeins of geese returning to their Maryland marshes and fields. With the return of the wild, migrating geese, the lady noticed a strange phenomenon. Whether on the pond or resting on her yard, the domesticated geese held themselves aloof from the others. There was also a difference in their appearance. Her geese were larger and had a more pronounced sheen to their feathers. The segregation was mutual for the wild geese would not mix with their more domesticated peers. There was no social reformer among them urging integration; so both groups were happy and content in their isolation, and showed no enmity toward each other. The lady reasoned that nature knew best and that not only birds of a feather, but of a breed also, should flock together.

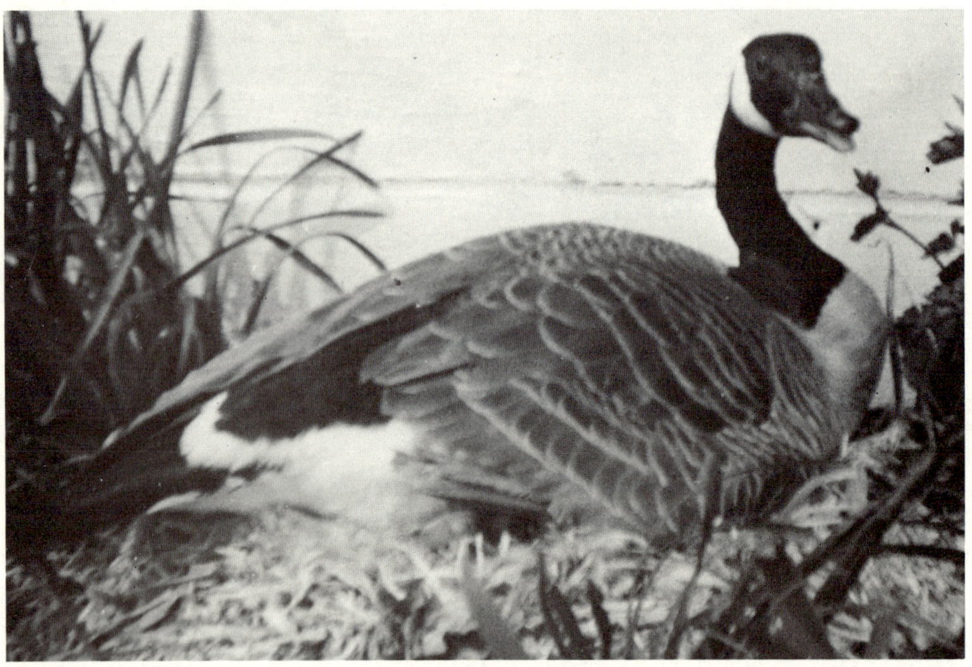

Fig. 2. Mickey. Note the feather design.

The next season the good lady placed a mallard's egg among Minnie's clutch. It hatched just as successfully as the others. Minnie did not notice the difference at first, but later the difference became more pronounced. She could not account for this strange little fellow developing differently from the rest of her brood, but being a good mother, she made allowances for him. When the time came to take her goslings to the pond, the mallard lagged behind. Minnie dropped behind and with her beak nuzzled him forward, tumbling him over at times. His ineptness vexed her, but with persistent care and abiding patience she urged him to keep up with the rest. Because the mallard was always behind, the lady named him "Tugboat," but Minnie was always doing most of the pushing. Minnie took her chores as a mother seriously, but Tugboat sorely troubled her. She finally gave up in disgust and let him travel at his own pace. If he wanted to march to the beat of a different drummer, he could do so with her blessings. Anyhow, Moses was now entering her thoughts again. She had neglected him too long. But Moses had been in one of his indifferent moods and had not been worrying about anything—not even being ignored by his family. He had made friends with Mickey, who was not such a bad guy after all, and the two of them explored the pond and the surrounding shores together. Concerning Minnie and her brood, he could not care less. Occasionally, Tugboat would separate himself from the goslings and join Moses and Mickey. He was a peculiar little fellow with a green head and a white neckband, clearly not a goose at all. Minnie's previous year's brood did not mix well, probably because of the generation gap, so the social relations on the pond were not too encouraging. The goslings were growing new feathers and were trying out their wings. All in all, each had his own problems, but above all there was harmony among them. There was never an anxious moment.

This true story is told to provoke respect and a deep sense of identity with Minnie and her family. The Canada goose is a wise bird, sociable, and easily domesticated by persons who understand wild creatures. He will become friendly enough to eat from one's hand and will desert his kind to be with his benefactor. A gaggle of geese feeding or resting on the grass or water is a wonder to behold. Just as interesting is their flight, flying low in the air. Carve several of them, a carved beauty of softwood, and squeeze several duplicates of polyester filler.

PART 2

Polyester Filler

Before the carving begins, a brief discussion of polyester filler should prove helpful because it will be used in several operations of carving described in this book. It not only offers an entirely new approach to the carver's art, but greatly facilitates his efforts in correcting mistakes and filling unwanted cavities. It is a very useful medium, but unfortunately it is slightly toxic and must be handled with care by most people, especially those who have an allergy condition. Read the directions on the can and obey them. Most carvers should wear a mask while sanding the material or have the carving near a vacuum exhaust outlet. The author touches the mixture without harmful effects, but contact is unnecessary, and when the fingers must be used, they can be shielded with wax paper. This added caution should not alarm the carver as the author has been using polyester filler for many years.

Polyester filler is available in cans. It is used extensively by automobile body and fender workers to mend dents or damaged parts caused by collision. It has taken the place of lead for this purpose and does a more satisfactory job. It sticks, or adheres, to almost any clean surface. It is ideal for making birds' legs and feet. A tube of colored paste called a "hardener" (benzoyl peroxide) is supplied with each can. About 2″ of the paste is sufficient to harden a batch of the filler the size of a golf ball. Mix the paste and polyester thoroughly until the color becomes uniform throughout the mixture. Apply to the crack or depression with an artist's pallet knife, or with some other suitable tool when squeezing a mold. In about 10 to 15 minutes the filler will harden, depending upon room temperature, at first soft enough to cut easily with a sharp knife or chisel, and later hard enough

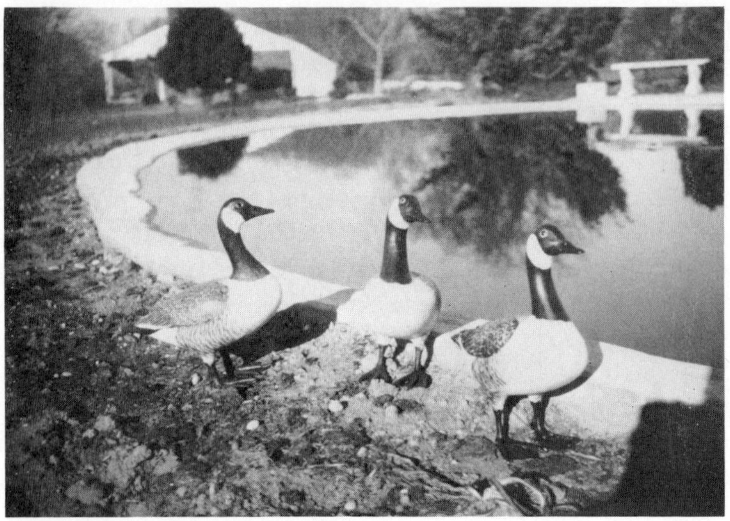

Fig. 3. Polyester duplicates.

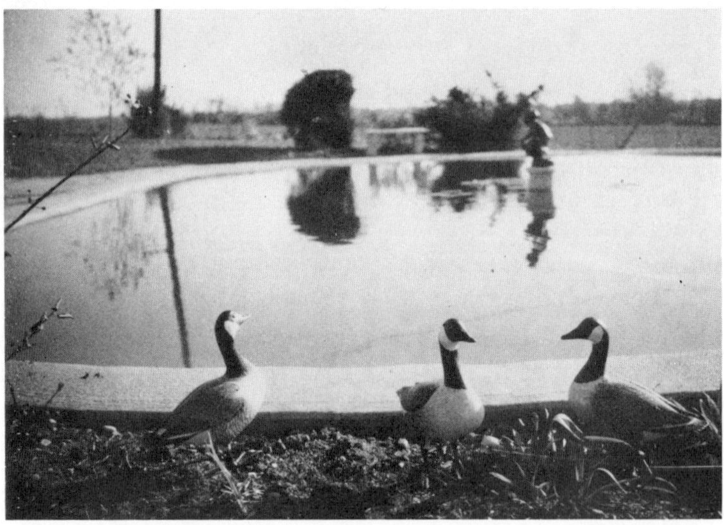

Fig. 4. More polyester duplicates.

to file or sand. The material has about the same density as poplar wood, but somewhat more abrasive, dulling the tools faster. The Canada geese (Figs. 3 and 4) were squeezed from Martin-Senour's polyester filler, "Payday." Several other concerns manufacture polyester filler and they all work with little or no degree of difference. (*See* Appendix.)

Carving a Canada Goose

A full size Canada goose measures 16-25 inches in length—from the tip of its tail to the end of its beak. It has a wingspread of 50-68 inches. The body measures 7-9 inches wide and the height is slightly smaller than the width. These two dimensions are about the same, usually, and if the carving is proportioned in this manner very little, if any, realism is sacrificed. Birds vary like people in their bodily measurements, so there is an appreciable margin for differences.

The drawing (Fig. 5) is meant to serve two purposes. The first, primary purpose is to carve a realistic goose of some desired size; the second is to use this carving as a pattern to form negative molds into which polyester filler may be squeezed to form duplicate models. The crosshatched sections between the wing tips and the thighs are left in the mold to form "draft" so that the carving (pattern) may be removed without damage to the mold in the first instance and the squeezed model which has been formed in the second.* These spaces, if carved out correctly, would lock the pattern in the cement and the molded bird in the mold. The negative surfaces must be eliminated and the best way to do this is not to carve them in the first place. All surfaces should retreat from the center or parting line of the carving.

First draw the silhouette picture on cardboard and cut it out with a sharp pair of scissors. Figure 5 has been designed to facilitate this operation. The squares of the grid are sized to form a bird about one-half the size of a natural bird if drawn ½" apart. The goose in the photograph (Fig. 6) was drawn in a grid of lines about 1" apart. The goose is full size for a small specimen.

The side silhouette drawing of the goose should be all of the design necessary as two important dimensions have already been established. The third is merely an arithmetical calculation plus some anatomical knowledge of the model concerned. In this instance a front view of the bird is drawn on the assumption that the carver may be inexperienced.

A common mistake in carving birds is sharply outlining the folded wing at the sides where the soft feathers tend to rise above it. The contour where the wing blends with the feathers is concave.

Next, decide if all of the silhouette is to be included on one piece of stock, or if the neck and head are to be carved separately. Let us assume that the goose will be half-size and carved from one block. Prepare two pieces of softwood (basswood, sugar pine, white cedar, etc.) long and wide enough to include your whole drawing and half as thick as the goose is wide. Plane one surface of each piece of stock in a true plane and transfer the drawing to both boards, making sure that the drawings match when the boards are put

*If the draft sections were not left in, separate molds would be necessary to solve the separation problem. Instead of a two-part mold arrangement at least two others would be required, one between the thighs and the other between the wings. For experienced carvers these extra molds are recommended, but for the novice a two-part mold will probably present fewer problems.

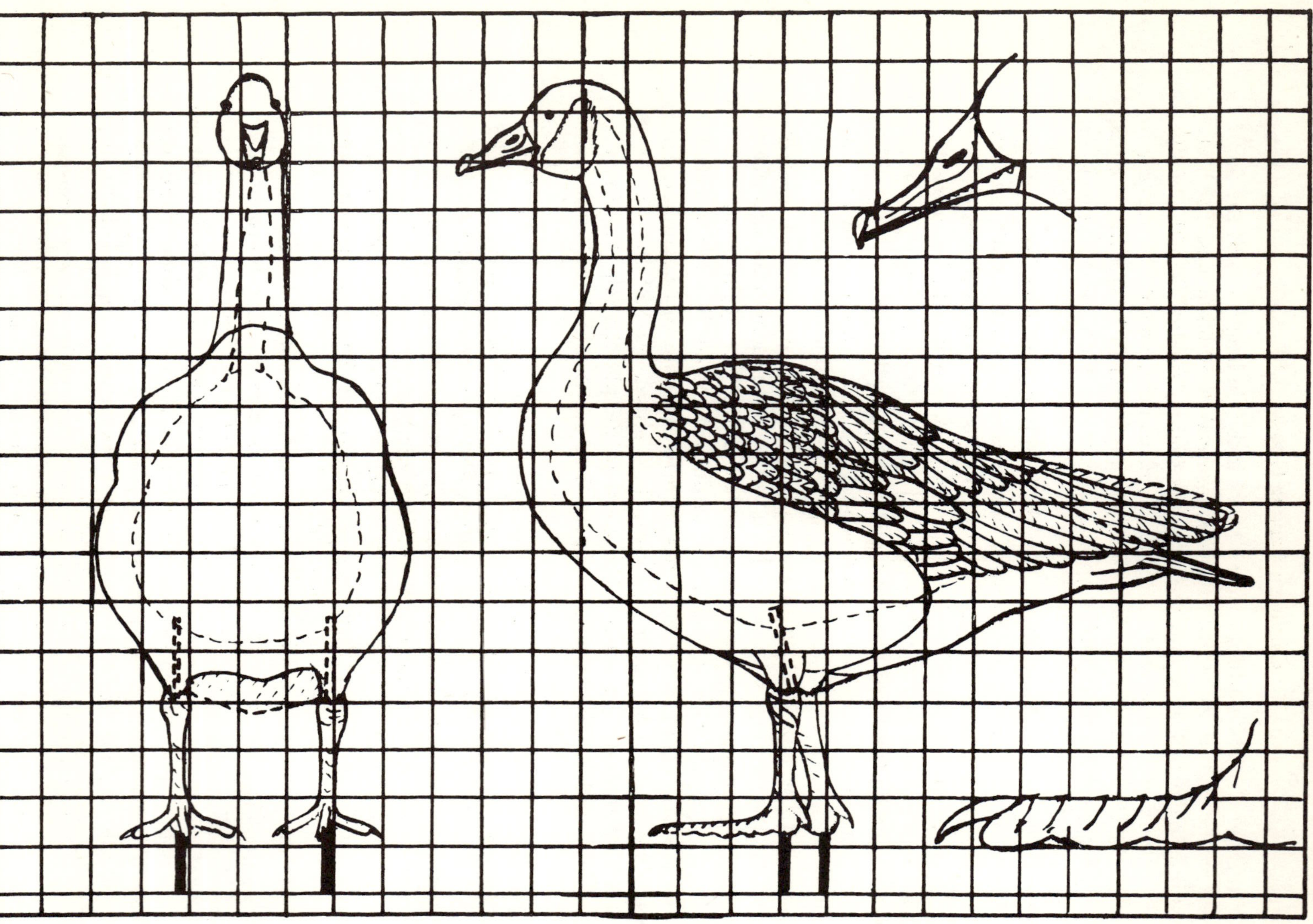

Fig. 5. Grid drawing for the carved Canada goose.

together. Cut out these profiles accurately, preferably with a band saw (otherwise with a coping or turning saw, or chiseling away the waste wood). When the profiles have been accurately formed, drop a dab of white glue at each end of one board only. Clamp the profiles together and allow the glue to set for about four hours at room temperature. The profiles are only temporarily glued to hold them together while being carved. Halving the bird in this manner has two distinct advantages: first, the center line is always visible, it cannot be cut away; second, when the bird has been roughly carved the two halves may be easily separated and hollowed out with a gouge.

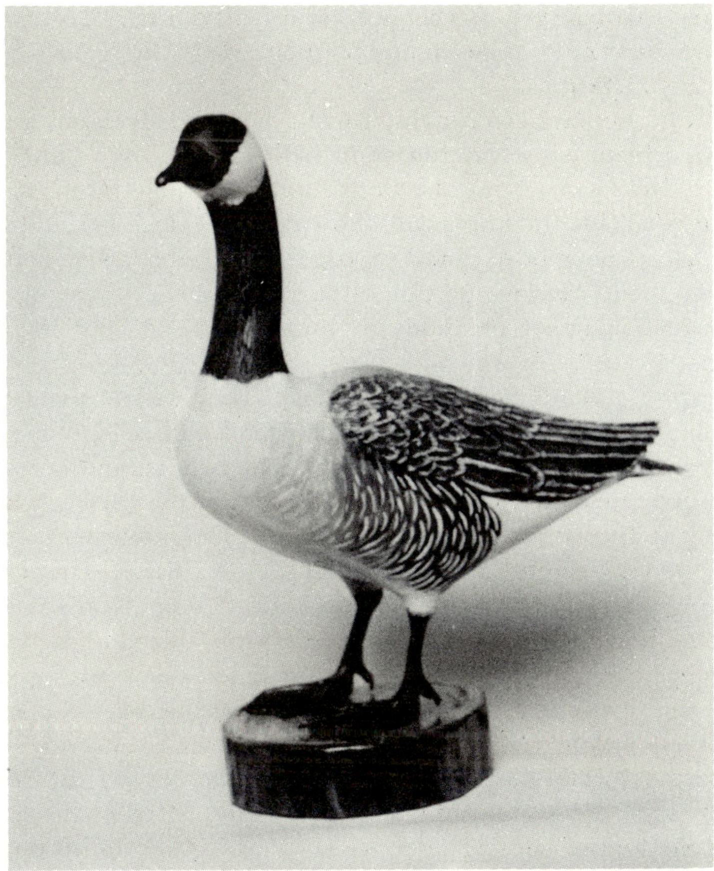

Fig. 6. Canada goose, carved by the author. Photograph by Brightwell.

After the profiles have set long enough they may be removed from the vise and the carving begun. Use any convenient method for carving the goose. The author starts in the middle and works down each side and toward each end. Carve all over the goose and not in a single location to keep the contours "tied" together and in proportion to the shape of the bird. During this operation some knowledge of the shape of geese is important. A ceramic model of the bird is helpful in learning about these general shapes. A model will be especially helpful in determining the shape of the front and tail parts. A Surform rasp will be very helpful in this operation. The rough cuts may be smoothed down later with a spokeshave. A fine cut rasp will be effective for detailed work. Always carve "downhill" to avoid splintering or roughing up the surface. The neck will prove to be the most difficult as the cross grain will break easily. Perhaps the neck should not be carved at all but left square until permanently glued together.

View the carving frequently from all angles to observe your progress. There is a restful satisfaction in studying your work. Some of your errors will stand out like sore thumbs, but no great harm has been done for there is considerable shaping yet to be accomplished during the first stages of carving. Perhaps as much time should be spent in viewing your work as in the actual carving operations.

When the goose has been roughly carved the two halves may be separated. Force a wide blade chisel in the seam between the thighs until the halves come apart. Next gouge out the body cavity leaving the thickness of the walls about ¾". This thickness will allow for some deep correctional carving when the halves have been glued together permanently. Ignore the "draft" sections left in the carving. Do not carve them, but let the gouged contours follow the real shape of the body at these points. Do not hollow out the neck either.

Every carver should have two sandbags. They serve as a good holding device while carving irregular shapes which cannot be held in a vise, and also as a soft rest for carving finished surfaces. The bags should be about 14" x 20" and filled three-quarters full of sand. Nestle the carving on a sandbag and gouge out the waste wood. Start in the middle and work forward and backward. Be very careful and always keep your fingers behind the cutting edge of your gouge, and do not gouge toward your stomach. Blood is a nuisance, messing up the carving and everything around it. Besides, the wound might be serious enough to interfere with your work for several days or even weeks. In any case, have a box of bandages handy.

Most carvers hollow out their birds. Not only are the carvings lighter, but they are less subject to checks and cracks. Most carvers, however, design their birds with the seam running horizontally (if there is a seam), the traditional method of carving a decoy. The author believes his method is less difficult both with respect to carving and the hollowing-out procedure. When the halves have been gouged out, glue them together permanently. The author uses white glue for this operation, but many carvers prefer an epoxy resin glue which is semi-waterproof.* The carving may be clamped in a good bench vise, but the neck and head should be tightly squeezed together with two C-clamps on the neck and one on the head. Let the carving rest in the clamps for four hours at room temperature before proceeding.

---

*National Casein, a urea-formaldehyde resin glue is sold under the trademark: "DR" Powdered Glue. It is very satisfactory.

Now the final carving operations are in order. The "draft" sections should remain in place. First, carve the neck which is presumed to be still square in cross section. The neck is not circular but egg-shaped. The windpipe and gullet parallel the neck bones, bulging this part of the neck. If desired these physical parts may be indicated lightly, but in any event your carving should be suitably elongated along this axis to allow for this anatomical variation. Sand the neck smooth after it has been carved and proceed with the head. The most important parts, determining the shape of the head, are the bill and eye cavity. The head of a goose is unlike that of a duck in many respects. It is of a different shape in fundamental contours, and its bill is heavier at the base in both directions. The shape of the bill is different also. If the bill is unsatisfactory after the first attempt, cut it off. Bore a suitable size hole in the head and glue in a birch dowel of suitable length and thickness. After the glue sets carve the bill all over again with better precision. The eye cavity is much the same as in other birds. It sets the eye below the surface of the head to protect it from danger. It begins at about the same level as the upper mandible, follows the contour of the head and disappears in the back of the neck on about the same level as the lower mandible. The most pronounced depth is at the location of the eye. From this location the cavity tapers in both directions toward the surface. The eye cavity gives the head a definite shape and, of course, determines the location of the eye. The shape and location of this cavity is, therefore, highly important. Concerning the bill, another suggestion is made. The author often cuts off the softwood bill of his birds and substitutes one of hardwood, birch, cherry, or any other tough wood. Such a bill will take a lot of punishment without splintering.

At this point be sure you have a goose head. If not, work on the carving until you do. Fill in the low spots with polyester filler and cut down the high spots. There is no part of the goose more characteristic of the bird than the head. Sand the head smooth. Be especially careful where the head joins the neck. Carve this location as if it had grown in place.

Inserting the Eyes

The eye is set in the cavity just discussed, and deep enough to protect it from harm. At a point not quite in the center of the cavity (lengthwise) drive a 1″ brad. Stand back and observe the locations. They will probably not seem to be just right. The right location, basically, is where they should be to a trained eye. But even a novice can discern a misplaced one. A general rule to follow is to locate the brads on the level of the nostrils and in the center of the cavity arc. After studying the position, decide whether the location should be higher, lower, farther back or more advanced according to your feelings. When the locations have been determined, drill a 1/8″ hole perpendicular to the surface of the head, and deep enough to extend beyond the bottom of the glass eye. Next, determine the size of the glass eye and bore a hole with a sharp auger large enough for it to slip in freely.* Cut the wire attached to the eye long enough to bend on itself (this wire should enter the 1/8″ hole and help to guide the eye). Mix up a small batch of polyester filler, enough to fill the holes of both eyes. Fill one hole at a time and insert the glass eye. Press in place with a flat surface until the eyebrows and cheek surfaces are touched. Be sure the eye sets correctly. If the eye is higher than the eyebrow, the effect will be "popeyed"; if tipped in either direction, forward or backward, the bird might look cross-eyed or otherwise ridiculous. The adjustment cannot be made after the filler sets. The entire eye will have to be removed and the job redone. Install the other eye before the filler hardens. After the filler sets, pare off the surplus with a sharp knife. During the painting operation the eyes may be ignored as the paint can be scraped off after the bird has been completed.

Carve the primaries and secondary feathers of the wing (Chapter 15, Fig. 15) and the large feathers, decreasing in size farther up the wing. If, by chance, you are carving from a mounted specimen, revise your drawing to suit or conform with the real bird. The shafts of the feathers may be scored in with a V-tool. Remember that the barb surfaces are slightly below the shaft and not just separated with a groove. The barbs are very close together and angle toward the end of the feather. Have a typical feather near you while you carve. The barbs may be carved in lightly with the V-tool, but discriminating carvers use an electric pyrograph which has a wedge-shaped, skewed burning end. A satisfactory job may be done with a sharp knife, drawing it over the surface at the determined angle. Care must be exercised in using this method as the feather is easily chipped. A Moto-tool equipped with a burr that is wedge shaped may be used too, but a steady hand and a uniform direction of the scoring is necessary. The barb grooves should be lightly carved.

Remember that the feathers grow on a bird like shingles installed on a roof designed to shed water. Have this thought in mind while carving feathers.

After the carving of the goose has been completed (except as before specified) apply a good coat of wood sealer. All reliable paint companies sell this product and are all satisfactory. After the sealer has dried thoroughly the next logical step would be installing the legs, but as stated in the beginning, the carving is to serve two purposes. The carving is now at the "pattern" stage and should be used to form the negative molds. Turn to the section of this chapter entitled "Making the Negative Mold" and proceed with the directions for making them.

Let us now assume that the negative molds have been made. The carving of the goose may now continue. Finish carving the neck. First cut it in half

---

*The J.W. Elwood Supply Co., Inc., Box 3507, Omaha, Nebraska, 68103, has an eye chart in their catalogue which gives the sizes and colors of most birds' eyes. This chart is reproduced in *Creative Bird Carving*, by William I. Tawes; Tidewater Publishers, Box 109, Cambridge, Md., 21613.

with a saw. With a suitable size auger bore holes in each section, down to the body of the one, and up to the head in the other. (Make the holes as large as possible without cutting through the "skin.") Cut a steel reinforcing rod which will extend in both sections. Mix up a batch of polyester, enough to fill both holes. Fill the holes, lifting the material in with a pallet knife. Insert the reinforcing rod and place the two sections together. Be sure the joint is well coated with the filler. Turn the head in a desirable position, press in place, and allow the filler to harden. After the neck has rested for about one hour at room temperature it should be ready to carve again. Notice that there is a twist in the neck now and the sections are out of line. Correct this malformation so that the neck looks natural. Sand to a smooth finish. The neck which was the weakest part of the bird is now as strong comparatively as any other part. With a V-tool, or a Moto-tool burr score in the long narrow feathers of the neck. These grooves should be unequal in length and twisted to conform to the new shape of the neck. These grooves should be carved closely together so that they have a feathery appearance. A cut-off disk used with the same electric carving tool works very well, also, for cutting in the grooves. These disks will cut deeper and faster but they are brittle and must be used with care. Let this technique of feathering disappear beyond the white patch on the head and at the base of the neck on the body.

The "draft" sections may now be removed and the carving continued in these parts. The carving between the thighs will be simple, merely shaping the insides of the thighs and chiseling the belly down to proper contours. Carving the space between the wings is much more difficult. Carve the underside of the wings to conform to their top sides. A coping saw will be useful in this operation. Saw out the rough wood and finish with a sharp fine-cut rasp and carving knife. This operation will leave the wings free of the body at the rump, as the back tapers toward the root of the tail. Incidentally, the feathers of the tail should be carved.

Drill a small pilot hole in each thigh for the legs. The direction of the holes should follow the center of the thighs. In one direction the angle will follow, and be parallel to the axis (central) of the goose, but in the adjacent direction the angle should be at an appropriate angle with the body (the angle of the thighs); that is, the goose should stand with its legs about parallel, bent gracefully at the knee toward the front of the bird.

Next, with a sharp auger bore holes large and deep enough to receive the leg rods, plus enough space to receive a film of polyester filler (1/8″ larger than the leg rod will allow 1/16″ of polyester to fill in the difference). This extra space will also allow for some adjustment when the legs are installed.

Making the Legs and Feet

Figure 7 shows the principal operations in making the legs and feet. Bird carvers use various ways of forming these members, from poured lead castings to fabricating them entirely of wood—even metal. The author tried

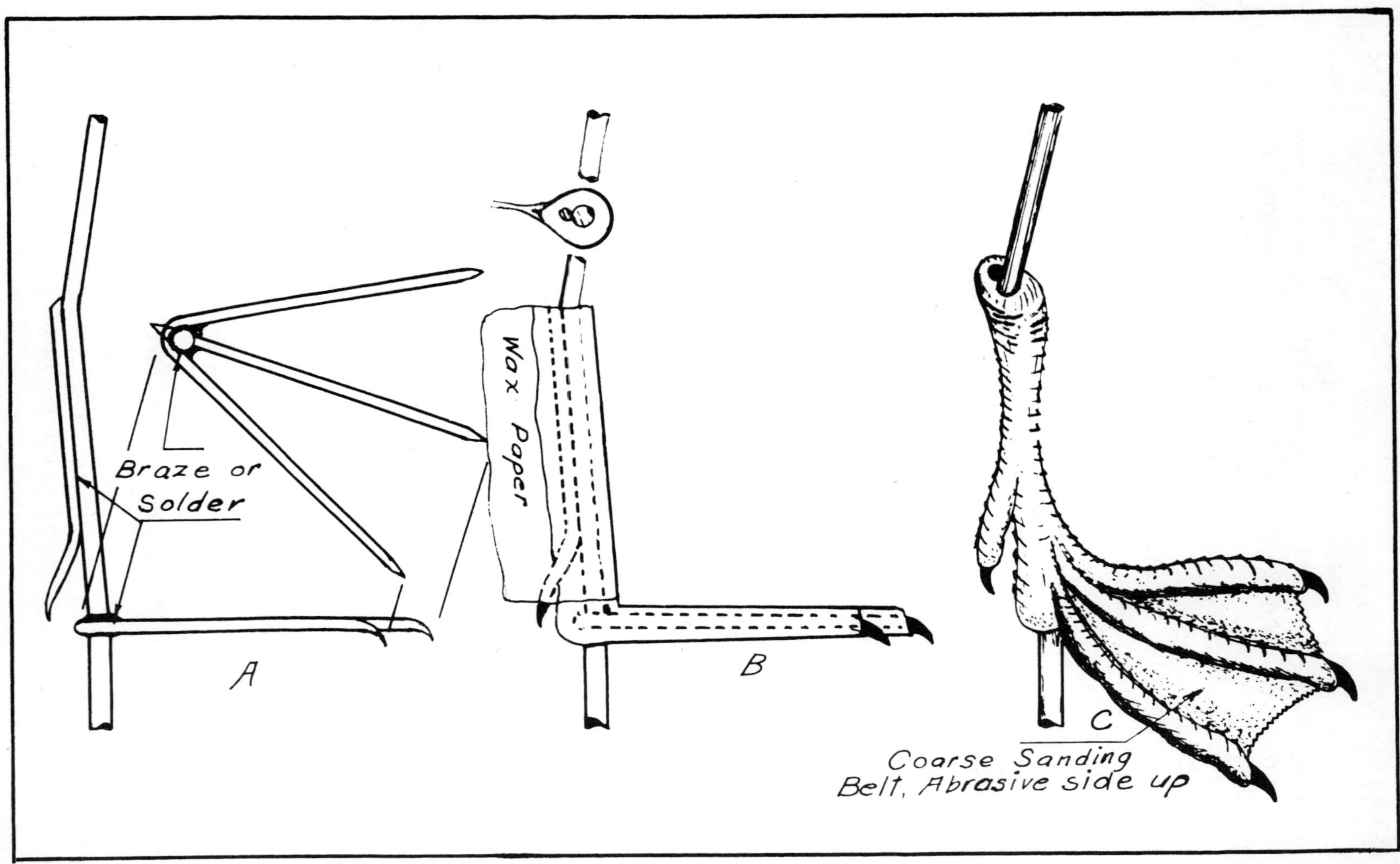

Fig. 7. Method of making polyester filler legs and feet.

all methods and has now settled on the technique explained in this section. These legs and feet are strong and as realistic as the carver is clever, and as easy as carving wood. Also, brazing or soldering wire toes to a heavier rod makes for a more flexible job during the forming operation. If the carver does not have an oxyacetylene welding outfit he should use clean brass or copper wire. Solder does not adhere well to steel. In both instances melt enough metal on the joints to insure a strong job. Do not use acid-core solder. It is dirty, messy and otherwise unsatisfactory. Use solid-core solder and a paste flux like the plumbers use to make sweat joints. A flux coated brass rod should be used for brazing if possible. Otherwise, the fluxing must be done in the old-fashioned way. The legs of a full size goose are about 4″ long and the middle toe the same size. Bend the toe wires around the leg wire. Arrange the toes in position (including the middle toe) and braze or solder them in position. The heat for the soldering may be from a soldering gun, an automatic blowtorch or any number of soldering devices. After the toes have been either soldered or brazed in place they may be cut to size and the claws formed by flattening out the ends and either grinding or filing them to shape. Bend the toes over the horn of a small anvil. The cross section of a bird's leg is not round. In the back a column of tendons controlling the feet are located giving the leg a somewhat horizontal teardrop shape. A wire should be brazed or soldered to represent these tendons and one end formed for the fourth toe.

After the toes and legs have been either brazed or soldered, cut pieces of wax paper measuring the length of the toes in one direction and long enough to wind around the toe leaving ample room to be held by the fingers while the filler is squeezed in place. The polyester filler does not mold well self-contained. It must be confined in a mold of some description; hence the wax paper to hold it in place. Mix up a batch of the filler and spread enough of it on the wax paper to cover the wire toe concerned. Place the toe on the filler and bring the ends of the wax paper around it. With the fingers grasp the loose ends of the wax paper and squeeze the material around the toe, making sure that most of it is located on the bottom of the wire. Each toe may be consecutively molded while the material is soft, but the legs must wait until the material on the toes sets. While the material is hard enough to remove the wax paper the toes may be shaped roughly with a sharp knife. Next prepare the wax paper for the legs. Spread enough of the material on the paper to form one leg. Place the leg upon it and bring the wax paper around it and squeeze in position with the fingers manipulating the molding operation. When the polyester has set enough for the wax paper to be removed, trim to shape with a sharp knife. There will be several places which must be patched. With a pallet knife spread on these spots enough filler to round out the contours. Approximately an hour later, the filler will be hard enough to file with a fine cut rasp. As the outside toes are mechanically straight, bend them toward the middle toe for a more natural position. If the polyester filler cracks no damage has been inflicted. Simply fill them up with the same material. During the filing operations a mask should be worn as the dust is highly toxic to some individuals. File the leg to shape. Repeat the operations on the other leg.

Next, put a web on each foot. An old coarse portable sanding machine belt will serve very well. With a solid end punch perforate a hole in one end large enough to receive the tang of the leg. Practice this procedure by punching the hole on the end grain of a block of wood. Place the sand-cloth in position, sanded surface up, and mark out the shape of the web. Cut the web to shape and glue to the feet with contact glue. Constantine carries a veneer glue in pint sizes that is very good. Apply the contact glue to all surfaces to be glued, both the feet and the web. When the glue ceases to be tacky to the touch (after approximately 15 minutes) press the web in place.

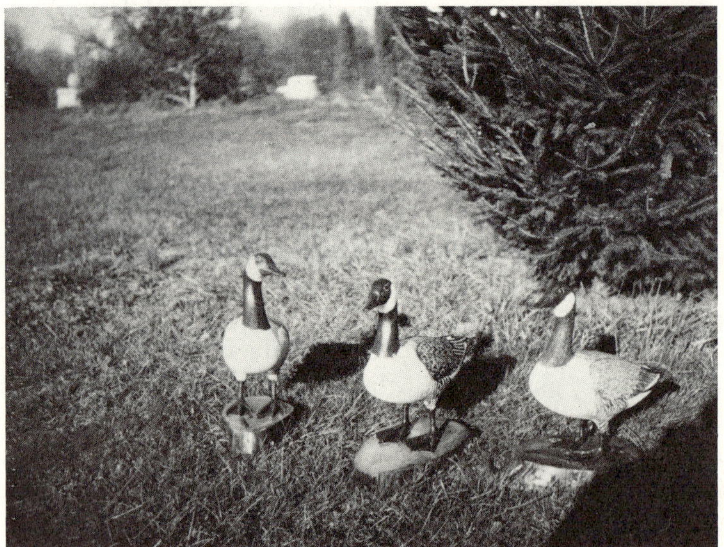

Fig. 8. Polyester duplicates mounted on bias-cut bases.

Remember the right contact must be made the first time as the bond is instantaneous. With a fine cut rasp trim the web to conform with the foot, stroking toward the toes. There will result an undercut where the web joins the bottom of the toes. This space should be filled with polyester filler. Fashion a piece of sheet metal about ¼″ wide at one end and round off in a semi-circular shape. Use this improvised tool to form the fillets. After the legs and feet have been formed make the perch or plinth.

Carvers design various types of perches. Probably the most common is driftwood. Certainly a pretty piece of driftwood will do very adequately. A combination of driftwood and a formal plinth is also popular. The most convenient perch is simply cut from a log on the bias and finished naturally (Fig. 8). The bark edge is trimmed to remove the loose bark, but otherwise left as is. Wild cherry, which is native to almost all states, is excellent for making perches. If a shaper or electric router are available a very formal perch may be made. Irrespective of the type of perch have it ready before the legs are installed in the carving.

Drill two holes in the perch for the tangs of the legs. Drill them perpendicular to the surface and just large enough for a friction fit with the tang of the legs. They should be about the same distance apart as the holes in the thighs and with the same offset. Make any adjustments necessary in the shape of the legs to allow the goose to pose naturally. Do not allow the toes to extend beyond the perch as they will tangle with almost anything that passes nearby. Next, mix up a batch of polyester filler and fill the holes in the thighs. Be sure the holes are filled. Spread some of the filler on the bare wires or rods of the legs and insert them into the holes in the thighs. While the material is still soft insert the tangs of the legs into the perch and adjust the goose in a desirable position. Remember that the holes in the thighs were made extra large for this purpose. The surplus filler may now be spread around the joint and to form the knees which, of course, are larger than the leg cross section. Before the polyester hardens be sure that your goose is not wing-footed or pigeon-toed. Several applications of the filler may be necessary to form the knee. When the material has hardened file the knee joint to shape. The final operation is painting the goose. Now the fun begins!

Painting the Goose

First, check your carving for unfinished spots or tool marks. Be sure you have a nicely sanded bird. Do not depend on paint to cover up your errors. It will not!

If possible have a mounted specimen before you while you paint. The next best guide is a colored picture by a recognized authority on wildlife. Bob Hines who illustrates for the U.S. Department of the Interior is such an artist. Walter A. Weber who, before he retired, illustrated publications of the National Geographic Society is another. Probably the most famous is Rodger Tory Peterson. There are several others. The author used as his guide a painting by Arthur Singer. While the author was familiar with the color and markings of the Canada goose he felt that a guide was necessary for an authentic presentation. First, prepare your pallet (several thicknesses of newsprint will do) with the necessary colors. They may be either oil or acrylics. The discussion which follows will have both techniques in mind. Oil paints are more flexible because they dry slowly, but the acrylics dry fast and the painting of the bird may be continuous. Your pallet should consist of black (either ivory or mars black), white, burnt and raw umber, and burnt sienna. Have a container of turpentine or water convenient depending upon the type of medium used. Incidentally, the goose in the photograph was painted with acrylics. Both oil and acrylics will work well in a wet-in-wet (alla prima) situation. The dark brown of the sides which curve from the thighs to the beginning of the primary feathers is tapered to a white color on the front of the goose by brushing together the two colors, burnt umber and white, blending them to an even consistency. This ground color may be the first step in painting the bird. The ground color for the wings and back should be burnt umber as it is the most prominent color. A black ground coat should be applied to the neck and tail feathers, also the legs and feet. The feathering may begin with the second coat of paint and continue for as many coats as are necessary to achieve a satisfactory job. Difficulty with a certain spot may, in the end, have several coats of paint which may really enhance the appearance of the bird.

Feather the primaries and the large carved feathers of the wing. Your brush strokes should be in the direction of the barbs. A clever technique is to have two contrasting colors on your brush at the same time and stroke in the barbs. Experiment on your pallet newsprint first. Your aim should be to have the barbs show naturally on the feather. Remember the shaft is usually lighter than the ground coat of the feather and should be merely suggestive in most feathers. The main feathers of a goose are fringed with an off-white color. This color is obtained by mixing in a small amount of burnt sienna with your white paint. Use your newsprint pallet for mixing to determine the right shade. If you are clever enough you may stroke in this fringe with a brush, somewhat dry. The color should not have a hard outline but be a continuation of the barb appearance. Painters possessing less expertise should use a very small brush and stroke in the barb fringes stroke by stroke. For the novice considerable experimentation will probably be necessary. But, patience and persistence is the open sesame.

After the carved feathers are painted, sketch the others on the wing. Probably the best technique in doing this is by the use of a very small brush and black paint. The under edge and the tip of the feather is stroked in (in the direction of the barbs). The strokes should not be long, about 1/8" will probably be enough. Each row of feathers should be pronounced as in your colored picture. Next stroke in the off-white colored fringe above the black strokes. (In oil paints the colors are allowed to dry before stroking in the next coat.) These black strokes will give depth to the feathers. Now paint in the principal feather color, stroking always in the direction of the barbs radiating from the shaft. Watch the area of the black strokes and do not entirely eliminate them. In an appropriate place sharply strike in the shafts.

Perhaps the novice should use oil paint to stroke in the off-white arcs (feather tips) on the sides. These arcs may be more pronounced than those shown in the photograph (Fig. 6). They may touch at the ends, but not be too regular in design. Let us assume for the moment that oil paint is being used. Stroke in a few arcs carefully. Then take a coarse-haired fan brush and drag across the arcs carefully toward the tail, being sure that you just break through the off-white outlines. Study your work at this point. Do the arcs look like the ends of fluffy feathers? If dragging across the arcs does not result in the right technique, take a very fine round-haired brush and break the back outlines of the arcs with it. The paint must be wet, otherwise the brush will have to be supplied with the arc colored paint. Continue this feathering technique through the dark brown into the lighter color and into the white as it approaches the breast. Watch the density of your color as the arcs should gradually disappear as the white of the breast is reached. The under parts of the body are mostly white and notice there is a white patch at the root of the rump of the tail feathers.

The white patch at the cheeks should not be a harsh outline. The black paint of the neck should be dragged into the white, giving a hairy appearance. The white cheek color continues under the head until it nearly meets, but is separated by thinly spaced black feathers being dragged into the approaching colors. The underside of the bill is nearly black (pure black will be satisfactory).

Now study your painting job. Touch up any spot that does not look natural. Continue this check-up observation over several days at convenient intervals. The author observes his birds while eating, so three times a day he studies his work and usually sees where improvements may be made.

Painting the goose realistically may prove to be more difficult than the carving. This is a natural situation for most carvers. Even a highly skilled artist might have difficulty painting a realistic bird. The technique is entirely different. A famous bird carver of the author's acquaintance requested a professional wildlife artist to paint one of his carvings. The artist took the carving home with him and returned it several weeks later. It was a miserable job! The artist was in no sense an abstractionist, but a good real-life painter. He found out that a flat canvas was not the same as a three-dimensional carving. The carver painted over his work and began the painting over again from scratch.

Anyone can, with practice, do a fairly presentable job. Skill in this activity comes with experience; eternal patience is the key which unlocks the art; and persistency is the magic that uses it to perfection.

Finally, after several days, observe your carving again. You will probably see patches that may be improved. Do not hesitate to make these improvements, for they may be the extra touches necessary to lift your carving from the level of mediocrity to professional dimensions.

Making the Negative Mold

Making a negative mold is a simple task for anyone with some knowledge of foundry practice. Making a casting is merely making an impression (depression) in molding sand by means of a pattern, and pouring metal into the cavity left after the pattern has been removed. No attempt will be made here to describe the process of green sand molding in detail. A brief sketch of the operations involved should be helpful, and sufficient, for an individual clever enough to carve the likeness of a Canada goose.

Foundrymen use special molding sand which does not concern us at this time. His tools are few: a flask, composed of a "drag" and a "cope"; a rammer, one end round (the butt) and the other wedge-shaped (the peen); a number of trowels and slicks, and a few other molding gadgets. A pattern, the exact replica of the subject to be cast, is essential. It is usually split and the two parts held together with short dowel pins.

The drag of the flask is placed, top part down, on a bottom board and the flat section of the pattern located in the central area. A fine dusting powder is blown over the pattern followed by finely riddled sand over the entire surface. Properly tempered molding sand is then shoveled into the drag and peened around the pattern in several stages until the drag is full and running over. The surplus sand is struck off with a straightedge. More sand is riddled over the surface and the molding board is seated on the drag. The whole assembly is then carefully turned over to expose the half-pattern embedded in the sand. Next, the doweled section of the pattern is placed over its "mate" and the cope section of the flask dropped in place. The pattern is again dusted to facilitate withdrawal from the mold. Fine seashore sand is riddled over the entire surface of the drag to form a parting plane. The sand will allow the cope to be lifted off with a clean separation. Molding sand is riddled over the surface as in the first instance and peened tightly around the pattern. Before the sand is shoveled into the cope, however, a sprue pin is located near the pattern and molded in the sand. The sprue pin forms the sprue hole into which the metal is poured. When the cope has been rammed tightly the top is struck off as before and a depression cut around the sprue pin to form a well, and to enlarge the pouring space. A steel wire (about No. 10 gauge) is thrust down over the pattern area but not deep enough to touch it. This operation is performed several times to provide escape vents for the hot gases formed by the molten metal. This procedure prevents the casting from "blowing."

After the sprue pin is withdrawn, the cope is carefully lifted off the drag and placed nearby on its side. If the cope-half of the pattern is withdrawn also, then both halves need to be removed separately, a procedure which is sometimes very tricky. The pattern is gently rapped to loosen it from the sand and then carefully lifted out. Some repairs are usually necessary and should be made at this time. The spoon, trowel and slicks are the tools used for this purpose. A gate is cut in the drag part of the flask leading from the pattern to the sprue hole, the depth near the pattern depression being smallest. This precaution allows the metal to be thinner at this point, permitting the gate to break off easily when the drag is "shaken out." The cope is replaced in its original position and the flask clamped together. If the casting is heavy, a metal weight is placed over the cope to prevent the sand from lifting. The mold is now ready to pour with molten iron, bronze, or any other metal. (*See* article in *World Book Encyclopedia,* entitled "Casts and Casting.")

The process is about the same for casting negative molds. First, construct a frame large enough to contain the goose with some room to spare. The depth of the frame should be the thickness of the goose plus 2″. The sides are made of softwood ½″ thick, and the ends ¾″. Nail the sides to the ends, being careful not to drive nails in the middle sections of the boards. Rip the frame apart on a table saw, making each section the same depth. If a table saw is not available the frame will have to be ripped apart with a hand saw. Dress the sawn edges so the frames will fit together accurately.

At each corner of the drag section glue and nail ½″ cleats projecting ½″ above the top edge. Chamfer the inside edges to allow the cope section to drop easily. These cleats will allow a perfect register of the two molds when assembled.

Place the drag section on a flat board (a drawing board will be just right). Sprinkle some fine bank sand into the drag about 1″ deep. Place the goose pattern upon the sand, leaving space at the close areas of at least 1″. Before adjusting the goose pattern, rub it thoroughly with paste wax and allow to dry for a few minutes until it will polish smoothly. This procedure will allow the goose to separate from the sand (and cement) easily. Be sure that the center seam of the goose is level with the top edge of the drag. This is important as one-half of the pattern should be in each section of the flask. When the goose has been properly adjusted, sprinkle more sand in the drag and ram it firmly around the goose. Continue this process until the drag is full. Strike off the drag with a straightedge, and trowel the surface smooth to do a good job. One-half of the goose carving (pattern) should now be exposed above the surface. At least three register holes should be cut in the blank areas. Do this with a quarter. These semi-spherical holes will help line up the two halves of the mold should the sides become damaged. Place the top frame (cope) in place. It should drop easily upon the drag.

Next, thoroughly mix one-half Portland cement and one-half clean masonry sand together. Add water until the mixture is rather light. With the fingers, flick the cement on the goose until the surface has been thoroughly covered. This process will prevent air bubbles from forming on the surface of the mold. After the surface of the goose has been covered the rest of the cement may be poured in gently until the cope is full. Strike off the top and smooth with a trowel.

Plaster of Paris is usually used for this kind of work, but is hard to obtain in rural communities. Portland cement sets up slower, but otherwise, serves the same purpose.

Cut suitable reinforcing rods of steel, two for the length and two for the width. Bend them in a bow slightly, to allow them to be dropped deeper into the cement. They should not touch the pattern and they should be at least 2″ shorter than the respective lengths and widths of the cope frame. Force the rods into the cement. Allow the cement to set for 24 hours at room temperature. Then the cope frame may be lifted off. The goose pattern should remain in the cope but no great harm has been done if it should remain in the sand. Turn the cope over on its side and remove the drag from the molding board. Carefully turn the cope over and place on the board with the pattern side up. Clean the surface thoroughly. Wax both the surface and the pattern and polish when dry. Clean the drag frame and replace it on the cope. Repeat the process of flicking the cement on the pattern and filling the drag with it. Drop the reinforcing rods in place and strike off the surplus cement. After the cement has set for 24 hours the flask may be separated. Prepare four thin wedges (about ¼″ thick, 1″ wide) and place two at either end of the flask. Gently tap first one and then the other working around the forms until separation is achieved. The goose pattern may now be in either mold. Perhaps the form in which the goose is held should rest another day as the cement is yet quite brittle. The goose pattern is finally removed by prying it out of the mold with a chisel. Do not worry about scarring the goose pattern. The damaged spots may be repaired with polyester filler. When the goose pattern has been separated from the form or mold the results should be very pleasing. The goose pattern may now be carved to completion as explained in the earlier part of this chapter.

Squeezing in the Polyester Putty to Form a Duplicate Goose

Correct any blemishes which may appear in your molds. Rub them down with paste wax and give them a shine after the wax has dried. This procedure is necessary to keep the polyester filler from sticking to the surfaces. The wide gap between the thighs must be corrected, the only difficult task in the whole squeezing process. Cut a piece of copper or aluminum screening to fit over the space plus some overlapping of the material. The top edges should be the same height as the molds. Fasten in place with the polyester putty or filler.

About two cans (quarts) of the filler will be required to squeeze one bird. Mix a batch of the material thoroughly about the size of a golf ball with an inch and one-half to two inches of hardener. With a pallet knife, plaster the wire screening with the filler until the gap is repaired and the thigh formed. Do one mold at a time. Be sure that the top edge of the screening is filled even with the top of the mold. Hold in place if necessary until the filler hardens. A stick of suitable length propped against the opposite side will hold the screening in place. Apply the filler liberally at the thighs and belly, as much as will hold properly of itself. As the filler hardens continue to build up this area until completed. In the meantime squeeze in the filler on some other surface of the mold before it hardens. A tablespoon is helpful in spreading the filler over concave surfaces. Have several pieces of wax paper handy to use under the fingers. Squeeze the filler to a thickness of ¼″ approximately. Under the tip of the wings the polyester filler should be spread on heavily as this part of the goose will have to be recarved. As much as 1″ might be necessary here. Otherwise, squeeze on the material evenly and continuously until the mold has been covered completely. When the mold has been completely covered with the polyester filler, be sure that the top edges are even with the surface of the mold. Near the body section of the neck fill in solid for about an inch. The reason for this procedure will be evident later. Reexamine your work. If it appears to be suitably done lay aside and begin the other mold. Repeat the entire operation of the first mold. When completed, mix up a batch of the filler, enough to form a ¼″ bead around the entire seam of the bird. If possible this mix should be light, that is, with a small portion of the liquid medium included. Spread the bead rapidly before it hardens. Drop the other half of the mold in place. The bead should fill in any irregularities and at the same time weld the two halves together.

Allow the molds to set for at least two hours before separation. Remember the polyester filler does not harden quickly in a cool room, and when it does harden does not lend itself to sanding until several minutes later.

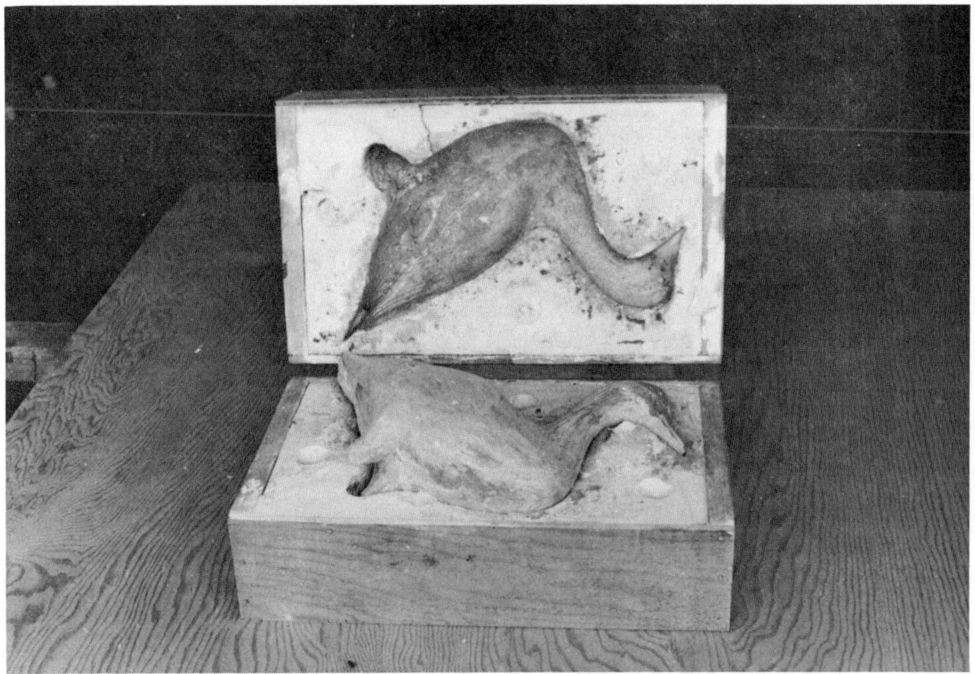

Fig. 9. Negative mold. The drag shows a squeezed goose in place. The cope section shows the negative depression.

The molds are separated as in the first instance. Use the four wedges in the same manner. The molds will separate easily, and if you have done your work satisfactorily your duplicate will be well formed and a close replica of the original carving. As one-half of the duplicate still remains in one mold it has to be pried loose. This will not be difficult. You may even be able to lift it out with your fingers (Fig. 9).

Your duplicate, like a metal casting, will be full of "fins" at the seams. A sharp key saw will be helpful in sawing them off. After such irregularities have been roughly cut off, a sharp, fine-cut rasp may be used to smooth off the surfaces. The thigh section will have to be carved to the proper contours, and the section at the wing tips will require considerable carving as there is much material to be removed. A sharp rasp and chisel will be desirable tools. Rasp and chisel the back down between the wings until it ends properly with the tail. Undercut the wings as in the original carving. In fact carve the duplicate until it is in every respect an exact copy of the carved goose. You will probably, while carving the back, cut through the filler into the body cavity. This should cause no sweat! Cut a piece of screening a little larger than the hole to be filled. Suspend it from a piece of the wire raveled from the screening and fastened in the middle. Insert the screening and pull in place with the single wire. The screening itself may be coated with the filler before being inserted. With a pallet knife fill the hole with the filler and allow to harden. The wire screening will prevent the filler from falling through into the body cavity. Continue your carving after the filler has hardened.

After your duplicate goose has been rasped clean, it should be sanded smooth. Be sure you are wearing a dust mask for this operation because the dust is toxic. Next saw the neck off in the middle. With the pallet knife drop polyester filler into the holes of both sections. If the holes are not large enough carve them to proper diameter. The filler will not drop into the body because of a precaution taken previously. Have a reinforcing rod handy and long enough to be included in both sections. Apply the filler to both joint surfaces and squeeze the parts together. Turn the head in a desirable position and allow the material to harden. Allow about 30 minutes for this operation depending on room temperature.

It is obvious that the neck may be sawn off in several sections and positioned in several appropriate curves before fastening back together again. This technique will give variety to your duplicate models.

After the neck joint (or joints) has (have) hardened sufficiently, carve in the long narrow feathers as in the original carving. Some additional carving of the neck will be necessary at the joints so that the twist in the neck will look natural. The hair grooves should follow this twist and the carving operations repeated as in the original model. Perhaps the disk cut-off of a Mototool will be the best method of doing this work. Without this carving device the work will have to be done with a V-tool.

The eyes are installed next. Perform this operation as in the original carving. Drill the 1/8″ hole in the center of the cast eye and proceed as before in installing the eyes. You may find some cavities in the head requiring more filler to do the job, but no more difficulties otherwise.

The legs are installed exactly as in the original carving. Prepare your perch and mount your duplicate.

Finally, your duplicate is ready to paint. Follow the instructions already given in the earlier section of this chapter. You might have learned from this initial experience. Do not be surprised if your duplicate looks even better than your carved model. Now hang out your shingle and sell your birds. You can afford to sell them much cheaper, and so far as looks are concerned they should appear as a professional carving.

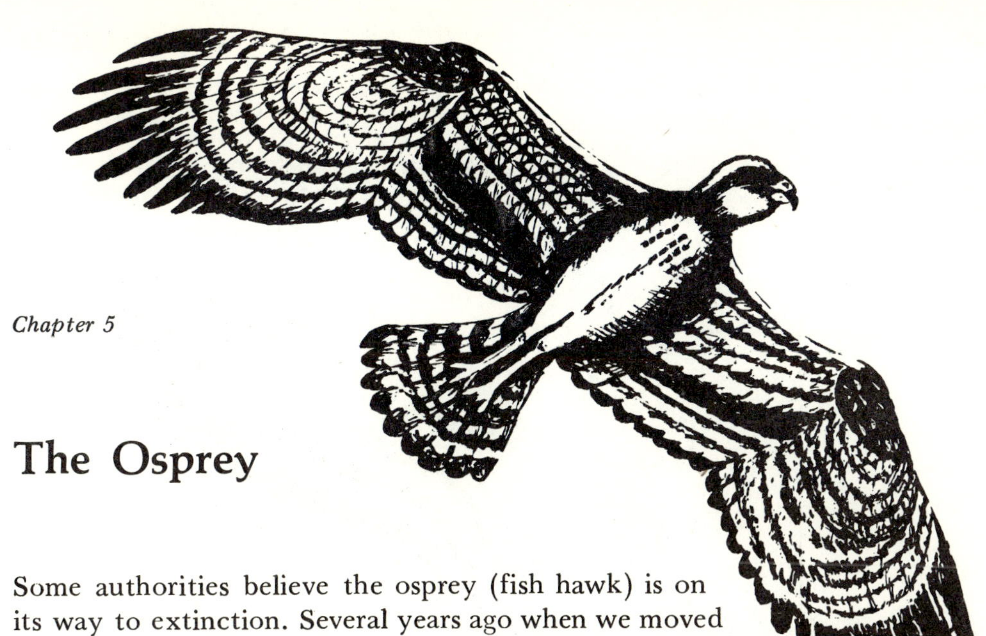

Chapter 5

The Osprey

Some authorities believe the osprey (fish hawk) is on its way to extinction. Several years ago when we moved to a farm on Southeast Creek, a small estuary of the Chester River, a pair of ospreys had a nest in an old dead tree across the waterway from us. Their untidy nest of sticks and rushes was repaired each season with more sticks and rushes. The female laid her eggs, and after they hatched we could watch from our shore the development of the young. We could watch them jump up and down testing their wings until they were strong enough to leave their nest. In the meantime both parent birds fished for food, the mother biting off measured bits for them to swallow. For three successive seasons we noted their return and watched as they fished our creek. They would fly 50 or more feet in the air until they spotted a fish, then like a sinker would drop, feet first, and plunge into the water splashing spray in every direction. Upon surfacing they usually had their fish and would take off toward their nest.

Ospreys will build their nest on any suitable flat surface that will support their sticks. How they get them to rest firmly in the crotch of a dead tree is one of nature's secrets. The wooden structures built by the lighthouse authorities to hold the equipment for their gas lights, which guide navigation through waterways, are favorite building sites. The light tenders on their rounds, until a few years ago, would destroy the nest, eggs and young, if there were any. No estimate is available of the number of nests destroyed by these government light keepers, but enough have been destroyed to make a significant depletion of the flock. This practice is now prohibited, but the great harm that has been done cannot now be corrected. Probably the most destructive factor in the life of the osprey has been insecticides, which find their way to the rivers and creeks where ingested by small fish which in turn are eaten by both the adult and young birds. The results may be sterility for the grown ospreys and death for their young. Also, if the eggs are laid under such conditions the shells may be too weak to protect the fetus, in which case the results are the same. So, the osprey and other fish-eating birds are having difficulty to survive.

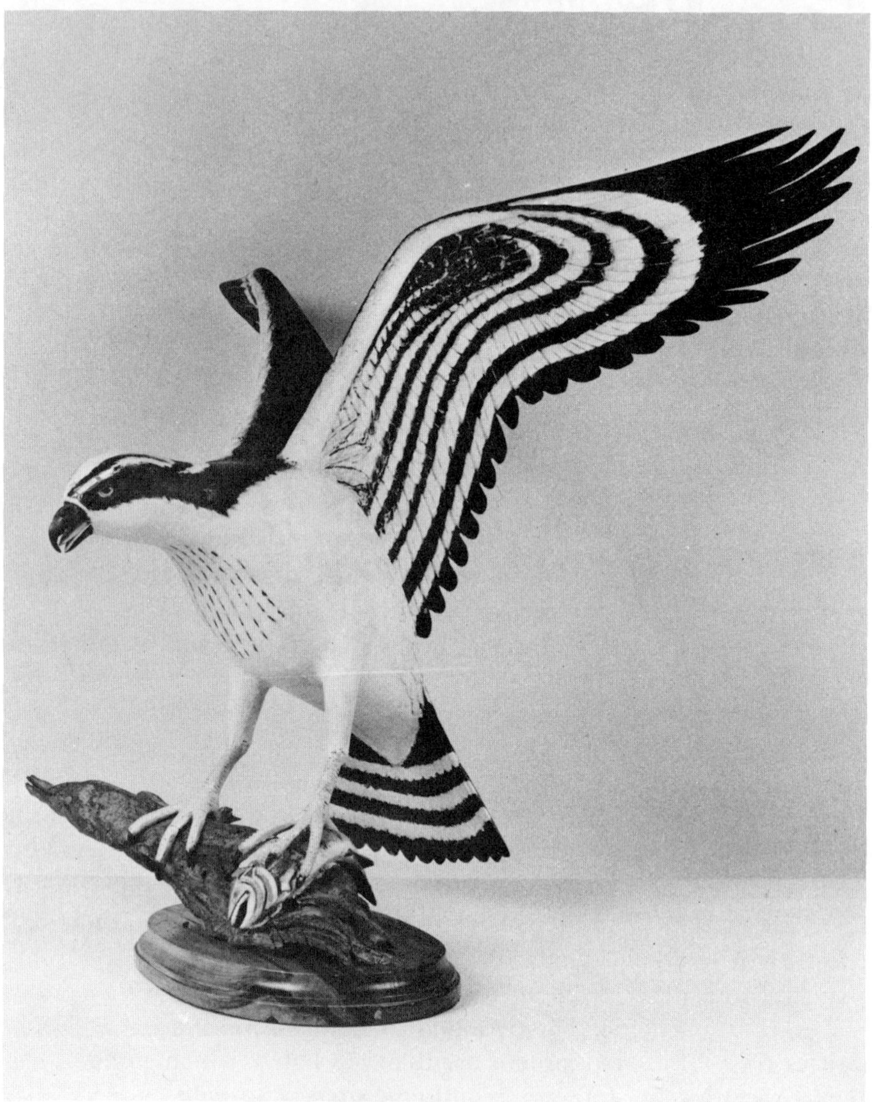

Fig. 1. Osprey (fish hawk), carved by the author. Polychrome white cedar. Photograph by Tawes Photographic.

What a pity! The osprey is a magnificent bird with a clarion call, not too shrill, but a melodious sound which seems so appropriate in a saltwater shed. It is already missed along the tributaries of our part of the Eastern Shore. "Ole crooked wings" as it is sometimes called because of the conspicuous crook in its wings, used to be a familiar sight, but now very seldom is it seen or heard. The crook in its wings and the black "wrists" are the distinguishing features which set it apart from other closely related species. The wings are held in an arched position as illustrated in the photograph (Fig. 1). Like the owl the outer toes can be rotated either forward or backward. When fishing they have two toes in front and two toes behind.

In 1967, our ospreys did not return to their nest. We never saw them again. Rodger Tory Peterson states in one of his articles that when he moved to Connecticut there were, in a ten-mile radius on the lower reaches of the Connecticut River, 150 active nests. Ten years later there were only 17. The harmless bird has become a victim of its poisoned environment. It may never recover and be seen again in great numbers.

Carving the Osprey

To carve the osprey of this chapter advantage must be taken of the procedures discussed in the previous pages. Prepare the two blocks which will form the body. White cedar, white pine, or any softwood will be satisfactory. After the surfaces, which will be glued together, have been planed to a smooth finish, apply the template or profile drawing and trace the design accurately. Cut out the design on a band saw. Glue the two halves together temporarily, and when the glue has set carve the body of the bird roughly to shape. Next split the halves apart and hollow out the waste wood, leaving plenty of space for the gluing operation which will follow. If the mortise for the wings is to be cut on a band saw, this operation should be done while the halves are apart. Lay out for the mortise. Tip the saw table to the proper angle and proceed to cut the mortise. The mortise should be about ½″ wide for a full-sized bird and as long as the wing tenon is wide, which is in turn as long as the wing is wide. To make the problem more complicated the tenon has the same camber as the wing. To make this "sticky" job easier the wings should be carved first. Be sure you have the angle in the right direction when cutting the mortise. Cutting through the back of the bird to reach the mortise offers no problem as the saw kerf will be reinforced by the adjoining half of the body. After the mortises have been cut the two halves may be glued together, permanently, and the carving completed except the areas around the wings.

If the mortises for the wings have not been cut, this operation is the next step. Carefully lay out the mortises and use any of the accepted methods for cutting them out. Probably the simplest way is to bore holes along the center line of the mortise the same diameter as the thickness of the tenon and at the proper angle. Bore these holes adjacent to each other to facilitate the removal of the waste wood. Remember the mortises must have the same cambers as the tenon of the respective wing.

The wings have a deep camber—nearly prohibitive in a life-sized bird to be carved from one block. The wing blanks should be bent to shape. This is an easy task after the clamping forms have been made. Determine the camber of the wings and construct the form as shown in the photographs (Figs. 2 and 3). Probably the easiest way to make this form is to glue together a number of blocks which have already been shaped to the approximate profile. Sawing blocks (about 2″ thick) wide enough to form both the top and

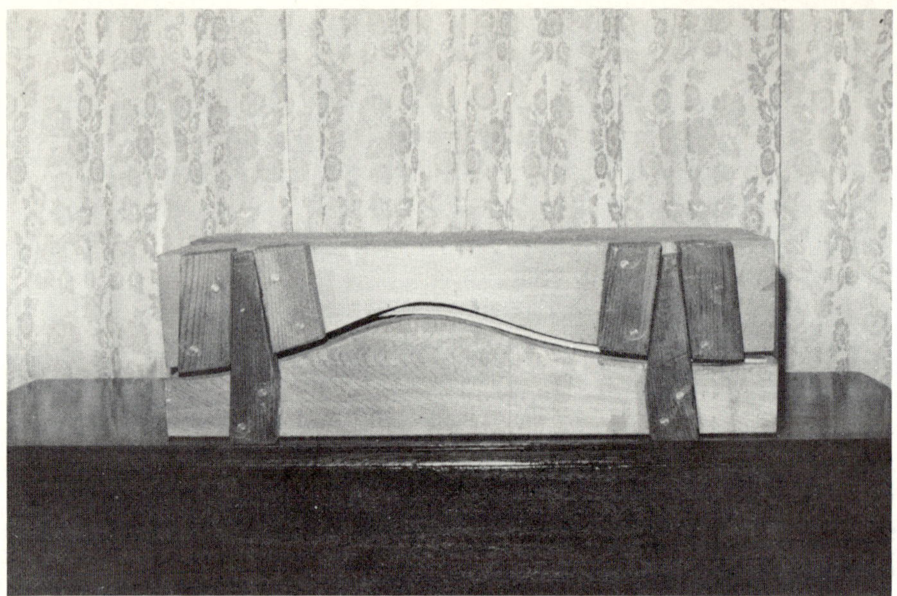

Fig. 2. Form for bending wings; wing blanks in place.

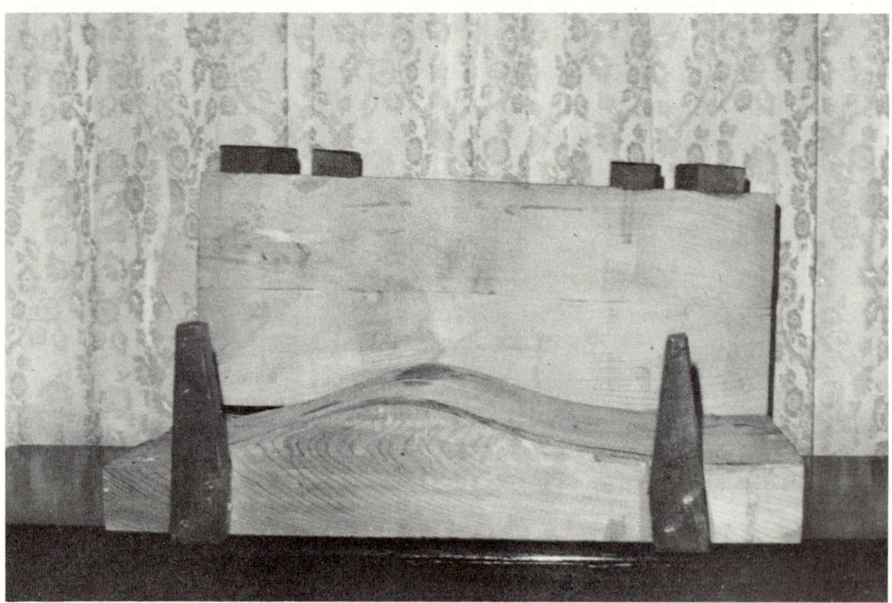

Fig. 3. Form open, showing wing blank.

bottom pieces is not a difficult problem. When the proper number of blocks have been prepared and sawn to the proper curvature, the bottom pieces may be glued together, and then the top pieces. When the glue has set the two matching pieces may be rasped to a smooth finish, put together and the cleats installed. These cleats are a "must." Without them you will have difficulty keeping the top and bottom parts of the forms in their proper position while being clamped. Two heavy bar clamps, one for each end, will be sufficient to clamp the two forms together. Prepare a number of soft-wood veneer strips wide enough to include the wing design (poplar veneer 1/8" thick is sold by concerns that sell veneers). Glue the adjoining surfaces of two pieces of the veneers and clamp them together in the form. When the glue has set the shape of the veneer will remain. Glue two more pieces of veneer, also the adjoining surfaces where they are to be bent to the part already formed. Again clamp the forms together. Repeat this operation as many times as is necessary to form the correct thickness. Remember there is a right and left wing, so the bent pieces should be laid out accordingly. Lay out for the feathers after the wings have been carved to their proper shape.

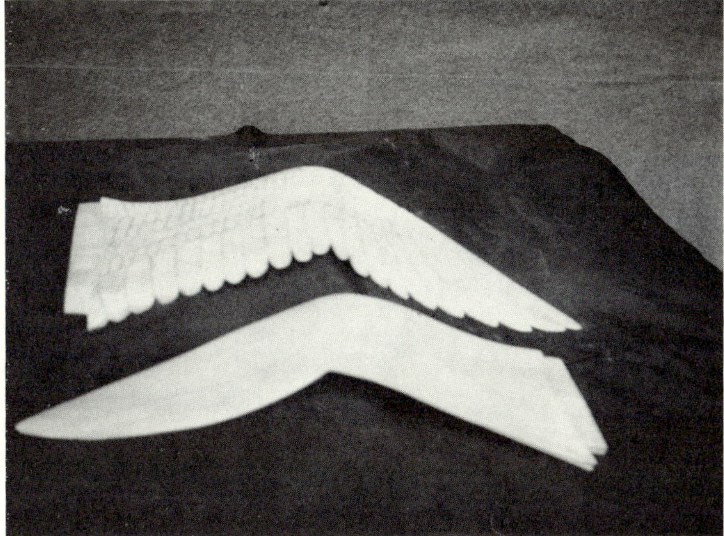

Fig. 4. Bent wings shaped and carved.

Cut the feathers with shallow strokes of the V-tool. The feathers should have a shingle effect when carved, that is, one feather should overlap the other. The wings are easier to carve before attached to the body. Do not let your impatience spoil this procedure (Fig. 4).

The tenon of the wings should be cut the old-fashioned way. In an operation of this kind there is no satisfactory machine method. There are too many curves to follow. The tenon should be the same size as the mortise, of course, and the same camber in both directions. Fit the wings in place. Polyester filler will be a great help in smoothing out the contours after the wings have been glued in place. Finish the carving in the wing area.

Next make the legs and feet. Follow the directions already given in the chapter "Canada Goose." Likewise install the glass eyes as explained in the previous chapters.

The fish in the photograph (Fig. 1) is a yellow perch. It was used to add some color to the carving. The perch and driftwood are fastened together as one unit, which in turn is fastened to the base with a long screw counter-bored from the bottom. If a suitable piece of driftwood is not available the perch may be fashioned from a tree limb. It should be rustic, however.

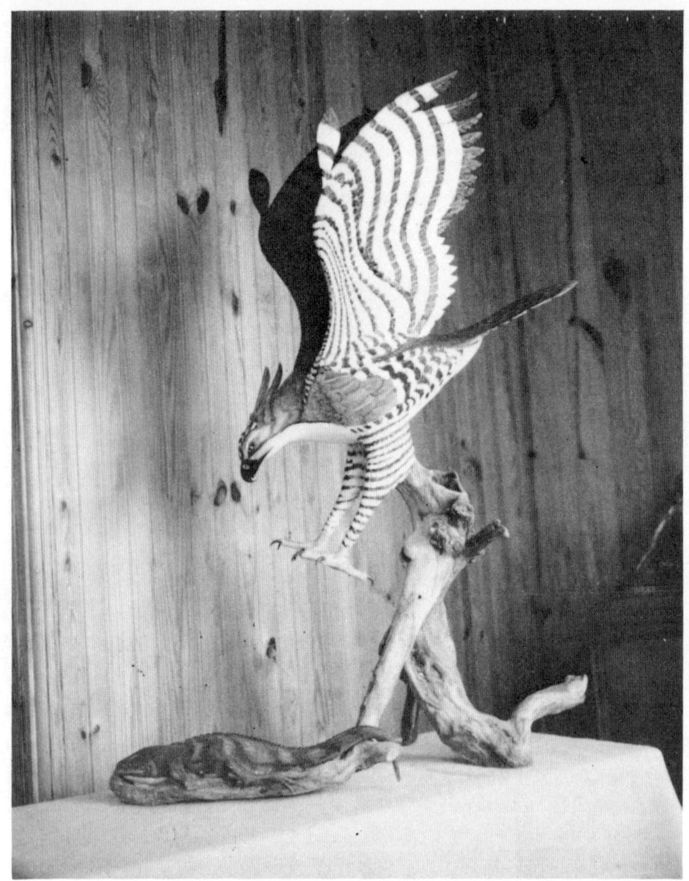

Fig. 5. Ornate eagle hawk, carved by the author.

If the bird is carved full-sized you and the family may have to move out of the room where the carving is displayed (Fig. 5). But the carving will be beautiful and cause much attention and praise, especially from conservationists and bird lovers in general.

The squares of the grid were drawn 3/8″ (Fig. 6). Grid squares ¾″ will make a nice sized carving, but if the bird is to be carved life-size the squares should be 15/16″. The length of an adult osprey is 22″ and the wingspan is 54″.

Painting the osprey is not as simple as it may appear. First, a very smooth, unblemished surface is required. All tool marks should be sanded out. Then, a thorough coat of wood sealer should be applied. When thoroughly dry the carving should be rubbed down with steel wool (000) and the steel shavings blown away. The feathering should not look mechanical or give a zebra-like appearance. Have a good painting near you to guide you in painting the

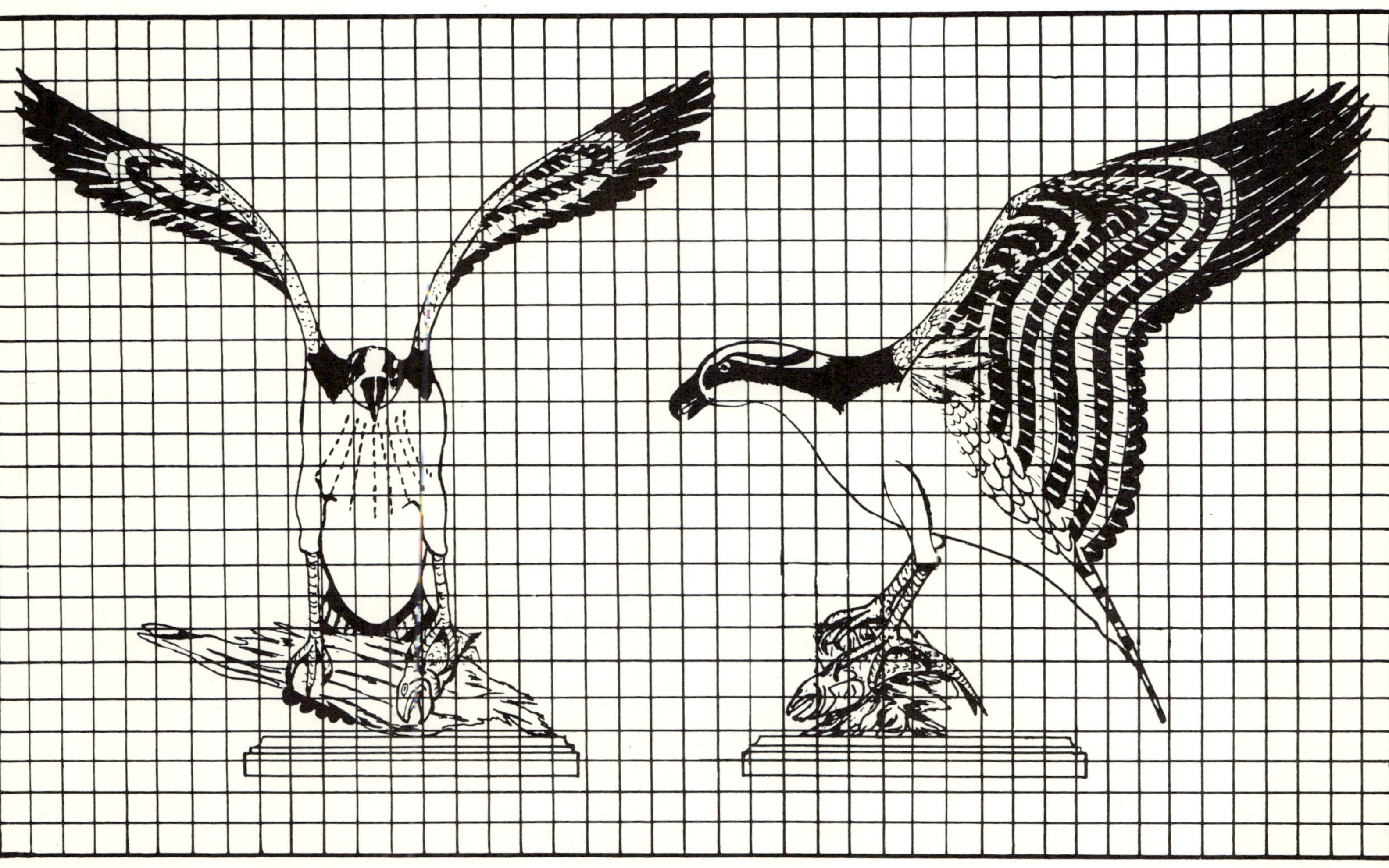

Fig. 6. Grid drawing of the carved osprey.

feather patches and also for proper coloration. Remember that feathers are made up of barbs and your brush strokes should indicate this composition. While the tail and wings appear to be composed of simple stripes they are actually feathers of very irregular outline, individually. The white patches are not flat areas but brushed in with feathered strokes. Some experimentation will be necessary to achieve this effect.

Chapter 6

The Great Horned Owl

As usual in these discussions of suggested projects the emphasis will be in part on related material which educators say is an important aspect of motivation. Certainly the carver should not be entirely ignorant of the figure he desires to carve. In this project the owl should not be a stranger in your shop. Read all of the available literature concerning owls. You will be surprised, not only with what you learn, but your increased interest and appreciation of the bird. Your carving effort will have an added stimulus.

Several years ago I exhibited a great horned owl at the Brandywine Art Festival in Wilmington, Delaware. A lady down the aisle from me came over and said, "That's an interesting piece of sculpture you have," indicating the owl.

"Thanks," I replied, "I am glad that you think so."

"You know," she continued, "we have one of these birds which comes and goes like any other member of the family. He eats with us and hangs around the house most of the day."

She continued to tell me about her bird as if he were indeed a member of the family. I know another family that has a whole backyard full of them. They are so tame that they beg for food. The lady of the house feeds them mice and raw meat. The great horned owl is indeed some bird! Did you know that the Smithsonian Institution had owls in the tower of the castle some years ago? They were so messy that the custodians shut them out and they were not allowed to return home. Then the rodents took over. The waste cans attracted hundreds of mice and rats. Then there was a decided change of feeling. A mated pair of owls were obtained from the zoo and were caged in the castle until they learned to call it their new home. A recent issue of the *Smithsonian Magazine* states that all is well with the owl family. They fly about at night and the trash cans are free of rodents. During the last few years our people have become ecologically conscious. Instead of casting out wildlife they are landscaping their property to encourage it to thrive, with a fervent hope that it will.

The ancient Romans had little respect for the owl. They let superstition control their thoughts concerning the bird, believing that it augured ill to those unfortunate enough to become fouled up with it. An owl alighting on a rooftop presaged death. Even in our time some people connect the owl with death. A current best seller is, *I Heard the Owl Call My Name.* In ancient Greece the owl was considered a wise bird. Plato quotes a proverb of his day, "Like taking owls to Athens." The bird is identified with Athena, goddess of wisdom. Modern people, especially in the New World, associate the bird with witches without losing any of its wise characteristics. Let us sing together the ditty:

> A wise old owl sat on an oak
> The more he saw the less he spoke;
> The less he spoke the more he heard;
> Why aren't we like that wise old bird?

Now, do you feel in the mood to carve an owl? If you do not it may mean you have had a bad day, so put on your night clothes and go to bed.

You should know something about owls before you attempt to carve them. You must have an insistent urge to carve them with feeling. Then even the wood will respond to your chisels. Copy the results of your research for your admirers and prospective customers. The information will make good conversation, for some of your visitors will be well informed—even to the extent of quoting the Latin names of the birds you carve. I have found that a prepared sheet of interesting facts about a carving and the subject it represents is very well received and often clinches a sale.

A phenomenon which often happens to carvers is to respect the lives of their subjects, and all wildlife. They tend to become ardent conservationists. Two of the best known carvers of wildlife on the Eastern Shore of Maryland expressed their feelings to the author one day concerning a Canada goose the younger brother was carving. "I've killed my fair share," said the younger, "but I will never know how I was able to do it." This sensitive individual learned so much about his bird that he became conscious of its welfare. He distributed at one of the wildlife shows the sentimental poem *Remorse,* by Truman Reitmeyer, which concerned the death of a pair of Canada geese he had shot. This was strange literature to pass around among the viewers of a show which had for its objective more ducks to shoot. Having a sympathetic feeling for your subject will give your efforts a reverent turn of direction, adding a spiritual drive to your carving tools, and bringing to a more perfect fruition the form of your dreams.

A few weeks before Christmas (1973) a building developer and promoter from Philadelphia visited my showroom of carvings and paintings. He took a long look at my great horned owl with up-stretched wings (Fig. 1). He turned to me and said, "May I go home and bring my wife to see your carvings?" He was visiting his wife's folks who lived in a nearby village. In a little while he returned with his wife, a beautiful woman, and they spent a full hour observing the various carvings. The owl intrigued them most. They stopped before it and studied it carefully.

"How much do you want for this bird?" inquired the wife.

"It is not for sale," I replied, "but I will carve you another for $500.00."

Usually this kind of declaration ends the conversation in this direction, but neither batted an eyelash.

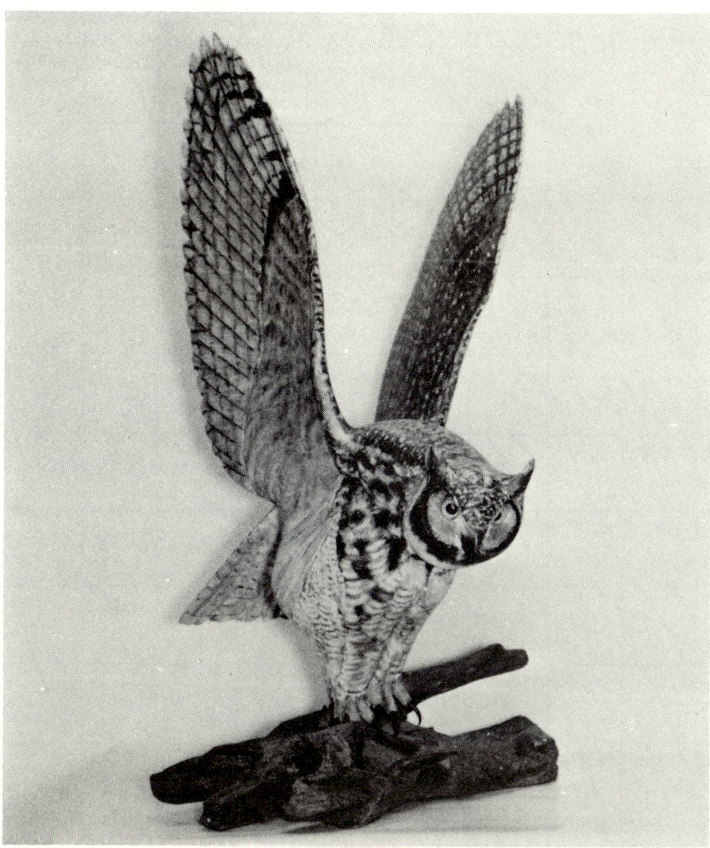

Fig. 1. Great horned owl, carved by the author. Photograph by Brightwell.

"I want my owl to have wings that are nearly closed—but not quite, standing almost erect, and his head turned nearly at right angles. Can you do this for us?"

They confessed that they were owl buffs and had collected over four hundred of them, mostly ceramic models. Before they left I promised them a bird within a few months, carved according to their directions. Their commission offered quite a challenge to my carving ability. I spent many sleepless hours trying to visualize every feature of the bird. Then one day in January I saw the model I wanted in my barber's shop. It was pictured on a calendar painted by James Lockhart, that versatile wildlife painter whose

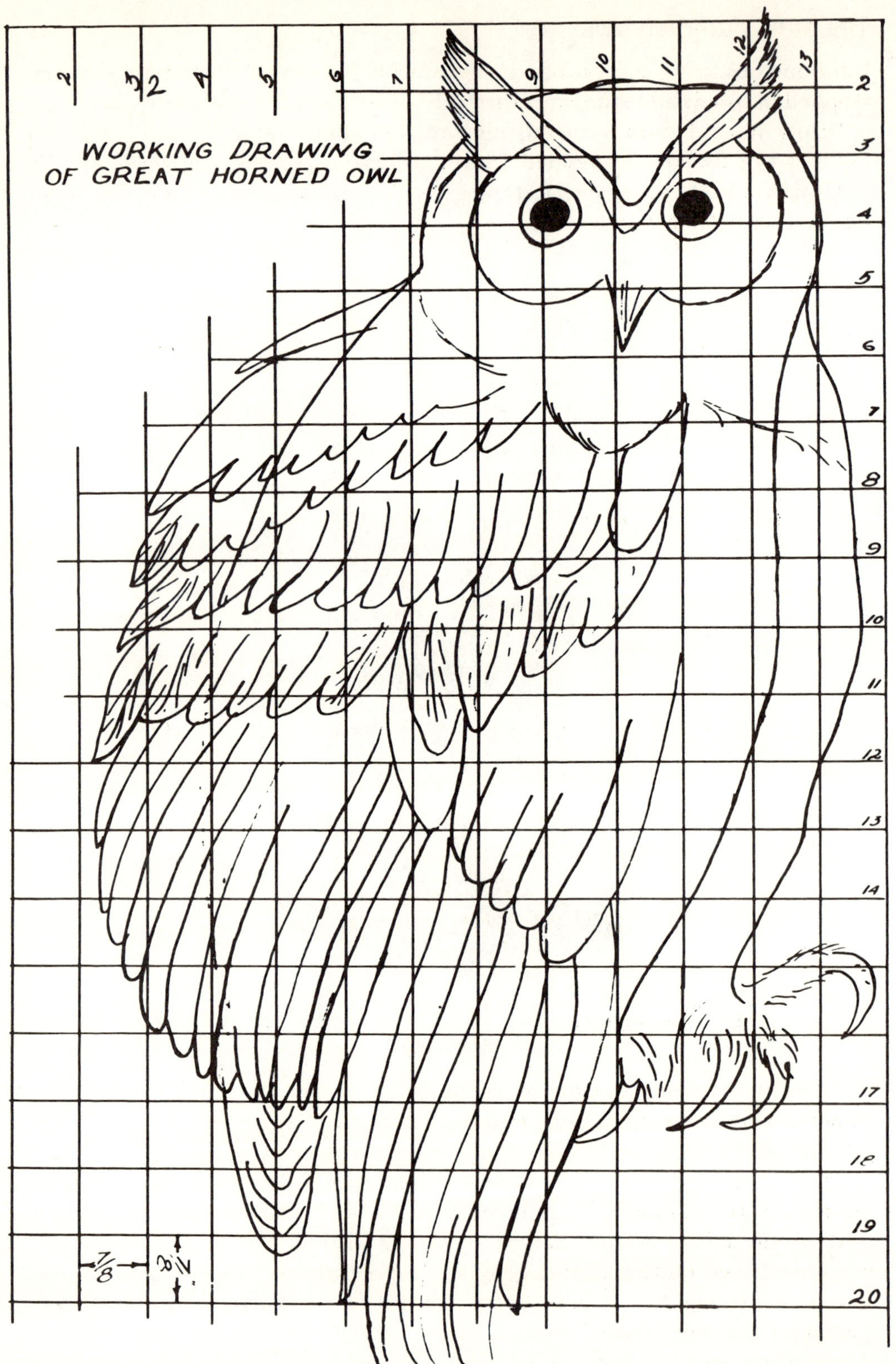

Fig. 2. Working drawing of the great horned owl.

superb work has won national recognition. He was recently quoted in *American Artist,* "If I can successfully paint a flower, an animal, a weed, or even a withered leaf, perhaps I can show others that the world around us is really beautiful." I do not know how to contact Mr. Lockhart, but I feel he will not object to my using his painting of the great horned owl for the basic

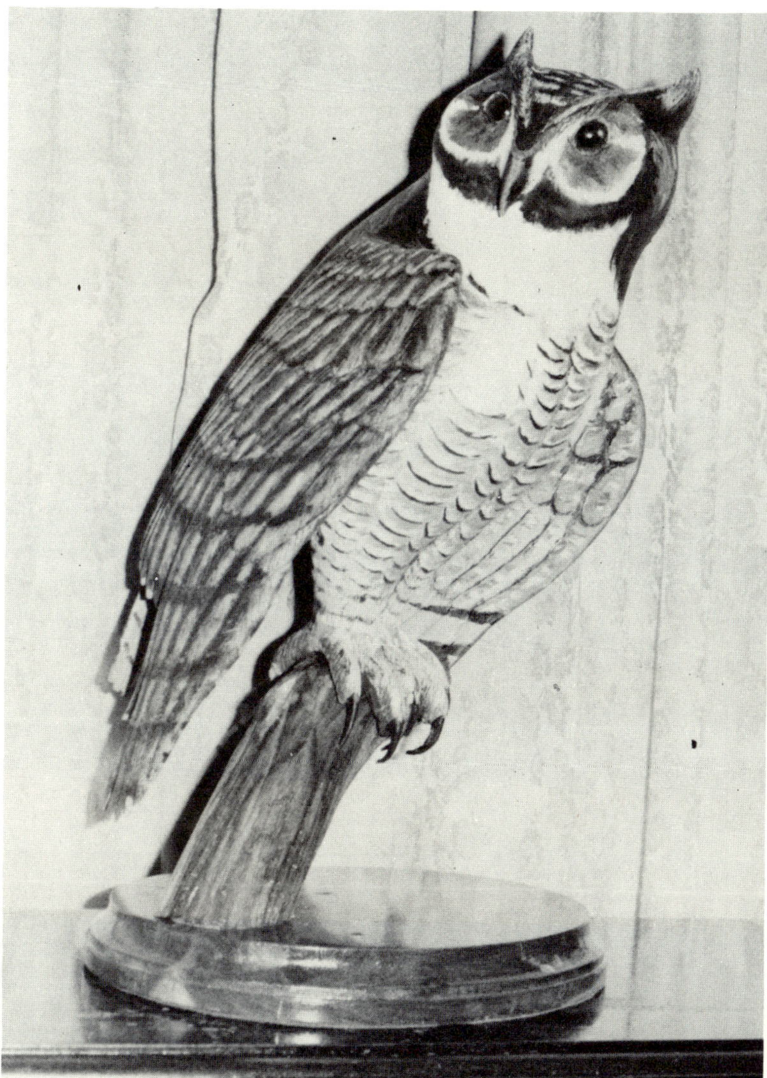

Fig. 3. Great horned owl, carved by the author.

ideas of the lady's carving. The carving will give his picture a third dimension, and I hope if he should chance to see it, it will not be too displeasing to his artistic feelings.

Figure 2 shows the original working drawing from which the various templates or profiles were drawn. These, of necessity, were somewhat modi-

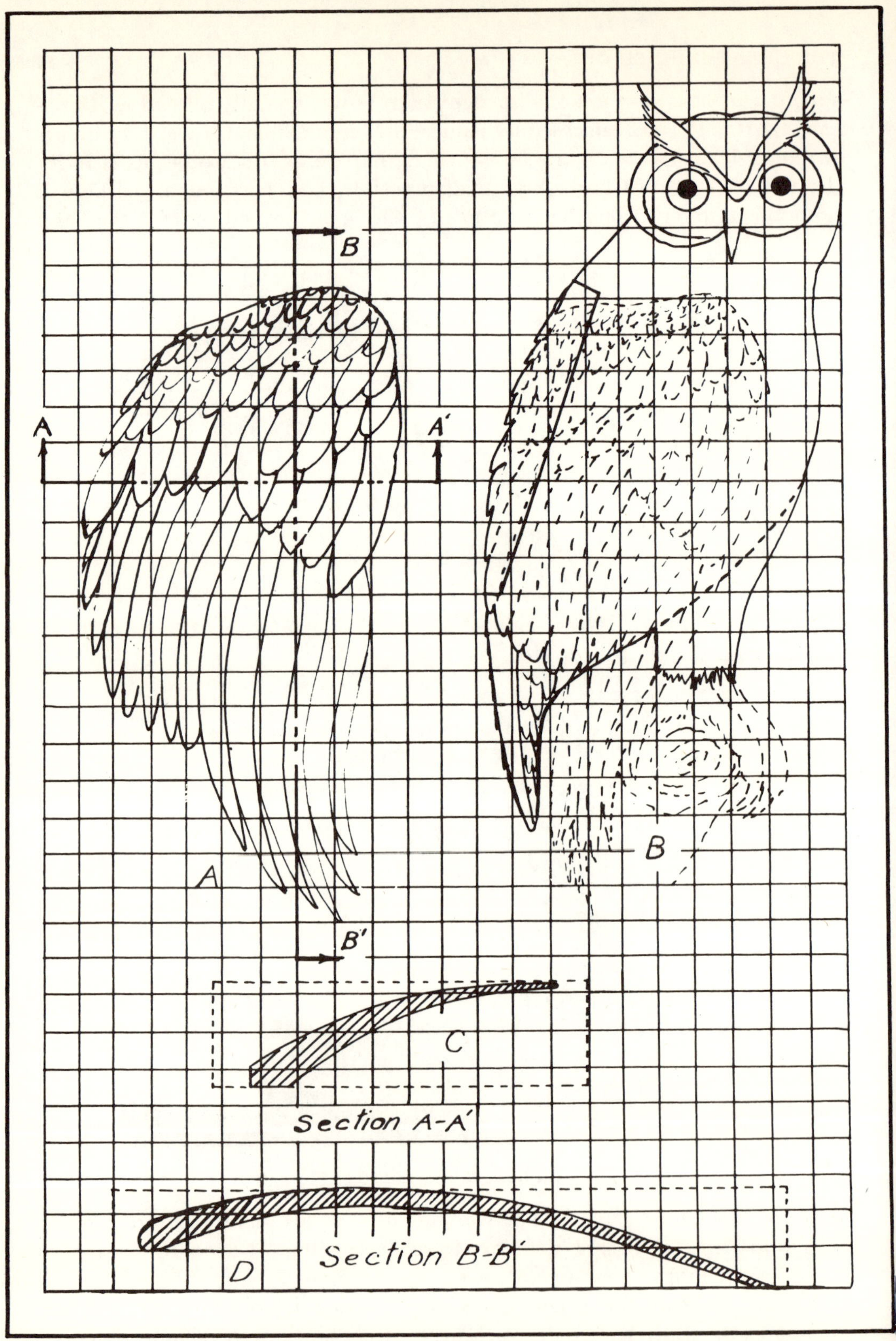

Fig. 4. Profile drawing for the great horned owl. Squares are 7/16″. Solid lines represent the carved bird; the dotted lines indicate the wing as it fits the body; 7/8″ squares will make the owl full-size. Cross sections show camber of the wings.

fied, for the airy fine lines of a painting cannot be duplicated in sculpture. However, the photograph of the finished carving (Fig. 3) will indicate to some extent Mr. Lockhart's owl's likeness and, I hope, please the owl collectors, man and wife.

The bird was somewhat difficult to carve. Several times I was tempted to toss the whole work into the fireplace. But one of the saving graces of a woodcarver is his bulldog tenacity, and his stubborn pride of allowing no problem to conquer him. You do not become a good woodcarver by throwing your work into the fire. You just keep carving along!

The first step in carving the owl has already been discussed: the background material. The second step is preparing the design and profiles, and the third is when you bite into your wood with your tools. Follow the routine operations of carving most of the polychrome figures of this book. Surface two boards, long enough and wide enough to receive your profile drawing (Fig. 4) and thick enough to carve one-half of the bird. (The wings are carved separately.) Cut out the profiles accurately on a band saw, preferably, and glue them together temporarily with a dab of glue on each end of one profile. Clamp the two halves together with a C-clamp at either end. After the glue has set carve the body and then the head roughly to shape. Note that the head is turned nearly at right angles with the body and that the twist in the neck should be indicated from the very start. The head block should be formed before the real carving begins. The block form should be the size of the head in all dimensions, and turned nearly at right angles with the block of the body. Before carving the body, note the segment-like space which is left flat at the root of the wings. Leaving this area flat, on both the body and the wings, will greatly facilitate the carving effort later when the wings are attached.

The body should be carved roughly first, but do not forget the twist of the head. The depression of the breast should turn naturally toward the center of the beak side of the head. The uncarved head may be used to clamp the body in the vise while being carved. After the body has been carved (roughly) the head should be shaped. Some neat carving ability will be required in this effort, but patience will help you to succeed. Control the twist of the neck. Let the carved depression stop at the neck in front of the beak. Remember that the eyes are protected by the eyebrows and cheeks and that the disk-like depressions which contain the eyes should not be carved too deeply. Note too, that the ears are made up of several feathers coming to a point.

Some clamping of the head may be necessary after the head has been roughly carved. During this process the beak may be squeezed flat. Do not let this "hurt" bother you for the softwood beak should be cut off anyhow and another of hardwood substituted in its place.

After the body and head have been roughly carved, split the halves apart and hollow out the waste wood. A wide fishtail gouge (2″) is suitable for this operation, but do not cut toward either your fingers or your body. Leave

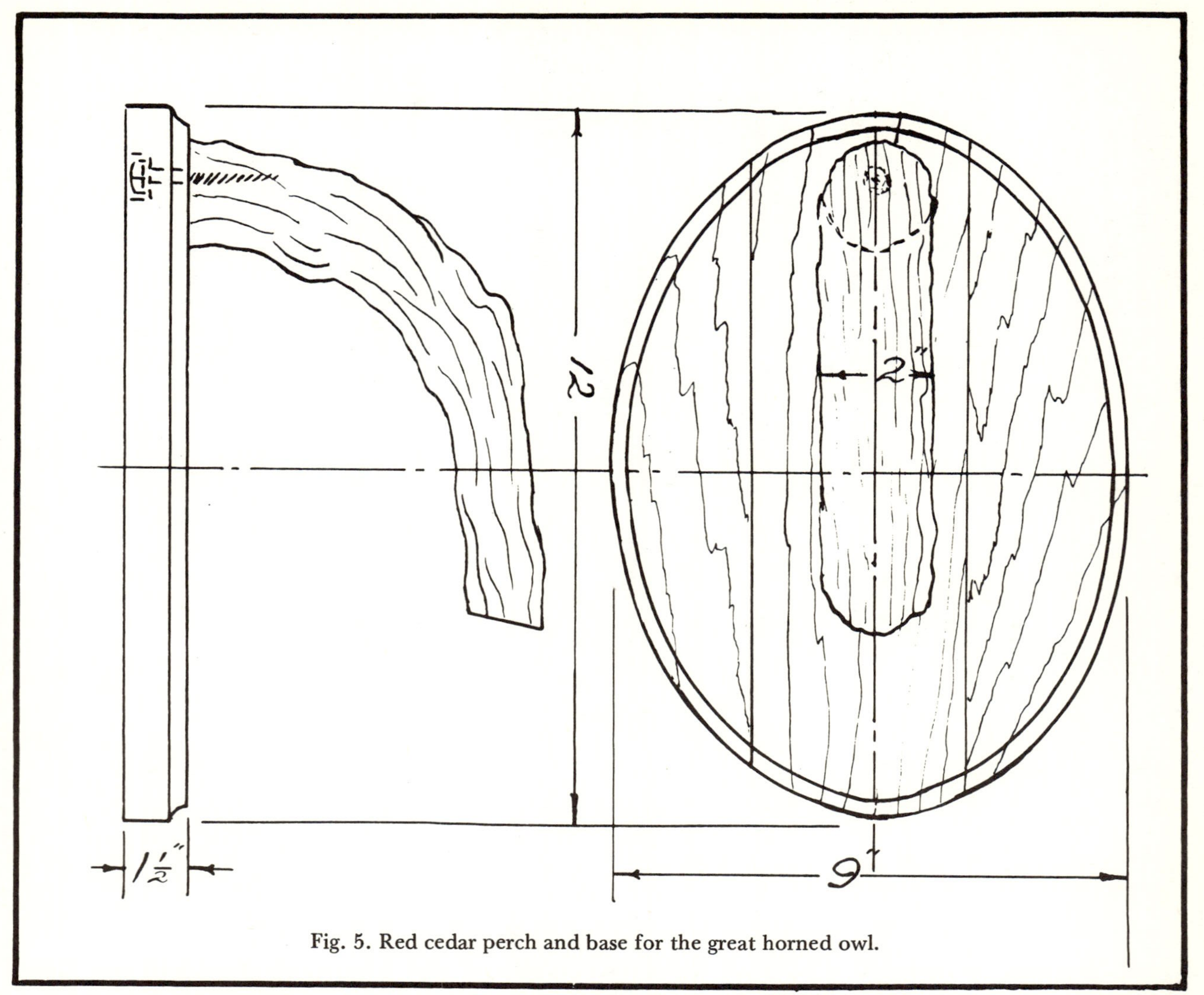

Fig. 5. Red cedar perch and base for the great horned owl.

enough space for gluing the parts together again and for some deep carving which might be necessary. Now the halves may be glued together permanently.

After the glue has set, carve the body to its final form. Finish carving the head. Locate the eyes carefully and bore holes for them large enough for a slip fit. For proper size and color consult the eye chart in J.W. Elwood's catalog (*see* Appendix) or the same chart in the author's book on bird carving. Bore the holes deep enough to allow the polyester filler to spread under the eyes. Fill the holes with the filler and press the eyes in place. Be sure that they do not appear "popeyed" or "goofy." After the eyes have been inserted the beak may be repaired. Cut a piece of hardwood the size of the beak, allowing for some waste. Prepare the head for the beak and nail it in place. The beak should have holes drilled in it for the nails (two nails will be sufficient) and the joint thoroughly glued. The nails will sufficiently clamp the beak in place. After the beak has set it may be carved to shape. Finish carving the head after the nails have been withdrawn from the beak and the holes filled with filler. Some careful carving will be necessary around the ears and perhaps some carving will be necessary to make the twist in the neck more natural.

The Legs and Feet

Refer to the chapter on the Canada goose for the method of making the legs and feet. The basic process is the same. Shape each toe (talons) before brazing them to the leg rod. The leg rod should be 3/8″ and the toes ¼″. The middle toe should be about 4½″ long and the others shortened accordingly. The back toe, of course, should also form the leg tendons and be brazed to the back of the legs. Heat the ends of the toes red hot and form the talons with a hammer on an anvil. The talons may be smoothed down with a file afterward. Be sure to shape the talons before assembly to save yourself considerable work and frustration. The tang of the legs should project down into the perch at least 1½″ and the legs about 1″ up into the thighs. The toes should be bent to fit the perch after it is ready and before the legs are fixed in the figure.

The Perch and Base

Prepare stock for the base of the carving. Figure 5 shows three boards glued together for this purpose. Three boards are less likely to warp than one wide board. A board tends to straighten its annual rings no matter how well seasoned the board may be. However, a quartersawn board may be used without danger of warping. After the glue has set cut out the oval shape and cove designed edge. If you do not have a shaper, cut the concave shape by hand or change the design. Dress the base smoothly and finish natural in the usual manner.

The shape of the perch should be a bent limb. It need not be seasoned for

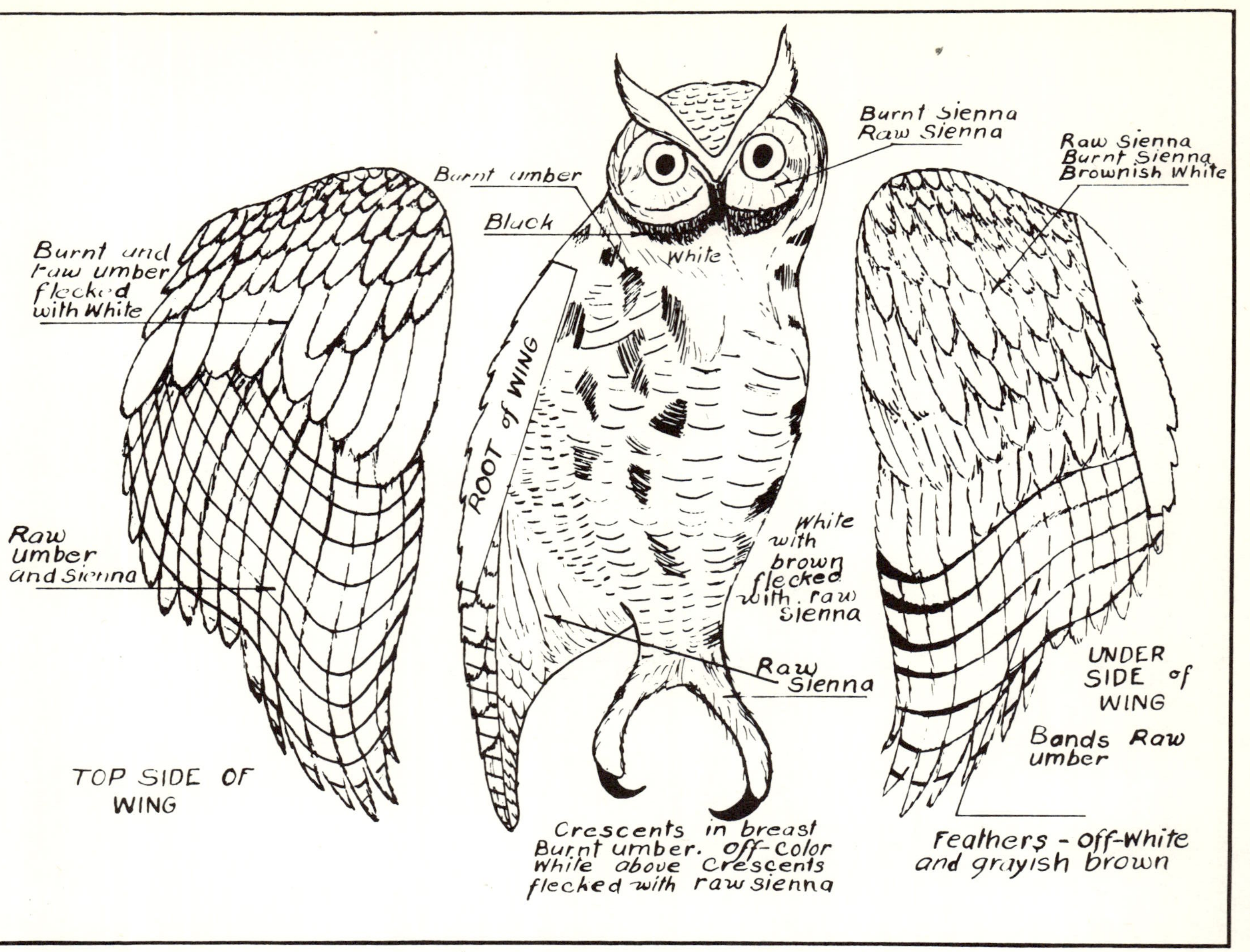

Fig. 6. Color scheme for painting feathers.

if it checks or splits no great harm will be done to the general appearance. This particular part is supposed to be rustic. Peel off the bark and groove it with a parting tool to bring out the shape. Do not leave the perch "hairy" for it should be varnished to make it dustproof. The perch must be shaped in the fashion shown so that it will not interfere with either the wings or the tail. After the base and perch have been made assemble them as indicated in the drawing (Fig. 5). A 3/8″ lag screw 3″ long will be just about right. Bore a hole in the base at the proper location and deep enough to sink the head and washer below the bottom surface, and large enough to receive the washer, leaving enough room for a socket wrench. The shank hole should be a slip fit as always in this type of construction. The hole for the threaded portion should be the size of the core of the screw at the beginning of the third thread, that is, slightly smaller than the core of the lag screw. Locate the holes for the leg tangs. Do this by placing the carving on the perch in the desired location and marking off the center of each leg. Drill the holes at least 2″ deep. Place a piece of wax paper over the holes (cut out the tang holes) and insert the leg tangs. Be sure the legs and toes are in proper position. Next bore a hole in each thigh of the carving 3/16″ larger than the leg rods and as far up as the leg rods are to penetrate. Fill the holes with polyester filler and carefully press down over the leg rods. Hold the carving in the proper position until the filler begins to harden. Allow about two hours after the filler hardens to mold the toes to shape. Apply the polyester filler to the toes. (The wax paper will protect the perch.) Form the toes until they look natural. Mold the legs to the thighs and join them with the toes, remembering that the feathers, fine feathers, cover the entire length of the legs. Next score in the feathers. The cut-off disk of a Moto-tool will do this operation with ease.

Next carve the wings (Fig. 4). Remember to leave flat the segment where the wings join the body of the bird (Fig. 6). Carve the cambers as indicated. Carve the feathering pattern on the underside of both wings. This operation is easily accomplished. After the wings are assembled the remaining space will be too small to guide your tools with proficiency. The feathering design is indicated in Fig. 6.

To fasten the wings to the body, first plane the segments on both the body and the wings so that the wings will be open and set at a desirable angle. Increase or reduce the angle of the joint to suit this requirement. Drill at least three holes in each wing segment the size of the box nails to be used. Cut six masonite washers (squares 1/8″ x ½″ x ½″) to be placed under the head of each nail and drill them with the same size drill. Place the wing in position—the exact position—and drive the nails down into the body about 3/8″. Withdraw the nails and coat the segments with glue (both body and wing). Replace the wing and after locating the holes, previously made, drive the nails down tightly. The body may be placed in a vise for this operation. After the glue has set repeat the procedure for the other wing. This time use your sandbags to hold your carving in place. Allow the wings to set overnight. The following morning the nails may be withdrawn with a claw hammer and the wings tested for strength. They should be as strongly fastened as if they were carved from the solid block. Complete the carving around the wings where they are fastened to the body. When completed there should be no evidence of how the wings were attached. If the outside surface of the wings are not finished smoothly do so at this time. The sanding operation may be eliminated, as the feathers when carved will require this treatment. Lay out the feathers. (I believe, however, that the patch of feathers above the primaries and secondaries are not far enough down. Drop them down about two rows, the extra rows being carved at the top of the wing. The underside wing arrangement seems to be correct.) After the feathers are drawn start carving them by first cutting around the under part of each row of feathers with a V-chisel. When the operation is completed the feathers will look like the siding on a house. This step is the first in the overlapping technique. In carving the feathers the tendency will be to carve them too deeply. Do not score them more than 1/16″. At the tips of the primaries and secondaries, chisel and file the feather openings to shape, joining the contours of those on the underside. Give the upper and underside parts some relation to each other. Now carve and carve, one feather over the other, like shingles on a roof.

Painting the Color Patches

The most difficult job for most carvers is painting the feathers in a realistic manner. Follow the scheme suggested in Fig. 6. First, as always, give the carving a thorough coat of wood sealer. Allow to dry until the surface is quite hard. Then rub down with steel wool (000) or worn sandpaper until the surface is even and without dust spots or other blemishes. Blow off the steel shavings. Next brush in the feather patches with either oil colors or acrylics. Use the feathering technique of stroking the brush in the direction of the barbs. For the beginner, oil colors may be easier as the feathers may be outlined and a dry stiff-bristled brush dragged through the outlines, giving the feathers the appearance of their barbed construction. The brush should be wiped dry after each stroke with a soft dry rag. If acrylics are used the barbed edges should be stroked in with a very fine brush following an imaginary outline. Reread the painting directions for the Canada goose. While the color scheme for the owl is indicated in Fig. 6, the technique and realism for satisfactory effects must be achieved by the ingenuity of the painter. Only practice, and more practice, can develop this art to proficiency. Have a good picture of a horned owl near you while you paint. If possible have a mounted specimen to guide you, for you will discover that one picture differs from another in color and feather design. Learn to highlight your work for no feather is perfectly flat either in shape or color. Consider the bronzed grackle. He is jet black fundamentally, but what a riot of colors in the sun! All shades of purple, blue and green. The owl is a medley of many colors without the benefit of reflected light, no area being exactly alike. The ground colors are most evident, but there are some pastels. Painting in these colors to look like feathers is no mean trick. Some feathers have definite patterns as indicated by the dark crescents, while others somewhat ruffled have less definitive shapes. On the body of the owl most feathers blend in harmoniously to form nearly a motley pattern of white, raw sienna, burnt umber and some burnt sienna. Paint them in carefully and you will have a beautiful bird.

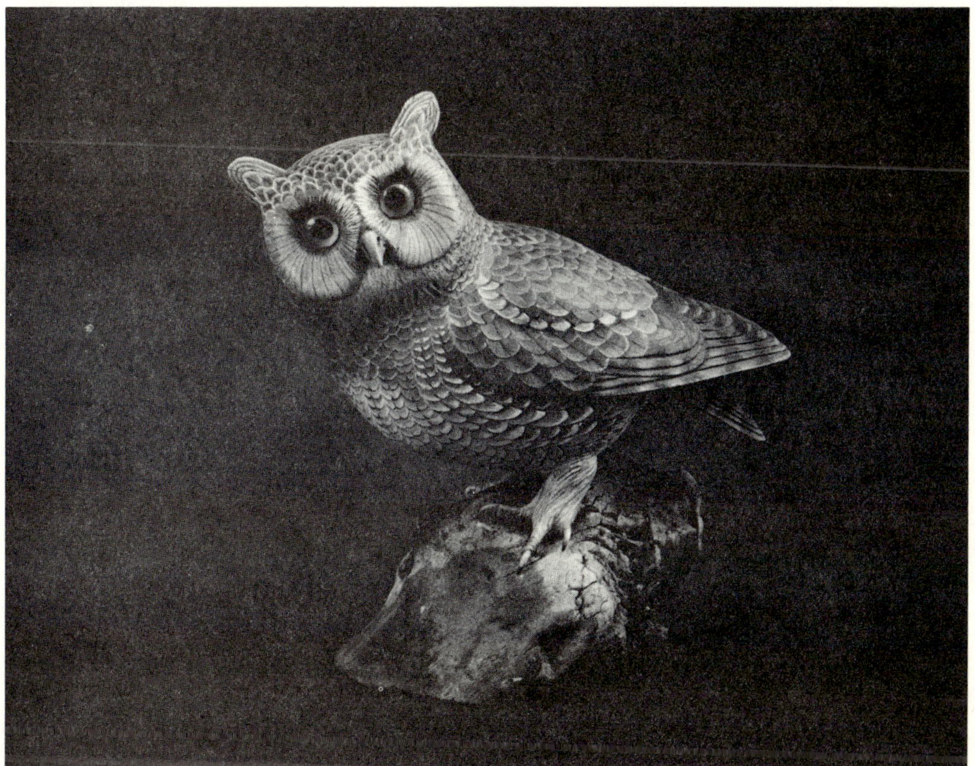

Fig. 7. Screech owl, by Davidson B. Hawthorne.

To make feathers look overlapping when they are not carved in, a dark shadow under the tips will be effective. The shafts of a large feather may be dashed in with a flat sharp brush filled lean with raw sienna after the painting has been completed. This procedure should improve your work if it is done with imagination and skill. Stand off and view your work often. You will observe where improvements may be made. You will discover your sins of omission and commission.

Touching the carving is a part of the appreciation process. The usual rule of "Please do not touch" should be ignored in your work. "Sculpture must be lovely to touch," says Brancusi. Touching should never be discouraged, even if it means as much wear on your work as on the big toe of St. Peter at the Vatican. The wear, however, should not be allowed. Always keep the surface of your carvings protected with a coat of wax—ordinary floor wax. Rubbing down each application to a smooth, soft finish will not only protect the surface but improve the looks of your work.

Now, if you have done your work well your visitors will rub their fingers over the surface of your bird and wonder how you were able to do it; how you made the feathers so real; the carving so realistic in form. Keep your carving out of sight from the outside, or you may have every horned owl in the community fluttering at your windows trying to get near your bird.

Chapter 7

The Pelican

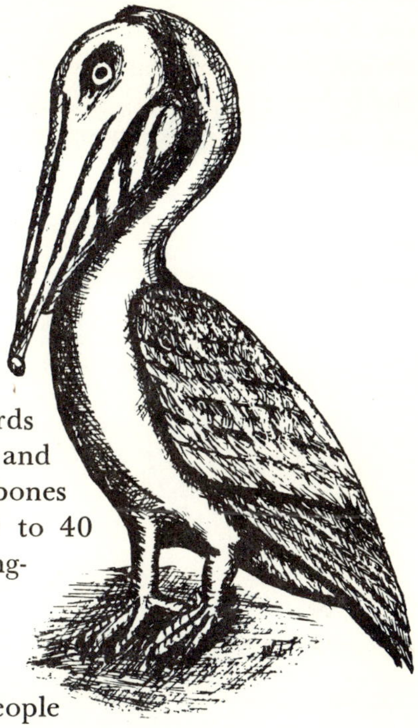

"What a wonderful bird is the Pelican. . . ."

The pelican belongs to a large family of birds ranging from the tropic-birds to the gannets and boobies. It is one of the oldest birds. Its bones have been found in Oligocene deposits 30 to 40 million years old. It is a large bird with a wing-span of as much as nine feet. The brown pelican is now on the endangered list, but the white pelican seems to be holding its own. The brown pelican has interested people most, probably because of its size and religious connotations. Because of the female's favorite pose, holding her beak close to her breast, she was thought to be pious. Early observers thought she plucked blood from her body to nourish her young. This faulty observation led to the analogy of the sacrificial blood like unto the allegory of Christ who shed his blood for the salvation of all mankind. This bird of "Christian Charity" so impressed the early settlers of Louisiana that they adopted the bird as their state's symbol. How these early people of Louisiana conceived of the bird's kinship with Christ is difficult to imagine. But for students of superstitious ideology and folklore such concepts are common. The owl, for example, has always been associated with wisdom. It was the symbol of Athena, who was the goddess of wisdom in ancient Greece.

The pelican is an awkward bird provoking a humorous attitude on the part of its observers. Despite the well known limerick, the beak is not used to store food except temporarily for her young. The pouch is used as a dip net to drain out the water after the fish is caught. The grotesque bill is reminiscent of the extinct flying reptile, Pterodactyl, and its clumsy movements on the ground are hardly more graceful; but once airborne the bird is a rhythm of motion. It is a familiar sight in southern waters and interest in the bird never ebbs.

Fundamentally, however, the bird is a scavenger. It combs the beaches and shore waters for offal, dead fish, or any such waste cast off by fishermen or other natives. It cares not for carrion like the vulture but instead fresh food of the estuaries. In this respect it is a very beneficial bird, and it belonged to the ecological society centuries before the problem of pollution was ever conceived by man. The pelican, therefore, is an important link in the balance of nature. In this capacity it does indeed embody some ideas of Christian charity, but not because of any religious feelings or interest of its own.

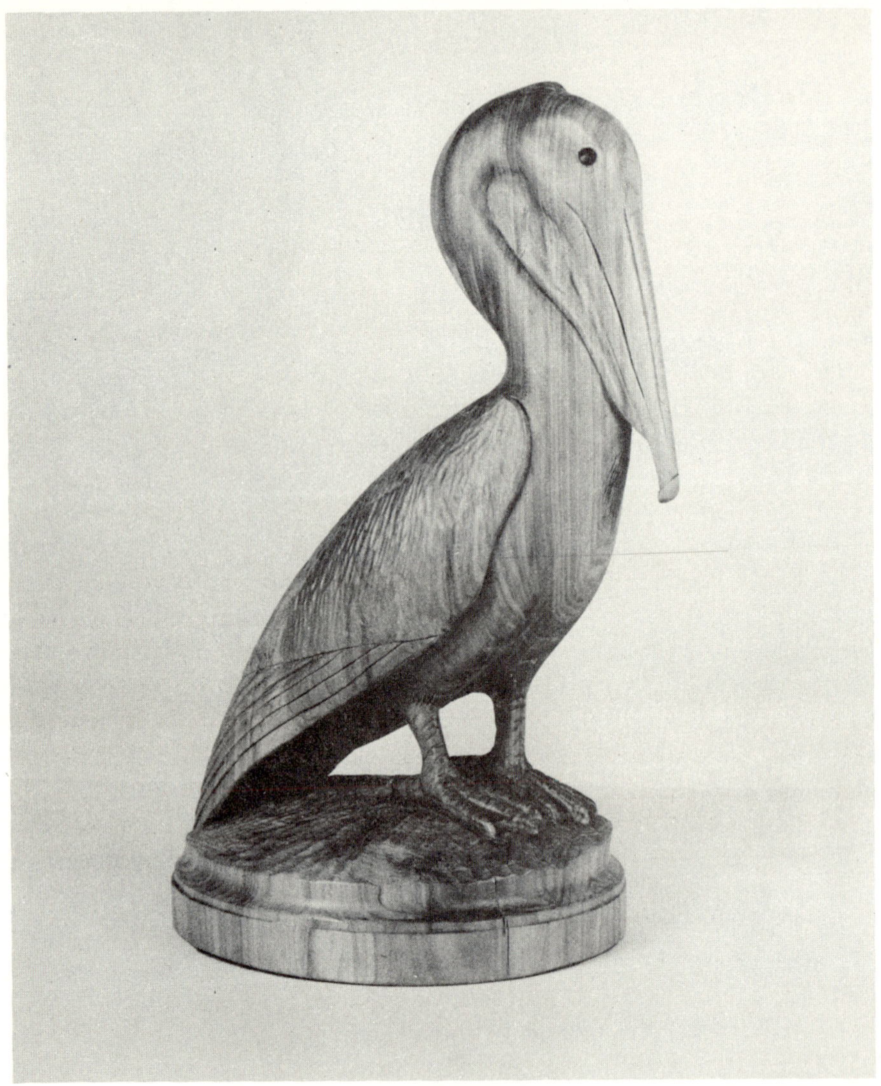

Fig. 1. Pelican; natural finish, carved from red cedar by the author. Photograph by Tawes Photographic.

Carving a Pelican from a Solid Log

This project (Fig. 1) differs from the previous carvings in some respects. It will not be laminated or painted in realistic colors. The bird will remain natural in finish and little effort will be made to carve the feathers realistically, the favorite treatment for most women collectors. Men usually prefer their models painted, but not the distaff side of the family who has her tastes conditioned to harmony in her furnishings (Fig. 2).

If the drawing in the grid (Fig. 3) is figured for a life-size bird (L 41″, W

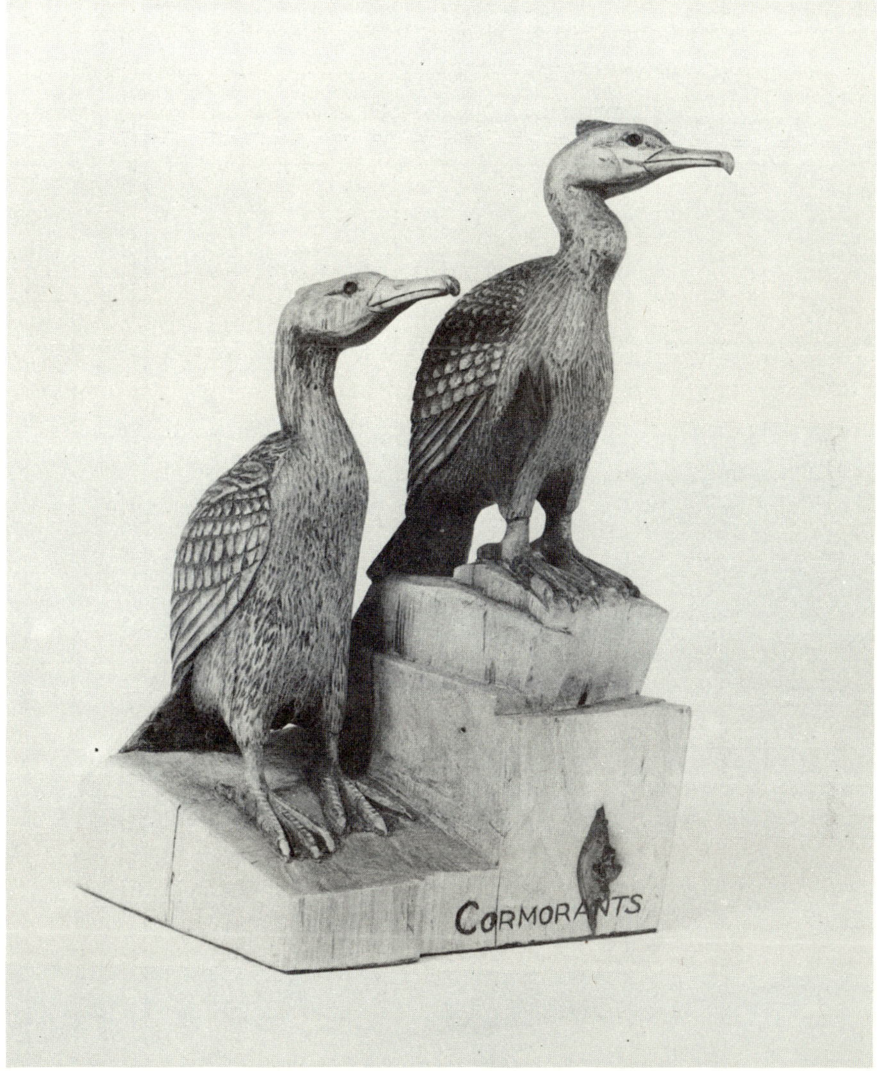

Fig. 2. Cormorants carved from an oak railroad tie by the author. Photograph by Tawes Photographic.

90″), the carving will not be too large because the "pious pose" and closed wings make the carving compact, occupying little space. First, however, the size must be determined and the log selected accordingly. Drawing the silhouette plan will help you decide on the size you desire. Be sure that the log has been seasoned over a long period of time. A log stored in a dry place for about ten years would be desirable. As the carving is not hollow the

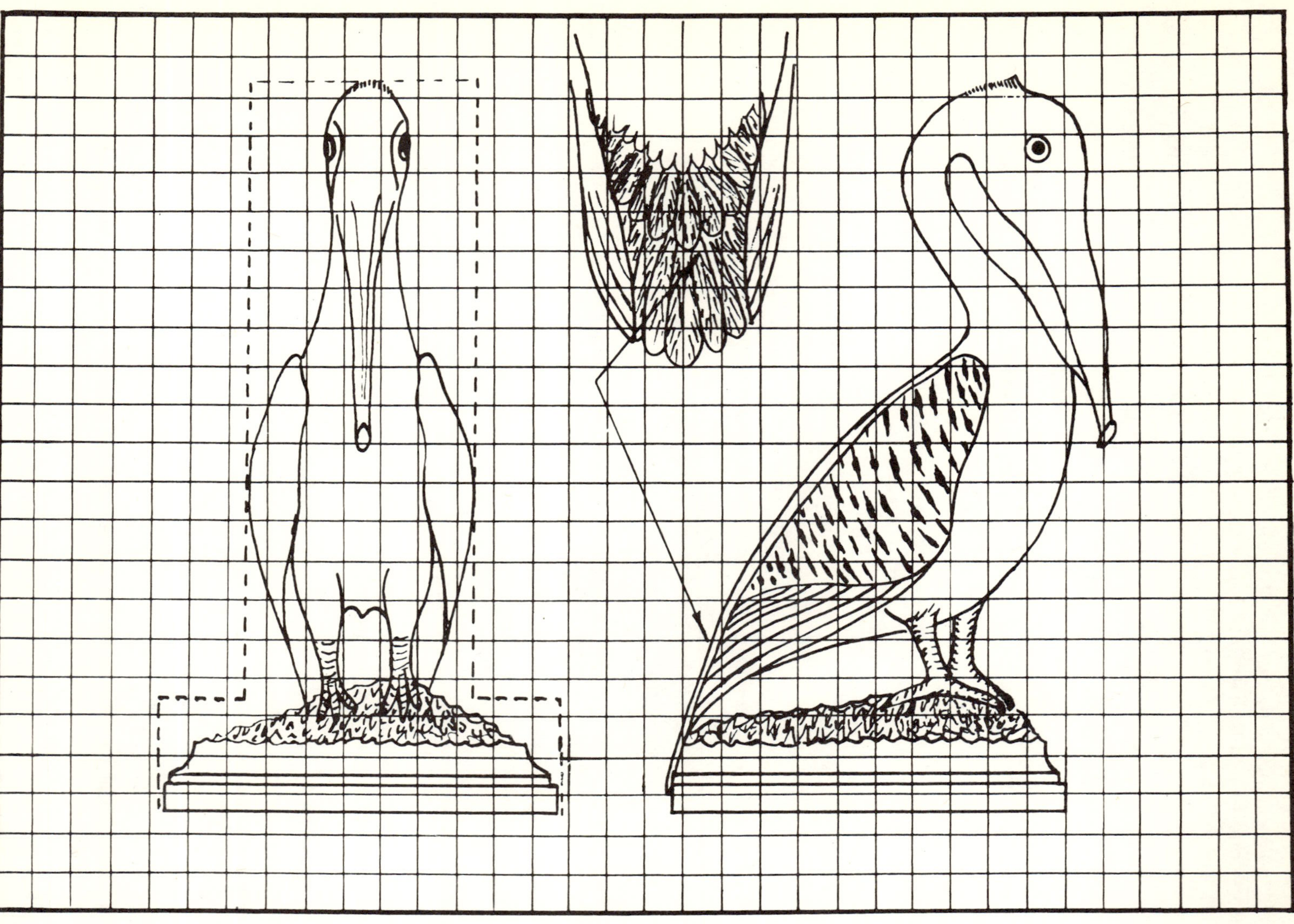

Fig. 3. Pelican carved from a single log.

tendency to check will be appreciable. If the log has knots be sure they do not appear in awkward places throwing the carving off balance. A log with knots is not objectionable because of the swirling grain around them but they can play havoc with the general appearance of the work.

Observe the dotted lines in the left-hand drawing. These lines represent the cuts necessary for removing the slabs of the log, leaving two parallel surfaces between which the pelican is carved. The profile or silhouette drawing may be placed upon one of these surfaces and traced. When this step has been completed the adjacent, barked side may be sawn at intervals down to within a quarter of an inch of the outlines drawn on the adjacent surface. When knocking out the waste wood between these horizontal kerfs, be careful not to split into the area of the drawing. When the front and back shapes have been roughly carved the bird will begin to assume its natural form. This operation is not as simple as it may sound from this discussion. Rounding off the corners and removing all chips which are not pelican requires some skill and imagination. Much of the rough carving may be done with a Surform rasp and the conventional steel, single cut type. Many of the bold curves may be removed with a fishtail gouge, followed by a spokeshave. Finishing the surface of this type of carving may be facilitated with the use of a cabinet scraper.* This useful tool is little understood or appreciated by the average carver. Every carver should have a supply of them in various gauges, sizes, and shapes. The base may be left in log-shape until the carving is nearly completed. The final carving should be done when the whole figure can be viewed without any unfinished parts.

Notice that the tail is a part of the base. The space between the tail and the legs will require some skillful carving. Do not cut these pierced parts about the legs until the figure has been nearly completed. Then the waste wood may be removed with more confidence and ease. An auger bit of the proper size (depending upon the size of the figure) will remove much of the waste wood safely. An ordinary 8″ single cut rasp and a rat-tail will be handy too, but the finishing cuts should be done with a sharp gouge and fine sandpaper held over the convex surface of a rasp. Between the legs is an equally difficult place to carve, but with a little patience and skill one can manage. Notice that the top surface of the base is elevated and formed of gouge cuts, or depressions, which should be sharp and crisp.

---

*To sharpen a scraper (a plain sheet of tool steel in various gauges, sizes and shapes) first file the edges square. Whet the edges on an oilstone, then with a burnisher begin turning over the corners to form a sharp hook. The burnisher should be held slightly downward at first, gradually increasing the angle until the burnished edge is about 45 degrees. A steady, uniform pressure on the burnisher will do the trick. To be sure you have a hook take the point of the burnisher and insert under the turned-over edge and trace the entire length. If you have done your work properly the turned-over edge will be razor sharp, and will smooth any contrary spot of swirling grain. The edge when it becomes dull may be burnished flat with the surface and turned over again. Finally the edge will have to be refiled, honed and the edge turned over again.

Locate the eye cavity and carve with care. The fabricated eye should be below the eyebrow and the cheek. Locate the exact spot for the eyes, and bore an auger hole ½″ deep the exact diameter size of the eyes.

The eyes are made of a piece of white wood (holly is ideal) rounded off like a dowel to fit the hole of the eye. An easy way to make this dowel is to cut a piece of stock slightly larger than the hole and as long as necessary to handle easily (about 4″). Cut off the corners to form an octagon cross section. Cut off the corners again and sharpen one end. Next drill into a piece of scrap iron (½″ thick) a hole of the proper size. Drive the sharpened end of the dowel into the hole and continue driving it through to the very end. The emerging dowel should be just the proper size, smooth and round. Glue the surfaces and drive the dowel into the eye holes. Cut the dowel off about 1/16″ above the surface. Mark with a center punch and drill a smaller hole in the dowel for the pupil of the eye. The hole should be small enough to leave an area for the iris. Form the dowel for the pupil out of ebony, if possible. In any event make this pupil dark enough to form significant contrast. When glued in place cut the black dowel off even with the iris and round off the eye in a button shape. This method of making eyes will apply for all natural finished carvings. Do not use glass eyes. I did until every sensitive artist who viewed my work criticized the technique.

Now the base may be carved to completion. Turn the carving upside-down and locate the center of the carving. Inscribe a circle with a pair of large dividers or a beam compass, the proper size. Cut off the waste wood carefully with a saber saw or chisel it to shape. Smooth the edge with a spokeshave. If you have a power shaper the concave curve may be shaped in the base with ease. If you do not have this useful tool the curve may be cut by hand with a gouge. Also, the edge design may be changed to suit the taste of the carver.

Notice that the feathering of the wings is conventional and no attempt is made to realistically carve the feathers. The feathering is done with long gouge depressions cut in the direction of the feathers on a real bird. The tail, on the other hand, is carved with realistic feathers as shown in the insert drawing on the grid.

Sandpapering is done with production paper. Sandpaper per se is almost obsolete. Whenever the word is used in this volume, production paper is indicated. Sand until scratch-free. Remember to use your scraper. Be sure your carving surface is perfect for your observers will examine your work closely, especially the more talented ones.

Finishing Techniques

After the carving has been sanded to a very fine finish, give it an adequate coat of wood sealer and allow it to dry thoroughly. When dry enough to work on (24 hours should be sufficient) rub down with steel wool (000). Blow off the steel waste and examine the carving for other imperfections.

Eliminate all defects. Next apply a coat of clear varnish or lacquer with a soft, clean brush. Do not make the coat "fat" and avoid "curtains" and "fisheyes." When the varnish has dried for two or three days in a constant room temperature, it should be hard enough to rub down with steel wool. Blow off the steel waste and other dust. Repeat the varnishing or lacquering process. Each coat of finish should be rubbed down with steel wool to give "teeth" to the surface. Ordinarily three coats of varnish will be sufficient. The last coat should dry for several days and be rubbed down with pumice stone and linseed oil. Do not rub too hard—a gently circular movement with a cheesecloth wad will do the trick. When the surface has become soft and velvety in appearance, a generous coat of floor wax may be applied. When this has hardened sufficiently it may be polished with a soft cloth as in polishing shoes.

Now your carving should be a fine example of the carving and finishing art.

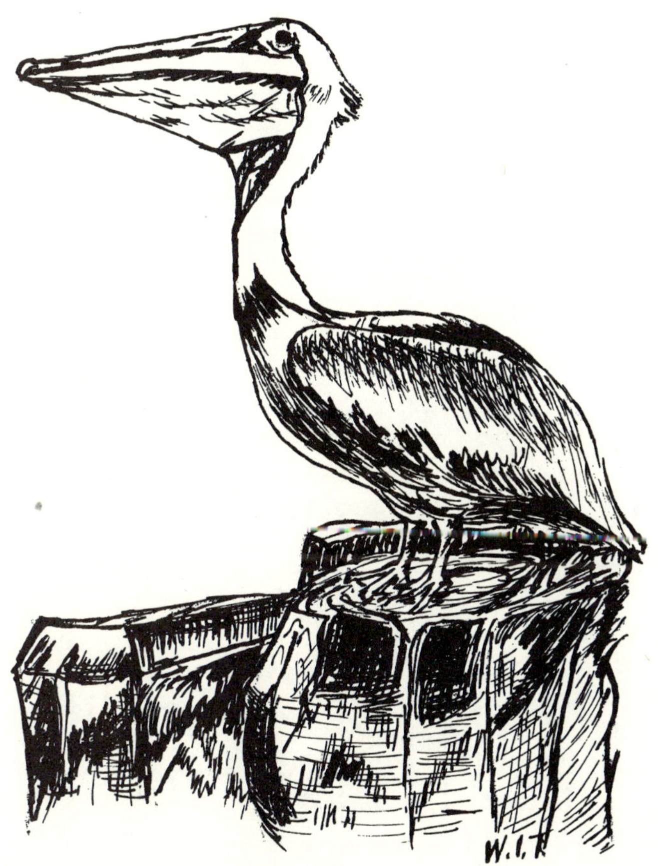

Figure 4.

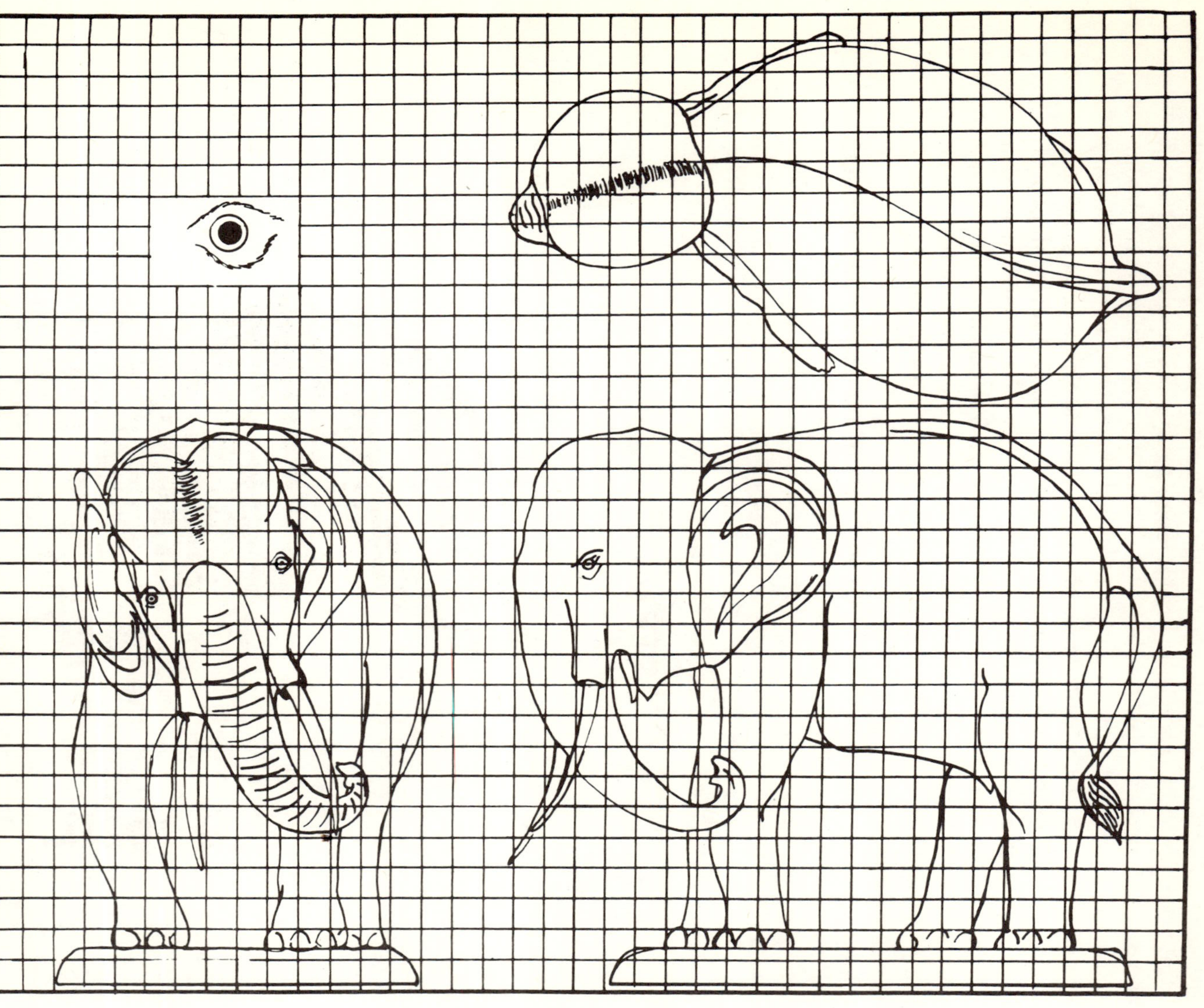

Fig. 1. Grid drawing for carved elephant.

Chapter 8

Elephants

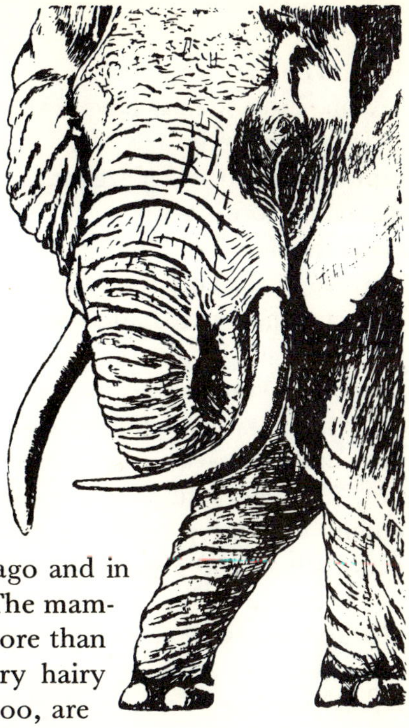

> Elephints a-piling teak
> In the sludgy, squdgy creek. . . .

The elephant is an echo from a far distant past. Its closely related prehistoric mammoth lived in Asia about 3,000,000 years ago and in North America about 2,000,000 years ago. The mammoth, extinct for thousands of years, was more than twice the size of present-day elephants, very hairy with large, upturned tusks. Our elephants, too, are very extraordinary animals, being the largest of the four-footed land creatures. They are the main attraction in zoos and circuses, due not only to their size but also to their body characteristics and intelligence. The Indian variety is easily tamed and have been used for centuries in the dense forests of India and Indochina to pile logs. They have been and still are a great service to man. They can drag several tons and lift tremendous weights. The African elephant has much more difficulty adjusting to the life of the zoo or circus. They are rarely used to perform labor. The male is especially a fierce animal in the wild—some of them are not even accepted by the herd. They are called *rogues* and "sleep wherever they want." The females of the African species are the elephants usually seen in zoos and circuses; some of them are so tame that children are allowed to feed them and ride on their backs around the park.

Before our era, elephants were used in warfare. The invincible Hannibal took 37 elephants with him across the Alps. But they probably all died during the winter, for despite their thick skins, they are as subject to frostbite as a garden pea. Hannibal's father, Hamlicar, used elephants with terrible effect in fighting the barbarians near Carthage. He armed their tusks with swords and his soldiers fought from the elephants' backs.

For the carver there are a few facts which should be noted. The Indian elephant's back is arched higher than its shoulders, while the African elephant's greatest height is located at the shoulder. The African elephant has two nearly equal finger-like knobs at the end of its trunk, the Indian but one. The African elephant has three nails on each hind foot and four on the front. The Indian elephant has four nails on its hind feet and five on its front feet. The ears of the African elephant are much larger than those of the Indian. Both species have small eyes compared to their great size.

Determine the size of your carving from the grid drawings (Fig. 1). Before reproduction the squares measured 3/8 x 3/8 inches. This size is very appropriate for ordinary use as an ornamental carving. For special purposes the elephant may be either enlarged or made smaller by increasing or decreasing the size of the squares.

Draw the profile of your carving accurately. (Use a stiff piece of cardboard.) Use the profile as a template and draw the outlines on a prepared block of wood (red cedar, mahogany, walnut, ebony), cut to size with two smooth, parallel surfaces. Cut the profile accurately on a band saw. In all projects discussed in this book a band saw is presumed to be available. If it is not, in some instances a coping saw will do, but in heavy stock neither a coping saw nor jig saw will be desirable. The last resort is to cut out the profiles with a hand saw and chisel—a slow, sometimes unsatisfactory procedure.

The waste wood between the legs (lengthwise) is best removed with a backsaw and a narrow gouge. In some close places part of the waste wood may be removed with an auger or drill bit. Do not hug the profile lines too closely. When shaping the third dimension, study the other views carefully. Notice there is a twist to the body causing the head to turn to the left. Mark out the shapes carefully and cut out the waste wood. The process of rounding out the carving is the next procedure. Use a sharp knife, rasp, and files. For removing a thick mass of waste wood use a Surform rasp. Do not cut below the skin. Do not cut the tusks as part of the carving. The tusks should be formed of holly or some tough white wood and set in the tusk sockets later. Try to get the grain to run in the curve of the tusks. They are easily broken off otherwise. The carving should be ready to varnish before the tusks are inserted. Smooth the surfaces with fine sandpaper (production paper). Carve in any final skin effects such as hairs in the tail or wrinkles over the body.

The eyes, too, are made separately. First make a dowel of the proper diameter from holly or some other white wood. A birch dowel will do very adequately if holly is not available. A dowel may be easily made by squaring up a piece of stock slightly larger than the finished piece. Next cut off the corners and make an octagon-shaped stick. Cut off the corners again to make a nearly round pin. Drill a proper size hole in a piece of scrap iron and drive the pin through it. The resulting dowel should be round and comparatively smooth. Bore or drill a hole the proper size where the eyes have been located. Bore the holes ½″ deep, glue and drive the dowel in place. Cut the projecting dowel (iris) off 1/16″ above the surface. Mark with a center punch and drill a smaller hole for the pupil. This wood should be ebony; if unavailable, use any dark wood. Make a dowel of this wood as before, and when completed drive in the hole and cut off even with the iris. Shape the eye with a knife and file. Carve the eyelids and wrinkles around the eye.

A base is not necessary in this carving, but it will make a more stable carving that will be less likely to tip over. If the base is carved, follow the drawing, rounding off the top edges as in antique furniture (Fig. 2).

On the bottom of all bases a piece of pennant cloth should be glued in place. This technique will not only keep the carving from scratching the furniture but add a professional touch to your work.

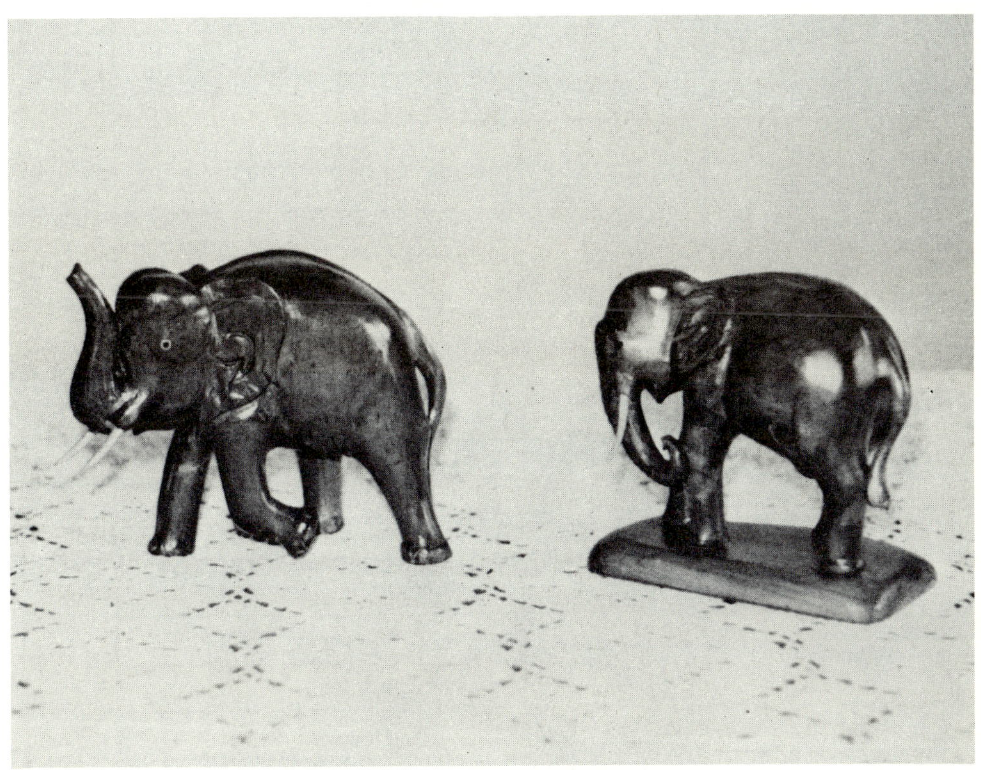

Fig. 2. Elephants, carved by the author.

The elephant was designed for a natural finish, but it might be carved of softwood and polychromed. In this case use the hollowing-out technique described for birds. In either case the finished carving should be pleasing to the eye and not an object indicating little proficiency. For finishing a carving naturally, the following procedures should be performed:

1. Be sure you have a smooth unblemished surface. Seal with a good wood sealer. When thoroughly dry rub down with steel wool and blow off the steel dust.

2. Apply a clear coat of varnish with a soft clean brush. Rub down with steel wool after the finish has hardened sufficiently for this process (two or three days depending upon room temperature).

3. Repeat the above process for each remaining coat. Usually three coats of varnish will be sufficient. The final coat may be rubbed down with pumice stone and linseed oil, using a cheesecloth wad.

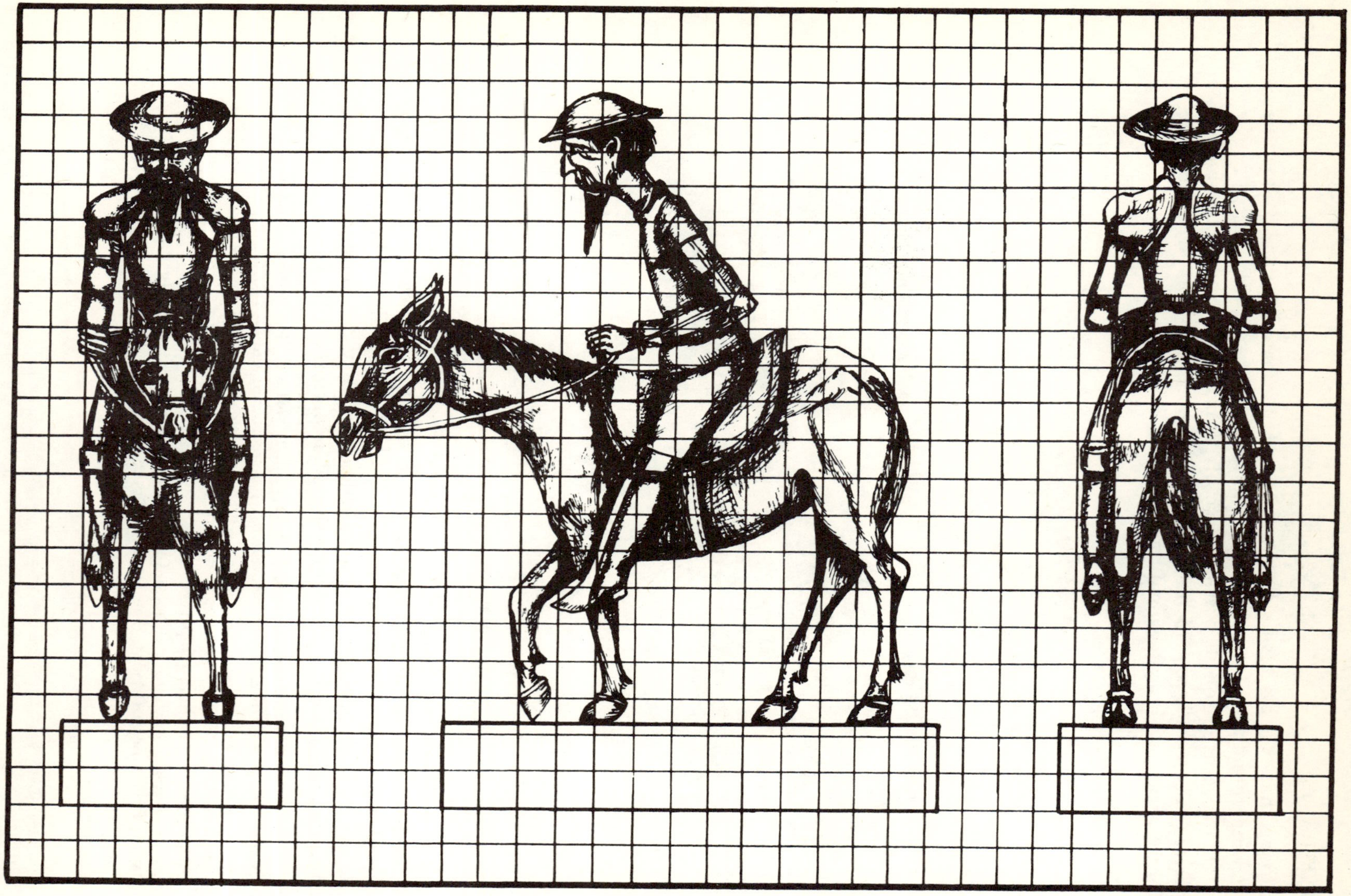

Fig. 1. Grid drawing for carved Don Quixote.

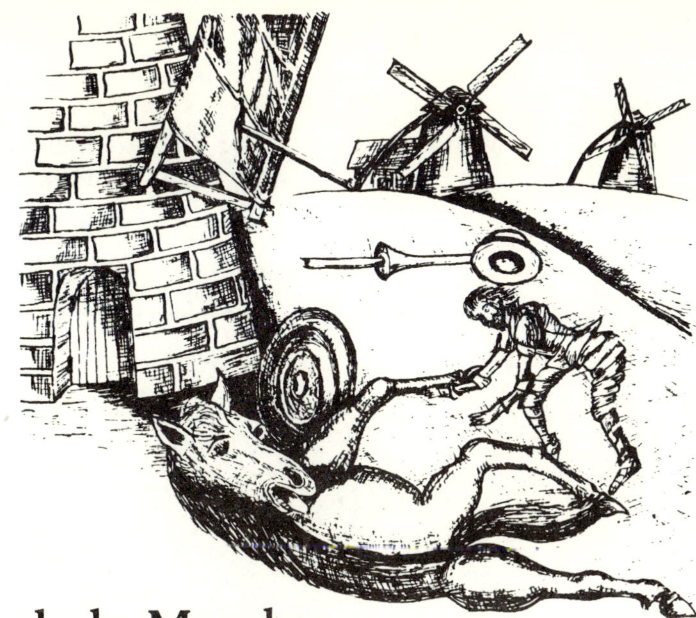

Chapter 9

Don Quixote de la Mancha

Few people these days read Cervantes' satirical novel, *Don Quixote.* While we, too, try to solve our problems by "tilting at windmills," we do not laugh at our madness with the sanity of the Spanish novelist. Few of us have had to experience the penury and bad luck of his bedraggled life, which makes the story all the more pertinent. Cervantes spent his entire life in and out of the shabby nakedness of a debtor's prison in Valladolid. The chances are that he began and wrote his famous story while under imprisonment.

Don Quixote read too many romantic books on knighthood, causing this simpleminded man to fall "into one of the strangest conceits that ever a madman stumbled on in this world." Completely deprived of his wits, he set out to right the wrongs of his world and to avenge the injuries inflicted upon his people. Like the knights of yore he set out on his old nag dressed in a suit of armor, with his fat squire, Sancho Panza, on a crusade to win fame and renown. His absurd adventures, tragic and comic, satirized Cervantes' own life which, to a more or less degree, paralleled the experiences of us all at one time or another.

The story which began as a burlesque grew into "an analogue of all mankind's adventures on this earth." Cervantes' satire on the books which had addled the brains of his hero evolved into humorous and enchanting contrasts between the lantern-jawed knight and his fat squire. Influenced by the ludicrous satire of Cervantes' mockery, his readers were able to laugh at their own follies and take themselves less seriously.

Now that you have a thumbnail sketch of Cervantes' knight, carve him and his old nag. Knight and nag have been favorite subjects over the years. Perhaps you would like to add a jousting lance held in his right hand and steadied by his arm and body. I did not think of the idea while planning the design.

Figure 1 is a grid drawing of the knight which will make an interesting carving. Again, the grid lines were 3/8″ when drawn, and grid lines 3/4″

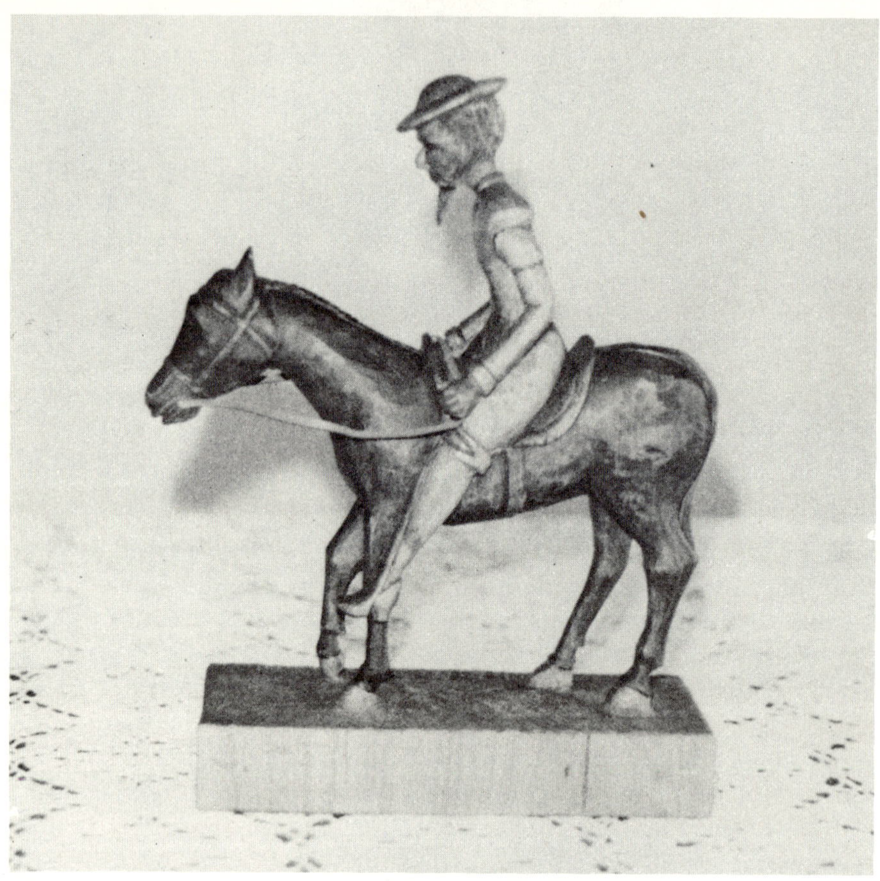

Fig. 2. Don Quixote, carved by the author.

apart will make a nice sculpture. Refer to Chapter 10 for directions. The block should not be in two parts, however, as the carving does not lend itself to this technique. Be sure that the grain of the block runs in the same direction as the legs of the horse. Be sure you have a nag of a horse when finished. Carve him rather bony and remember that Don Quixote should be slim and lean, too. The photograph, Fig. 2, shows the author's carving done in polychrome. He used white cedar for his medium which worked up very well. Read the chapter on carving the human figure (Chapter 13) for some help in carving the knight. Some carvers show an arc (a lance damage) in the helmet. It usually looks like a slip of the knife. It has been omitted in this work but, of course, may be put in if desired.

Allow much of the wood to remain natural in finish. Color some parts for emphasis.

Figure 3 shows an interesting carving by the author. Don Quixote and his squire, Sancho Panza (astride their nags) were carved after the manuscript was submitted to the publisher.

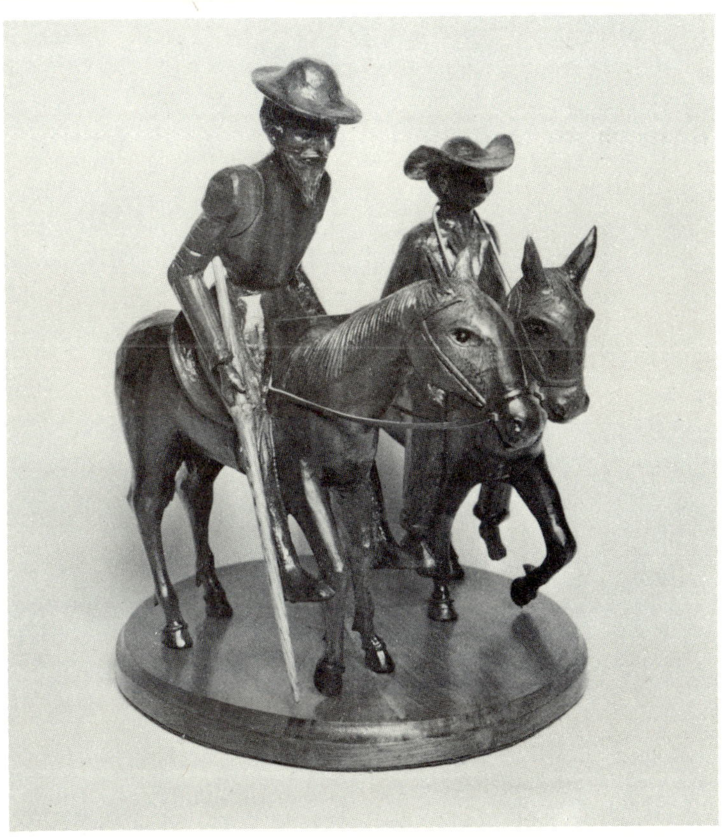

Fig. 3. Don Quixote and his squire, Sancho Panza, carved by the author. (Medium: Monkeypod from Hawaii.) Photograph by Brightwell.

Chapter 10

Adios Harry

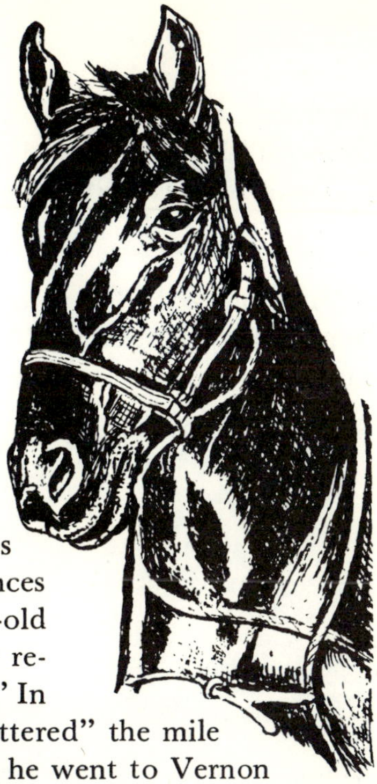

In an article written by Jeremiah Tax, *Sports Illustrated,* July 23, 1956, he states: "Adios Harry . . . holds 12 world pacing records at distances from a mile to a mile and a half and, as a 5-year-old in his prime, he is odds-on to lower the few remaining marks in the book before he goes stud." In an eight-day period at Vernon Downs, he "shattered" the mile standard five times. His record was 1:57$\frac{4}{5}$ when he went to Vernon and 1:55 when he left—close to four lengths per second and more than ten lengths faster than it had ever been raced before.

During "Little Brown Jug" week (1954) at Delaware, Ohio, Harry had so many visitors that he became upset and tried to kick his way out of his stall. He kicked his left hind leg through the wallboard of the stall and badly injured himself. He came within an ace of being scratched at the last minute but Harry, with a slight limp, paced his way in three successive mile heats totaling up to a world record for 3-year-old colts. Despite a hurt leg, he won the coveted "Little Brown Jug" trophy.

At the peak of his career, Adios Harry held 15 national world records, probably the highest of all time. Even more astonishing is the fact that some of his records have not been broken. But Adios Harry does not race any more. Several years ago he was given a cozy stable and a large paddock belonging exclusively to him and scores of mares are brought to him each year to be bred. His offspring dot the Atlantic seaboard and beyond. While they have never achieved their sire's reputation, they have won many awards. Yes, Adios Harry is now a gentleman of leisure, just waiting around anxiously for his next affair.

Adios Harry, the muscular son of Adios and Helen Win, was bought at a sale in Harrisburg, Pennsylvania, by Howard Lyons in 1952. Mr. Lyons knew his horseflesh and took his young yearling home to be trained for harness racing. In the meantime, the horse was named Adios after his sire and Harry after Harry Truman, a name to be remembered in the all-time annals of harness racing. Mr. Lyons is dead now, but his sons, Luther and John, have taken over the work of breeding horses. As many as 400 standard-bred horses may be stabled at the farm at one time to be either bred or trained for the races. Luther probably knows as much about horses as his father, so Sugar Hill Farm is in good and capable hands.

There is more about training horses for the respective harness races than meets the eye. Just recently, Luther explained to me some of the tricks. "Did you know," he said, "that the way a horse is shod influences the way he uses his legs? There are many tricks to make a pacer or trotter handle himself just right in the harness, making every movement count." Do you know the difference between a pacer, a trotter, and just natural running?

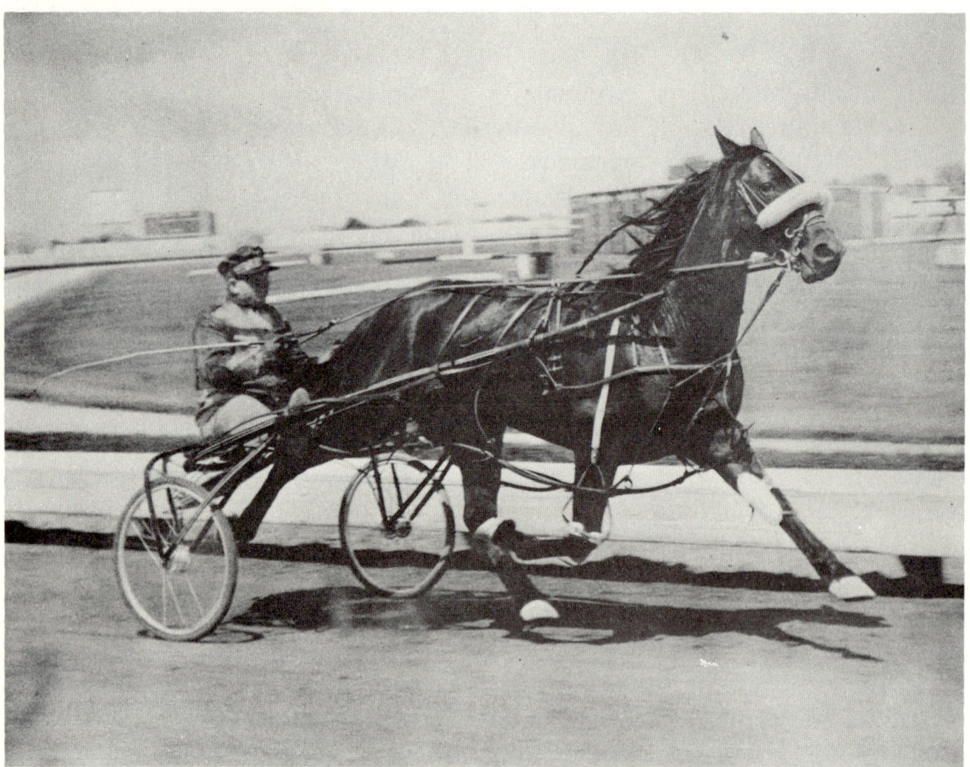

Fig. 1. Adios Harry, world's fastest pacer, "doing his thing." *Courtesy:* Luther Lyons.

The trainer of each has his own secrets of teaching his horses to run with efficiency and the least amount of effort. To train a pacer (Adios Harry is a pacer, Fig. 1) requires considerable time and "know-how." The legs of each side must move together and while racing, the stride must not be broken. While the legs on the right side are stretched forward, the legs on the left side are stretched backward; that is, the legs on the same side must move together. On the other hand, a trotter lifts the front leg on one side of the body and the hind leg on the other side at the same time. The two legs hit the ground together. In either case the movement is rhythmical and streamlined. The movements of a trotter can be very wasteful in time and energy.

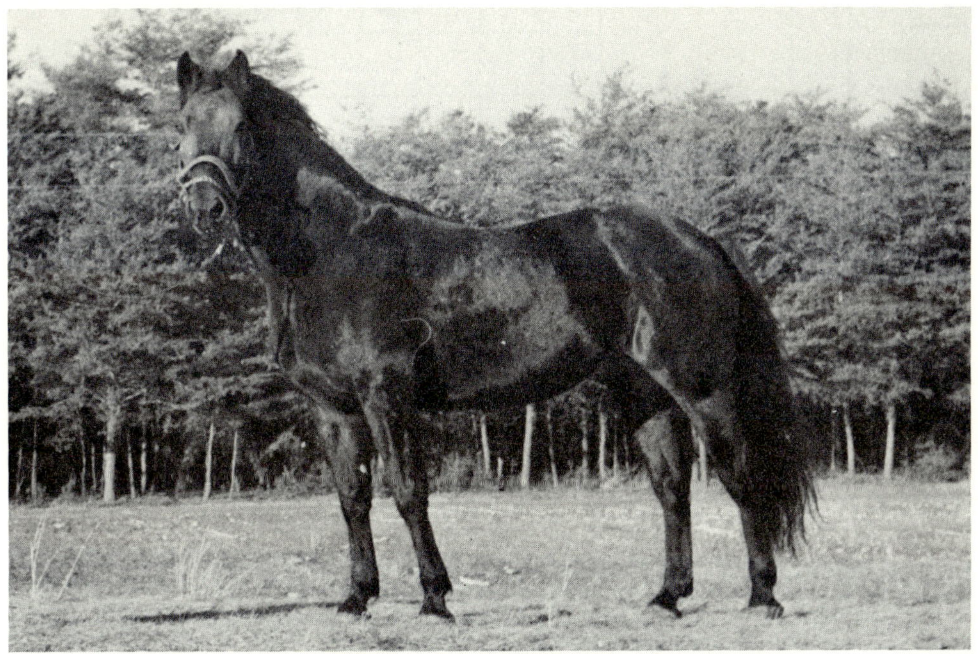

Fig. 2. Adios Harry. *Courtesy:* Luther Lyons.

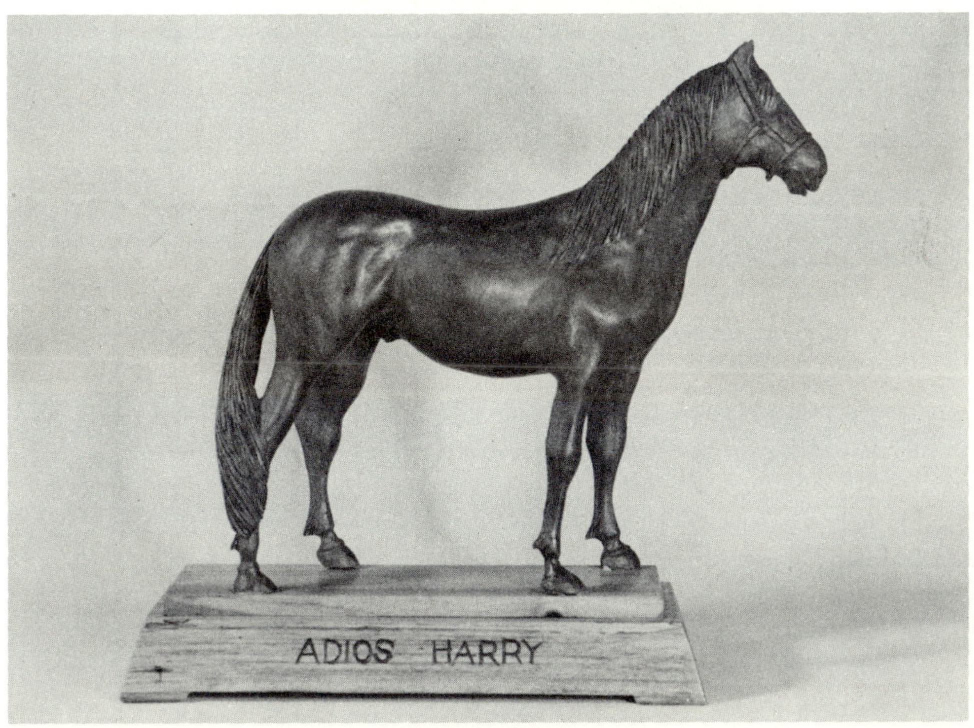

Fig. 3. Adios Harry, carved by the author. *Courtesy:* Luther Lyons. Photograph by Robert J. Bennett.

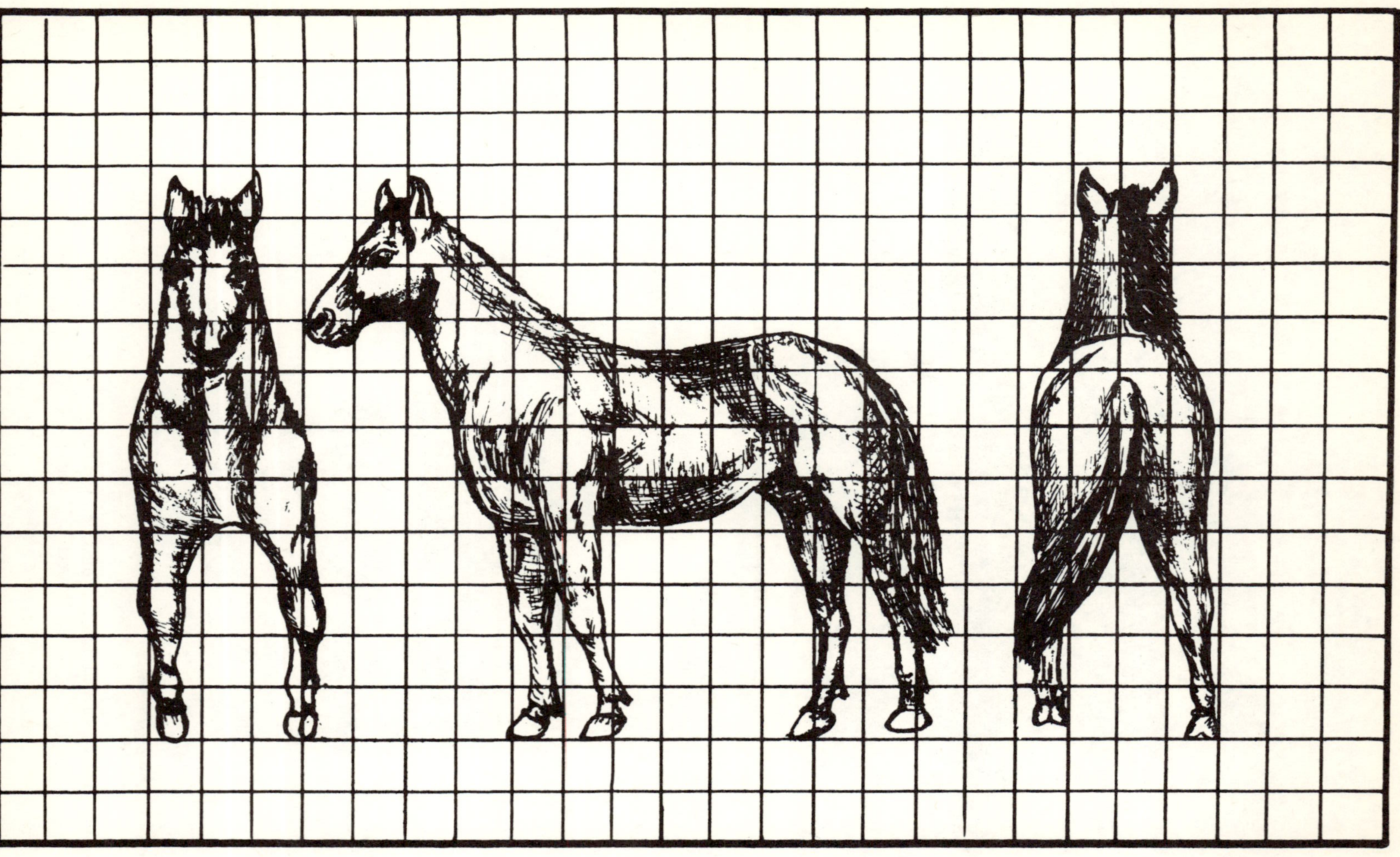

Fig. 4. Grid drawing for carved Adios Harry.

The trainer has to symplify these movements to eliminate unnecessary motion. The running gait of a horse is a galloping procedure—both front feet forward at the same time while the back feet are gathered under the body. Both the back and front feet move together. The gallop is a natural gait for a horse when it wants to go places in a hurry.

About a year ago, Luther requested me to make a carving of Adios Harry. He loaned me a number of photographs from which to draw profiles to obtain the likeness of his famous horse (Fig. 2). Later, after the horse was roughly carved, I visited Sugar Hill Farm to sketch in the muscle bulges. Adios Harry is a large horse—much larger than one may imagine. He is still full of life and could probably kick the soda out of a biscuit without cracking the crust. So, while Luther held the halter, I sketched in the muscles. A photograph of my sculpture of Adios Harry is shown in Fig. 3.

Study the line drawing in the grid picture. Before reproduction, the lines were drawn 3/8″ apart. The horse measured nearly 5″ long. Drawing the grid lines ¾″ apart will make a nice size carving (Fig. 4).

Draw two profiles of the horse full-size on cardboard, one for each side. Next prepare two black walnut blocks, one-half the thickness of the horse with enough extra to allow for carving. Dress the adjacent surfaces of the block to a true plane so that they may be glued together. Draw the profiles on the prepared blocks, making sure that they match when placed together. Saw out the profiles on a band saw accurately. Place a dab of glue on each end of one block and clamp the profiles together with a C-clamp, one at each end.

After the glue has set, the carving may begin. Lay out the third dimension and remove the waste wood. Carve the general shape of the horse carefully. Do not carve the legs until the rest of the horse is finished (roughly). The legs are somewhat fragile so as much wood as possible should be left on them until the horse is nearly completed.

After the horse has been roughly carved, the two halves may be separated and hollowed out, leaving about ½″ of the stock around the body. Glue the profiles together again, this time permanently.

Sharp gouges, regular chisels, and a fine-cut rasp are used to carve the finishing touches. The mane and forelocks should be left raised until the last minute when they may be carved with a V-tool and the cut-off disk of a Moto-tool. The eyes, nose, and the general shape of the head are difficult areas to carve. Be careful with the halter gear. The loops under the jaws should probably not be cut through, but left with a thin section of the wood remaining. Of course, the loops may be formed with shavings glued together and bent to the proper curve. After being formed, they may be glued in place. The head of a horse will test your carving ability. Forming the hooves is much more difficult than one may think. The trick is to shape each one properly and in the right position with the respective leg. The muscle bulges are best carved with a sharp shallow gouge. In a few depressions, a deep-turned tool may be used. Sand the carving carefully with the grain. A strip of sanding cloth held down on the surface with the thumb and drawn through the confined space is a good technique; it is not only efficient, but provides greater control in finishing deep contours. Be sure all tool marks have been removed before finishing.

Give the horse a natural finish. If carved of black walnut, linseed oil and pumice stone followed by paste wax will provide an excellent finish.

The photograph (Fig. 3) shows Adios Harry mounted on a base of English walnut. Construct the base and finish with a clear varnish or lacquer. When

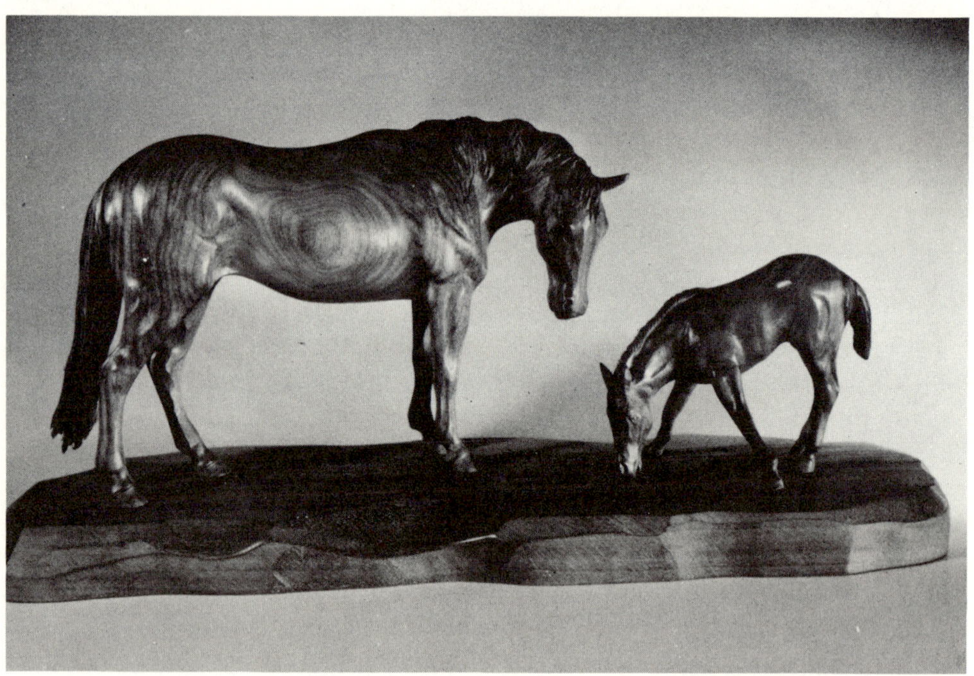

Fig. 5. "Growing Up," by M.E. Brasher. Brasher considers his work sculptures and not wood carvings despite the similarity of techniques. "I arrive at the final definition of form through my own worked-out techniques which might not qualify strictly as wood 'carving'," he says.

Mr. Brasher is a disciple of beauty and in his work he aims to achieve this quality so "that they (the sculptures) will afford others pleasures similar to mine to permanently enjoy." As the photograph "Growing Up" shows, his horses are, indeed, beautiful.

Mr. Brasher is a prolific artist. He publishes a catalog of his carved animals and birds containing more than 60 pieces of sculpture—all comparable in beauty to "Growing Up."

dry, mount the horse on the base in his proper location. Trace around the hooves with a soft lead pencil. Drive a six-penny wire nail in the center of each hoof print down about ¾", and leave ¾" more above the surface. Cut off the head. Next, drill through the center of each hoof and up the leg a hole larger than the diameter of the nails, far enough to include the nail studs with 1/8" to spare. The sculpture should fit over the nail studs without binding in any direction. Fill the holes with polyester putty and place the horse over the nails and press in place. Rub away the surplus putty and allow the rest to set up hard. Now the horse and base are securely fastened together.

Study the sculptured horses of M.E. Brasher, Fig. 5. His sculpture "Growing Up" is an excellent example of the sculptor's art. Notice the hooves. They are well done and the pose is excellent too.

Figure 6 shows a carving of a horse in an interesting pose. The horse is rearing on its two hind legs with its tail to hold it in position.

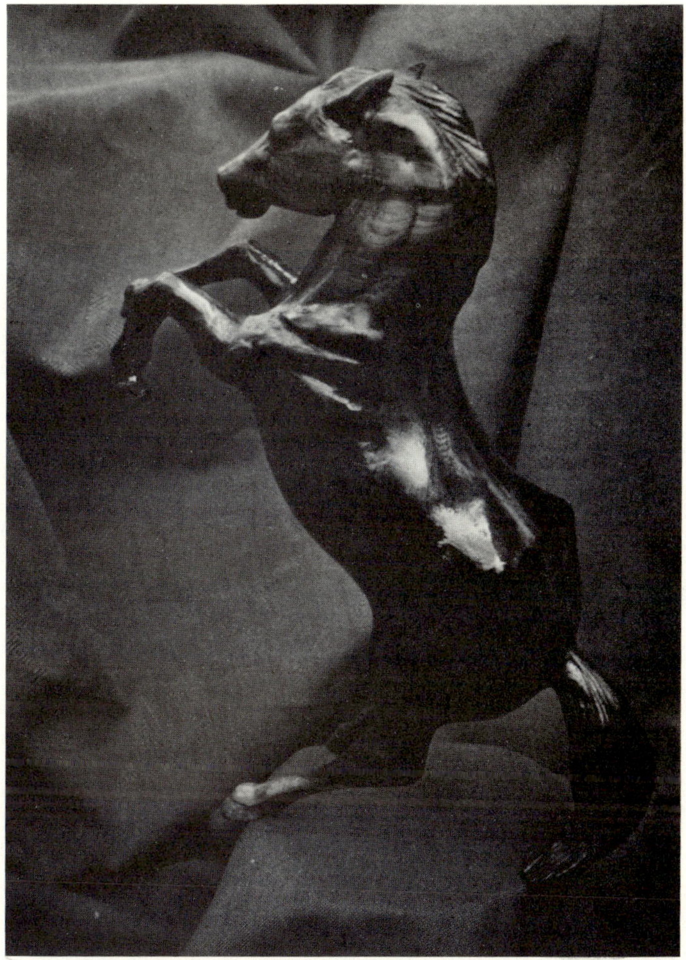

Fig. 6. Horse, rampant, carved by the author.

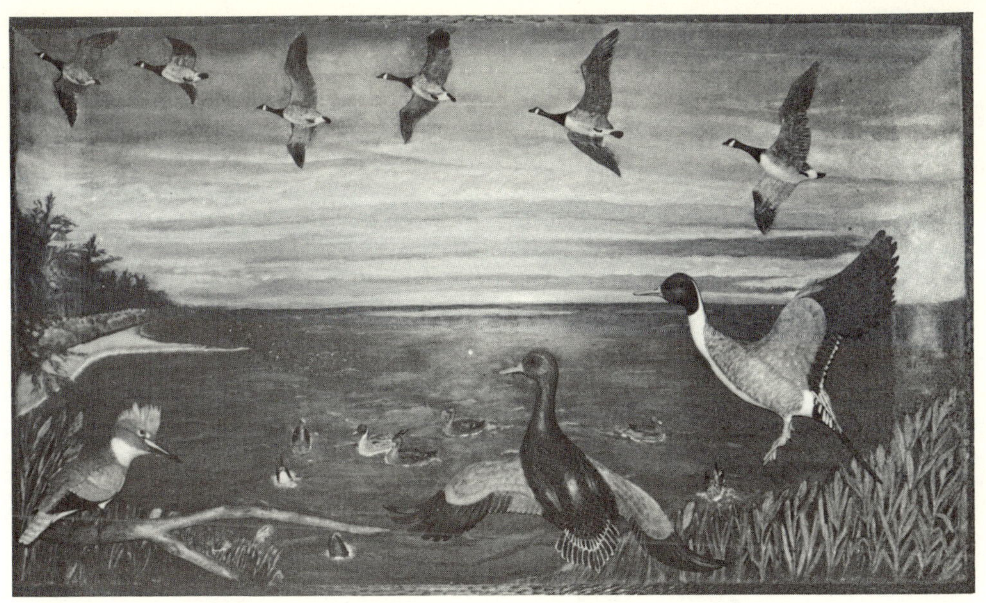

Chapter 11

Plaques

Plaques and panels are carved to hang or fasten to a wall, either in- or outside of a building. They are not "sliced-through" compositions along the central axis, as many people believe. The novice who attempts his first plaque usually makes this mistake. The carvings composing a plaque have their own rules of perspective and should look natural projecting from their backgrounds. They should have sculptural qualities, tone value, and composition, the same as sculpture in the round. Perspective is highly important—even more important than in a painting, having patches of light and shadow. As has been stated in a previous chapter, a plaque is a cross between a painting and sculpture in the round in many respects. As in a picture, foreshortening is necessary at times requiring greater skill with the chisel than with the brush. To make figures stand out naturally is no mean trick. The art requires considerable know-how and insight. One side of the figure might be below its central axis while the other is far above it. Retreating figures will appear as being one behind another because of the carved planes, although there is little difference in overall projection. This phenomenon is quite evident in Fig. 1. Generally speaking, the carving technique is the same, but keep the perspective in mind as in a painting, and let the planes fall where they may. The plaque should give the illusion of the figures situated before a wall or in a pastoral scene without distortion. They should look natural and as though they are a part of the setting. Notice this technique in Frederick Brunner's *Last Supper* (*see* Fig. 12).

The tonal quality of a relief carving is achieved by allowing the light to fall on two sides of a figure, which, in turn, requires them to be slightly turned toward the light, one way or the other. High relief carving is carving in the round to a great extent, and every artist knows that light falls on various planes of a sculpture.

Plaques and panels are carved in various degrees of projection from the background. Probably the most common is low relief (bas-relief). The frieze around the Parthenon at Athens is low relief. It was probably carved by Phidias during the Age of Pericles. By definition, a frieze is a horizontal panel between the architrave and the cornice of a building. The figures on all coins and medals are struck in low relief.

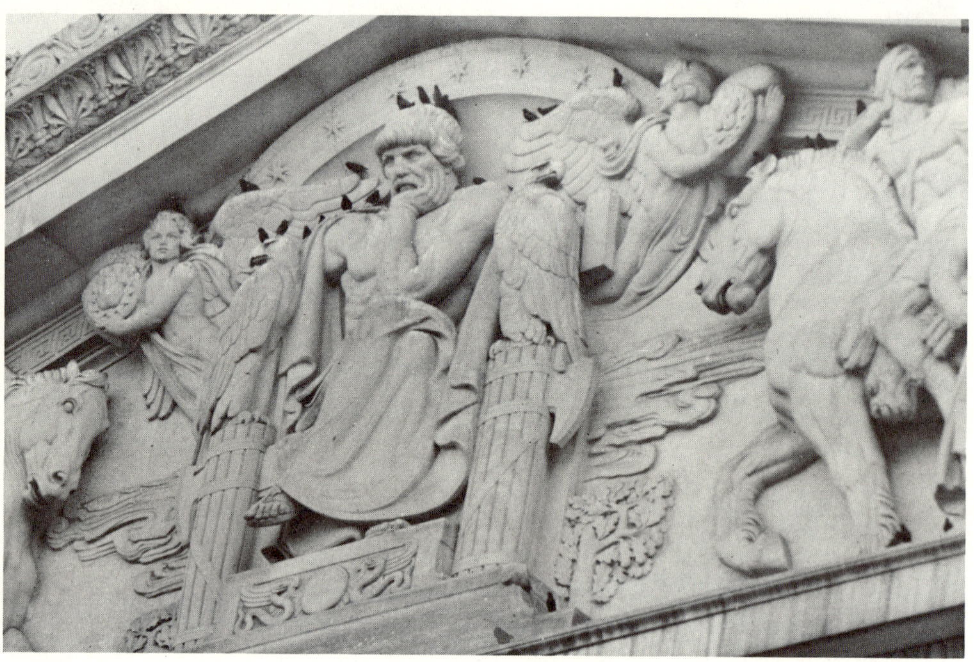

Fig. 1. Granite frieze on Archives Building, Washington, D.C. Associated Press Photo.

The frieze on the public building, Washington, D.C., shown in Fig. 1, appears to be half-relief (mezzo-rilievo) which projects to a height between the low relief and high relief (alto-rilievo) from the background.

The most primitive relief is hollow (intaglio-rilievo); depressions are scratched, cut, or pressed into the background. The artists of the Stone Age used this method to scratch or etch their symbols on the walls of their caves. Children use this method today and, of course, it is an important technique in jewelry design. Many architectural titles are carved in hollow relief, for machine sandblasting makes this technique a simple task.

I wanted to illustrate an excellent example of panel carving, a religious subject, by Luca della Robbia, but the curator of the Art Institute of Chicago, where the carving is on loan from Italy, informed me that the

Institute is not permitted to release photographs of art it does not own.* The panel depicts five boys singing from a hymnal. The carving is a superb piece of work, "The youthful voices are vividly suggested by the individual faces." The picture may be seen in *The World Book Encyclopedia* under "Sculpture."

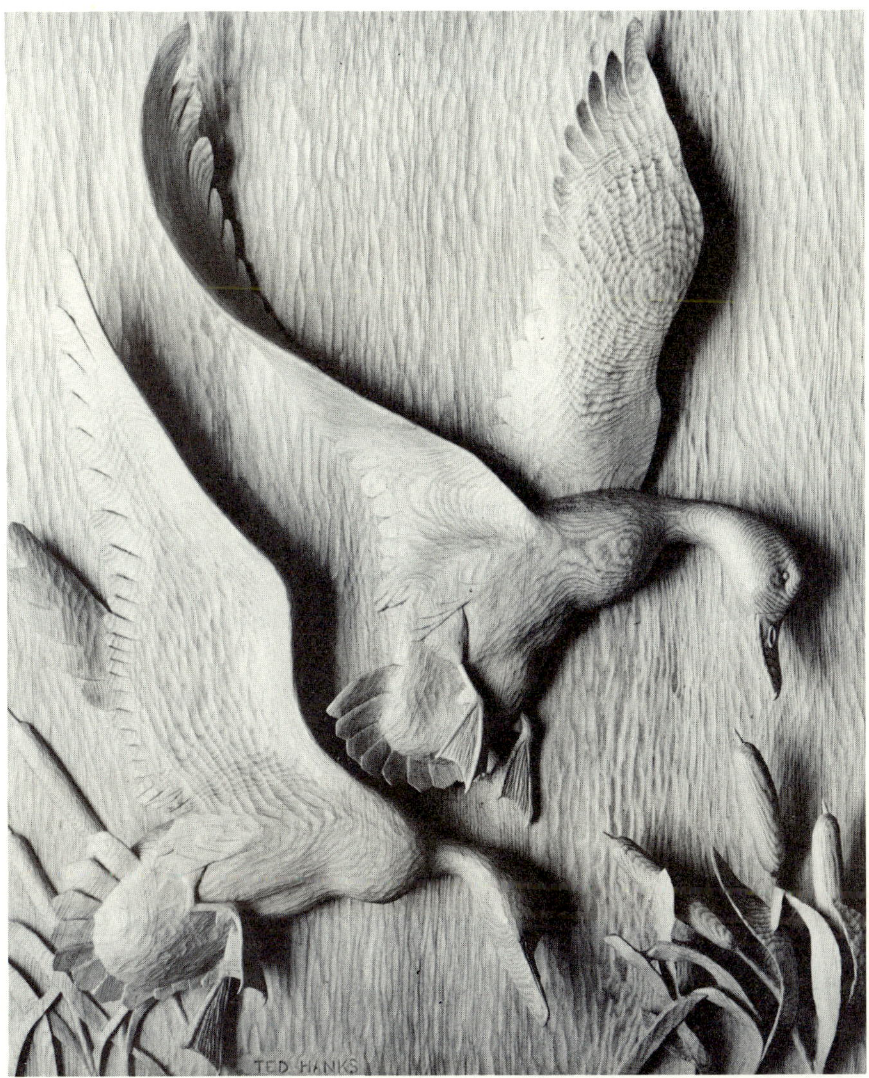

Fig. 2. "Ducks Dropping In," by Ted Hanks.

The Field House at the Naval Academy, Annapolis, Maryland, to which reference has already been made, has a carved architectural plaque cemented

*After the unpleasant experience of trying to obtain photographs from foreign museums while writing *Creative Bird Carving,* I decided that the picture was not worth the expense and the effort. There are too many problems of currency exchange and language difficulties.

in its façade (Fig. 2, Chapter 3). The carving is of Hercules. The battle club symbolizes his victories as a warrior, the laurel wreath is the sign of his supremacy as an athlete. As you travel around the country, notice the plaques and panels of private and public buildings and study the techniques used. In this way you will not only increase your appreciation of this form of art, but also your knowledge of subject matter and the methods of application.

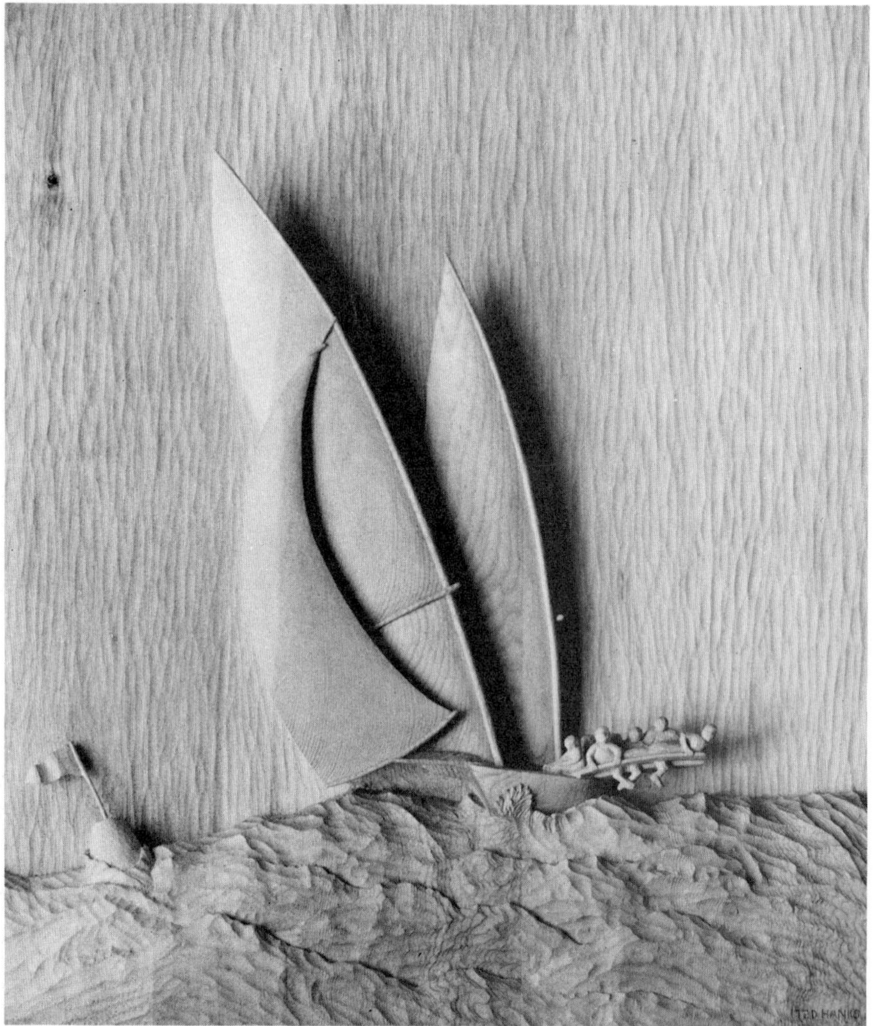

Fig. 3. "Log Canoe Race," by Ted Hanks.

Most of the friezes, plaques, and panels designed and used for public buildings today are abstracts, or near abstracts. It seems that artists of architectural designs have dismissed any form of art that appears real. Some of this work is very clever and executed by extremely skilled craftsmen. It should not be adversely criticized. There is a mechanical "twist" which probably fits more into the scheme of building techniques. Balancing heavy parts of a building on the heads of sculptures of human figures does seem farfetched. But, even so, how would Phidias feel about the matter!

This chapter is more concerned with plaques and panels designed for the interiors of homes and public buildings. They are made of wood and usually are given a natural finish. Examples of the natural finished plaques are represented in Figs. 2, 3, and 4, by Ted Hanks and Robert H. Burgess, respectively.

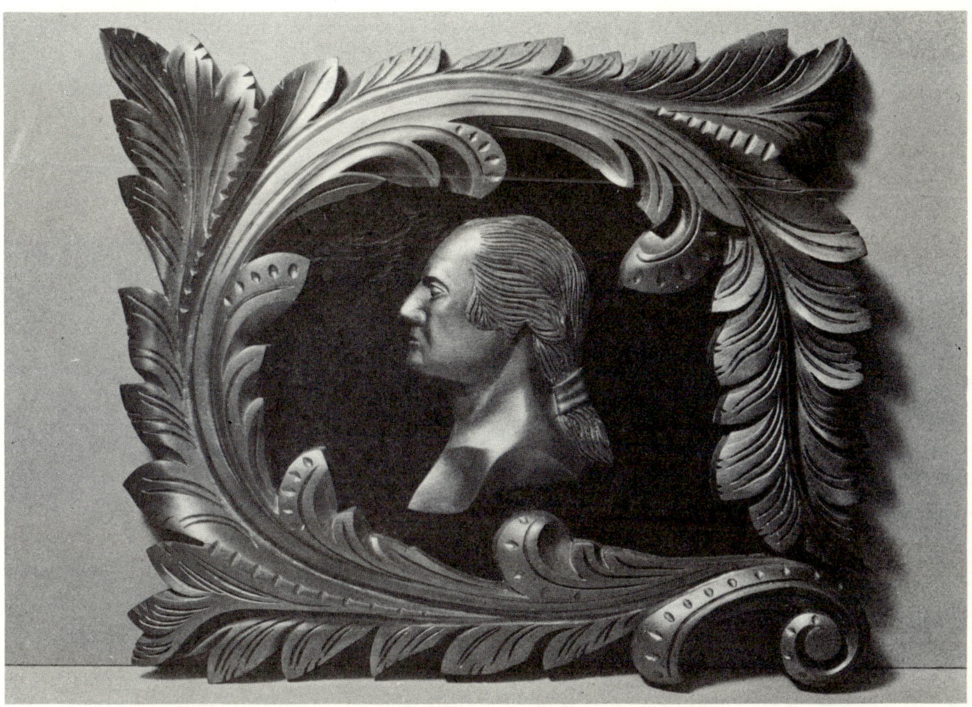

Fig. 4. Portrait plaque, carved by Robert H. Burgess. White pine; 18″ square. This plaque is an exquisitely carved portrait of George Washington. It is beautifully designed and skillfully carved. Mr. Burgess is Curator of Exhibits at The Mariners Museum, Newport News, Virginia. You will recall that he carved the figurehead of the ketch, *Valkyrie,* discussed in Chapter 3. Mr. Burgess runs a tight ship as "Captain" of the Museum and fills in his leisure time with his jackknife and chisels.

I have always liked the plaques carved by Ted Hanks. He is an ex-Navy man and has never lost the salt of his imagination. He has had varied experiences and is talented in several media. Both he and his wife, Consuela, are excellent watercolor artists. His wood is usually white pine and he gives his plaques a natural finish, allowing the grain to come through to enhance his work—even to supplement it in some areas. There is not much evidence of sandpaper for he creates his forms with clever gouge strokes, keen and fine, creating a texture that is quite intriguing. In observing Ted's work, any person ought to be moved to "carve up a storm" in his own imagination.

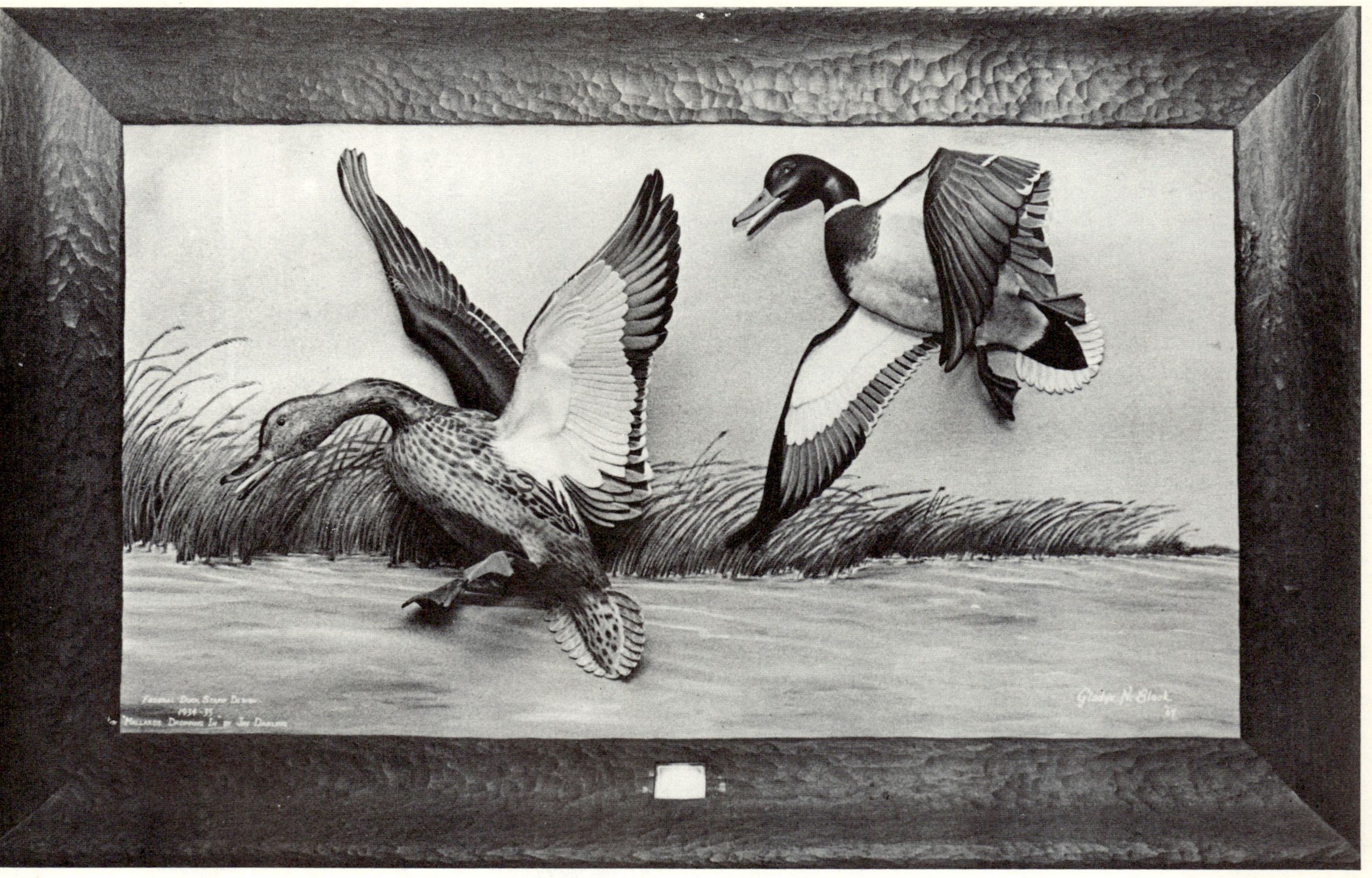

Fig. 5. "Pair of Mallards Dropping In," by Gladys N. Black.

Ted's work is represented at various places along the Atlantic seaboard, especially on the Eastern Shore of Maryland where he once lived. Ted Hanks' plaques may be hung anywhere for they have universal appeal and do not require any particular setting. The same may be said of Robert Burgess' portrait carving, but to a lesser degree. It is, however, more appropriate in a building that is in some way associated with George Washington. The two pictorial plaques, too, have general use, but would be more appropriate in some buildings than in others.

Two pictorial plaques are also represented, one by Gladys Black (Fig. 5), and the other by the author (*see* chapter headpiece).

Probably the country's most talented woman wildlife carver is Gladys Black. Her plaque, "Pair of Mallards Dropping In," is taken from the 1934-35 Duck Stamp, designed by "Ding" Darling, a Pulitzer Prize winner whose cartoons were syndicated by the *New York Tribune.* The photograph was reproduced in *Creative Bird Carving* but it deserves another exposure. It is an example of a pictorial plaque. The ducks are carved in the round, full-size, and painted realistically. The reeds and water were painted in. Notice the construction of the frame around the background—a concave surface skillfully highlighted with keen gouge strokes. Invisible wrought iron brackets hold the carvings in place. The whole composition is a complementary third-dimensional interpretation of "Ding" Darling's dream.

After publication of *Creative Bird Carving,* the author considered what could be done with the carvings which he had used for illustrations. Gladys Black's work gave him inspiration. A picture was designed for the background and a frame was made of soft pine 1½″ thick and rabbeted on the underside to receive a piece of plywood ¼″ thick. After the frame was put together and the plywood glued in place, it measured 30″ x 60″. The frame was gouged out in a concave curve which feathered into the plywood, and all signs of construction were concealed. The panel was given a coat of sealer and, when dry, a ground coat of green paint (acrylics). Then the picture was painted as illustrated. The various birds were superimposed on the surface and screwed fast from the back with countersunk flathead screws. The reeds were carved from the frame stock (*see* chapter headpiece).

To fasten a plaque to a wall requires a special technique. Hanging with eye screws and wire is unsatisfactory. A plaque should fit flat against the wall. The author uses a keyhole steel plate arrangement (not less than 20 g.). The plate is made as shown in the accompanying drawing.

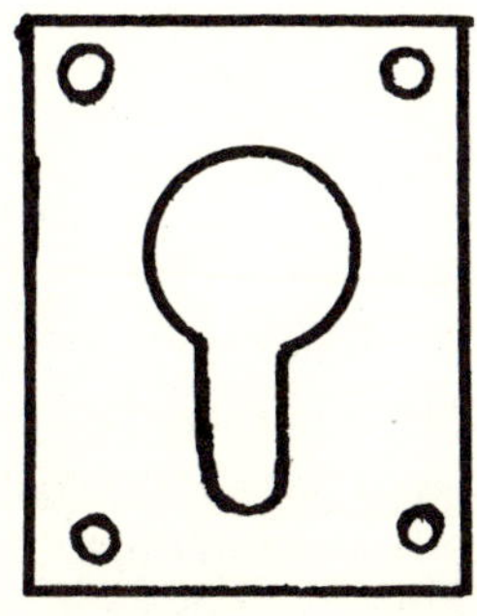

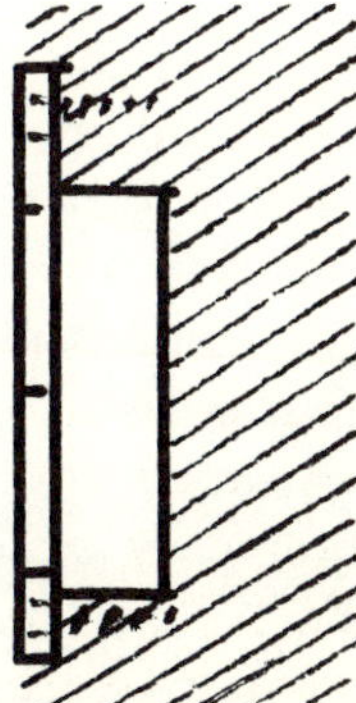

The plate is set flush with the back of the frame and enough wood is removed to allow a roundhead screw to move freely (including the head). About 6″ from the top of the frame is a good location for the plate. Of course, the screws in the wall must be exactly the same distance between centers as the holes in the plate.

My first experience with a plaque was in the late thirties (Fig. 6). The architects of the school building where I was a teacher had left a circular niche in the pediment a brick deep and 36″ in diameter. There was no immediate need for the niche at the time of construction. In 1938, the Seniors were casting about for a suitable memento to leave the school after graduation. The Superintendent suggested that a school seal be made for the

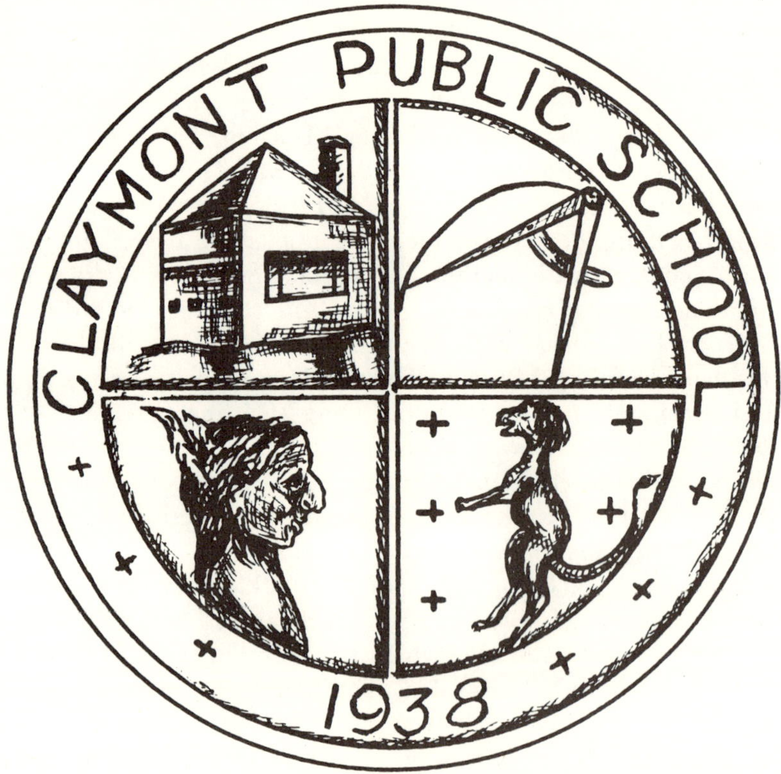

Fig. 6. Claymont Public School plaque, designed and carved by Seniors.

niche in the pediment. The idea was immediately accepted and a group of boys and girls were assigned the task of designing the plaque. They decided upon a seal of four *charges* depicting what they considered to be historic incidents concerned with the school district. Near the boundary of the district was a prerevolutionary fort called the "blockhouse." Portholes for muskets still were visible from the outside walls, and the colonial furnishings remained inside. The blockhouse became the first charge. The northern boundary of Delaware is an arc, the center of which is located at New Castle. For several miles, the arc designated the northern boundary of the School District. A pair of dividers inscribing an arc became the second charge. Chief Naaman was a colonial chief of the Indians in this part of the state, so his bust became the third charge. I have forgotten how the fourth charge was determined. So far as I know, it had no particular significance. It was probably borrowed from a family seal. The stars which do not appear in any of the other charges seem to testify in favor of this speculation. In any event, a lion, rampant, became the fourth charge. The next step was to design the charges and carve them for a pattern. The Art Department assisted in this project along with the Seniors' committee. The designs were carved in my shop by the members of the Senior class. They were in low relief. A circular disk 35″ in diameter was made of ¼″ plywood, bounded by an edge 1″ wide and 5/8″ thick glued on the plywood, making a 7/8″ thickness at the edge. The quadrants were sectioned off with ½″ x ½″ strips and the carved charges were glued in place. The background was stippled to give it some texture, the sharp inside corners were filleted, and the edges were rounded slightly. The whole plaque was given several coats of shellac and rubbed smooth with steel wool. The pattern was then taken to the bronze foundry and a casting was made from it. The shop boys did a good job and so did the foundrymen. It was a beautiful job when wirebrushed clean and very little repair work had to be done. Four lugs had been cast in the back near the rim ¾″ thick. These lugs were drilled and tapped for a ½″ machine bolt. I shudder, even now, when I think of working in the pediment over the third-story rooms on a jury-rigged scaffold held in place with rope thrown over the parapet and tied to vent pipes on the roof. The custodian helped me swing the heavy plaque in place and locate the bolts in the tapped holes. Holes ¾″ in diameter were drilled through the brick wall with a star drill. The plaque was bolted in place without incident. All is well that ends well! The plaque still fills the niche of the Green Street school which is now only a small unit of the school system.

Study the plaque illustrations accompanying this chapter. They will help you to see how different techniques are used to good effect.

As stated before, the emphasis in this chapter concerns plaques and panels carved from wood for interior decorations. If plaques are desired for exterior use, they should be cast of bronze metal (Fig. 8) or be made of stone and cemented in the wall. Quite often heavy slabs of sandstone or other media are cemented in the wall and the carving is done later by skilled sculptors. This type of plaque making does not concern us here. But cast plaques will be briefly discussed. The media will be Portland cement in one form or another. Exterior carvings take a lot of weather and temperature punishment. "Neither snow, nor rain, nor heat, nor gloom of night" should affect these ornaments in their appointed places. Cast friezes or plaques are easily made from negative molds, cast from a pattern of wood. In Chapter 4, negative molds are discussed; the principle of casting negative molds for plaques is no different. Once a pattern is carved, making a negative mold is comparatively simple. Be sure there are no negative edges in the pattern. If there are, fill them in with some sort of filler which may be removed easily. As in all such casting work, a separation paste or liquid must be used to

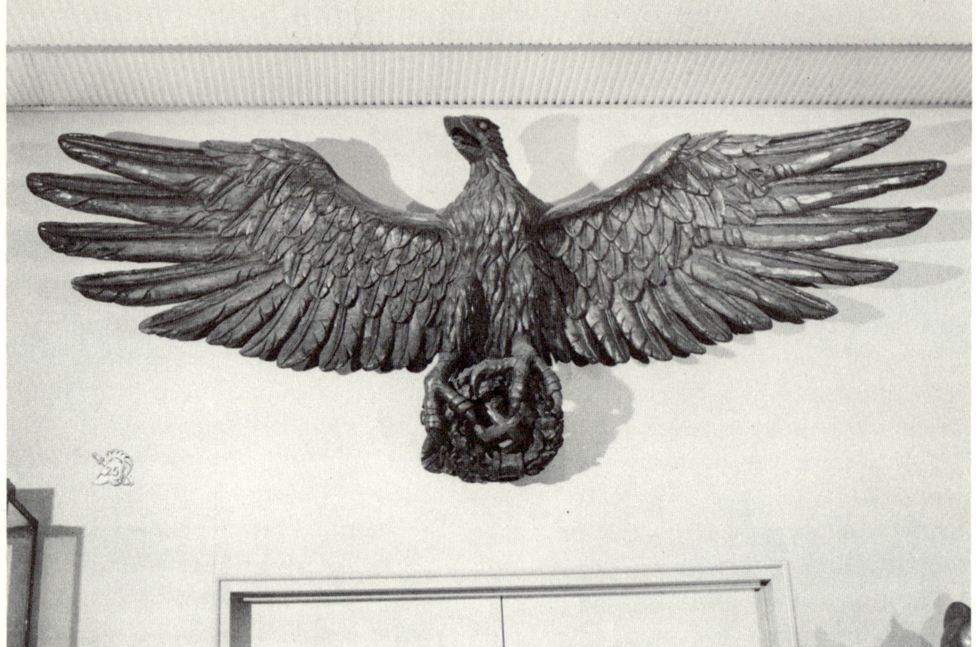

Fig. 7. German National Insignia, Third Reich. Taken from the Headquarters of the 107th German Infantry Regiment by officers and men of the Third Army. General George S. Patton, Jr., presented the eagle to the United States Military Academy.

The insignia is almost 10 feet long and carved of white pine; natural finish. It represents the best of this type of carving. *Courtesy:* The United States Military Academy.

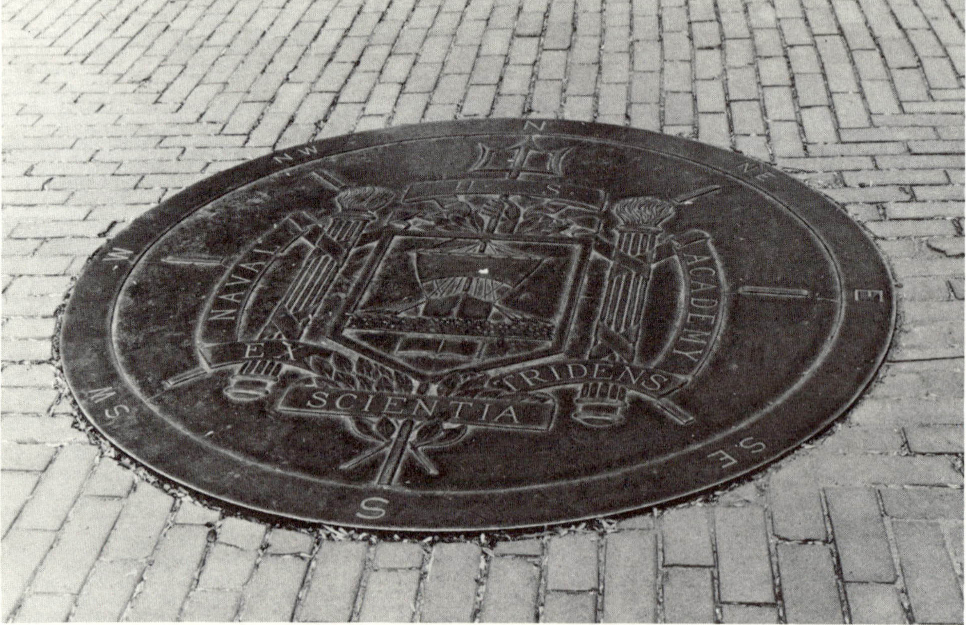

Fig. 8. Bronze plaque cemented in the walk, U.S. Naval Academy, Annapolis, Md.

insure a clean parting of the pattern and mold in the first instant, and a parting of the mold and Portland cement plaque in the second.

Once the mold is ready, a cement mix of Portland cement and sand is pounded in the form (add only enough water to hold the particles together). A rammer with a 2″ peen and mallet end is used to pack the sand tightly. This mix gives a more porous texture to the casting which is preferred by many sculptors. When a looser mix is used, care should be exercised to avoid air bubbles in the casting. Splash on the first application of the cement until the pattern is covered; then the rest of the mixture may be poured in. Strike off the surplus as the back of the plaque must be in a flat plane. If it is to be cemented in a wall, it should be one brick thick. If it is to be hung free on a wall, a hanging arrangement such as just described should be cast in the back of the plaque. Holes for bolts are usually cast in the plaque.

If the casting is more than a foot in either direction, a piece of baby-chick wire should be cast into the cement. Use plenty of reinforcement steel in large plaques but have plenty of cement space between them. For example, do not use hardware cloth; the meshes are too close together—I have had castings to split along the plane of the wires.

A suitable cement mixture is as follows:

1 part white Portland cement
2 parts fine masonry sand
2 parts marble chips or very small pebbles
Add dry coloring powder
Mix thoroughly before adding water

The mix may be varied to suit certain requirements. For example, the sand may be equal parts of sand and marble dust. The marble chips (or small pebbles) may be eliminated altogether. Use the dry coloring powder sparingly as it tends to weaken the cement. Experiment with the cement mixture and the whole technique until you hit upon the combination which works best for you. Remember that cement is not a very sympathetic medium for sculpture and it must be used in accordance with its nature. Incidentally, some sculptors use equal parts of Portland and Keene cement.

Gelatin molds are used in many professional jobs of casting cement instead of plaster of Paris which is generally used for mold making. Gelatin molds are more flexible making negative surfaces less critical.

A carborundum block will be necessary to remove any lumps or to smooth out the surfaces in critical places. The edges of a cement casting (frame) should be rubbed smooth for contrast.

Now that you have been informed of the general principles of casting cement plaques, go to it and good luck. Meanwhile, the author will labor with you afar off sculpturing an 80-ft.-long, reinforced cement dinosaur on his front lawn.

Carl Boettcher

For a glimpse of Carl Boettcher's work, I am indebted to A.G. Ivey, Director, University, North Carolina News Bureau. His article appeared in *Chip Chats* Magazine, May-June 1973 issue. Mr. Ivey gave his kind permission to quote from his story.

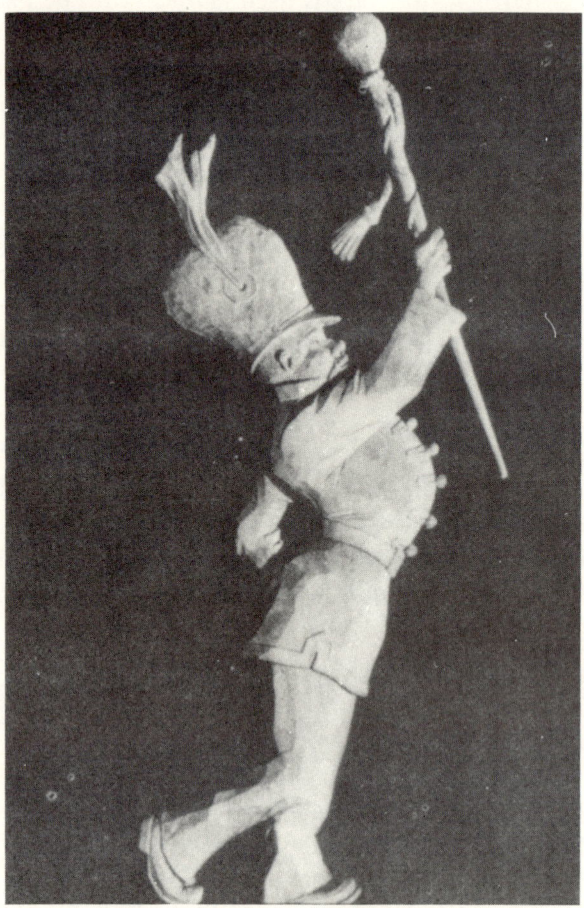

Fig. 9. "Band Leader," by Carl Boettcher. *Courtesy: Chip Chats* Magazine.

Sensing the trouble just over the horizon during the exultant days of Hitler's Third Reich, Carl Boettcher emigrated to the United States. He settled in a small town in the foothills of the Great Smokey Mountains. From the start he was looked on with suspicion, and when World War II became imminent, he was more than a stranger to them. "When I go down the street they look at me and whisper 'zzzt'," he explained to William Carmichael, Jr., vice president, University of North Carolina, who was passing through the town.

"Come to live in Chapel Hill," said William Carmichael. "That is where the university is. We need good craftsmen like you. And people in Chapel Hill are all so strange and talk so funny that nobody says 'zzzt' at anybody else."

Carl Boettcher moved to Chapel Hill. He began carving for the university. Among his carvings is a giant plaque, "The Circus Parade." It seems that each

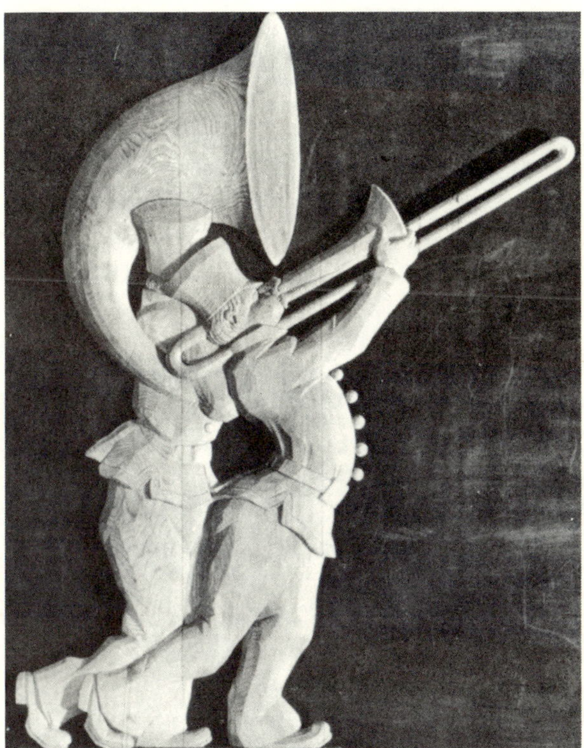

Fig. 10. "Follow the Band," by Carl Boettcher.
Courtesy: Chip Chats Magazine.

figure, or group of figures, was carved separately and superimposed upon the background. The plaque now decorates the walls of the Carolina Inn cafeteria at the university. Two of the figures on this plaque are illustrated here to indicate the master's technique in this medium of carving art. "The Circus Parade" was estimated to be worth $300,000 in the 1940's. It is worth much more now.

Carl Boettcher died of cancer in 1952.

Frederick A. Brunner

Frederick Brunner has been called "The Complete Woodcarver." He was born in the city of Metz, Alsace-Lorraine, in 1901. He began his apprenticeship there at the tender age of fifteen. Three and one-half years later he became a full-fledged journeyman. He worked in several countries, including Germany and France. After coming to America in 1923, he worked as an architectural craftsman in church shops in Boston and Cambridge, Mass., and was soon recognized as an advanced worker in his trade.

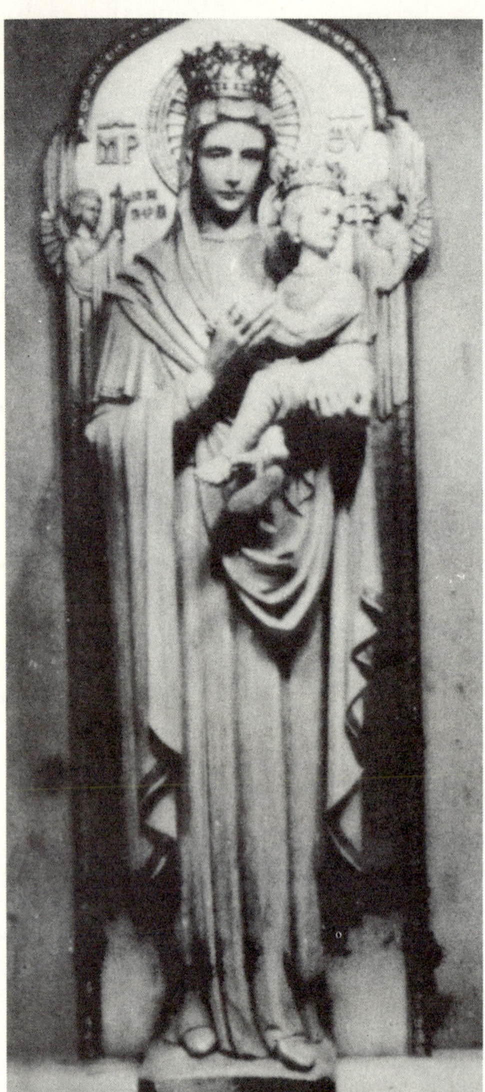

Fig. 11. "Madonna and Child," Our Lady of Perpetual Help High School, New York. *Courtesy: Chip Chats* Magazine.

As the photographs indicate, his work usually depicted ecclesiastical subjects. During the 1920's and 1930's he was employed in carving projects for many outstanding buildings, including the Riverside Chapel, The Cathedral of St. John the Divine, St. Patrick's Cathedral, all in New York; Harvard University, Princeton University, and many others.

In 1950, the Brunners moved to Westwood, Mass., where Mr. Brunner has his studio and workshop.

There is a serious quality to Brunner's work which smacks of the old masters. His figures look real, yet there is a contemporary flavor in the statue of the "Sacred Heart," and the pediment in reredos, Merrimack College Chapel, Merrimack, Mass.

After a trade experience of nearly a half-century, Mr. Brunner has become a master woodcarver. His *Manual of Wood Carving and Wood Sculpture* should be in the possession of every individual interested in learning to carve on a high level of efficiency. A study of his work should be an inspiration to all persons interested in wood sculpture.

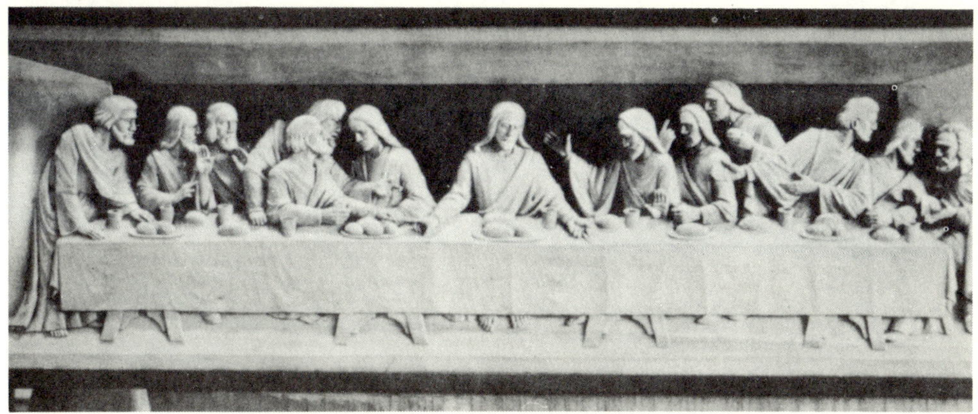

Fig. 12. "The Last Supper," Sacred Heart School, Fairhaven, Mass. Five feet long, 2.5-inches, thick stock. *Courtesy: Chip Chats* Magazine.

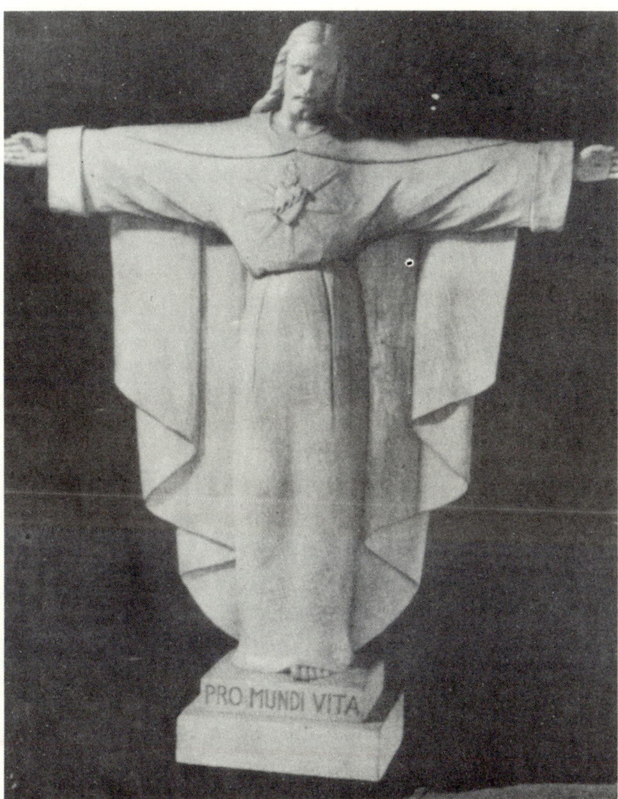

Fig. 13. The five-foot-five "Sacred Heart," Albany, N.Y. reveals a beauty that only comes from years of study. *Courtesy: Chip Chats* Magazine.

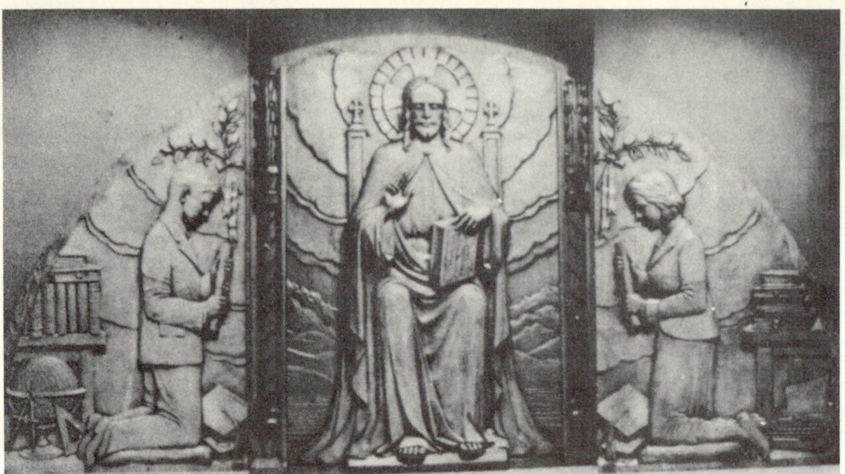

Fig. 14. Pediment in reredos, Merrimack College Chapel, Merrimack, Mass. Carved in 1955; 11 feet wide. *Courtesy: Chip Chats* Magazine.

Chapter 12

Woodcarving and Sculpture

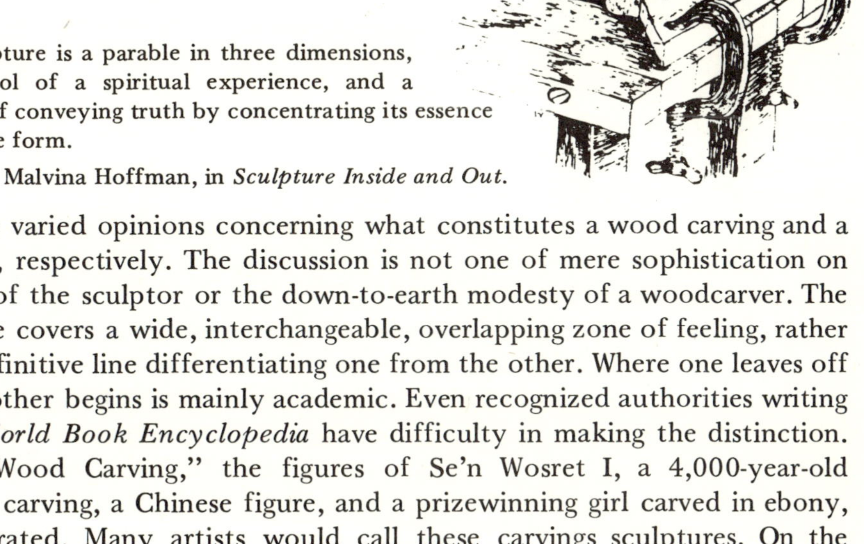

Sculpture is a parable in three dimensions, a symbol of a spiritual experience, and a means of conveying truth by concentrating its essence in visible form.

Malvina Hoffman, in *Sculpture Inside and Out.*

There are varied opinions concerning what constitutes a wood carving and a sculpture, respectively. The discussion is not one of mere sophistication on the part of the sculptor or the down-to-earth modesty of a woodcarver. The difference covers a wide, interchangeable, overlapping zone of feeling, rather than a definitive line differentiating one from the other. Where one leaves off and the other begins is mainly academic. Even recognized authorities writing in *The World Book Encyclopedia* have difficulty in making the distinction. Under "Wood Carving," the figures of Se'n Wosret I, a 4,000-year-old Egyptian carving, a Chinese figure, and a prizewinning girl carved in ebony, are illustrated. Many artists would call these carvings sculptures. On the other hand, the carvings of Riemenschneider are called sculptures and illustrated under this title.

In this work there will be no effort made to distinguish one art from the other. If the sculpture is in wood, the author sees no belittlement in calling it a wood carving, which is really what it is.

In another section of this book some thoughts concerning how to appreciate and enjoy a carving were discussed. It was an indirect approach, a sort of critique on how to evaluate a work of art in order to appreciate it. The art of appreciating and enjoying a carving is one thing, but the ability to carve it is quite another. Appreciation and ability to create are different aspects of the total conception. Given the prerequisites of a sensitive feeling for art, creativity is off to a good start.

Talent, like appreciation, may be unconsciously developed by pursuing related activities. It is never a sudden emergence due to an emotional experience, or an inspirational awakening. What may seem to be instant talent is a display of hidden, unexplored abilities which have been acquired over the years. Many bird carvers have confessed to the author that they never carved a chip until they read his book, *Creative Bird Carving*. That may well be, but in every case there was an active or inactive area of carving ability and artistic temperament which had not been focused on any particular art. What they did after reading the book was to purposefully guide and direct their efforts toward their new objective and found to their surprise that they had the ability to carve birds. They already had the spark. All it required was a little fanning to cause it to flame.

For older persons starting from scratch (if such a beginning is possible), the spark first has to be struck. Then with persistence, patience, and much labor, they, too, will be able to carve, hopefully, on a very high level.

If fate has the budding artist in its keeping, and it usually does to those who try, the spark may not only flame but even leap into incandescent brightness. Then his every word will be weighed heavily by the critics, and if fate still continues to call him her own, his every word and act will embody artistic truth itself. Here is the moment of decision! Just ahead there is a fork in the road of destiny; one leads to an increased perception and development of his art (the route of the old masters), and the other (because of unreasonable conceit, or some other shortcoming), leads to his own decadence and the art he personifies. This latter road is often chosen. It has happened over and over again throughout history. Picasso, so far as this writer is concerned, is an example in our own time. This talented artist became so "far-out" in his theories and work that only his worshiping disciples and some of the pseudo critics supported him. For some strange reason, the monkey-see/monkey-do followers continue to proclaim his "divine" insight and authority in promoting his ridiculous ideas and creative work. How are the mighty fallen! The arts decay; the people forsake their gods; their time-tested traditions and other age-old signs run their course, in an age-old matrix of national decay!

The history of western art began in the Stone-Age caves as has been indicated. The artists were probably the "priests of the temple" for their art had a religious significance which was to continue to the present century. Their god-symbols were petitioned to help and protect them in the dangerous adventures of their rugged existence. Their symbolic art followed the forms of nature and indicated to a surprising degree their knowledge of the anatomy of their subjects. What happened between these prehistoric origins and the golden age of Pericles we do not precisely know, but surely as the races developed more individuals practiced the art of carving and painting, and some, no doubt, became very talented artists. There is every reason to believe that this development was an up-and-down process following the age-old pattern of decay and revival, for the recapitulation of modern art indicates this recession and procession. Much so-called modern art is but the regression to a former technique.

The climb to excellence is a difficult, stony adventure, but the Greeks did it a few hundred years before our era. They were followed by the Romans. Many of their sculptural masterpieces still exist and may be found in museums all over the civilized world. Then the arts and the nations plunged into the Dark Ages. If the truth were known, art with its patron, religion, probably led the way to religious tyranny, ignorance, and destitution. One has only to read and study *The Divine Comedy,* by Dante (1300 A.D.), to get an idea of the religious concepts of the age—the unimaginable tortures of an everlasting hell and the temporary, but horrible, sufferings in a purgatory to refine the spirits of the saved and make them spotless before heaven. If there was anything left of them, they were indeed burned clean! One marvels at the courage and sacrifice which brought about the Renaissance. You may be assured that the way flowed with the blood of these brave souls.

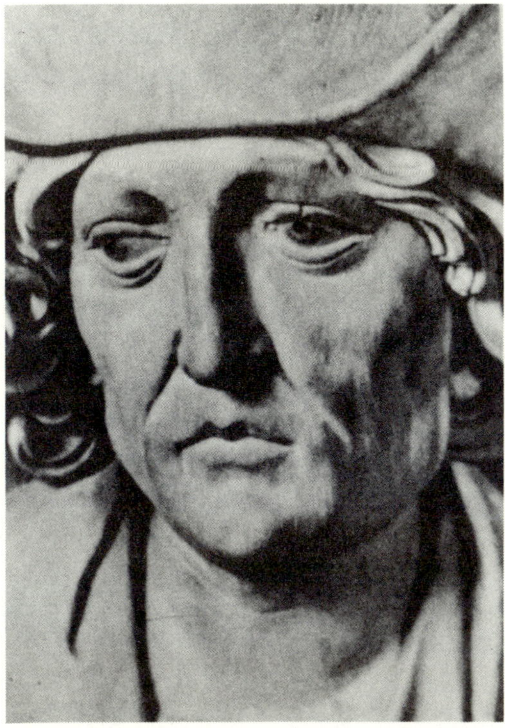

Fig. 1. Carving from Marienaltar in Herrgotteskirche, Creglingen, by Riemenschneider, is believed to be a self-portrait. *Courtesy: Chip Chats* Magazine.

When artistic creations began to surface again, the sculptures were dead, stiff, straight-line figures, more or less stylized. This fact is illustrated by early Gothic sculptures and the development of the art to the latter part of the century when figures began to assume a more natural, realistic appearance. They were lighter, livelier, and carved with flowing curves. It is significant that art led the way to the Renaissance which was climaxed by the works of Leonardo da Vinci and Michelangelo. The themes and drives were still religious. Then came another decline in what the art critics describe as the *baroque* and *neoclassic* periods. The decline was not as obvious as might appear, at least to the layman. Giovanni Lorenzo Bernini carved the towering altar of St. Peter's Cathedral at Rome and the beautiful sculpture of *Daphne and Apollo.* Jean Antoine Houdon graced the neoclassic period along with several other famous sculptors.

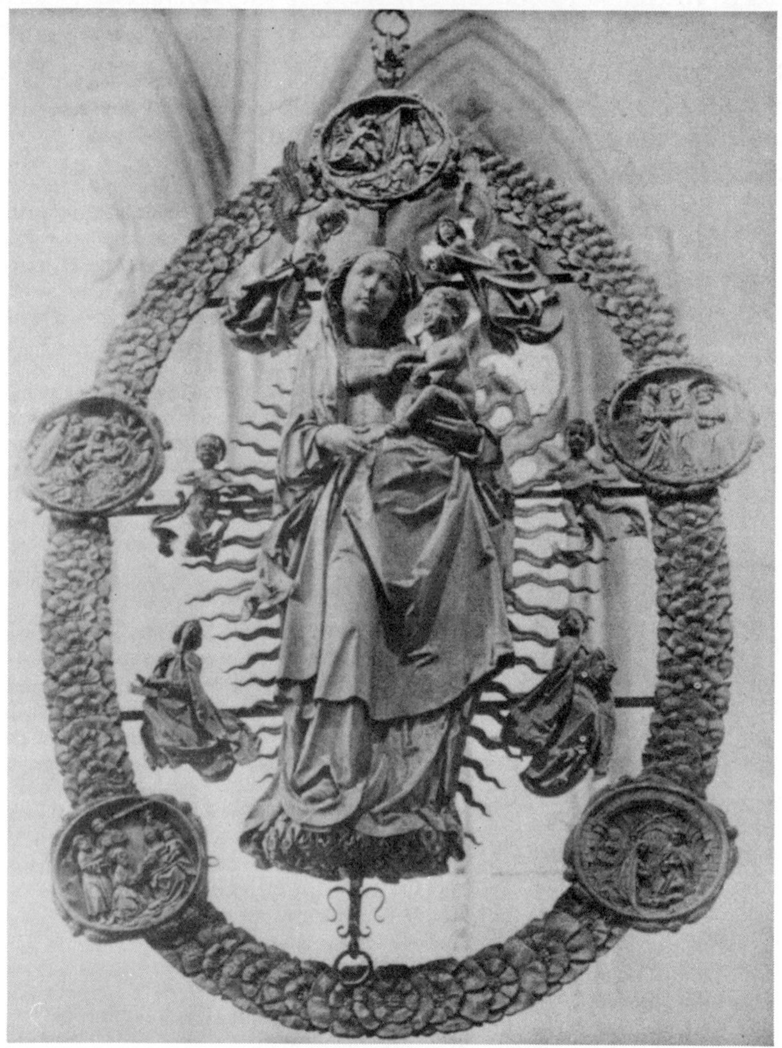

Fig. 2. "The Holy Virgin in the Rosary," by Riemenschneider. *Courtesy: Chip Chats* Magazine.

In a work of this kind, two woodcarvers whose skills and techniques have become legendary should be mentioned. The first of these early carvers was Tilman Riemenschneider (1460-1531). He carved the altars in almost all of the famous churches in Germany. His Madonnas, single figures, and monuments are found in many museums which survived the war. He lived ahead of his time. He did not paint his carvings; he wanted the bare wood to be seen in all of its natural beauty. When the altar work of the church in Munnerstadt was ordered painted by the Commissioners, one can imagine how

Riemenschneider felt. Ironically, years later when the artist became famous, the same church paid to have the paint removed and the carvings restored to their former luster.

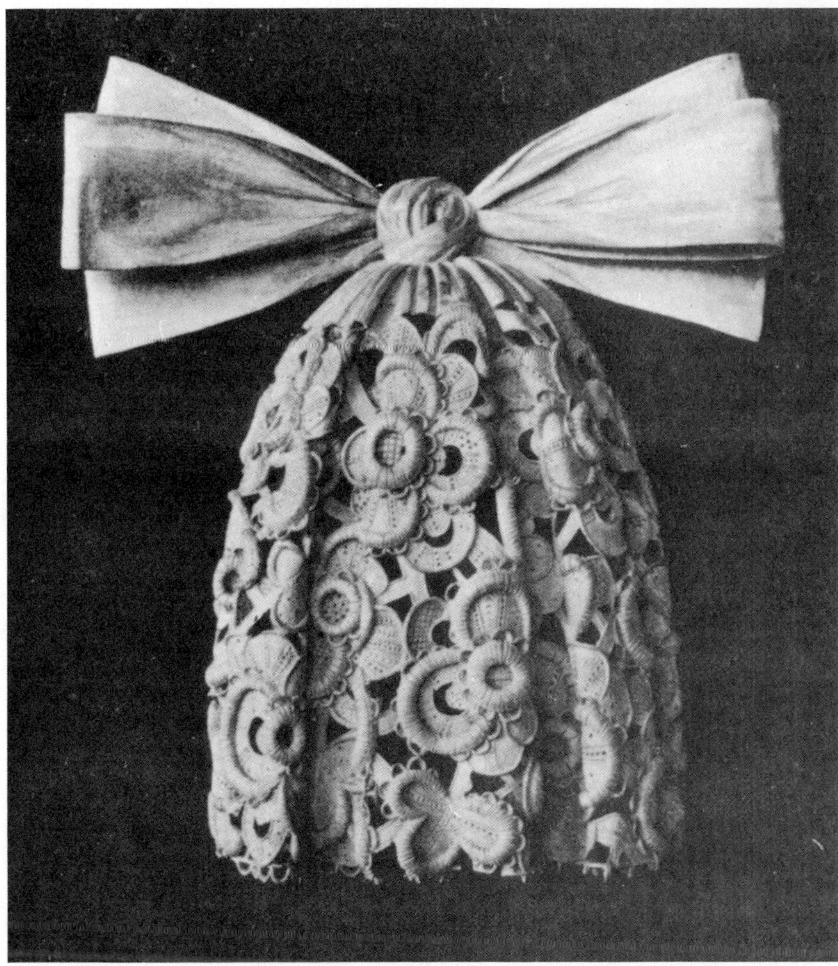

Fig. 3. Cravat carved by Grinling Gibbons, Victoria and Albert Museum. *Courtesy: Chip Chats* Magazine.

Figure 1 is a carving believed to be a self-portrait of Riemenschneider. Figure 2 is a photograph of a famous wood carving entitled: *The Holy Virgin in the Rosary*. It hangs from the high arches of the Gothic apse, The Pilgrimage Church of St. Mary in the Vineyard. Riemenschneider was primarily a stone sculptor but he was better known as a woodcarver.

As well known, and perhaps just as talented, was Grinling Gibbons (1648-1720). He dominated the Jacobean (or Restoration) period. He has been called the greatest of all woodcarvers. He worked with Sir Christopher Wren. He had private commissions in Canterbury Cathedral, Windsor Castle, and Cambridge University. He became the master carver of George I. He is best known for carving the stalls of St. Paul's Cathedral in London. An example of his work is illustrated in Fig. 3.

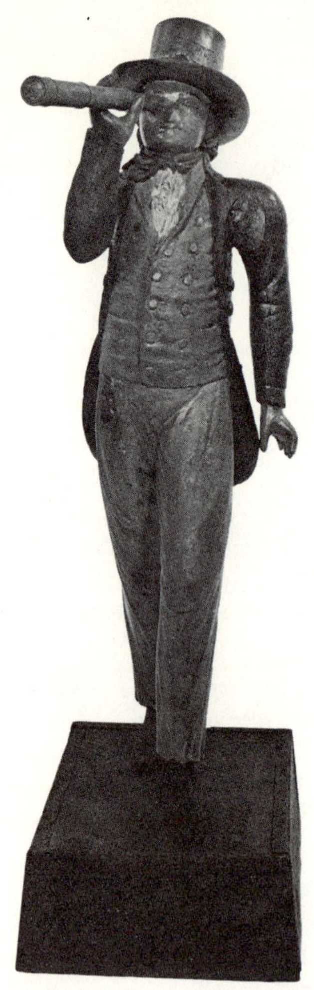

Fig. 4. Ship chandler's sign, polychromed wood, 66″ high, c. 1850, probably New England Collection, Rudolf F. Haffenreffer, 3rd.

Sculpturing in the United States began with the shipcarvers of colonial New England. In Chapter 3, the reader learned that according to the records the first figurehead was carved for the 30-ton pinnace *Virginia* in 1607. This was before the Pilgrims landed at Plymouth Rock. The trade came to flower in the mid-1800's and was influenced by neoclassicism in Europe. Between this period and the early colonial days there must have been some good carvings which have been lost to history. The knife was as much a part of colonial life as the flintlock, so some good carvers must have developed. The figureheads, many of them, have come down to us, but other types of carvings are scarce and the carvers are virtually unknown. The ship chandler's sign (Fig. 4)) is a good example that has weathered the years, but the sculptor is unknown. One Wilhelm Schimmel is noted by name because of his notorious personality. He wandered all over central Pennsylvania carving lions, eagles, parrots and other subjects, for booze and board. There are a few carvings in museums from Vermont to Virginia, and some have been preserved by collectors, but the total is small.

During the figurehead period, which came to an end when steel hulls and steam superseded wooden hulls and sails, there were many works of exceptional sculptural quality. William Rush of Philadelphia became known as the first sculptor in America. He was commissioned by the U.S. Government to design and carve figureheads for the new navy. He sublet many of his commissions to carvers—some as able as he, perhaps.

As noted elsewhere, most sculpture in the States was influenced by the neoclassicism then current in Europe. There were a few carvers who may be properly called sculptors in any definition of the word who did not carve figureheads. Horatio Greenough (1805-1852) designed the Bunker Hill Monument. He was also a portrait sculptor and carved the likenesses of many well-known Americans. He carved the colossal statue of Washington which stands in the Capitol building at Washington, D.C. Hiram Powers carved the *Greek Slave*. He also carved portraits and figures. Other sculptors of the

1800's were William Wetmore Story, Randolph Rodgers, and Harriet Hosmer.

Frederick Remington achieved fame for his bronzes of western figures and is probably better known than most artists of the period. He also painted western scenes.

None of the aforementioned sculptors were as famous as Augustus Saint-Gaudens who carved the grieving figure on the Adams Monument, or Daniel Chester French, the creator of the Lincoln Memorial. Gutzon Borglum is popularly known as the sculptor of the heroic figures of the Mt. Rushmore memorial. Other sculptors of this period were Paul Bartlett, George Gray Barnard, Henry Augustus Lukeman, and Lorado Taft.

There are few sculptors today who make any effort to carve realistically, irrespective of their medium. The trend is toward the abstract where skill is not so essential. Probably the best known sculptors are Jo Davidson for his portrait figures, Paul Manship for his *Prometheus* fountain in the sunken plaza in Rockefeller Center, New York City, Gaston Lachaise for his bronze *Figure of a Woman,* Mahonri Young for his realistic figures in American sports, William Zorach for his *Mother and Child* in marble, and Robert Lorent for his torso figure cast in aluminum. Many of the sculptors named above are now dead. They were outstanding for their period and were in contrast with the mediocre art of the other current schools. Jacob Epstein, who was an American citizen before he moved to England, should also be mentioned. His work has been controversial, but his rugged figures indicate a masterful skill. Malvina Hoffman is included in the *World Book's* list of modern sculptors. The author has leaned heavily on her work and writings. Her *Sculpture Inside and Out* should be in every sculptor's library. She also wrote *Heads and Tails.*

Most modern art is a story of decadence. It is sponsored by unskillful men and women and is in itself an excuse for poor craftsmanship. As this manuscript is being written, the Associated Press (May 1974), London, captioned a news item: "Sculpture Exhibit Stinks." The sculptors used perfume, sometimes noxious scents and aromas, to aid gallery-goers in achieving "total ambience." The exhibit was sponsored by the Royal Academy of Art and the responsible sculptor, Geoffrey Clarke. *In Passage of Moments,* Clarke's largest work, sold for $2,400.00, including the aromas of coffee, tobacco, cooking sherry, grass, and woodsmoke.

Current sculptors just cannot perform on the high level of work comparable to the artists of the Renaissance and the neoclassic periods. On a still lower level of competence, the work is merely trash. Particularly irritating to the author are the so-called sculptors who coil together wire and rods without knowing the fundamentals of oxyacetylene welding and call their fabrications highfaluting names which have no relationship whatever to their dangerously twisted metal. I am not even moved by the famous sculpture, *Bird in Space,* by Constantin Brancusi. It is indeed a superb carving and the critics say that it suggests motion, therefore the poetic name. *Spaceship* would be more appropriate, for there are few birds in our atmosphere above the first thousand feet and there are *none* in space. One wonders if the carving would have been noticed if carved by an unknown whittler.

At a recent Arts Show the first place in sculpture was won by a painter who had superimposed a small black square (about 36″ square) in the upper left-hand corner of a white canvas. I forget the name given to it. An artist standing by remarked, by way of explanation: "He was the first to think about it." Two fine sculptures carved from a walnut log were judged third best. A moulded form of Sakrete cement with finger scrolls pressed into the surface while it was still plastic was awarded first place and the silver award. A bouncing piece composed of deformed, reinforcing rods bent into coiled hoops was selected for second place. It was hardly worth its place on a junkpile except for the scrap steel it contained. But this was during the era when a famous artist could walk into a grocery store with a piece of paper and charcoal, draw a few lines and curves, sign his name, and walk away with his arms full of groceries. If the decadence of art is indeed a sign of national decay, our country is on a toboggan sled sliding toward the valley below. Time! O Time, be merciful unto us! Forgive us of our sins of commission and omission—

All of this is not to say there is not any good art being created at the present time. The mantle of authority, however, rests on the shoulders of mediocrity. The best is not in the ascendency. Much of the art that is good is suitable only for architectural application. Some carvings in both wood and metal show considerable skill and artistic quality. I wanted to portray the abstract metal sculpture located in the middle of the fountain at the Civic Center in Philadelphia. I consider it to be a fine example of free art. The authorities of the Civic Center were cooperative, but the artist was not. Several weeks later I was more successful when I learned, quite by accident, of the work of Ted McKinney of Houston, Texas. His abstracts are refreshing and carved with exceptional skill (*see* section on McKinney). Current art is too recent to be judged properly. However, little modern art moves me to tears, or, as the younger generation says, "Turns me on."

Criteria of a Good Carving

A good carving should be immediately recognized because of its outstanding craftsmanship and theme. If seriously conceived, the message should be evident to the appreciative observer. "Let me tell you a story about her ('Goin' Home,' Fig. 5)," says John Rood, author of *Sculpture in Wood*. "I had a very specific idea in mind when I made this sculpture, but did not give her the specific title then because I felt that this woman pertained to something so local that not many people would understand. When she was first exhibited in New York, an acquaintance of mine—one of those sophisticated, rather brittle New York business girls (or so I had always considered her)—came in. This was the first figure to catch her eye. 'Good Heavens!' she exclaimed, stopping in front of the sculpture, 'you've done an old coal picker.' That was, of course, the idea that I had in mind and Coal Picker was the right title."

On February 4, 1974, I wrote to John Rood for permission to use his wood sculpture "Goin' Home" in my new book. My letter traveled from one place to another until March 1, when it was received by him in Scarborough, Tobago, W.I. He readily gave me permission to use the photograph and stated that he would be in Minneapolis on April 15th to prepare for his show at the State University.

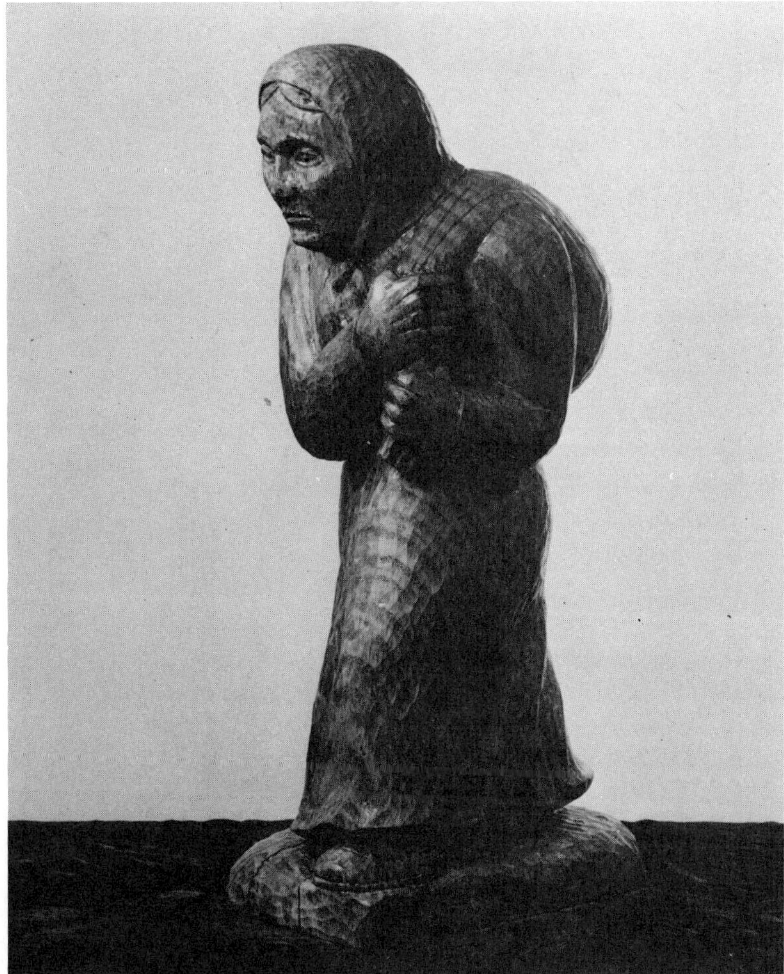

Fig. 5. "Goin' Home," by John Rood. Oak; approximately 18″ high.

In his lengthy letter, he described his work and told of his fight against cancer for four years. "But," he said, "there's life in the old boy yet." Less than three weeks later, his talented widow wrote and informed me that John was dead. His bout with cancer had finally ended.

Mrs. Rood sent me the glossy I desired and it is here reproduced—I hope, a fitting memorial to a great sculptor.

Most modern sculptors design their subjects compactly according to the static, orthodox rules; others are massively and tightly carved. Slobodkin says a sculpture should be strong, simple, and balanced. The Laocoön Group (Fig. 6), though probably the most striking composition ever carved depicting passion and pain, is not considered good design. The fight between Hercules and Hydra (Fig. 7) is in the same category. They are considered examples of the dynamic, Hellenistic style going too far. There are too many "flying buttresses," serpent heads, arms, and hands, all too easily broken off.

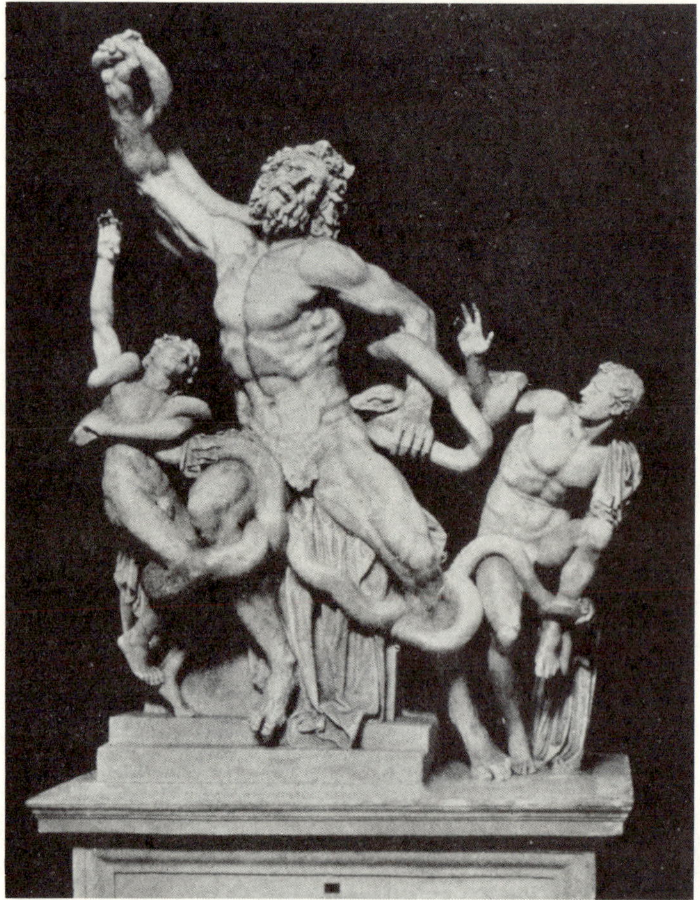

Fig. 6. "The Laocoön Group" (Vatican at Rome). Laocoön, a priest of Apollo, warned the Trojans against the wooden horse outside the gates of Troy. "I fear the Greeks, even when bringing gifts," he said. Later, as Laocoön worshipped, two sea serpents attacked him and his sons and crushed them to death. Believing this to be the punishment of the gods, the Trojans rejected Laocoön's warning and let the large wooden horse through the gates. During the night, the Greek soldiers concealed in the horse came out and captured the city.

The group was carved by Agesander, Polydorus, and Athenodorus, Rhodian sculptors of the third or second century B.C.

They are not "tight" enough. Yet, how could either of these masterpieces have been better conceived and carved to visualize the theme? Art critics say that *Winged Victory* is also overdramatic, but here too is a powerful sculpture even though it may be very dynamic. It suggests motion with better artistic feeling than Brancusi's *Bird in Space.* Would a static treatment have served better and at the same time expressed the same theme, "winged?" John Rood would not have chosen such a theme, and if he did, one wonders how he would have carved it. His subjects, like his carvings, are all strong, simple, and balanced.

Some modern critics do not approve of pierced parts, either. Others argue that the holes show the relationship of opposite sides and help to tie the

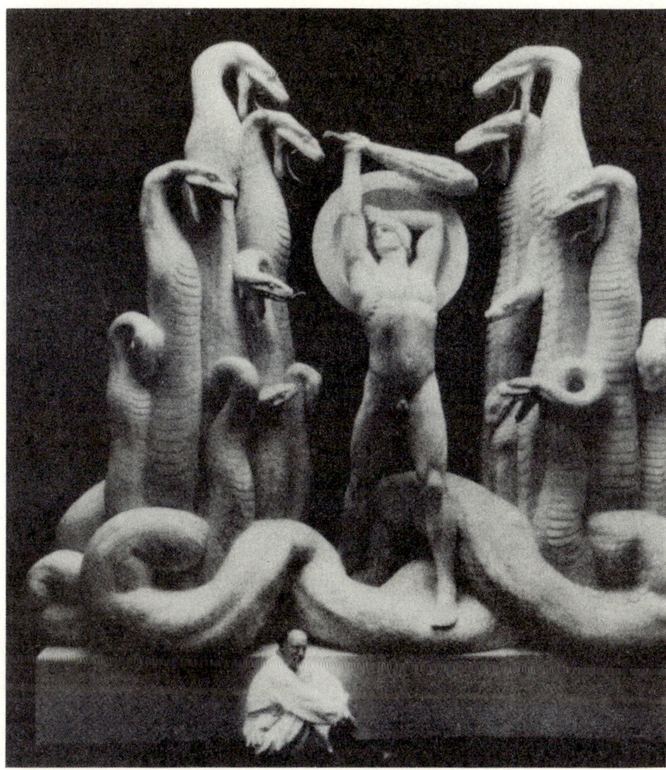

Fig. 7. "Heracles (Hercules) and Hydra," by Rudolph Tegner, Copenhagen. Heracles was the most famous hero of Greek legend. He became insane. When he regained his sanity, he sought help from the Oracle at Delphi. The Oracle told him he must serve the King of Argos for 12 years. He performed 12 great labors, the second being a fight with Hydra. Hydra was a nine-headed serpent. When one head was cut off, two grew back in its place. The ninth head was immortal. Heracles killed the monster, cut off the immortal head, and buried it beneath a rock.

A painting of Heracles fighting the Hydra reposes in the Boston Museum of Arts. It was painted by Sargent.

whole carving together. The author leans toward the latter view. The technique is exciting, both to carve and observe, relieving the monotony of form and lending more realism to the figure. Some critics may say that this is the crux of the whole matter: A carving should not be realistic; a camera shot would serve this purpose better. The weight that should be given to the creative aspects and the carving skills is another matter. This is modernism going too far. Almost any whittler can make a stab at the abstract for the goal or objective is not very important. After carving aimlessly, perhaps, for some time, he may have something that resembles nothing. Then he may give it some far-out title and achieve success. But, even to carve a good abstract that aims toward a certain objective requires skill and imagination—perhaps as much, or more, than a realistic work. However, this is seldom the case. Most of the work is unskillfully carved, without beauty of form, and sterile of imagination—a mere technique to conceal the carver's inabilities. Even the carver with little ability has a compelling urge to create. Having achieved success with little effort, he is not likely to labor to excel in his work, but will whittle away wasting material on forms without meaning and usually without beauty.

All sculpture need not be of a serious nature. Like the graphic arts, there can be a humorous objective. The chisel, then, must make every stroke in keeping with the theme just as a cartoonist would make every line of his pen provoke humor. This technique of sculpture is not easy, but there are many carvers using it successfully. I remember a carving of an old cowpoke I saw on Olvera Street in Los Angeles during the war. The memory of his exaggerated bowed legs, his drooping mustache, drawn leathery face, and general composition still provokes a chuckle. The figure was not only skillfully carved, it was comical. A Lurie cartoon can be skillfully drawn and be humorous, philosophical, and pregnant with meaning. A sculpture can be, too, if the artist holding the chisel has the mind-set of a Lurie.

Consider the artistry necessary to form a single detail—a feather, a fingernail, an eyelid, or any number of such details—and mold them in their proper place. The task is analogous to the words of a dictionary; useless unless they are combined in a phrase or sentence with meaning. The miracles of proportion, perspective, location of the masses, and poise are important aspects of carving a figure—expressing the thought, so to speak. Each element must be combined with a natural bent and become a harmonious part of the whole composition. A wing or an arm made too short strains the visual powers and marks the carver as a novice. Every member must be carved exactly right and reflect the natural form of the model. An eye must be located in the exact spot and formed to express the desired feeling. The whole must be a rhythm of grace and beauty even if the work does not depict a living creature. These are some of the more obvious elements which make a carving effective and forceful; a story told in wood, a recital without sound, moving and aesthetic.

A good carving has crisply cut lines and planes. There must not be any "hairy" cuts left by a dull chisel. The motif is a studied composition, definitive, and representative. The technique and skill of the artist is reflected in his work, for one carving differs from another according to its creator. (*See* photographs of Janel's work.)

Lines or planes improperly molded together distort the figure and otherwise destroy the effect of the various masses which comprise the carving. Rather than a feeling of wonder and appreciation, there is a strained visual concept displeasing to the observer. An effort is made to bring order out of chaos, but not for long. If the carving does not relate to the observer or lends nothing to provoke his appreciation and pleasure, he will turn away. The whole work is dismissed without a second glance.

A sculpture with missing parts does not confuse or disturb an observer quite so much as misplaced masses and unskilled work. A good carving with missing parts may be recognized and appreciated as much as the complete image, perhaps. This is especially true with respect to the broken classical sculptures of ancient Greece and Rome. It is true of modern sculpture where only the torso is carved, or a bust, or single features like the hands. A poorly carved image is like a miserably rendered musical composition—there is no joy in seeing or hearing it. Using the same analogy, an excellent carving is to the eyes what good music is to the ears. Both stir the emotions to awe and wonder concerning the skill of the artist, and a feeling of delight in his performance.

A carving has "skin." To cut through it to form a feather, a fold of fabric, or any overskin adornment is to cause the figure to figuratively bleed. The wound is noticeable even to an untrained eye. So near to nature must a serious sculptor carve that he literally follows the hands of the creative forces which shaped all things from the very beginning. The anatomy of all models must be strictly considered and be as evident in the carving as in the model. Even the prehistoric artists recognized this requirement. In many instances even the veins and muscles may become vital aspects of the creative effort. In all cases of figure sculpture, there are bones and muscles under the skin and these anatomical structures must be considered by the sculptor while he carves the respective parts.

The perspective of any carving must be imaginatively conceived and skillfully performed. The perspective of a bas-relief is not the same for either a primitive carving or a sculpture in the round. A stylized carving is flat with little thought of the third dimension. It represents man's first effort to represent the things of his world. Many of these compositions are still existent as artifacts of prehistoric civilizations. Foreshortening, a method use in painting, is usually necessary in bas-relief work. In fact, the perspective of a plaque straddles the art of sculpturing in the round and fine art painting. A carving in the round must be a good imitation of the project it represents. (Cubist, abstractions, and other forms of modern innovations have no place in this discussion. These forms have their own rules and techniques—or the lack of them—and do not concern us here.) If the carving is a serious effort it must possess the characteristics of the model so far as techniques are concerned. It must possess the third dimension without distortion or such other integrated imperfections. Each of the techniques mentioned has its place in art and, by the same token, its own laws of perspective.

Every carving has lines and planes peculiar to its subject. These elements create the form, the form first visualized in the artist's dream. Some have flat surfaces, others concave or convex, but they are usually a combination of all three shapes harmoniously molded together. When carving a bird in the round, the carver dare not sculpt a straight line or a flat surface. A bird is a symphony of curves; this is why it is so beautiful.

Finally, a good carving is a priceless possession. It represents the creative efforts of a sensitive, talented artist. Such artistic temperament and skill are awarded to only a persevering, energetic few who have labored hard to achieve a goal. In this creative effort, the artist has most nearly followed the hands of the Almighty in forming the likeness of the things of this earth, especially His living creatures, including man himself. To paraphrase some lines of Shakespeare: A carver's skill is an attribute of God Himself. An earthly power doth then likest God's when creative art reflects the miracle of His works.

Ted McKinney

The reader has learned that I am not too sympathetic toward abstracts in art. I have been told that my vision in this medium has been dimmed, not only by prejudice, but by a dwarfed artistic insight. There might be more truth to this criticism than I care to admit, but my emphasis has always been on the inherent shoddy craftsmanship, devoid of both meaning and imagination. Most abstracts are mere masks to cover a multitude of artistic sins.

Such is not the case with the sculptures of Ted McKinney. There are few artists with equal or greater skills and his subjects have meaning and indicate a sensitive, imaginative individual with mallet and chisel. He is an abstractionist, but a thorough craftsman who sees eagles in chicken bones or an art form in every burning bush. He is tireless, and has enough maturity to work long hours in his studio without losing interest in his work. While not formally trained as an artist, he is a true child of his social, inherited environment. His father was a free-lance commercial artist, and even now, in his eighties, paints in oils. His mother was a close relative of the great George Bellows. It is not surprising, therefore, that some of this artistic talent should rub off on the precocious Ted McKinney.

Ted majored in business education at the University of Pennsylvania, but he did take some art courses. During World War II, he was a naval aviator and survived 158 missions. He had enough free time to walk the Pacific beaches studying the forms of driftwood and seashells. This indication of his artistic temperament showing through was later to burst the seams of its confinement and express itself in beautiful art forms.

Following the war, he worked for a plastic manufacturing company on the east coast. But he soon quit this job and decided to start a new life in Houston, Texas, where he soon became one of the city's leading businessmen. He founded and developed a large fence company, which he continues to head, but now that he has become a brilliant star just above the art horizon, he thinks less and less of fences and more and more about his new interest in creative art.

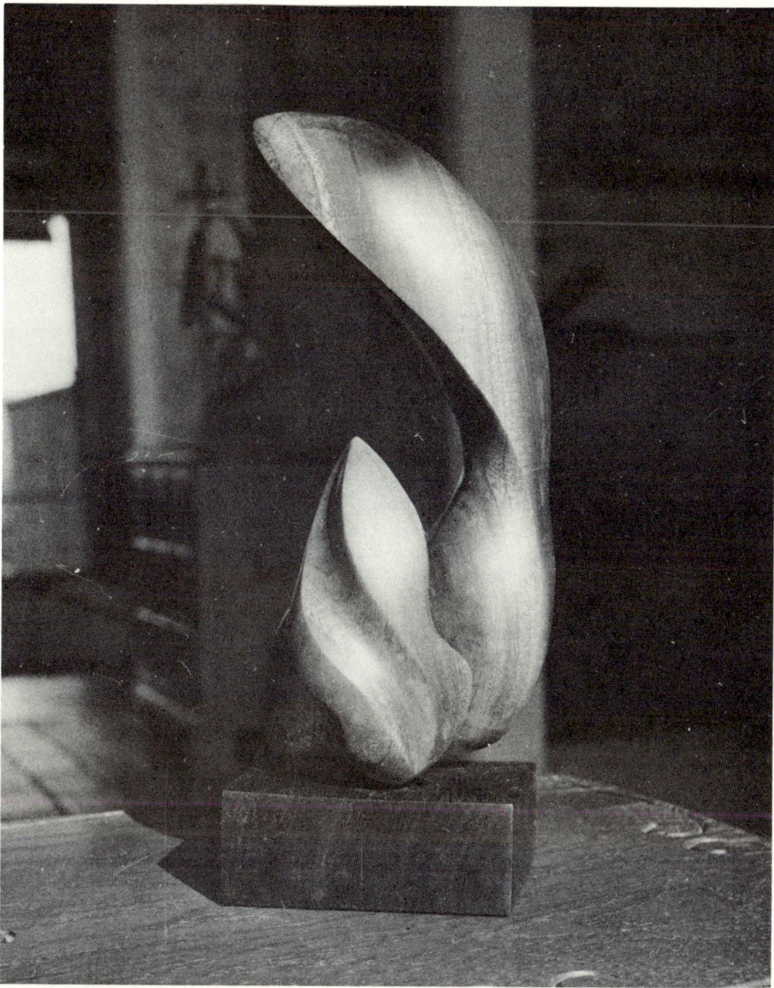

Fig. 8. "New Growth." This "realistic" abstract is somewhat like Constantin Brancusi's "Bird in Space." The resemblance is but a passing thought. There is more relevancy with the title and the form. "New Growth" actually looks the part. It resembles the skunk cabbage pushing up its coiled leaves above the muck of a stream in early spring. The skunk cabbage is an interesting plant and is among the first to respond to new life after the winter's cold.

This carving is not done in styrofoam, but from a wood resembling mahogany.

Ted is a perfectionist in his sculptural activities. Every line and plane must be just right and give the proper impression. He is concerned about the future of his work and mourns for the artists who use as their mediums wood and plastics which might last a hundred years. He wants his sculptures to last forever. For this reason, he has his carvings cast in either bronze or stainless steel. He dreams of archeologists visiting earth from outer space thousands of years hence and digging in the ruins of our civilizations to

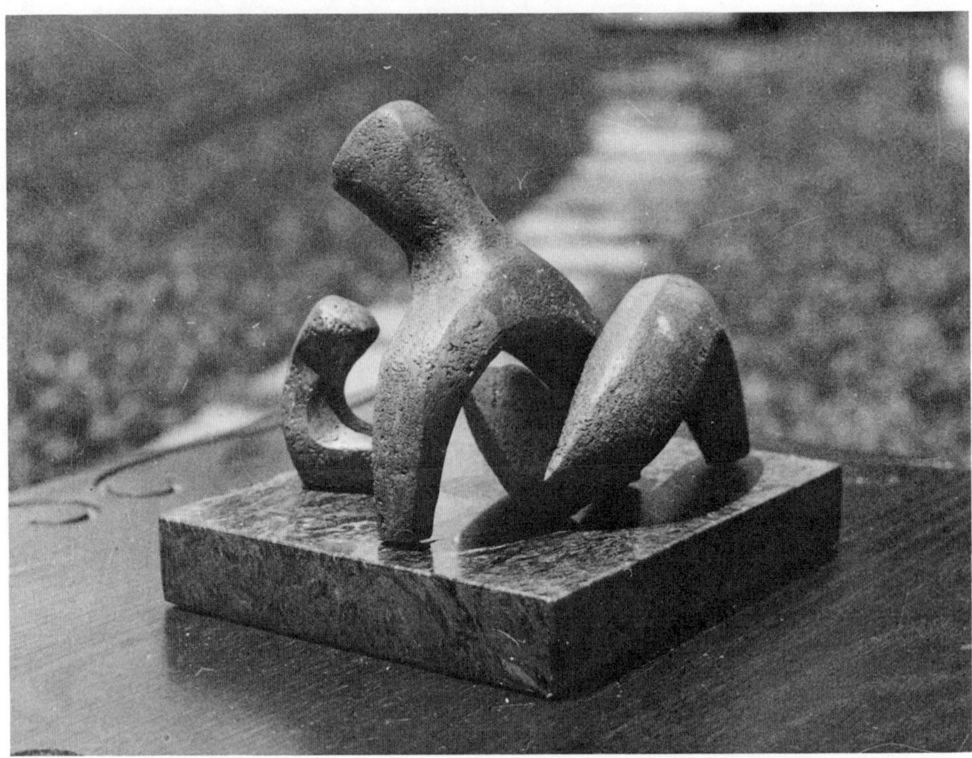

Fig. 9. "Three-Piece Figure." This sculpture is more like the typical abstract, expertly carved and representing no particular thing: animal, vegetable, or mineral. This is probably the reason for the nondescript title. The sculptor was too honest to pull out of space a name for the title without meaning. He could have called it, "All Gaul," which Caesar said was divided in three parts. "The Trinity" also comes to mind, but this title might have been offensive to some sensitive religious souls.

discover some of his sculptures. He says his stainless steel forms will last a million years unless melted down in bullets. Here he is slightly inconsistent in his thinking. His stainless steel sculptures would be more apt to run like water in the heat of nuclear fusion.

Usually, Ted's medium for carving his models is styrofoam. He sands his carvings glass-smooth and gives them two coats of wax which he rubs to a sheen like expensive furniture. He eagerly awaits the cast reproductions of his sculptures. The cast metal forms are polished and mounted on marble blocks. He has become so involved with his art work that it is his very life.

He says: "I have given a lot of thought to the thing which drives me so towards the sculpting. And I believe my own compulsion to create is because it gives me inner peace. This peace is achieved when I work with my hands to create."

There is a smack of impressionism in Ted's abstracts. In fact, each creation strongly suggests the subject he has in mind. His eagle carving, inspired by a chicken bone, really gives the impression of an eagle—rather like the images one sees in clouds forming in a summer sky. Unfortunately, this sculpture is not included here. (Figs. 8–10.)

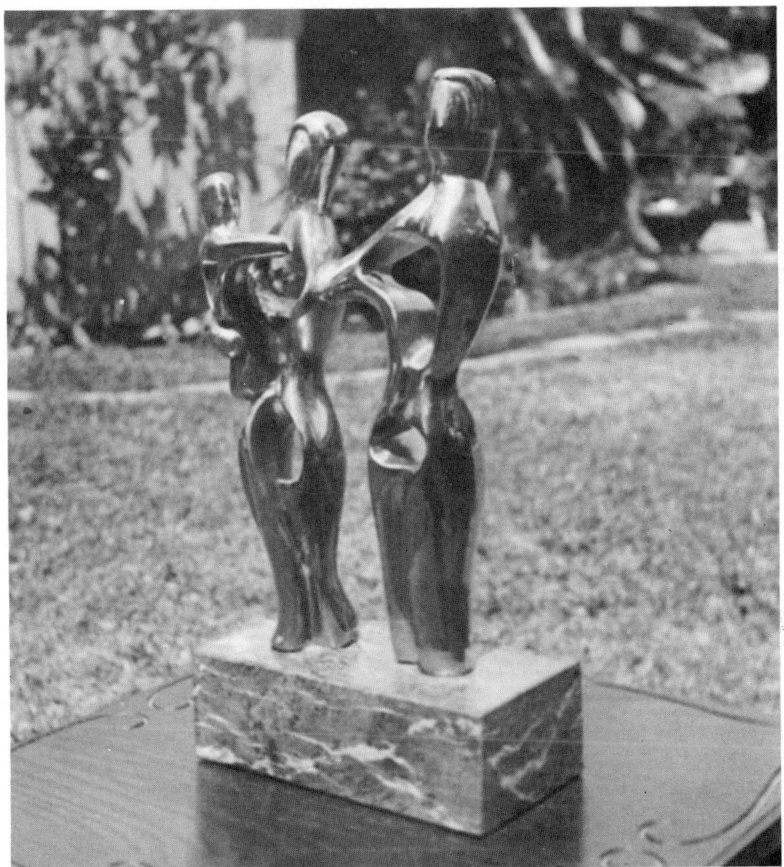

Fig. 10. "Family Group." This is a superb sculpture. Its title is relevant and suggestive. It gives the distinct feeling of father, mother, and child. The emphasis, however, should be on the beautiful curves and the design in general. It is an exceptional piece of craftsmanship. Notice the effective use of pierced parts which some sculptors deplore, but which here prove the point to the contrary. The famous "Reclining Figure," by Henry Moors, also makes use of empty spaces. The sculpture would fail without them and so would "Family Group." The carving is designed to be viewed from all angles and the holes tie the whole composition together in a unified design. The sculpture is several degrees to the windward of most abstracts.

Emil Janel

Emil Janel was born in Sweden. He now resides in San Francisco, California. He has carved since he was four years old and that was 72 years ago. His carvings are comparatively small (averaging about 15″), but thought-provoking and chiseled with a human, realistic bent; sometimes grotesque, sometimes pathetic, sometimes happy, but at all times the faces are lined with the sorrows or joys of the living. His subjects are usually old for, he says, "only age and experience give character, the young have little to say."

Meet three of Janel's little people, The Man with a Shovel, The Man with a Crutch, and a fellow who appears to be posing for his picture (Figs. 11–13). Photographs: *Courtesy* Maxwell Galleries.

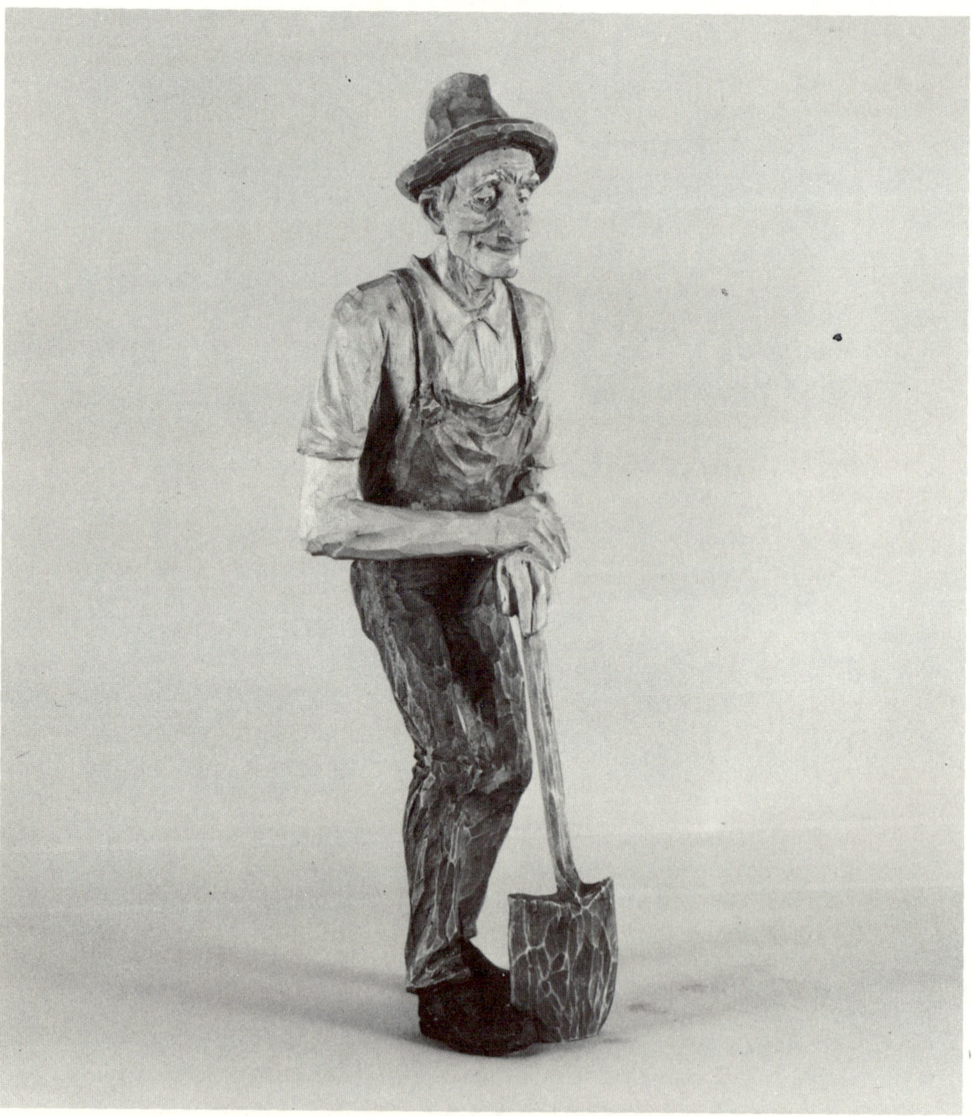

Fig. 11. "Man with a Shovel," by Emil Janel.

Emil carves from green alder. He makes every chip removed count toward portraying his characters. The lights and shadows in the photographs of his sculptures have the effects of a master painting, or nearly so.

In the summer of 1965, King Gustav Adolph VI of Sweden conferred on him the Knighthood of the Royal Order of Vasa in recognition of his outstanding work. He is exclusively represented by the Maxwell Galleries in San Francisco where some of his work is on exhibition in the newly decorated Janel Room.

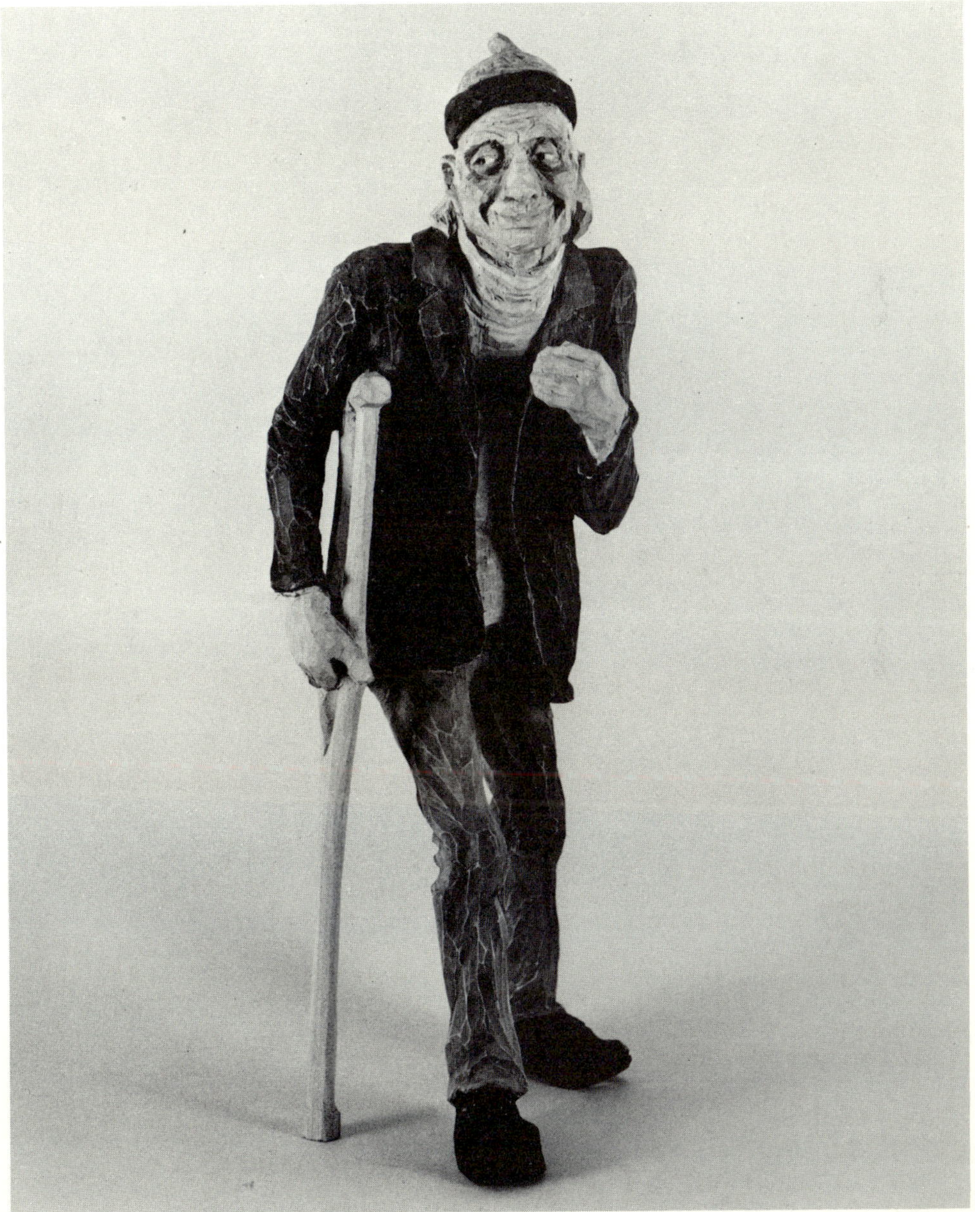

Fig. 12. "Man with a Crutch," by Emil Janel.

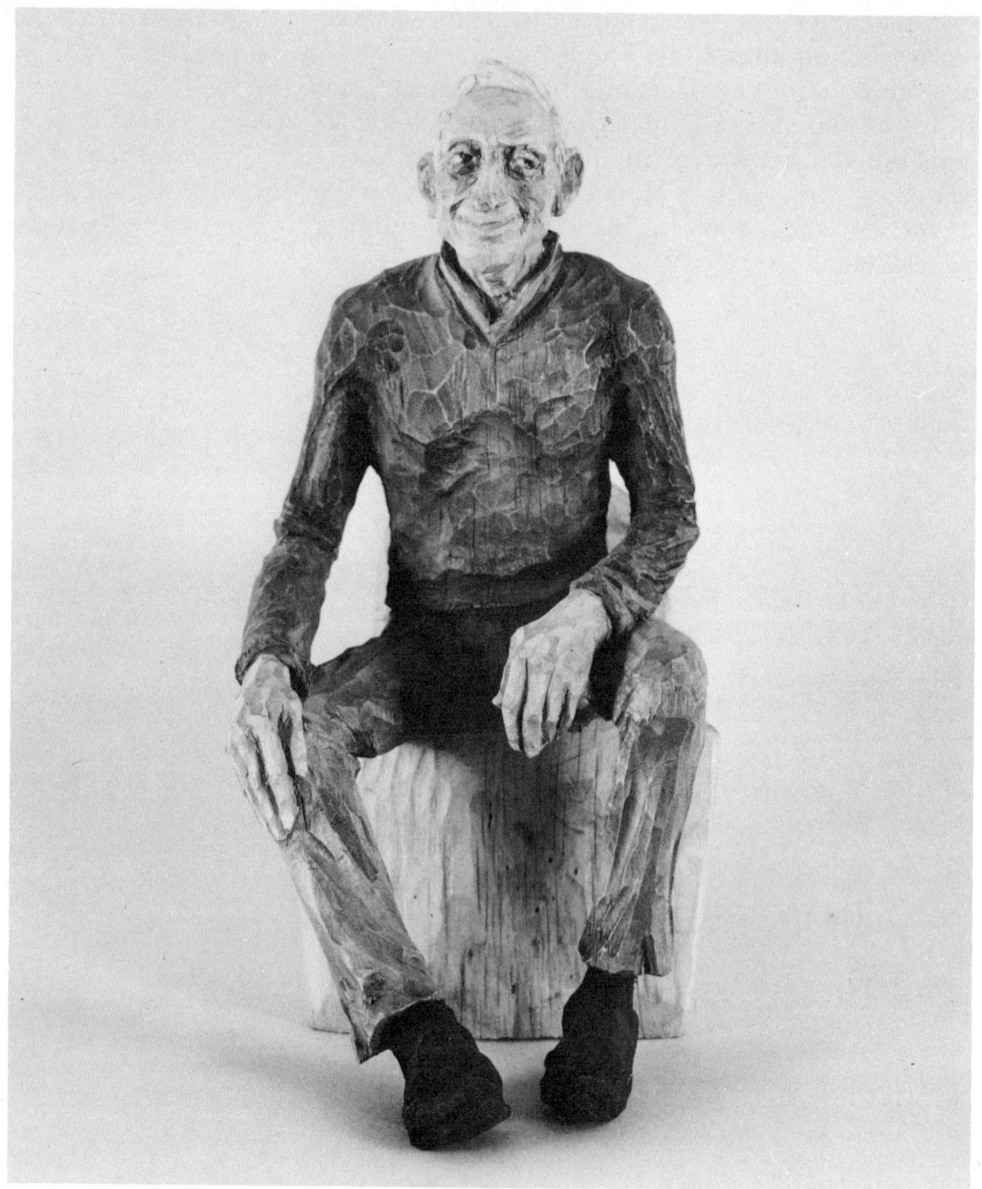

Fig. 13. "Man Posing for His Picture," by Emil Janel.

Donald Hord

Donald Hord was born at the turn of the century, so his work may be included as creative sculpture of the present period in America. He was an outstanding example of an individual who took advantage of his handicap.

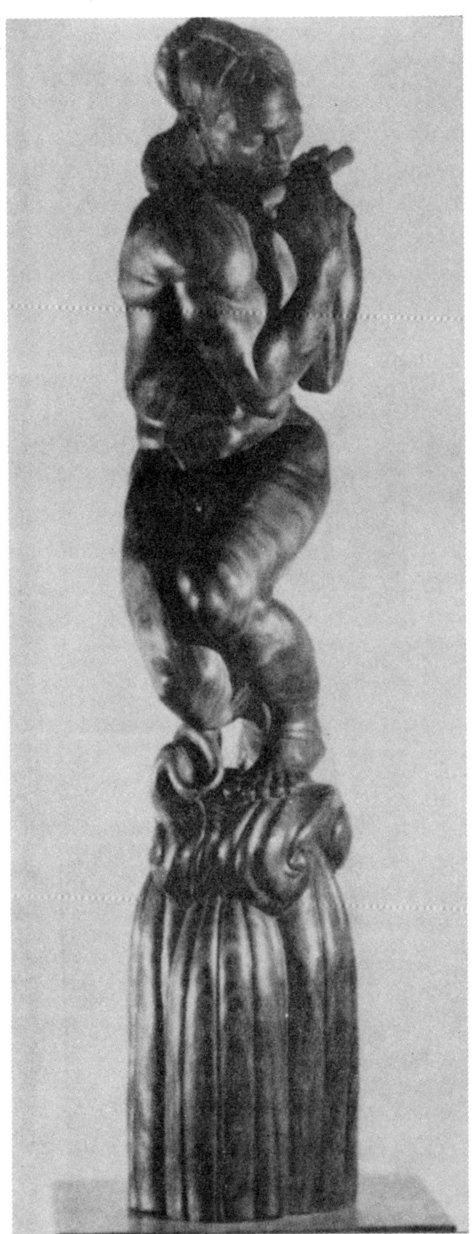

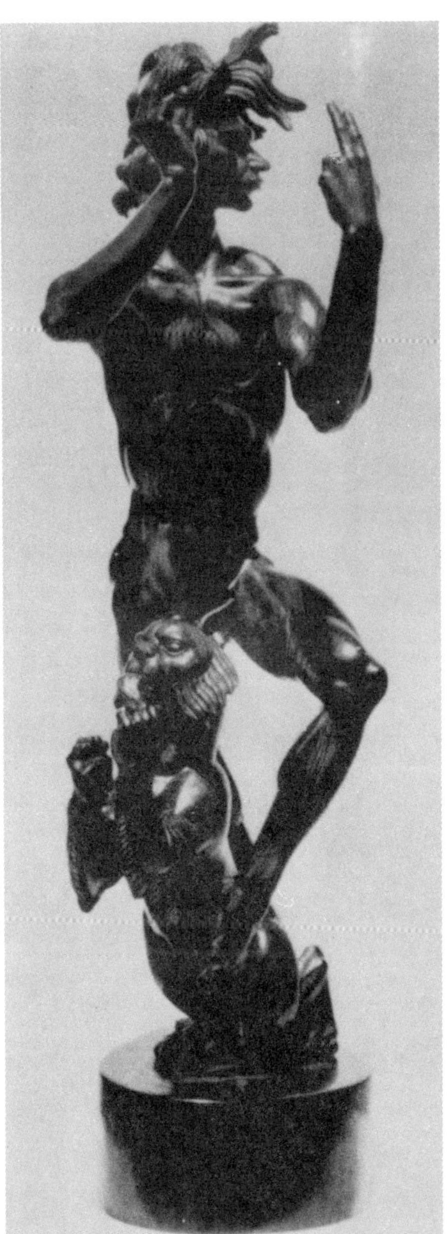

Fig. 14 (left). "Desert Night Wind,"—lignum vitae, 42 inches high. Goff collection. Fig. 15 (right). "Nagual By Moonlight"—rosewood; 42 inches high. This pre-Colombian nature-sprite and his inseparable companion exemplify the best in 20th century sculpture. Schlappi collection. Photographs by Homer Dana. *Courtesy: Chip Chats* Magazine.

At the early age of 14, he experienced a debilitating attack of rheumatic fever which caused him recurrent trouble throughout his entire life. But, paradoxically, because of his affliction he met the Muse that was to bring him both fame and fortune.

His preparation for his creative work was thorough. He attended the Santa Barbara School of Arts, studying under Archibald Dawson of Glasgow, Scotland. He studied at the Pennsylvania Academy, and the Beaux Arts Institute, New York. This formal training, along with his extensive travel in Europe and the Americas, prepared him for creating some of the best sculpture in contemporary America. He is presently a member of the National Institute of Arts and Letters and was elected to the Academician-American Academy of Arts and Letters.

As the accompanying photographs indicate (Figs. 14 and 15), his works smack of Hellenistic-Roman art, but he was especially influenced by the classical work of Michelangelo Buonarroti whose "forceful exercise of the . . . complex torsion of the axis of the body, . . . undulating line contour movement, were so fused with Hord's own individualistic style that they became literally his own." So says Prof. William D. Sturdevant. Paul Manship referred to Hord on occasion as "the founder of the American Renaissance."

Prof. Sturdevant says further: "Probably the most remarkable thing about Hord's sculpture is its profound kinship with nature. Each form is carved with a natural quality that carries with it the pulse of life, of movement, and vitality. Exquisitely stylized, each form is thoroughly expressive of a luxurious foliated rhythm that is present in all vibrant life forms."

Hord's forms have a modern twang too, yet embody all that is good in excellent sculpture. There is not only aesthetic vision but also remarkable craftsmanship.

Donald Hord's work may be seen in the Museum of Modern Art, New York City; the Roosevelt Museum, Hyde Park, New York; and other notable public and private collections in the United States, Europe, and the Orient.

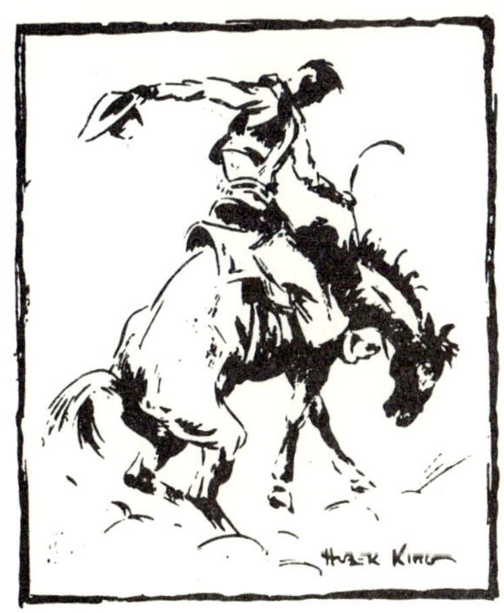

FIRE CRACKER

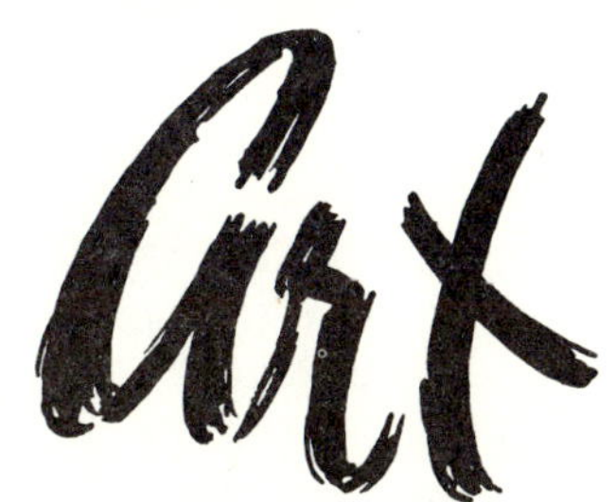

Exhibition From

the "STUDIO ON WHEELS"

HUBER KING

Huber King

The accompanying reproduction of a clipping is from a brochure announcing a Huber King "One-Man Show." The paintings are of the South and Southwest—realistic pictures, away from the smog of the cities.

Our immediate concern, however, refers to Huber King's wood sculptures. His portrait carvings not only reflect accurate and physical and anatomical details, but illustrate, also, the personalities of his subjects. Anyone who has followed the "Gunsmoke" TV shows can see these qualities in his sculpture of "Festus" (Fig. 16).

Huber King was formally trained for his profession at the Cleveland Art Institute. He has by this time probably outskilled his teachers. He has won numerous awards, best-in-the-show honors, and his work is represented in private collections all over the United States. His portrait sculpture of Will Rogers, a "best-in-the-show" selection at the International Wood Carvers Congress at Davenport, Iowa, now reposes at the Will Rogers Museum in Claremore, Oklahoma.

Huber King is a native Buckeye, an unusual realistic sculptor. He is a down-to-earth artist and a master carver.

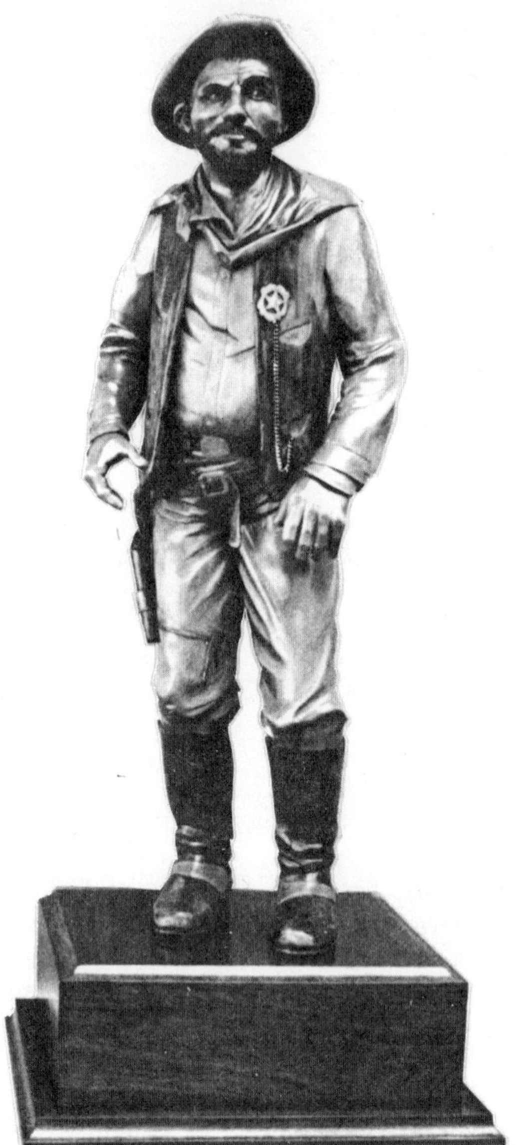

Fig. 16. "Festus," by Huber King.

Ray Wiltsie

Ray works in charcoal and tempera. He is a qualified photographer and is a professional writer. He started carving when only nine years old. He now swings a wicked knife, and as his carving develops he takes advantage of the grain in the wood. Here is an artist who emphasizes detail and uses the technique to make his carvings really come "alive."

A dog team recalls the famous Eskimo dog, Balto, that led a dog team carrying diphtheria serum 600 miles through an Alaskan blizzard from Nenana to Nome; also, the wolfhound, Aibe, for which King Connacht of Ireland was willing to pay 6,000 cows. Of course, the Prospector is a reminder of our own forty-niners. (Figs. 17 and 18.)

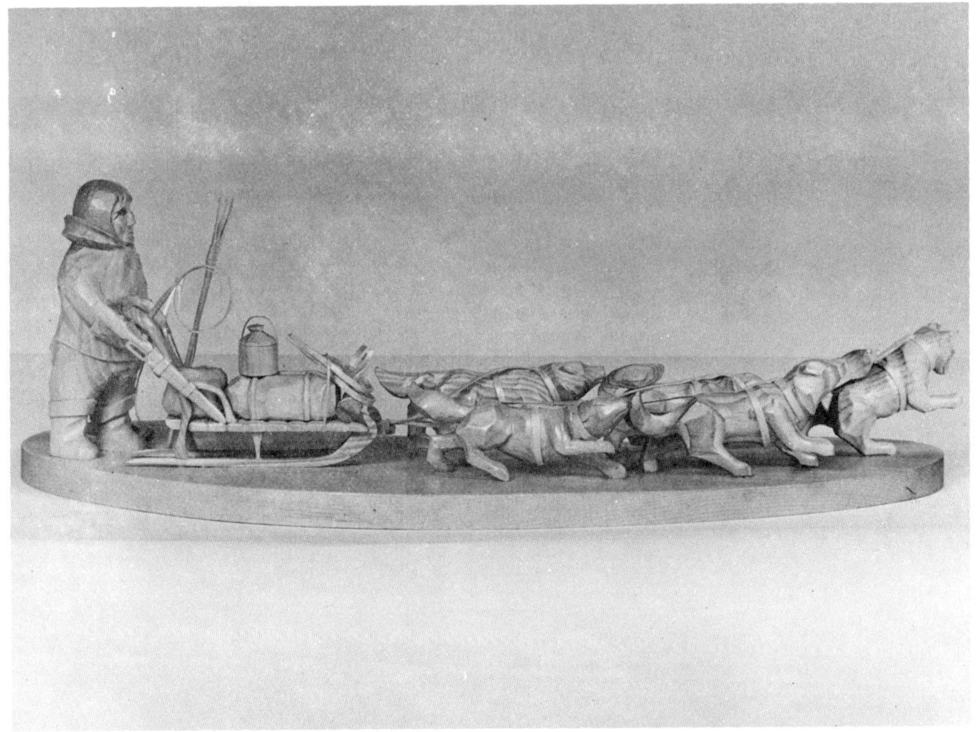

Fig. 17. "Dogsled Team and Driver," by Ray Wiltsie. Photograph by Tawes Photographic.

Ray's team started with the vague idea of a dog which grew and grew into a whole team of dogs, a sled, and a driver. Like Topsy, he says, his carvings just grow until a suitable composition develops. "A helluva way to start a carving," he confesses, but after reading reams of books concerning the subject, his method still persists. He advises one to visit museums for inspiration and learning the basic techniques of wood carving.

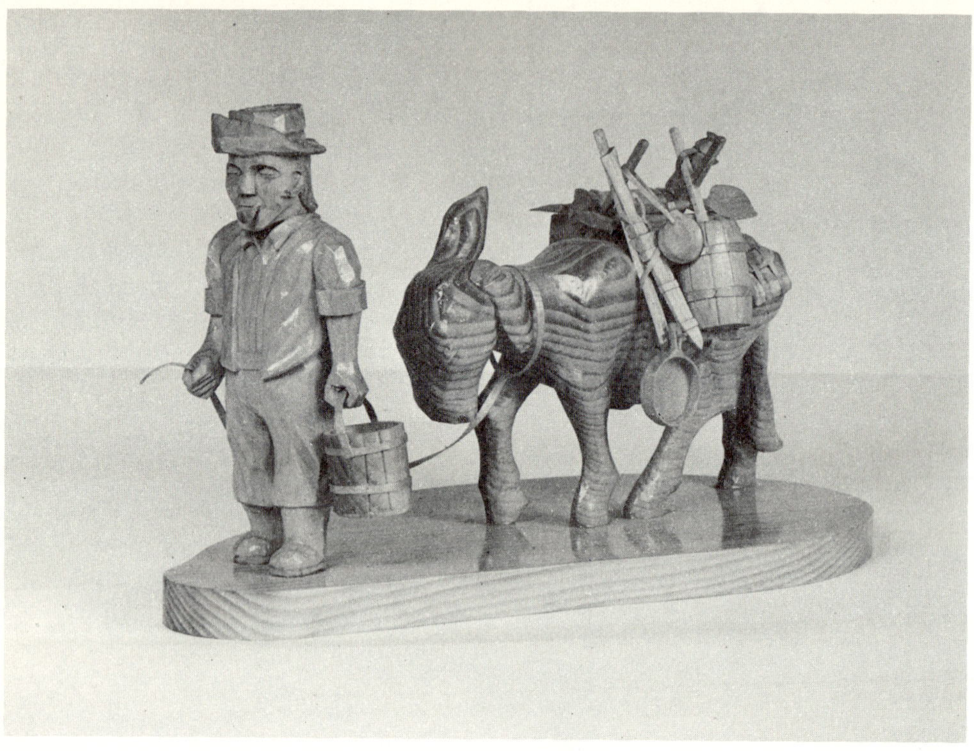

Fig. 18. "Prospector and Donkey," by Ray Wiltsie, Ontario, Canada. Photograph by Tawes Photographic.

Chapter 13

PART 1

Sculpturing the Human Figure

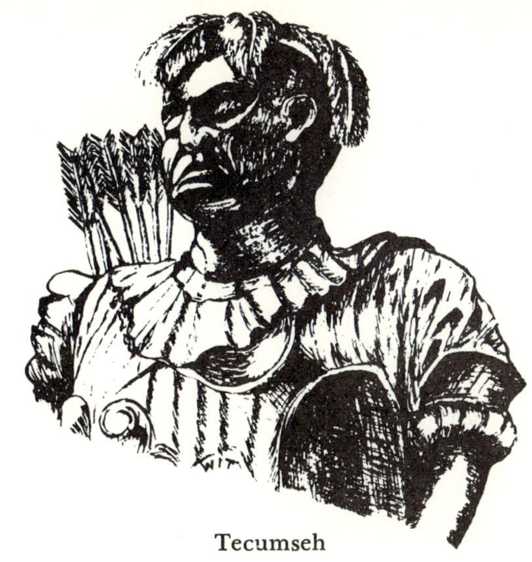

Tecumseh

Most sculptors use the head as the unit in proportioning the human figure. All of the old masters did. This flexible unit holds irrespective of the size of the carving. Perhaps the formula most often used is the one used in this text: 7½ to 8 heads for a full-length figure. Seven and one-half heads is said to be normal, but the Greeks preferred eight. Leonardo da Vinci used 7½ heads for his figures; Michelangelo, eight heads; and Jean Antoine Houdon, used approximately 7½ heads in his *Anatomy Figure.*

The number of heads determines the posture of a figure, whether it is squatty, lanky, or otherwise. As much as ten heads are often used—and for special effects, even more. The average scale of the human figure, according to Malvina Hoffman in her excellent text, *Sculpture Inside and Out,** is as follows:

7½–8 heads	=	height of the body
2 "	=	width of shoulder
1½ "	=	width of male hip
2 "	=	width of female hip
1¼ "	=	shoulder to elbow
1¼ "	=	elbow to tip of third finger

The distance from a point in the center of the brow to the tip of the chin often equals the length of the hand.

Figure 1 shows the proportions of various members of the body of a man. If the novice follows these measurements, he will have some extra wood to carve his figure to a more desirable shape. The idea, however, holds so far as proportion is concerned. Eight heads were used to scale these drawings. Of course, these measurements should be modified to suit special requirements. The female figure, for example, is different from that of the male figure. The lines and planes are smoother and the overall front appearance is that of a

*Last published by Bonanza Books, New York. Probably now out of print. *Heads and Tails* was written by the same author.

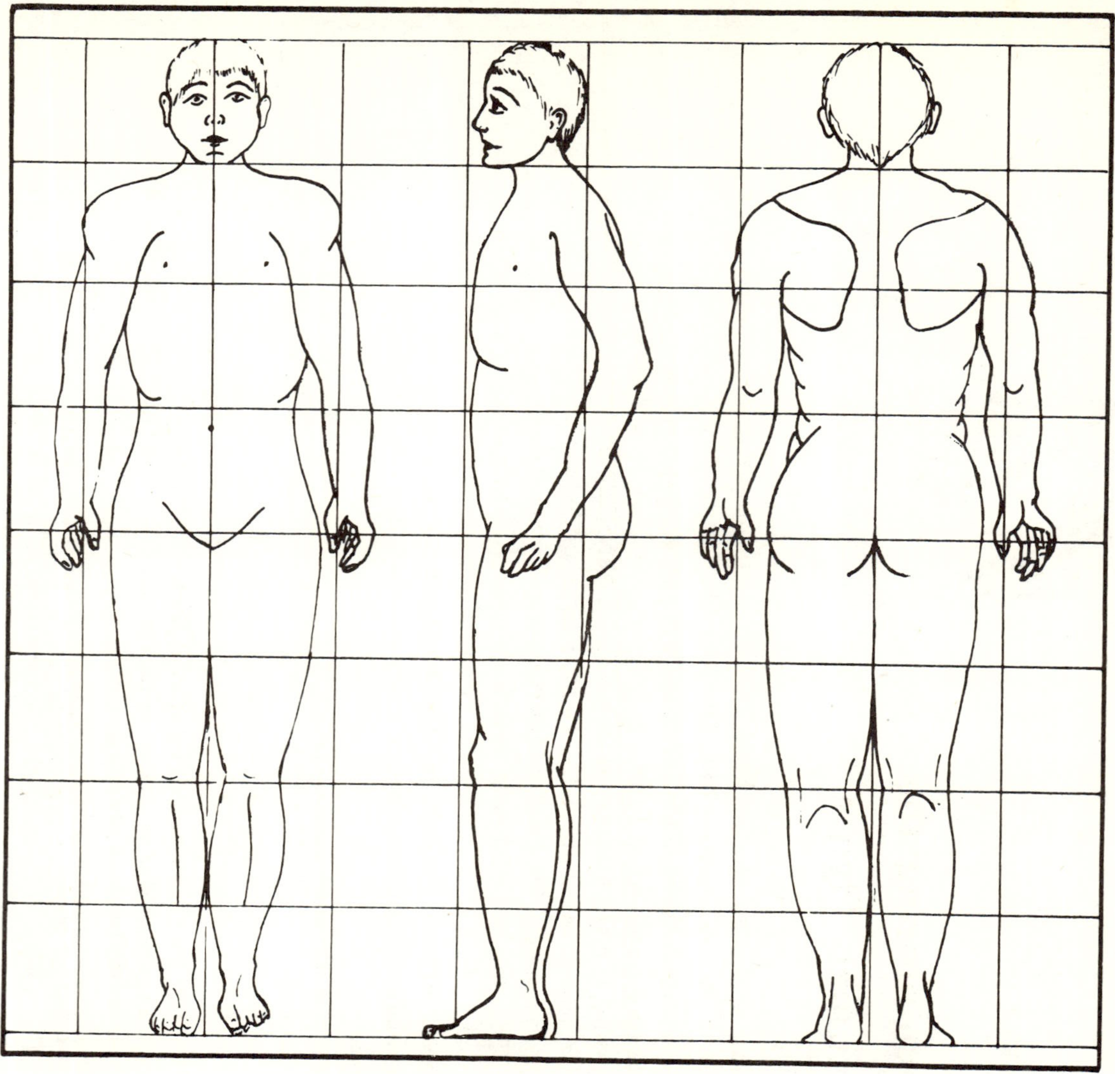

Fig. 1. Proportions of the human figure.

beautiful oval, the greatest axis after height being that at the hips. The geometrical figure of the male is a parabola, the greatest axis after height being at the shoulders. Also, the sculptor who carves an Amazon woman will lean toward more masculine curves in her poise, expression, and other characteristics. To quote Malvina Hoffman again: "When a model bears his weight on one leg, the angle of this leg should be in direct plumb line with the pit of the neck. The shoulder over the relaxed leg is naturally higher than the one over the standing leg. The curve of the spine and the instinct for balance are the cause of this."

The assumption is made that the carver has a live model available. Of course, this model is not absolutely necessary, but for authentic lines and planes there is no better way to give proper rhythm and poise to a carving. A mannequin is of little help in the skin and muscle effects of a carving. A satisfactory model is not very difficult to secure. Many individuals will pose just for a piece of the action. Some difficulty might be found in using nude models. In this event the wife might serve, or a professional model should be employed. The author uses a Polaroid camera to good advantage, requiring much less need for the model. If the carving is not too sophisticated a good carving by a professional sculptor will give the general planes and lines necessary for a presentable job; in fact, sculptural supply houses sell almost any part of the anatomy as well as the whole figure in plaster of Paris. Even pictures can be used if there is enough imagination to supplement the study. The author's wife modeled for his painting of Eve in the garden. The hose of a vacuum sweeper served as the serpent. The story is told that Michelangelo was asked who he used for a model in carving *King David.* He pointed to a decrepit old man at the far side of the studio who served in the capacity of a janitor. This model differed greatly from Israel's great King! Yet, all of the lines and planes were indicated in this old janitor, leaving only the master's imagination and knowledge of the human figure to translate them into a masterpiece.

Since a model is not always available, many sculptors express their ideas in modeling clay. Of course, a model should be used for this process also, but once the clay model is completed it is always at hand for study and guidance without the benefit of the actual presence of the model. When submitting work in competition with other sculptors, the idea of the subject is often expressed in clay. When molded in clay or cast in plaster, almost any professional sculptor can copy the form and carve it to any dimension. The main idea is the inspirational aspect, however, and it is this quality of form that wins the commission. If clay is to be used in your sculptural studies, a reliable text on the subject should be studied, and tireless practice expended in using this plastic material. (*See* Appendix.)

The face is the most important single phase of carving a human figure. It is the most difficult, too, especially if it is to represent a real person—a portrait sculpture. Every single nerve muscle must be in place and every chip removed must help to convey the desired effect. There are two important features which help more than any of the others in carving an expressive face. Probably the mouth is most expressive. It is merely a ball of muscles cut in half, fundamentally, but oh, how these lines may be cut to bring out beauty and character (and vice versa)! "There is something wrong with the mouth," is a frequent criticism. The eyes, which are deep holes in the face on either side of the nose, are likewise, fundamentally, depressions protected by the eyebrows above and the cheekbones below. A professional painter of the author's acquaintance first paints the eyes as deep depressions with alizarine crimson oil paint. Then with her skillful brush she molds the eyes to match those of her model. The folds of the eyelids, the convex planes above them, even the hair of the lids and eyebrows, are important. The eyes are below the bridge of the nose and vary in distance from each other according to the model. The nose projects from the face in various shapes according to race and individual profile. It is never sharp on the bridge. Most persons are familiar with the Roman nose which, of course, may now "turn up" in any country.

Usually a beginning sculptor will give a face a "pushed-in" appearance because of the nose. For a Chinese expression there should be a "depression" to a slight degree, but even a Chinese face possesses some clear-cut projection of the nose. As the head is being carved, frequent observations should be made of it from every angle. "Beginners," says Malvina Hoffman, "mold heads that lack solidity because of uncertain construction. Looking up from the chin is helpful in correcting this error." The profile of a figure should be boldly carved and clean. Some profiles form a smooth convex curve from the hairline to the tip of the chin, not considering the nose. Others are comparatively straight, and some might even be a concave curve which is emphasized in cartoons of witches. A weak chin recedes and a strong one projects. Again, conversely, the chin of a witch, usually, almost touches her hawk-shaped nose. Study the faces of individuals on TV shows to learn more about profiles and the general shape of the head. A silhouettist can make even this characteristic of the face favor the personality concerned. In cartoon carving the silhouette is very important. The cheeks usually indicate whether the model is obese or lean, and the hairdo (before the youth revolution) distinguished between the sexes.

The ears are important features of the head. Study their various shapes and relative positions. In general they are on the side of the head opposite the nose. Some extend above the nose and some below, but all are in this general direction, situated on the side of the head according to the model. Notice that some ears have conspicuous lobes while others have none at all. Like all other features of the face, the ears are highly important.

Some imagination is necessary in determining the pose of a figure. Whatever the pose, it should be graceful, balanced, with full consideration given to the joints and muscles concerned. It need not be a general pose, but a natural one—it must be for satisfactory results. If a model is being used, have the person assume many positions of his or her own free will. Study the various poses and decide which one is most suitable for the particular sculpture. Notice the grace and natural pose of a Hord carving (Chapter 12, Figs. 14 and 15). The animation, appeal, and fulfillment of the theme are embodied in the pose.

Before delving into the actual work of carving a figure, the novice (the professional artist need not be advised; he is already aware of the necessity of adequate preparation) should spend many hours contemplating his project. He should know that an idea must first be carved in the imagination before it is carved in any media. The initial glimmer of an idea might be very inspiring and intriguing, this is good—but it is not enough. The glimmer must assume a definite glow and finally flame in incandescent brightness. Then the urge to carve will be compelling; the hands will be eager to translate the ethereal form into substance. The chisel will then be guided in a more skillful direction for the subconscious powers have been set free to assist in the carving effort. A sculptor spends many sleepless hours forming the details of his dream after it has been conceived. The more sleepless hours spent in visualizing the completed work, the more moving the idea and the form it will assume. For, as Flaubert says (in substance), the idea and the form are one.

Think about the self-portrait of Riemenschneider (Fig. 1, Chapter 12) and carve it full-size. The picture will give you a good start and an objective. In the meantime, study the heads of persons near you. Make a number of full-size drawings, and when you think you have made enough preliminary studies, select a soft block of wood and go to work. Use the Hancock-Brushwood technique described in Chapter 3. Your first attempt may surprise you but the chances are that you will be disgusted. Here is the moment of decision! It is the moment to test your will to succeed, your "stick-to-itiveness," your bulldog determination to pick up another block of wood and start all over again.

PART 2

Indians

The aborigines which met the boats, *Susan Constant, Godspeed,* and *Discovery* at Jamestown (1607), and the *Mayflower* at Plymouth Rock (1620), should have done so with a shower of poisoned arrows. None of the adventurers should have been spared—no, not one. The open-arms' welcome of the Indians and their efforts later to save the colonists from starvation were paid back in full measure in the ensuing years by treachery, deceit, and massacre of nearly genocide proportion. The crusade of Chief Metacomet, of the Wampanoag Indians, began too late. In less than 300 years, the Indians of North America lost their country, and the remnants of the race were made wards of our government and placed on barren reservations. The evils which the Indians have suffered at the hands of the white man have few parallels in history. The story of the settlement of America, its expansion from sea to sea, and certain aspects of its economic growth is not one of which to be proud. Blood, deceit, and brutal force marked every step of the way. Even the most sympathetic of the bleeding hearts in the cause of justice for the Indian might deny this assertion, but the record is clear to any individual who cares to make the necessary research into our historical development. Most people will deny the facts with the fervor of a New Englander when he is told that the colonist at Jamestown had a *House of Burgesses* before the Pilgrims landed at the over size pebble known as Plymouth Rock. Also, while the colonists at Jamestown developed a solid economy on tobacco, Indian corn, and hogs, the *Puritans* were engaged in commerce on the high seas and the main traffic was in rum and slaves, with the blessings of the clergy.

The conquest of South America was even more cruel. Here the civilizations of an enlightened people were totally destroyed and the culture of a thousand years was forever lost to history.

So, the Indians as a race have become lost because of the aggressive powers of foreign legions—sometimes in the name of the Cross. But the end is not yet. In the evolution of time there is a retributive justice which will lay waste the conquerors. So history repeats itself *ad infinitum*.

The poet Longfellow seems to have had tender feelings for the Indians. His allegory of Hiawatha and Minnehaha is a poetic gesture in this direction; a story of the west wind, Mudjekeewis, who deserted Wenonah, child of the moon. Because she died of sorrow, Hiawatha set out on a long journey to find Mudjekeewis, his father, to punish him. He succeeds, and on his return home he meets Minnehaha, laughing waters; so, the story ends on a romantic note.

The Indian characters here discussed were carved with the same reverence as with a crucifix which, by the way, embodies some of the same symbolism.

First, let us carve Hiawatha, "skilled in all the craft of hunters." Carefully prepare full-size drawings of your proposed sculpture—front, sides and back views. Draw all parts to scale so they may be transferred to the log with dividers or calipers. A felt-pointed pen is preferable for drawing the pictures in their final development.

The carving technique discussed in this chapter is not *a la* Hancock-Brushwood, although the method may be just as practical and equally as good; it is not quite as professional. In this method there is danger of losing proportion (of the carved figure showing the sectionalized technique) and an indication of the sculpture being loosely tied together. This method is used, however, by some able sculptors and was used to some degree by the author in carving Minnehaha. The method discussed here embodies some techniques of both of the above methods, but more like the carving scheme of the old masters. The idea is to carve all over the figure in simple stages so that the sculpture develops as a whole rather than in parts. Beginning with the head, the figure is carved over and over again until it assumes its final form. With every pass, the log becomes more like Hiawatha, the first probably being just as important—even more so—than any succeeding stroke. Removing waste wood with safety is a major problem, and the greatest portion of it is involved in the first operation. The second operation is merely a refinement of the first, and so on.

Select a well-seasoned log (or build up a form similar to that used in carving St. Francis, Chapter 14) of a desirable wood, as long as the planned height of the figure and thick enough to include all structural projections. The author's log was 54″ long and about 18″ in diameter. Mark off the section for the head. This section should have a definite vertical length because it will be the unit controlling all other parts of the figure, as has been discussed previously (Fig. 2). The chinline should be approximately on

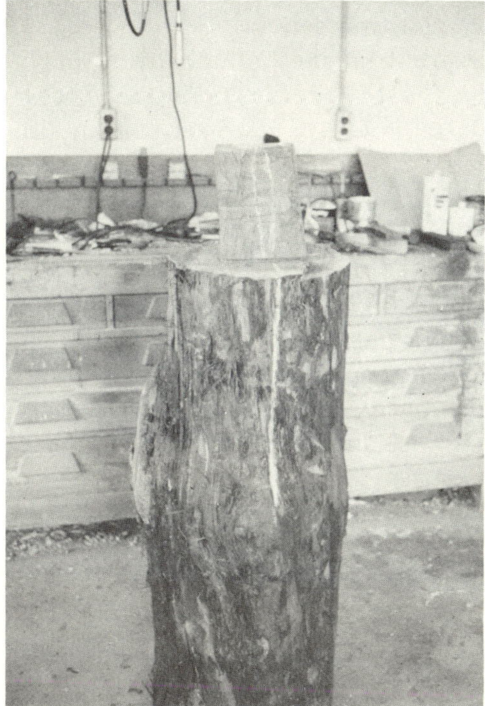

Figure 2.

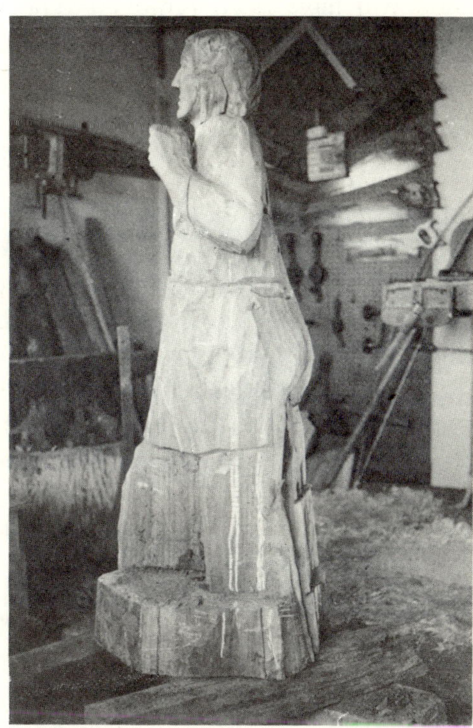

Figure 3.

a line with the top of the shoulders; or a little above, if the neck is to be long. Leave plenty of waste wood for future carving and correction. Cut out the form with a chain- or handsaw. In the hands of a competent operator an electric chain saw will save considerable work with a chisel. Rough carving can be performed with it, but be careful. Do not cut through the "skin."

In the second or third pass over the figure, carve the relief forms of the duck and the quiver across the back, and refine the contours of the arms and hands (Fig. 3). Remain alert for any projecting forms which could be accidentally cut off (for instance, the buttocks).

The figure should be left tied together at the feet so that it will stand upright while being carved. In fact, shaping of the feet may be left until the rest of the figure has been completed. It is highly important to keep viewing the figure from every angle as the carving progresses. Neither should the web between the legs be cut free for the first few passes over the figure; it will help to strengthen the figure and make it more stable for carving. Remember that the head is the unit of measurement and every member of the body is governed by this scale. For example, the shoulders are two heads wide—one head on either side of the center, vertical line. From the top of the shoulder to the elbow measures 1¼ heads; from the elbow to the tip of the third finger, 1¼ heads. Carefully follow the scale as indicated in the grid drawing.

By the time the third pass over the figure is completed, most of the waste wood will have been removed. The work should become more exciting as Hiawatha begins to come alive. The carving must now be more precise, making every chip removed count towards bringing out the form. Begin carving the head block with studied care. Cut the profile and be sure that it is Indian. The nose is comparatively large, the eyes deep-set, the mouth strong, and the cheekbone high. Study the discussion on how to carve the human figure; it should be of especial help in carving the head. After you have carved the profile, carve the front of the face. Carve roughly at first, gradually refining your work until the face stands out—alive. The eye cavity might prove to be most difficult. Remember the eyeball is a sphere covered mostly by the cavity and the eyelids. The techniques used on one eye should be repeated on the other. Avoid a bulged-eye appearance. The eyes are lower than the bridge of the nose, and the high cheekbone is formed by the eye cavity and the retreat of the face toward the mouth. Even the cheekbone is below the nose, and the furrows beginning at the sides of the nostrils and curving toward the ends of the mouth are significant. Carefully weld or mold the contours of the profile and the front of the face together in a unified whole.

The face is framed by the hair. The hair on top is higher than the skull form, and the line of the hair around the face is of various thicknesses, terminating in a bundle of hair on either side, tied with a leather thong. Be sure to allow for the relief of these thongs. The hair may be formed in general shape with a small gouge, but the hairs are formed with a V-tool and a cut-off Moto-tool, if available. An Indian's hair is not curly nor is it mechanically straight; give it a natural wave.

Observe the throat muscles of the people around you. Study your own and form these muscles on the figure with care. They are important. Notice how they mold in with the contours of the clavicle. Study the sternum, the rib cage, and the belly. The photograph shows the ribs too prominently; the carving fails in this respect. The skirt thongs help to point up the waistline and notice how the legs may be followed up the skirt. The hairs on the hide skirt are treated with short strokes of the V-tool. The skirt is torn in various places along the lower edge.

Use your own body to help guide you in carving the arm and leg muscles. (Do not be as rash as the author who exposed himself in his cold shop and lost two weeks' time with double pneumonia.) These muscles are prominent and must not be ignored. The hands are quite difficult. Bore a hole in the left hand and insert a dowel to simulate the stave of the bow. The grasping fingers will be easier to carve. The hands around the duck's neck should not be very difficult but the thumb might cause some trouble. Most of it is hidden (Fig. 4).

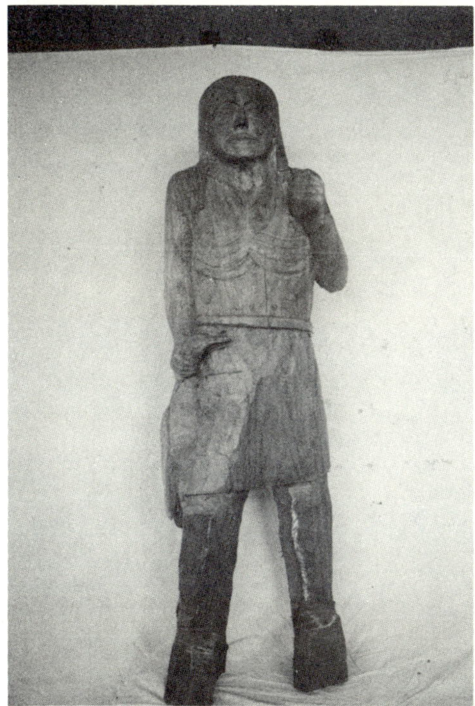

Figure 4.

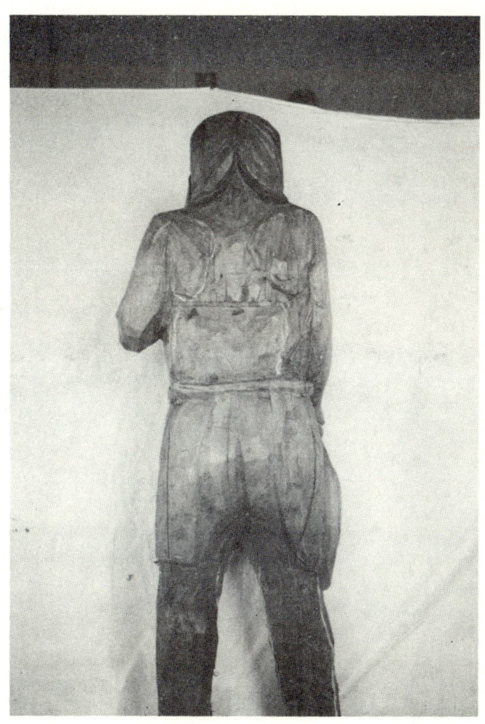

Figure 5.

The back of the figure has not been discussed. The quiver is the highest relief form. It should be conceived as being made of leather decorated with the usual fringe design. The arrows should be made separate and inserted in holes bored for this purpose. The shoulder blades are important. Locate them properly (see grid drawing). The protruding buttocks were mentioned earlier (Fig. 5). As stated, the figure was corrected to a more natural position. This portion of the figure is rather important as the apron or skirt is open here showing the nude form. Note that the quiver is not blocked out. It was forgotten, but due to the fact that plenty of waste wood remained, the quiver was carved without harm to the figure. Note, also, the belt thong that continues around the waist and the parting of the hair to droop over the shoulders. Cut the feet loose from the log and the web which connects the legs. Carve these parts to conform with the figure.

The feet are covered with moccasins laced together with rawhide laces. The photograph does not show the carving to good advantage here, but the carving of the feet was done cleverly and added greatly to the overall impression of "Indian" (Fig. 6). Incidentally, a simpleminded old lady visiting my studio saw the carving and threw up her hands with a chuckle: "Well I declare," she exclaimed, "he has finally got his bird!" The experienced mien of a good hunter did not come through to her.

The final sculpting of the figure is not only exciting, but a decided pleasure. Smooth every surface which should be smooth without leaving a tool mark; in places where the tool marks count, leave them without modification. Over the next few weeks occasionally observe your work and make any corrections necessary. Make the bow and fit it in the hand after the figure has been screwed to its base. The bottom of the bow should be anchored in the base. Insert the feather (or feathers) in the hair. Make these separately (Fig. 7).

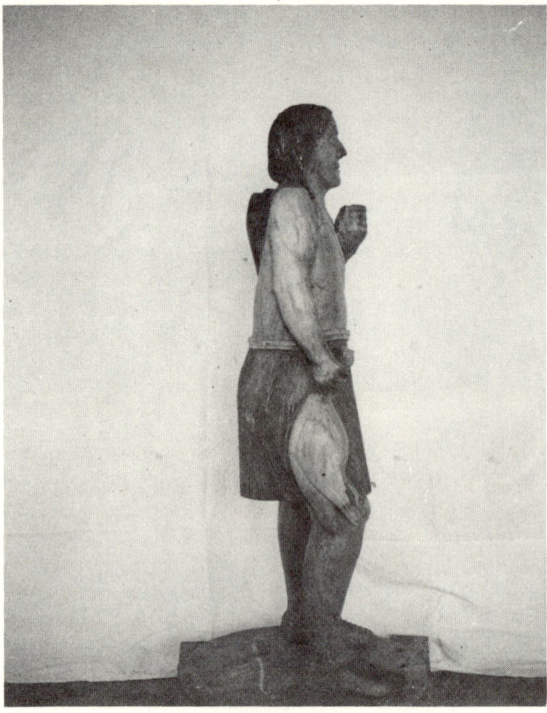

Figure 6.

Hiawatha is fastened to his base with lag screws. Bore the holes in the base large enough to accommodate a slip fit of the shank of the lag screw. Bore the hole for the threaded portion slightly smaller than the core, allowing the threads to cut their way into the material without splitting. Of course, a washer should be placed under the head of the lag screw.

The base is a surface board to which are glued and screwed (use flathead screws) two other sections made up of segments about 4″ wide. Design the base to conform with the figure.

The base should be finished before the figure is mounted on it. See directions for applying a finish in Chapter 7. Before finishing the sculpture, it should be mounted on its base over several layers of newsprint; then the finishing process may be performed without damage to the base.

At the start, the directions for carving Hiawatha seem to be different from those given for sculpturing Minnehaha. Instead of an up-and-down, overall

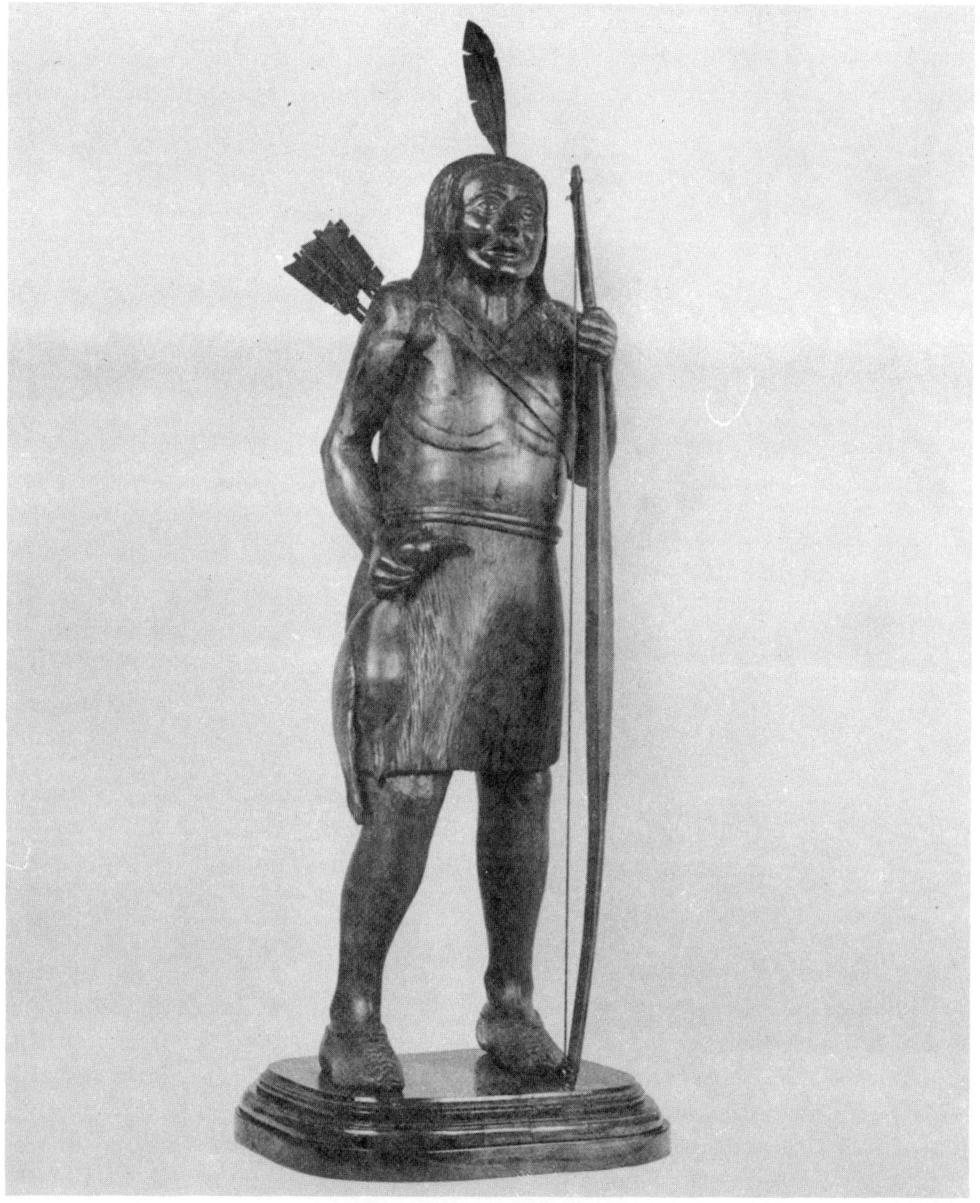

Fig. 7. Hiawatha, carved by the author from black walnut, natural finish. Photograph by Tawes Photographic.

procedure, as shown in Fig. 3, the upper part of the young maiden was carved almost to completion before the rest of the log was even marked (Fig. 8). But who can predict the way of a woman? She often takes a turn much different from that of the male; so there should be little surprise in her makeup. The sculptor, so close to the natures of both of his subjects, responded faithfully to their emotional needs. The creation of Hiawatha was over; so, in a way, Minnehaha was merely a rib taken from the body of the experience, which, of course, should result in a more spontaneous creation than the step-by-step carving of Hiawatha. So, when her head, her arms, and her breasts emerged from the solid log, the sculptor looked upon his work and found it good.

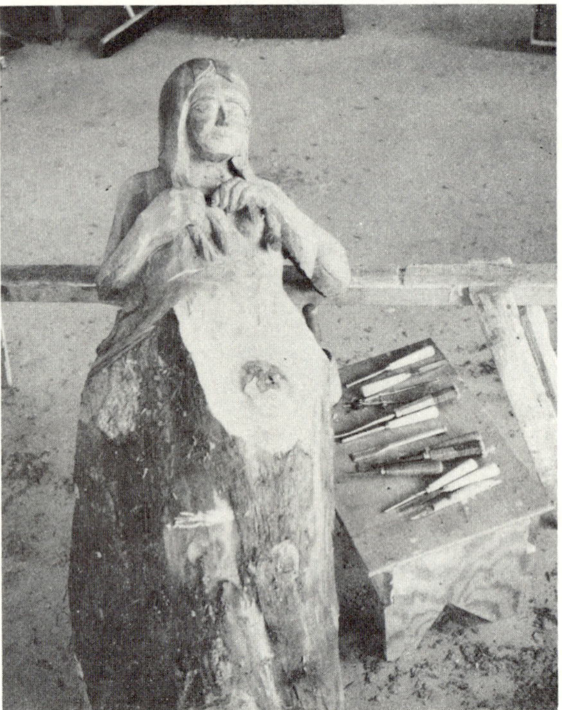

Figure 8.

But the carving procedures were really not very different. The step-by-step method was followed to form the upper part of the carving. The remainder of the log was marked off and the waste wood removed according to the guidelines of the drawings. Hoffman's scale proportions were faithfully followed, making allowances for the female figure. The overall, step-by-step procedure continued until the figure was near completion. Then, as in the Hiawatha sculpture, the final cuts were made, the figure sanded, and made ready for the finishing process.

In this work, a model was used and also a Polaroid camera. The details involved in braiding the hair, and the positions of the fingers and arms were much too difficult to carve from the imagination. To save time and fatigue of the model, closeup pictures were taken of the model's arms and fingers while braiding the hair. These pictures were very useful. Some artists disapprove of this technique, but it is convenient, practical, and helpful in solving many difficult carving problems.

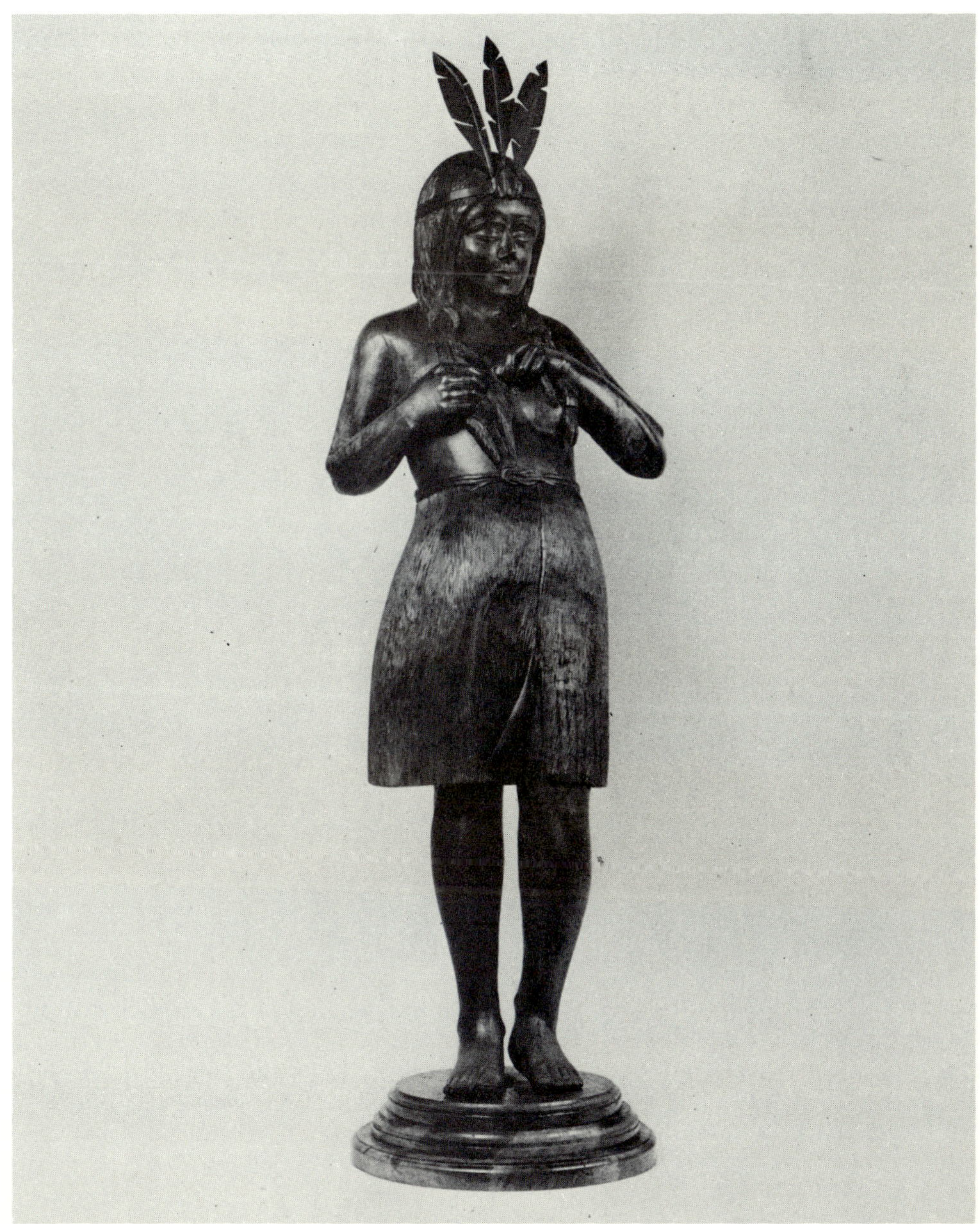

Fig. 9. Minnehaha, carved by the author from black walnut, natural finish. Photograph by Tawes Photographic.

The base of this sculpture is round like the base of St. Francis and may be constructed in the same manner. Minnehaha is mounted on her base (Fig. 9) as described for Hiawatha.

The main tools used in these sculptures were: Chain saw, handsaw, large fishtail gouge 3″, assorted gouges and chisels, mallet, spokeshave, surform rasp, and scraper.

A shipbuilder's adz and broadax are very useful, but dangerous. To remove large pieces of the log, the chain saw may be used directly or cut kerfs to desired depths a few inches apart and then knock out the wood with a flat chisel and hammer.

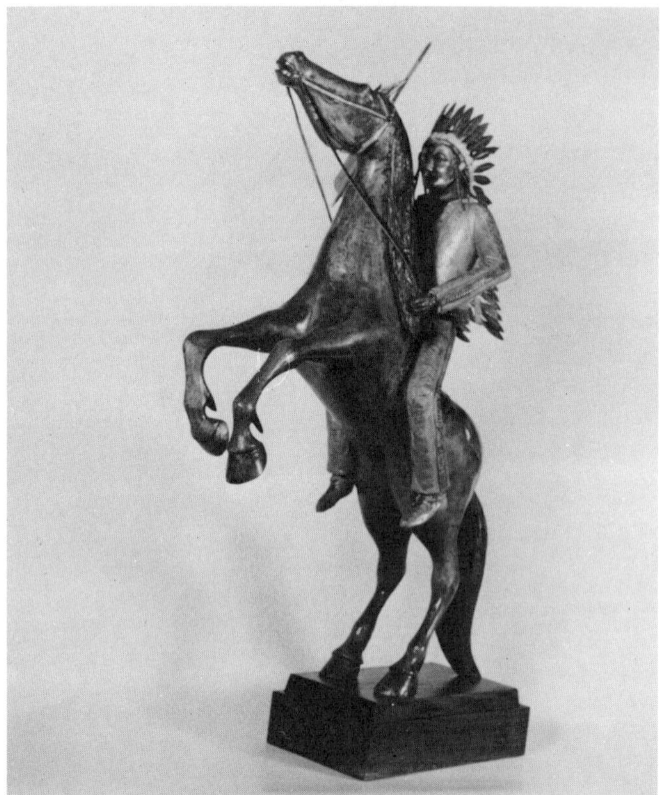

Fig. 10. Chief Crazy Horse, carved by the author from white cedar; oil-stained walnut for the tail and mane and mahogany for the horse.

Crazy Horse was Chief of the Minneconjou band of the Oglala Sioux Indians. As a boy he was named Curly. His father, Crazy Horse, gave his son his own name after his first great feat of bravery. Because of the son's unusual spiritual powers, the Sioux called him their "Strange One."

Chief Crazy Horse demonstrated his leadership ability at the battle of Rosebud, Wyoming, defeating General George Crook. Eight days later he led his Sioux and Cheyenne Indians in the battle of the Little Big Horn, killing General George A. Custer and his entire command (known in history as "Custer's Last Stand").

Chief Crazy Horse was murdered at Fort Robinson, Nebraska, by Indians of his own tribe—a fate not uncommon for great leaders of men. Photograph by Brightwell.

Chapter 14

St. Francis of Assisi

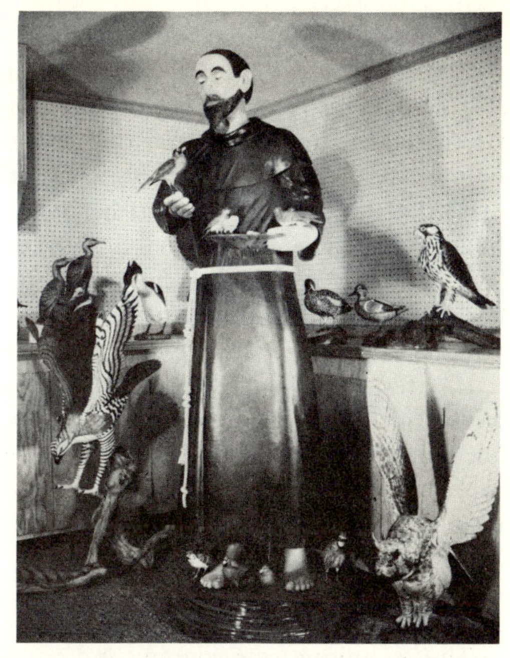

The author carved St. Francis to "reign" over his carvings in his showroom. At a recent Art Show the statue won the special award for sculpture and the best in the show. St. Francis has a great appeal to many religious individuals and some of them consider him to be their patron saint. He was born in Assisi, Umbria, Italy, the son of a rich merchant. He was a handsome lad, gay, and popular with his friends. After achieving success as a merchant, he became sorely troubled by the lot of the poor. He was subject to that strange phenomenon that many youths in every generation throughout history have experienced, and which is prevalent in our own times (along with some peculiar quirks of decadence and revolutionary techniques). Born of affluent parents, they become guilt conscious, disillusioned, or because of some freakish, far-out reason, they leave home and cast their lots with the poor or vagabonds. In our time they join antisocial organizations or communes and live paradoxical lives contrary to both their nurture and education. St. Francis became very sensitive to the plight of the poor in contrast to the wealth of others. Being of a strong religious bent, he began to have an aversion for his manner of living, and finally he was constrained to denounce his wealth and worldly position and cast his lot with the poor. He did not choose a commune or sex-joint to express his emotional conflicts, but even so, he has been termed the first "hippie" in history. He became the butt of his friends' jest and his father's scorn. He even took delight in their mockery for their reactions made him conscious of the fact that he was indeed now numbered with the poor.

Living such an exemplary life, he attracted many people to his way of thinking and soon had a large following. In 1209 Pope Innocent III gave oral approval to the Franciscans to found a religious order. The success of the order was immediate; the idea spread all over central Europe. In addition to being a fervent missionary at home, he went to Egypt and preached to the Sultan and at Damietta, he preached to the Crusaders. After visiting Palestine, he returned home in 1229.

Francis was never ordained a priest. He was, however, so reverent and absorbed in his religious obsessions that he desired martyrdom in their cause. He visited the unchristian East with this thought in mind.

It is said he received the *Stigmata* (the impressions of the sacred wounds of Christ) in 1224. He died at his beloved chapel, Portiuncula, on October 3, 1226. When the end came, he welcomed it with a cry: "Welcome, sister death." Two years later he was canonized by Pope Gregory IX and has become known as the patron saint of birds and animals—especially birds. Some modern writers have called him the first ecologist.

If after this sketch of St. Francis of Assisi, you are not impressed and would rather carve some other figure, do so. Little improvisation will be necessary for the principles of the design are very flexible, leaving only the superficial surface carving to transform St. Francis into a subject of your own choice, a character with whom you can more readily identify.

Carving St. Francis

The technique of designing and constructing the statue like a boat was the result of many sleepless hours spent in search of a method of designing the basic medium light enough to carry and at the same time one that would offer all of the advantages of a solid log. Having a background of boat construction, the idea occurred to build a timbered form consistent with the design of the statue and fasten "bulkheads" along the "keel." "Planking" fastened to the bulkheads would form the "hull" and the general shape of the figure. Having built up such a form, the fabricated structure could be considered a solid log and carved accordingly. The idea became the form, not only offering a new approach to carving large figures, but also solving the acute problem of securing suitable wood for sculptural work.

First, draw a full-size front and side view of the figure to be carved. These drawings will determine the number and position of the bulkheads. The bulkheads are shaped and then split so that the two halves may be fitted around the two uprights which form a double backbone for the figure (Fig. 1). To insure the strength of the bulkheads, they should be notched into the uprights, glued and nailed fast. The uprights in this particular instance were 3″ x 3″ redwood and as long as the figure was tall at the shoulders. The bulkheads should be at least 9/8″ thick to provide enough contact space for the glue and nails when fitting the "planking."

The shape of the bulkheads is determined by the drawings and the flow of the garment on the model. The shape of the waist should not be round but oval. The shape of the bottom bulkhead will also have a general ovate shape made up of concave and convex curves determined by the folds in the frock. The heavy fold over the right leg may be ignored for the time being as it can be added later after the garment has been formed. Notice that the frock fits rather tightly over the left leg, above the knee, for obvious reasons. Notice, also, that the feet have been carved on the uprights before they were assembled (Figs. 1 and 5). Use your own feet as models. Be sure that the shoulders are two heads wide. Allow for the planking which will be 9/8″ thick. If the uprights are separated two heads minus the thickness of the upright and planking, the distance should be fairly accurate. After the bulkheads have been securely fastened in place, nail the two uprights (at the top ends) the proper distance apart to hold them in place while the frock is being planked and carved. The head and bust of the figure will be carved and assembled later.

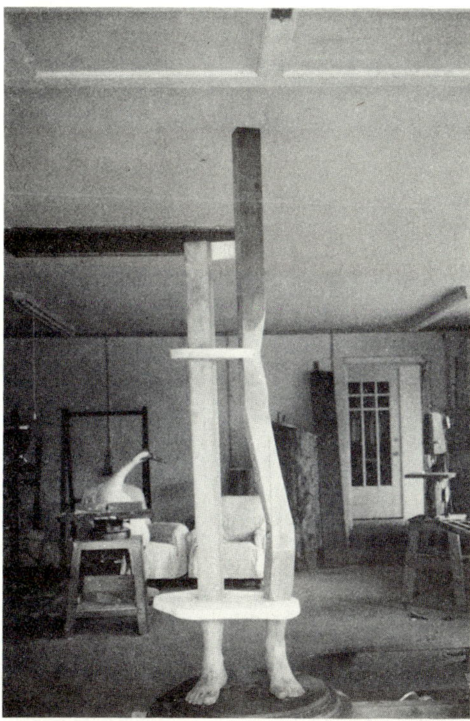

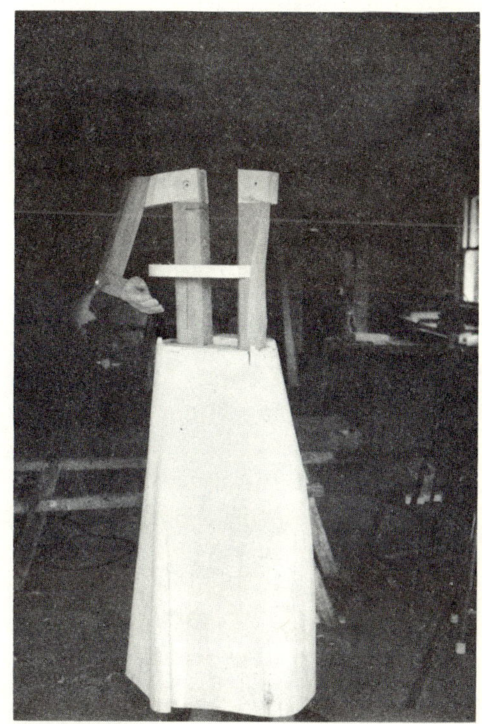

Fig. 1 (left). Feet uprights with "bulkheads" in place for the frock.

Fig. 2 (right). The frock is carved and the right arm is in place.

The next step is to decide if the rope is to be carved on the frock or fitted in place after it has been formed. A real rope belt with its double series of knots representing poverty, chastity, and obedience is shown in the photograph (chapter headpiece). But a better sculptural technique is to carve the rope belt in place while carving the frock. In this case the planking at these points should be thick enough to allow for the extra relief work.

The planking, or skin strips, should be about 9/8″ thick x 1½″ wide, on the average. The shape of the bulkheads will determine the sizes. Note that the top of the strips are tapered smaller than the bottom so that the seams will be perpendicular at all times. The strips are also beveled to fit tightly against each other as they are to be glued together. The strips are long enough to reach from the waist to the hem of the frock, leaving enough waste wood to even up the hem later. At the knee joint the strips will have to be cut and jointed to conform to the bend in the knee. Each piece will have to be jointed and fitted separately as it is fastened in place.

There should be no nails to gap the chisels and other tools, and clamps are not practical. The problem, however, is simply solved. Cut many ½″ x ½″ masonite squares 1/8″ thick, and drill a hole in them the size of the box nail to be used. Also drill holes of the same size about 1′ apart in the strips to be fastened to the bulkhead. Apply a liberal amount of glue to the seams and nail them together with the masonite-washered nails. The washers will permit the nails to be withdrawn after the glue has set. This clamping technique is an effective clamping trick when clamps are not practical. Also nail and glue

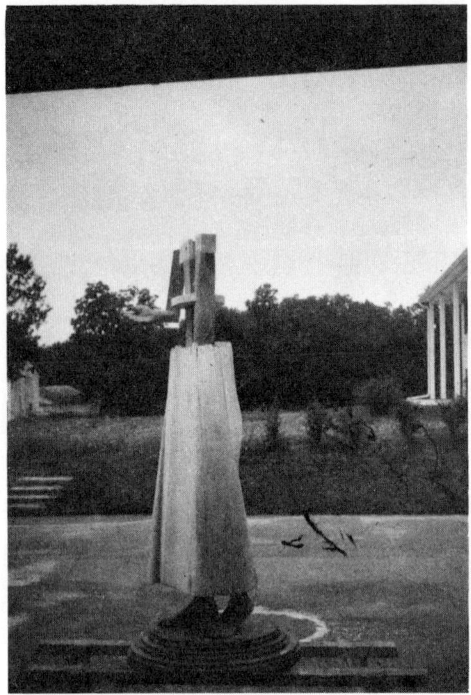

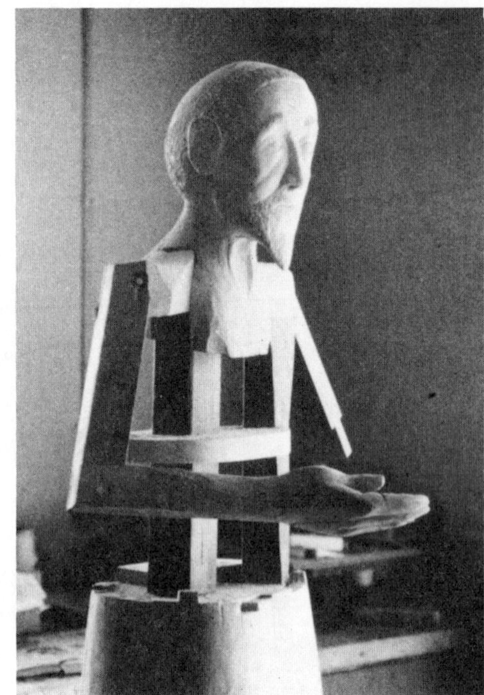

Fig. 3 (left). Side view of frock. Fig. 4 (right). Closeup showing how bust was installed. Notice right hand already carved.

the ends to the bulkheads. Be sure that the strip-ends and bulkheads are well glued before nailing in place with the washered nails. Allow enough time for the glue to set before installing the next strip. While one strip is setting up, work may be resumed by preparing more strips, carving other parts, or any number of other operations which must eventually be done. The last strip may be driven in place and only nailed at the two ends. After the planking has been fitted for the garment, the carving may begin. A Surform rasp will be very useful in this operation; also, a 2″ fishtail gouge, a spokeshave, and a few assorted gouges and flat chisels. If by chance a nail hole appears during this operation, ignore it. It can be filled later with polyester putty. After the frock has been sanded smooth, finishing nails may be used to strengthen the strips at the bulkheads. Drive the nails below the surface so that they may be covered with polyester putty. When finished, the frock should be just as acceptable as if carved out of a solid log and there will be less danger of checking or splitting (Figs. 2 and 3).

Perhaps the head may next be carved and fitted between the two uprights. Fit enough softwood boards together to form one-half of the head (thickness) and glue them together. Repeat the operation for the other half. After the glue has set, the two halves may be fitted together and glued temporarily as in the bird carvings. After the rough carving has been done,

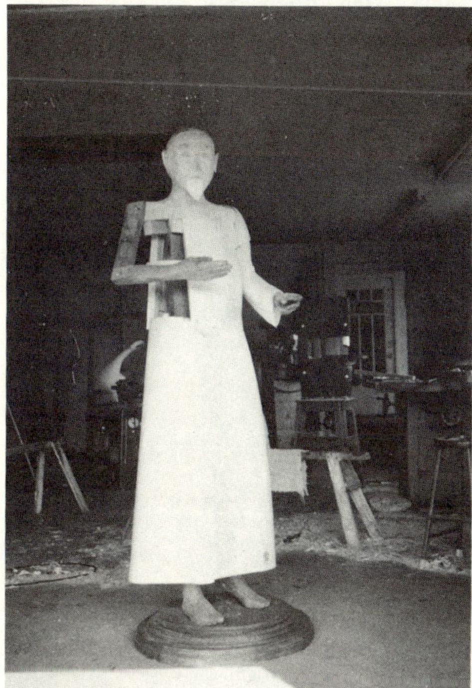

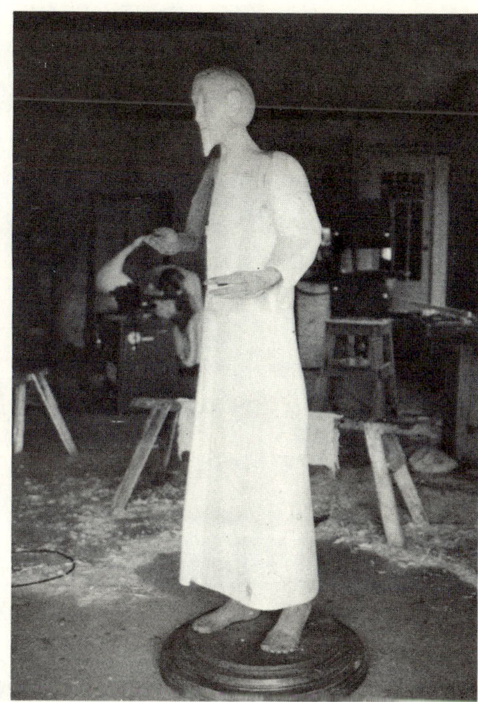

Fig. 5 (left). Blouse of garment nearly completed. The bust is in place showing how it is used as a bulkhead. Fig. 6 (right). Side view of figure.

the halves may be separated and hollowed out, leaving about ¾″ gluing space, and also allowing for additional carving. The two parts may be glued together permanently after the hollowing-out process.

If the author had his work to do over again he would not have given his model a trim, pointed beard. He would have made it sparser and more irregular. It is unlikely that the saint was so particular with his beard. The same may be said with regard to his hair, although he probably had his head shaven according to the religious custom of the times.

After the glue has set, the head and bust may be worked on again to achieve the desired features and to save time after being fitted between the two uprights. Remember the discussion in Chapter 13 concerning carving the face of the human figure. It is a difficult task, so take care. Fit the head and bust between the two uprights by making any or all necessary modifications. Notice how the neck welds in with the shoulders. Note, also, that two extra pieces (one on either side) have been added to form the shoulders (Figs. 2 and 4). Do not fasten the head and bust section in place as it might have to be removed later. The arm "bones" should now be carved and installed. The hands are carved before the assembly is made. The arm parts are glued and bolted together. A half-lap joint is probably the best construction. The head and bust may now be fastened in place. The shoulders and lower part of the

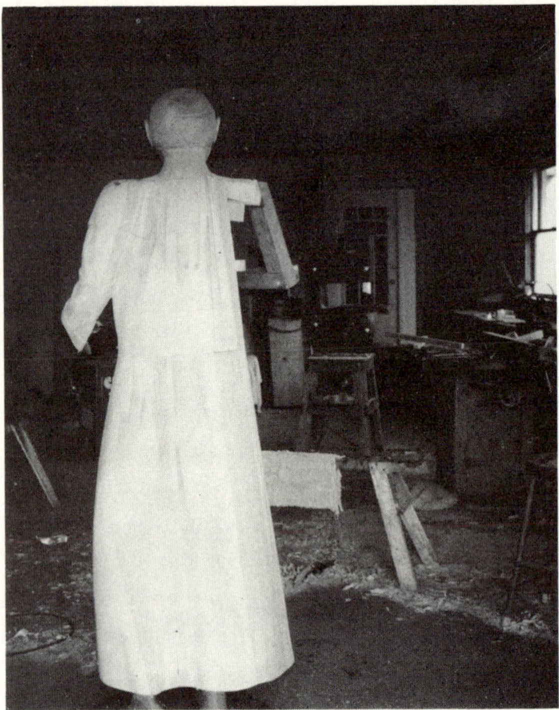

Fig. 7. Back view of figure.

bust will serve as a bulkhead for fastening the upper ends of the strips, forming the blouse portion of the garb (Figs. 5–7). The collar of the cowl may be carved later from superimposed stock.

The bulkhead at the waist will now require extra thickness to fasten the blouse strips. Cut another bulkhead, a near duplicate but only about 3″ wide. Drill holes (slip fit) for the flathead screws. Glue the 3″ segments to the waist bulkhead and fasten with flathead screws. The screws will pull the two parts together making a tight joint. The bulkhead is now double thickness. Before starting to glue the strips in place, check the poise of the arms. The right hand serves as a perch for the robin and the left hand holds a tray of bread crumbs against the body.

These members should be properly and naturally positioned, and not appear awkward to the observer. The tray is carved extra and fitted in the hand later. This is a very difficult task. In fact, a skilled cabinetmaker told the author it could not be done.

The strips of soft pine may be shaped and fitted like the frock to form the blouse section. Some neat fitting will be required at the union of the sleeves and body sections of the garment, but the job is not too difficult and any poor fitting may be corrected with polyester putty. Special care should be given to the sleeve wrinkles. The author observed a coat on a real model to get the natural effect. The joint at the waist between the two sections of strip must be accurate. No "sloppy" work will pass at this vital part of the sculpture. Be sure every flaw is corrected before the finish is applied; go over the carving with a critical eye. Fit the tray in the left hand. Here your carving ability will be tested. After the tray has been properly carved in place, notch it slightly in the garment. Cut the garment, not the tray. Glue and nail (finishing nail) in place. Cover the nail head with polyester putty. Be sure all holes are filled wherever they appear in the carving.

Form the heavy fold over the right leg and glue and nail it in place. After the glue has set, carve it to mold with the frock. Roughly carve and install the cowl and collar. Glue in place and nail fast. After the glue has set, carve to the proper shape.

Forming the Base

Sometime during the carving of the figure the intermissions may be spent in cutting out parts for the base for the Saint. Figure 8 is a drawing of the base details. These details should be sufficient to guide the good craftsman. However, some preliminary information might prove helpful.

When constructing a circular base made up of sectors, the big problem is a holding device for clamping the parts together. The author contrived quadrants and fastened the sectors together as follows: Joint the sectors accurately (1¼″ stock), three to a quadrant. Place in position and form a clamping device as shown in the drawing (use a piece of scrap plywood to mount it). The cleats should be as thick as sectors. A cleat is nailed at each end to prevent slipping. The pressure is exerted by two opposing wedges driven toward each other. Glue the joint surfaces liberally (place a piece of newspaper under the joints) and position in the device. Exert pressure on the sectors by driving the wedges toward each other. Do one quadrant at a time. Next, joint the edges of two quadrants and glue the edges. There will be enough holding spots to place a bar clamp for clamping them together. Be sure the edges fit in a plane. This position can be assured by clamping two clamps over the seam, one at each end. When the glue has set, joint the diameter edge. Repeat this operation for the other half and glue and clamp the two halves together. When the glue has set, inscribe the circumference with a bar compass and cut out with a band saw.

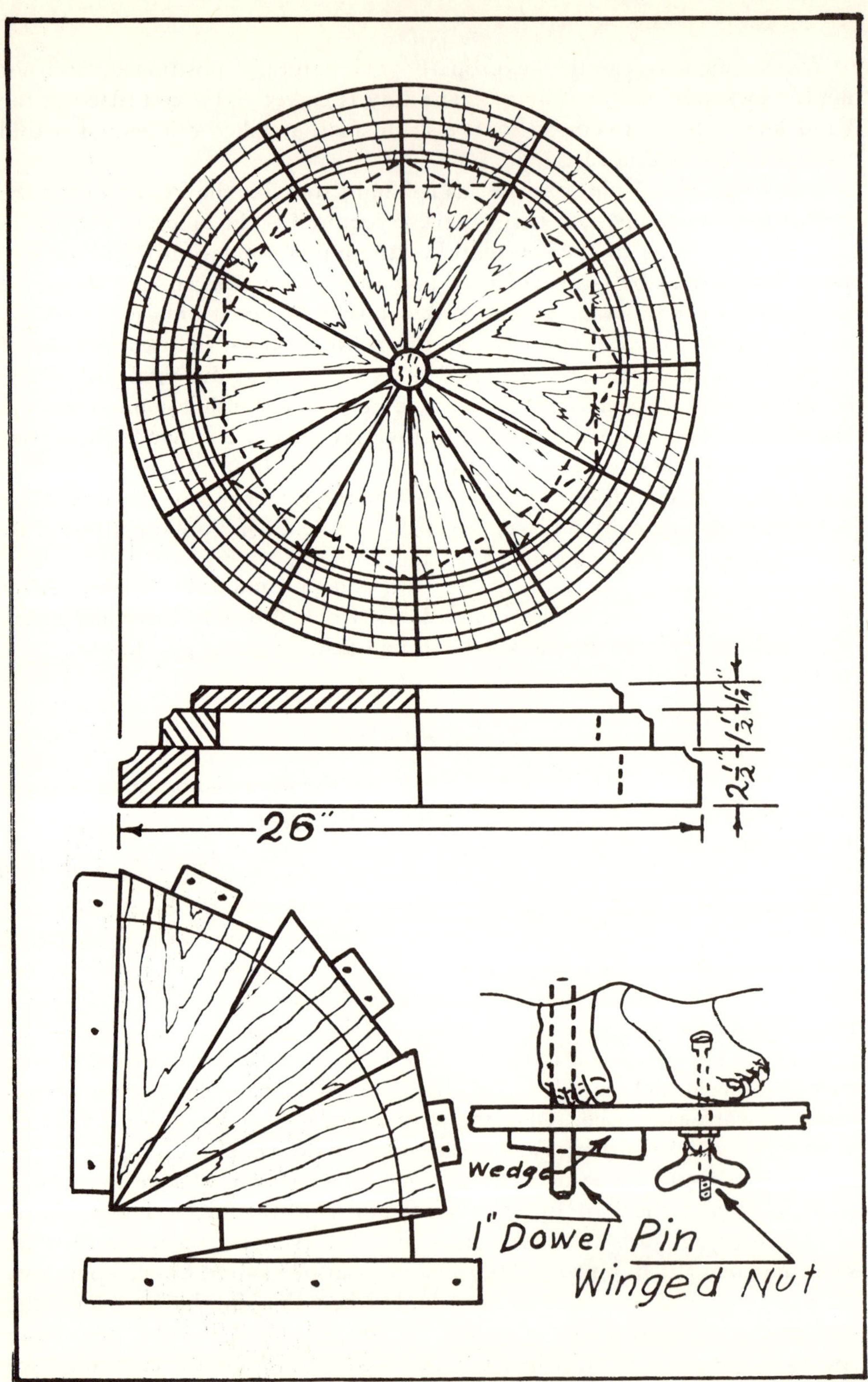

Fig. 8. Details of base for St. Francis.

Bore a suitably sized hole at the center and insert a plug to make a good job. Little surface finishing should be necessary. Sand smooth. Use a spokeshave to smooth the edge and cut the concave depression or core on a shaper or by hand.

The other two parts which make up the base are formed by cutting six segments each, as shown in the drawing. Notice that the hexagon shapes are staggered to increase the strength. The segments are glued and screwed to the top of the base already formed. This is a comparatively simple job but do it carefully. Fasten the middle section to the top and cut the core trim before fastening the bottom form in place. As the shapes are already formed before fastening to the top, they must be concentrically fastened together. Form the bottom and fasten in position.

After sanding all parts smooth, the base is ready for the finish. A clear varnish or lacquer finish is best. Proceed as follows: Apply a good coat of wood sealer. After it has set up, rub down with steel wool to remove any curtains, dust, or rough spots. Brush off the surface thoroughly. Next, apply a coat of clear varnish or lacquer with a clean soft brush. Avoid curtains, fisheyes, or other blemishes. Allow to rest for at least two days in a warm room; a cold room will prevent the finish from setting up properly, and the time required will be considerably longer. With steel wool or sandpaper that has already been used (a new piece of sandpaper might scratch the surface too deeply), rub down the surface lightly–just enough to give it "teeth." Apply another coat of finish and allow to set up properly. Repeat the teething procedure and apply a final coat of finish. When completely dry, this coat may be rubbed down with pumice stone and linseed oil to dull the bright shine.

Now the base is completed and it should be an example of good cabinet construction. The holes for fastening the statue should be bored next. Study the drawing detail (Fig. 8). Bore a 1″ hole for about six inches up the right leg of the figure and glue in a 1″ dowel pin, allowing 4″ to protrude beyond the heel. Cut a ¼″ slot (about 2″ long) 1″ down from the heel. This is for the wedge shown in place in the drawing detail. Locate the right foot on the base and bore a 1″ hole for the dowel. Insert the dowel and drive in the wedge. Turn the statue on the base until it is properly positioned. In the center of the left foot, near the origin of the toes, bore a hole ¼″ deep the size of a head of a 3/8″ carriage bolt. Continue the hole through the foot and the base with a 3/8″ drill. Insert a 3/8″ carriage bolt the proper length and screw fast with a wing nut. This wing nut might have to be fabricated. The hole in the left foot may have to be drilled from the bottom. The frock might prevent the counterbored hole from being bored from the top; if so, it must be gouged out with a gouge.

The holes in the base should be accurately located. This may be done before any holes are bored. Place the statue on the base in the proper position and mark around the feet with chalk. Remove the statue and locate the holes and bore them. The counterbored hole in the left foot is for the head of a 3/8″ carriage bolt. Bore deep enough to allow the head to sink below the surface. It may be filled with polyester putty later and trimmed off to conform to the rest of the foot.

After all of the holes are bored, mount the Saint and test out the fastening device. It should work perfectly.

Remove the figure and cover the base with heavy paper or several layers of newspaper to protect the base from sprayed paint. Fasten the saint back in place. He is now ready for the finish. The color should be very dark brown—almost black. Mask the flesh parts with paper and masking tape. After the garment has been finished, paint the flesh parts and hair by hand, using either oils or acrylics.

Birds should be carved for the tray and other logical parts of the figure to support the legend regarding the Saint.

Chapter 15

Metal Sculpture

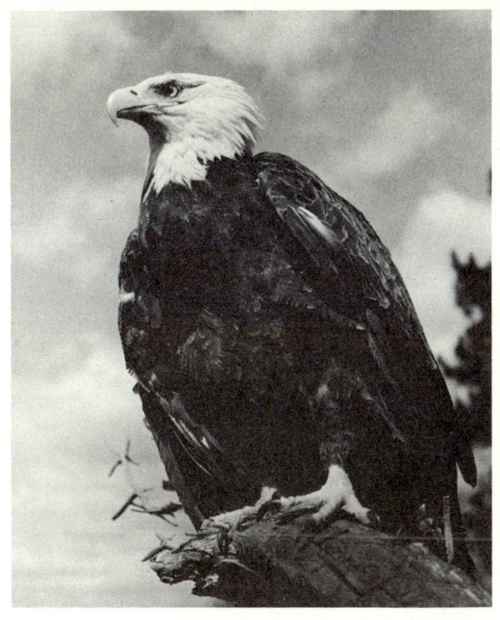

An American bald eagle. *Courtesy:* Michigan Department of Natural Resources.

The writing of this chapter recalls the fruitful years of the thirties when I taught metalwork to high school pupils and one summer session at Millersville State Teachers College. Working with a talented, active group of Industrial Art teachers was one of the greatest satisfactions of my life.

The work of a metalsmith and sculptor is an exciting activity and there are no bounds to the scope or possibilities of a creative and imaginative individual. Only the limitations of skill and energy slow down the creative efforts. The making of a simple candlestick can be as exciting as the fabrication of an intricate grill or the sculptured image of a bald eagle like the one illustrated in the Frontispiece.

Aside from a heating device and a heavy anvil, only a few small tools are necessary such as hammers, tongs, and an assortment of chisels, punches, and chasing tools. Most of the smaller tools are made by hand to accomplish special work and design. With these few tools and equipment a piece of metal may be fashioned into an article of utilitarian worth, or a priceless ornamental sculpture (Fig. 1).

I have used both the forge and the oxyacetylene blowtorch. Both have their advantages and disadvantages; either one supplies the heat necessary. The oxyacetylene outfit is more expensive to operate, but has more versatile possibilities. The forge is more romantic to use, less expensive to operate, but not quite as convenient or flexible in some instances. With the forge you do not have to extinguish the fire—merely turn off the blower, while shaping the metal. The gas heating device requires the flame to be turned off and, in the meantime, the metal is cooling. If welding by the contact method, this interval is critical when working with thin metal. The iron must be hammered together while at welding heat. Some artists prefer the gas method because of the type of work which they do and the instant availability of the method when only a small job is to be done.

At this writing, art metalwork is becoming more popular and metal sculpture has improved. Artists like Ivan Bailey have trained themselves for their

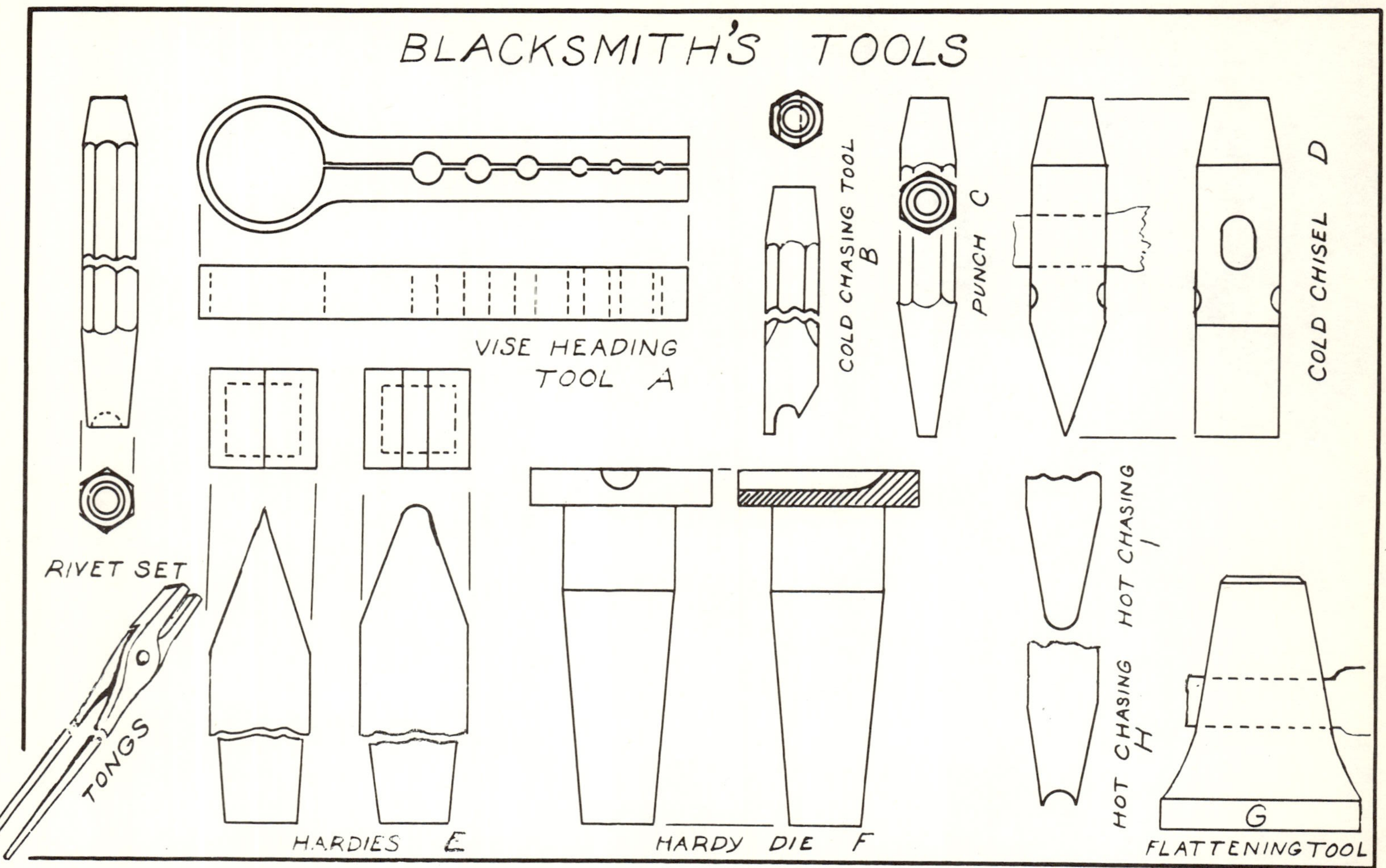
BLACKSMITH'S TOOLS
VISE HEADING
TOOL A
COLD CHASING TOOL
B
PUNCH C
COLD CHISEL D
RIVET SET
TONGS
HARDIES E
HARDY DIE F
HOT CHASING
I
HOT CHASING
H
G
FLATTENINGTOOL

Figure 1.

vocation and seem highly motivated and excited about their work. Unfortunately, all metals are now in short supply and very expensive. In recent months they have almost been priced out of the hands of all but the more affluent metal workers. But, hopefully, better times are ahead when inflation will not sap the limited financial powers of the average artist and he can once again return to his forge and art. The copper for the whooping crane (Fig. 2)

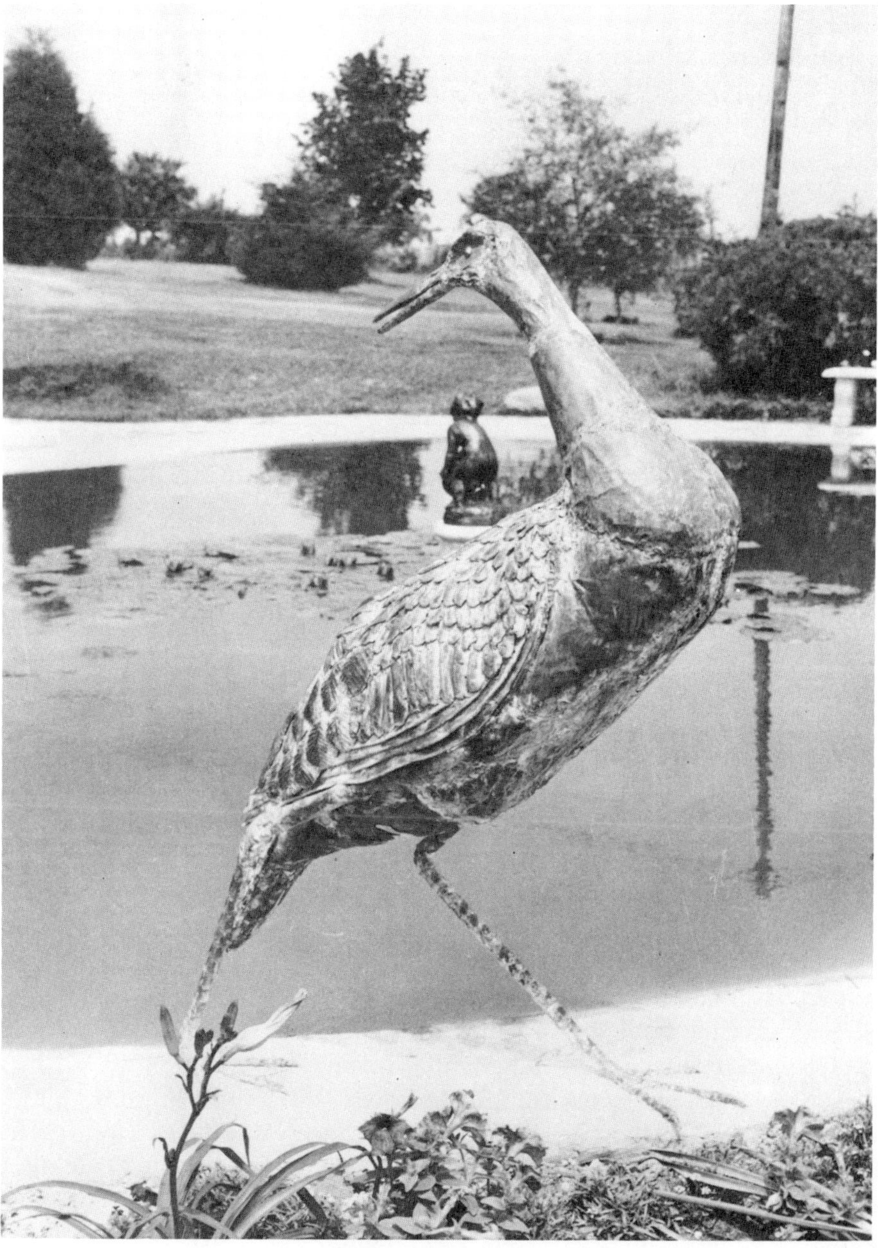

Fig. 2. Whooping crane, by the author.

cost over $125.00 ($2.45 per pound). The material for any type of sculpture has reached an all-time high. But there are some artists who have the "bug" and pay the price for their materials irrespective of the cost. Such an artist is Ted McKinney, the Texas abstractionist. After carving his creations he has them cast in bronze or stainless steel. His sculptures seem to require the lost wax process of casting, so his art is costing him a mint of money. But that is of little concern to him, for he sells his work at a flattering profit. He wants his work to last forever, he says, and his stainless steel sculptures will probably be around some place thousands of years hence to be excavated by archaelogists of a far distant age, long after our civilizations have moldered in the dust.

One can even become overenthused with metalwork without having either the talent or basic information for the art. Unfortunately, some individuals are ill prepared to forge metal in useful and artistic shapes. They are entirely ignorant of the necessary processes and seem unwilling to learn. The bouncing spring arrangement has been mentioned before and is a case in point. The judge of a recent show was more infantile in his judgment than in his knowledge of metal art. Metal sculpture, like all other art mediums, must obey the accepted rules of creative work. It must be aesthetic, skillfully perceived and executed, and indicative of some depth of imagination. If it does not "send" a sensitive person of artistic temperament, it should not be exhibited, but junked—a state where it will be judged solely on its intrinsic worth.

The anvil is the basic piece of equipment for executing metalwork. It has been ever since the crippled Vulcan hammered out armor and weapons for the mythological immortals. A skilled smith can form almost any shape on the various surfaces of an anvil. The anvil consists of a steel body with a cold chilled hardened face. The face has one square hole (hardy hole) for holding hardies and a round hole for bending rods and punching holes. Just below the face and between it and the horn is another flat surface for chipping metal. The angle formed may be used to bend metal in any type of curve. Hammering metal over the open angle is very effective, offering more control than over the horn. The horn, however, is probably used as much as the face of the anvil. It is the form over which most shapes in the metal are made with a blacksmith's hammer.

Hardies are made in many shapes for many uses. There are hot and cold chisel forms, veining shapes and dies for forming various shapes and impressions. They all have a tapered tang which fits into the square hole of the face of the anvil. Wooden forms for turning over edges and "bumping out" depressions are also fashioned to fit in the hardy holes. Most wooden forms may be held in a machinist's vise but not near so effectively. Hot punches and chasing tools are made of square stock (hexagonal or octagonal), fashioned after a hammer with wooden handles (*see* Fig. 1). To use such a tool requires a helper to either hold the material or strike the tool.

The height of an anvil is the distance between the blacksmith's fist and the floor (while standing erect).

Short hot pieces of steel must be held with suitable tongs; they must fit the material to be heated and formed. To hold the reins of the tongs tightly a ring is often slipped over them to relieve the muscles of the hand. In large forge work this technique is always used to hold the tongs together.

Forged metal must be quickly formed. Too much heat not only reduces the metal but otherwise makes it less responsive to the worker. When "bumping out" concave shapes, the metal must be annealed often. In steel, the metal after much use tends to crystallize; in copper, it pulls apart or stretches unevenly. To anneal steel, heat the material red hot and place it in a bed of lime to cool slowly. The opposite technique is used to anneal copper. Heat the metal red hot and plunge it in a container of water. The number of times the metal must be annealed depends upon the depth of the depression—how much the metal must be stretched.

Both steel and copper may be stretched to various shapes either by hammering or by pressure between dies. Automobile fenders and other deep-drawn parts are formed by huge presses several stories high exerting several hundred tons of pressure. The small shop artist may cut dies of various designs to stretch his own shapes. They should not, however, be over 6″ in diameter. A hydraulic press will be necessary. Hydraulic jacks may be purchased reasonably and they may be improvised in a holding device to press together the top and bottom dies.

Hammering metal to shape over wooden depressions has already been suggested. The method shows tool marks which are not objectionable. In fact, the depressions of a ball peen hammer are often intentionally made for ornamental effects. Metal may be stretched in almost any shape (*see* Figs. 2 and 28–30). There must be, however, considerable "know-how" to make a door knocker like those created by Thomas F. Googerty. When you can form sheet metal and bars into door knockers like those illustrated, you have arrived at your journeyman skills. When you can design them to look as attractive as Googerty's, you are an artist of metalwork.

A process of forming metal called "repoussé" is seldom discussed. In this method the metal is worked from the reverse side on a bed of pitch. (Light depressions, such as leaves, may be formed on a close-grained block of wood, end grain up.) The pitch will yield sufficiently with the tools used to avoid cutting or tearing the metal. Old masters, four centuries before Christ, performed amazing work using this technique; their figures and images are nearly drawn in the round. Some of these works may be seen in the British Museum and are known as the "Sires bronzes." The repoussé work of Samuel Yellin is excellent, as would be expected, but, unfortunately the photographs do not show this quality (Figs. 3–5). Working from the reverse side is difficult. Even the old masters melted off the pitch after forming their images and poured it in the cavities on the reverse side and touched up their

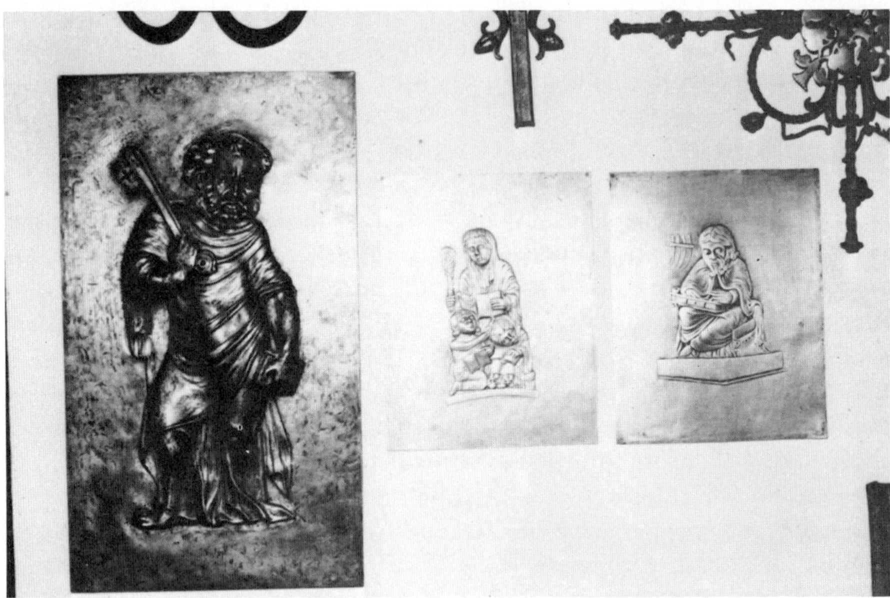

Fig. 3. Repoussé figures by Samuel Yellin.

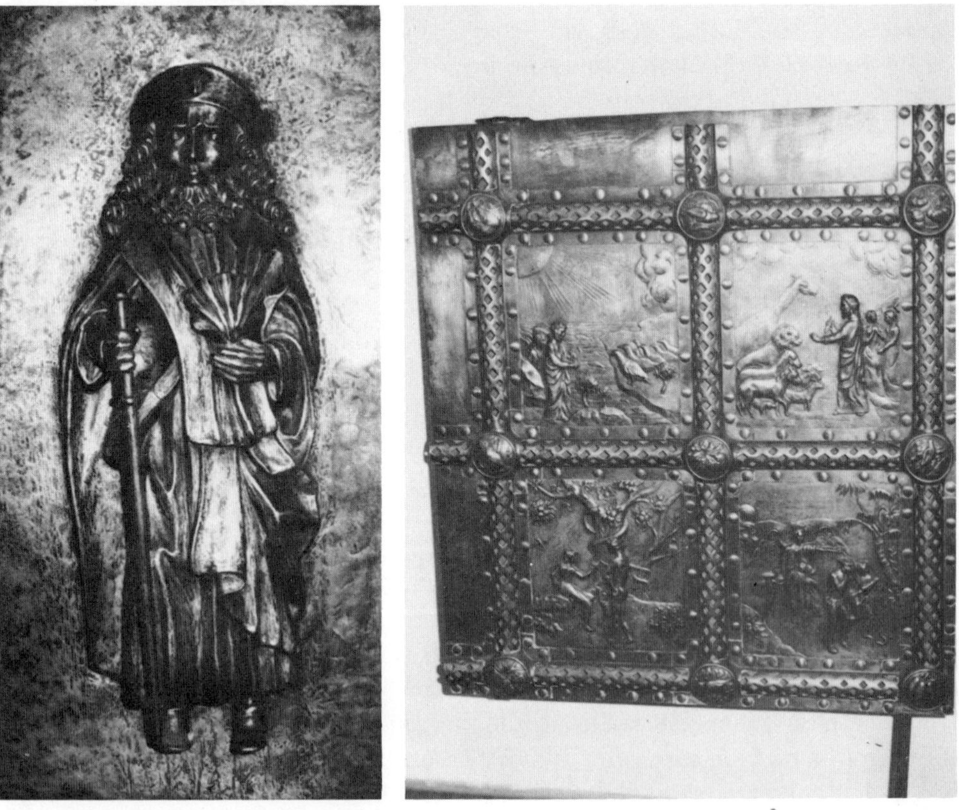

Fig. 4 (left). Repoussé figure of St. James Major, from a sheet of 1/16″ iron. Fig. 5 (right). Repoussé panels for a door by Samuel Yellin.

work from the right side. The Byzantine artist which excelled in all forms of metal work kept the repoussé art alive after the fall of the Roman Empire. In the 15th century, the artists of the Renaissance revived the art and brought it to flower.

This chapter is not intended to be an elementary treatment of art metalwork. The individual who desires to profit from this discussion is presumed to have had some previous experience in working metals. Therefore, explanatory details are brief, using the art of suggestion as the motivating drive. The emphasis is really on experimentation and exploration, for any adventure into the unknown is a courageous activity of excitement and expectations. So a minimum of detail in the projects illustrated (with the exception of the bald eagle) should not be too frustrating. Therefore, advance with your tools and imagination, brave one, and may heaven bless your every effort.

Fabricated Metal Sculpture

Giant Steel Eagle

The American bald eagle is an interesting bird and is the main project of this chapter (Fig. 6). Throughout recorded history more has probably been written about the eagle than any other bird. The prophet Isaiah, to express his thought of emotional regeneration of faith in the Lord, wrote: "They shall mount up with wings like eagles." Seventeen books of the Bible mention the eagle. The people of all ages, in every clime, used the eagle to symbolize *courage, strength,* and *freedom.*

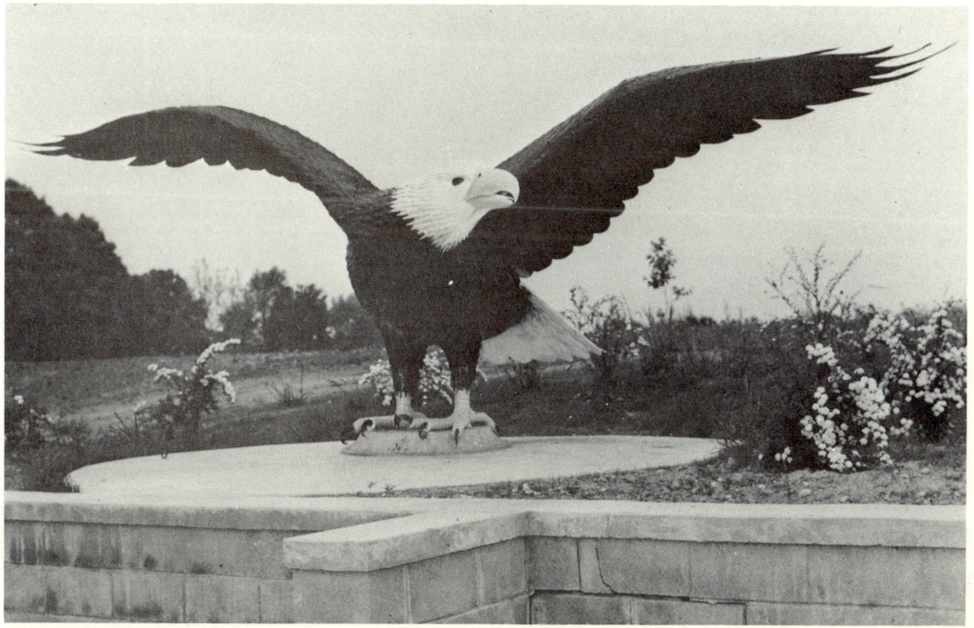

Fig. 6. Bald eagle fabricated of steel rods and sheet metal by the author. Wingspread, 20 feet; weight, about 1,500 pounds.

More than 3,000 years before our Christian era, the eagle was the guardian divinity of the people of Lagash, that ancient city of Mesopotamia in the valley of the Twin Rivers, probably the cradle of all mankind. Throughout the ages its divinity has hardly diminished in any country to which it was native. The Romans believed the eagle was the bearer of their souls to the stars. In fact, it symbolized the whole Roman Empire in the days of its grandeur.

Zeus of Greece and, of course, his Roman counterpart, Jupiter, were linked with the eagle. Before these gods finally perished, a God-child was born in Bethlehem. Some years later the onslaught of Christianity conquered these mythological gods and the civilizations they were ordained to protect and preserve. Only the eagle survived. He lost his divinity but not his soul.

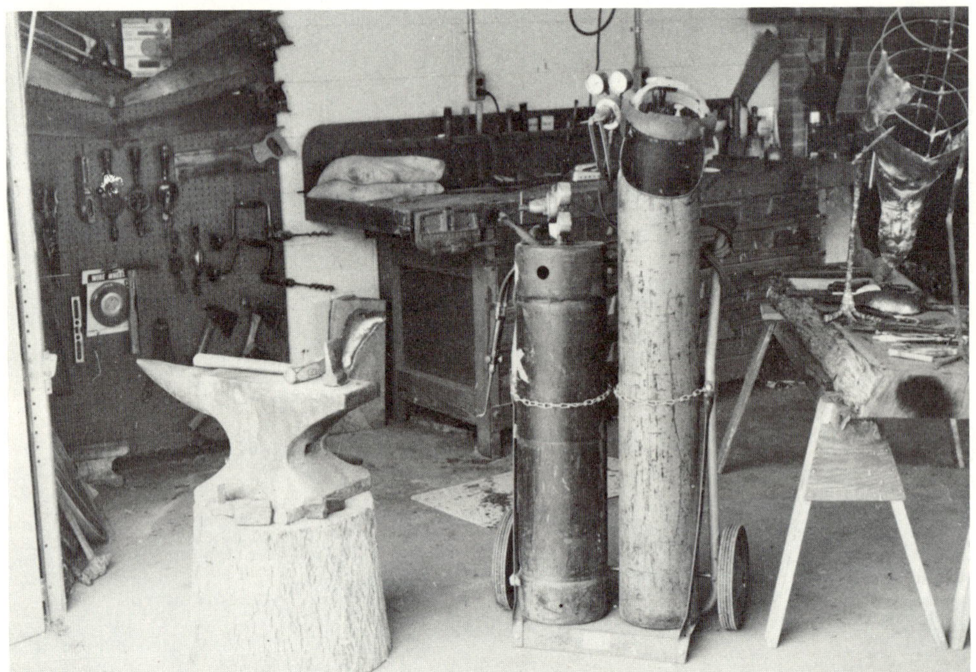

Fig. 7. View of the author's shop showing oxyacetylene welding outfit. Note skeleton of whooping crane (right) and sandbags on the workbench.

His symbolic traits could not be destroyed, and so his form has come down to us, not only in the flesh, but as symbols, or motifs on coins, stamps, seals, and other national imagery. Even our own national seal is dominated by the figure of an eagle. Its very name possesses a magic charm to thrill the soul of all patriots. Even our own Benjamin Franklin, that colonial giant among men, could not take this glory from him.

For several years after I began to carve birds, I had dreamed of fabricating a giant eagle. So, in the spring of 1971 I bought an oxyacetylene welding outfit and began plans for my steel bird. My shop was already equipped with a large anvil and other necessary tools for the work (Fig. 7) and during the early part of World War II, had supervised six teachers in gas and electric arc welding (around the clock) in a war production training program. So I was acquainted with both processes of welding and could do a presentable job in either process myself. Everything necessary seemed to be going for me, so I began building the form for the base of my giant bald eagle.

While every effort has been made to give enough detail in fabricating the eagle, only the gross ideas are sometimes given, leaving to the imagination of the artist the task of solving any problems which might arise—to correct any mistakes or take advantage of them. Mistakes are often an advantage. They may be like accidental strokes of a brush on canvas or a chisel on a sculpture, much better than the preconceived idea or intention. Rodin once told Malvina Hoffman: "Catch the accidents and convert them into science." It

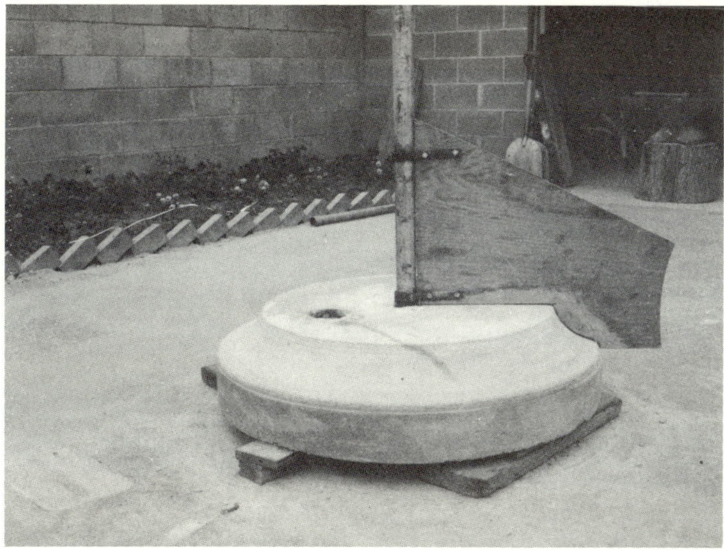

Fig. 8. Concrete base with sweep in place.

happened to me while attaching the skeleton of the secondary feathers of the right wing. I had designed the rods to be opposite those of the left wing. After the rods were welded in place, the "error" was discovered. They had been advanced up the body several inches, but *they looked just right.* Then the muscles of the wing were considered with the turn of the head. Of course, the right wing would be pulled forward ahead of the left wing due to the tension and the natural response of the wing muscles.

Figure 8 is a photograph of the cast concrete base showing the sweep in place. To receive some supplementary information concerning this method of working concrete, read Chapter 16.

To build the form for the base, proceed as follows: First, build a platform of tongued and grooved boards about 40″ square. Nail these boards to two 4″ x 4″ stock. Locate the center of the platform and screw down tightly a

1″ pipe flange. Screw into it a piece of 1″ pipe long enough to rise above the sweep. Inscribe a circle about 38″ in diameter and bend around it a piece of 1/8″ masonite, 6″ wide. Have the ends meet in a corner of the platform and fasten them to a bracket installed for this purpose. Install a bracket in each corner and nail the masonite to it. These four supports should be enough to hold the form in place as the cement will tend to pull the form in a circular shape. Next, locate the centers for the leg holes. They should be 15½″ apart and located in the center of the form. Turn on a lathe two disks, from 2″ stock, to fit loosely in a 3″ pipe. Nail these disks in place to hold the pipe forms. If a lathe is not available, square pieces of stock which will just fit inside of the pipe will be satisfactory. Cut two pieces of black pipe 3″ in diameter 1′ long. Wrap these pipes neatly with wrapping paper until the diameter has been increased about 1/8″. This operation will cast a hole into which the leg pipes will slip easily. The axis pipe should be treated likewise, so that it can be removed easily after the concrete has set.

Design and contruct the sweep as shown in Fig. 8. The hinges may be made from band iron 1/8″ x 1″. Fasten the hinges to the sweep with ¼″ x 1½″ R.H. stove bolts. The bottom edge should be shod with 1/8″ x 3/4″ band iron. Drive the nails in slightly countersunk holes and flatten the heads to conform with the surface.

The concrete mix is one part Portland cement, two parts sand, and three parts fine gravel. Mix thoroughly before adding water and use only enough water to bring the mixture to a stiff plastic. If the concrete is too loose it will not hold in place behind the sweep. Fill in the main part of the form. (Be sure the pipe forms for the pipe legs are in place.) Trowel in a batch of concrete near the center and start operating the sweep. Add concrete until the whole base has been swept to shape. Keep working the sweep after the concrete has been shaped to keep the material from falling. Several minutes will be required for the concrete to start setting up. Continue to rotate the sweep from time to time until the concrete starts to harden.

While the base is setting up, the two leg pipes (3″ x 54″) may be formed. First, cut four narrow V's 90° apart, in one end 4″ long. The wide part of the V should be about ¼″. After the V's have been cut, hammer the remaining segments toward the center of the pipe until the V-shaped slots are closed. This technique will make the ends of the pipes smaller in diameter and facilitate their entrance into the cast holes in the base.

The photograph in Fig. 9 shows the leg pipes in place and the ends burned off to conform to the shape of the body hoop. Burning off the ends is not necessary. Also, there should be two hoops of the same size tacked to the pipes, instead of one hoop, one on each side. Later, of course, these hoops should be electrowelded securely as this unit will carry the weight of the whole bird. All joints should be tacked first by the gas welding process, but later a professional electric arc welder should be employed to weld all joints securely. My welder said the eagle would never come apart but it might break up; he was thinking of metal fatigue caused by vibrations. However, over the past three years the eagle has never vibrated appreciably in the strongest wind. Incidentally, an aviator who saw the bird after the wings were installed said: "I hope you have a way of tying this bird down. His wings are set for an ideal takeoff." Fortunately, I had foreseen this problem and had one eyebolt welded under each wing to anchor the eagle to the pavement. But the necessity for that has never arisen.

After the toes have been designed and formed, they should be electrowelded in place and the scales spiraled around them. After this operation the leg pipes should be inserted in their sockets and remain there until after the bird is completely finished.

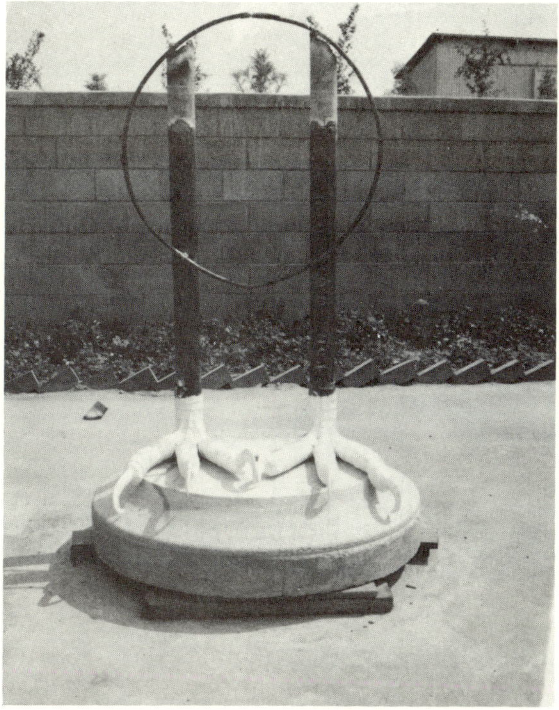

Fig. 9. Legpipes in place.

The middle toe is 16″ long, not counting the claws. A "V" should be cut in the end which fits against the 3″ pipes and the other end cut 45° with the long side down (bottom of the toe). The front of the toe should be covered with a convex piece of sheet metal stretched to the proper depth. To stretch this metal, proceed as follows: Cut a piece of sheet metal about 4″ in diameter. File the inside edge of a piece of 2″ pipe. Form a male die of wood about 6″ long and a little less than the diameter of the 2″ pipe (less two times the thickness of the sheet metal). Round off one end to a semispherical shape. Put the metal over the open end of the pipe, place the wooden die on top and drive the male die into the pipe. Even, solid strokes of the blacksmith's hammer will stretch the metal. Keep the outside metal from

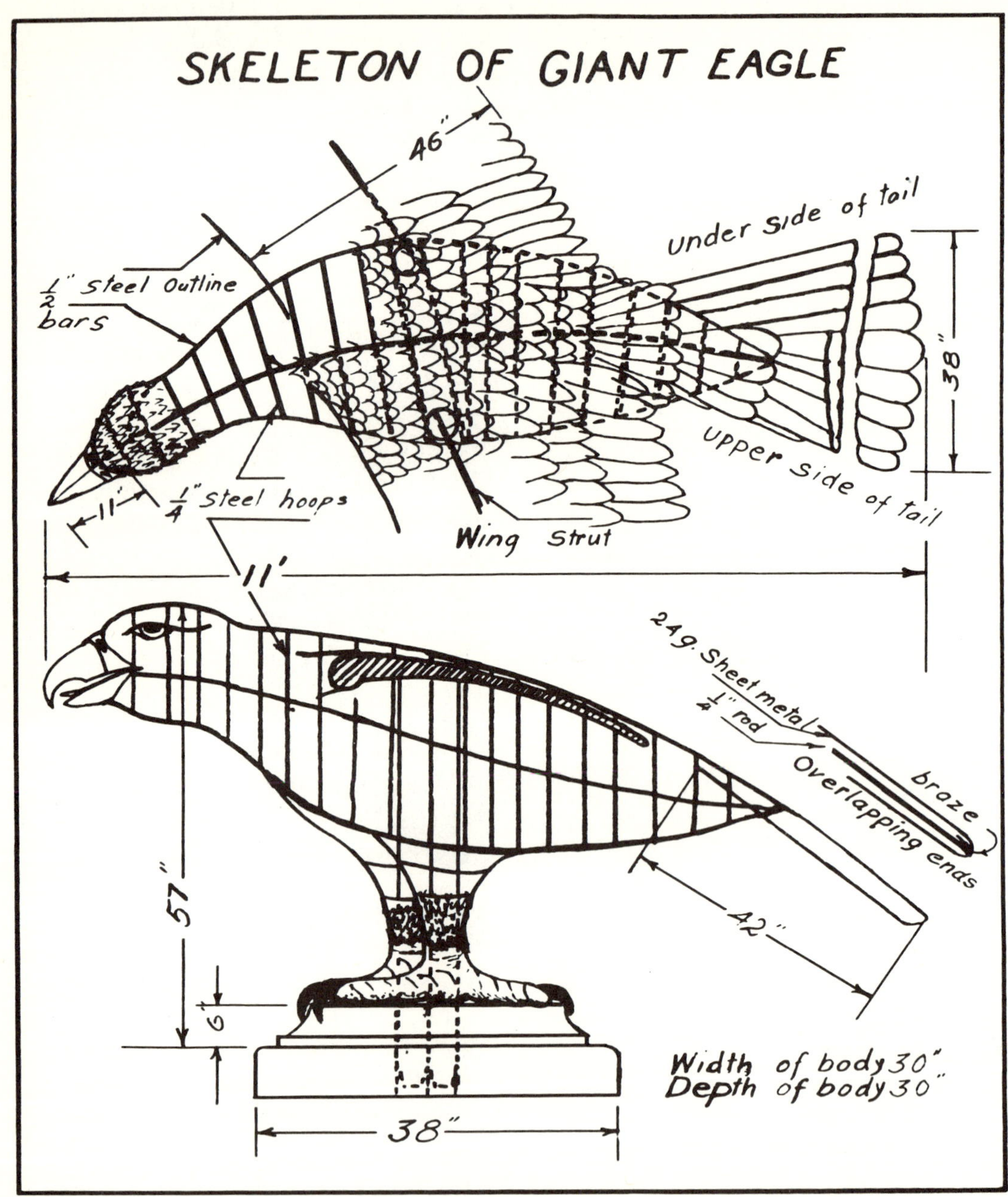
SKELETON OF GIANT EAGLE
46"
Under side of tail
1/2" Steel Outline bars
38"
Upper side of tail
11"
1/4" Steel hoops
Wing Strut
11'
24 g. Sheet metal
1/4" rod
braze
Overlapping ends
42"
57"
6"
Width of body 30"
Depth of body 30"
38"

Figure 10.

hugging the die. Keep the metal flared out so that it will be stretched rather than wrinkled. When the metal has been stretched enough, the die and the stretched form may be removed. Trim the concave formed metal and place over the toe end in a natural position. Braze in place. The other toes should be cut to conform with the middle toe (16″); that is, they should be shorter. The back toe is slightly higher up the leg and about the same length as the outer toes. In brazing the convex caps to the toes, the pipes should be heated hot enough to cause the coated brass welding rod to readily adhere to them. Then the stretched caps should be located in place and brazed fast. Be careful not to burn the sheet metal.

Next, cut strips of sheet metal (24 g.) 2¼″ wide and long enough to spiral around the toes for their entire length. Turn over the ¼″ hem and start the spiraling procedure on the bottom of the toe. The folded edge should be in the direction of the claw end of the toe and the distance apart should be a little less than 2″. Tack the spiraled metal in place as you proceed. The pipe should be entirely covered. Where the spiraled metal joins the legs, the scales should come together in a neat mitered seam. The toes (except the claws) may be completely formed before they are welded to the legs. This procedure might be easier than spiraling the toes after they have been welded to the legs. After the toes have been welded in place, the claws (talons) should be trimmed and adjusted to conform to the concrete base. Braze them in a neat bead to the convex form.

The claws should be carefully designed and two pieces of sheet metal cut to this shape for each claw (8 of them). The root of each claw should be 1½″ wide. Stretch the sides of the claws to a concave shape over the open jaws of a machinist's vise. When placed together, if the sides do not look right, correct your errors and start all over again. Then braze them together from the inside. Open the bottom edges to a desirable width and braze in the opening a piece of sheet metal cut neatly to shape. It should look like an eagle's claws.

After the toes have been welded in place, cut the claws to fit properly over the convex ends. Braze in place with a neat fillet. The feet and the lower section of the legs are the first parts of the bird to be finished. Give them a coat of white rustproof paint.

The photograph in Fig. 9 was referred to earlier. The two hoops, one on either side, are bent to shape easily over the open space of the anvil where the face drops to join the horn. By hammering the ½″ rod over this space, it will bend upward to any degree desired. A chalked design on the floor will aid in bending the hoops to shape. Another method is to use a machinist's vise, bolted fast to a workbench, to tighten two ¾″ bars (about 6″ long) about 2″ apart. Place the hoop bar between these two studs and bend to the required arc. Study the skeleton of the bird as shown in Fig. 10. Bend the "backbone" and belly outline steel as shown (½″ rods). Turn the head in the desired direction and degree. The front termination of these important bars should be welded to the front ¼″ neck hoop and a cross bar of ½″ steel rod (the front ends of the backbone and belly outline rods may be bent over to meet each other near the center of the neck and welded where they overlap). The two body outlines of steel should be bent and welded to the others at the end of the rump, as shown. These too may be bent over in the neck to meet each other and across the backbone and belly outline extensions. The fastening of these important bars should be strongly electrowelded joints.

Bend all of the ¼″ steel hoops to fit the outer sides of the outline bars. Cut the bars longer than necessary so that their ends will overlap, making welding an easier task. Decide the length of the exposed surface of the feathers. Suppose that generally speaking the exposed surface is 4″. Then the ¼″ hoops should be 8″ apart and the feathers cut 9″ long, leaving nearly an extra inch for the split end providing the loop around the hoop as shown in the feathering design, Fig. 15. More than 16 of these hoops will be required. Special hoops may be necessary in certain places, and there are many places which will require the ¼″ bar connections to which the feathers may be fastened. Your fabricated bird should now appear as shown in Fig. 10, excepting the tail form. The tail is formed with ¼″ bars as shown in the top view. Notice that there is a bottom and top, and that the tail has some camber. Generally speaking, the feathers are attached over the ¼″ lengthwisee bars at the center. The drawing does not show this design plainly—merely the feather outlines. The tail is easily formed over the guide reinforcing bars, however. The fabrication of the tail should be an exciting task. Design the first feathers to extend the entire length of the tail. Install the bottom feathers first. Only the crescent edge of the side feathers should be bound with wire. The outside edge should be folded over the guide bars and the other edges left plain. Working toward the center of the tail, the next feathers should be bound with wire except the edge adjacent to the center. The bound edge of the next feather should be brazed to this plain edge. The bound crescent edge should extend from the guide cross bars to make a streamlined finish. The central feather should be bound all around and brazed over the plain edges of the feathers located on each side. The result is a shingled effect with the central feather capping both sides. The top feathers are installed the same way. Be sure that the lower feathers are brazed securely to the frame bars. These bars should be located approximately in the center of the feathers (over the "shafts"). Several loops of sheet metal with the edges turned over in a hem should be used to fasten the feathers in places where brazing cannot be conveniently done.

The crescent, unbound ends of the first row of top feathers are bent over the lower tail feathers and brazed watertight. Only the side feathers need be as long as the tail, but long enough to extend well under the next row of feathers, 16″ from the end of the tail. Remember that the central feather overlaps the adjoining feathers which are brazed shinglewise toward the edges. The next row of feathers (8″ exposed surface) is installed in a similar manner, also, but the crescent edges should be bound with wire. The turned-over edges of the side feathers increase the tail's thickness as the rump is reached.

The triangular section under the rump is covered by a sheet of plain metal cut and bent to shape and brazed fast. Cut a paper pattern for this section to be sure that the metal will fit correctly when bent in position. The small undertail feathers may be brazed to this sheet metal until the ¼″ hoop is

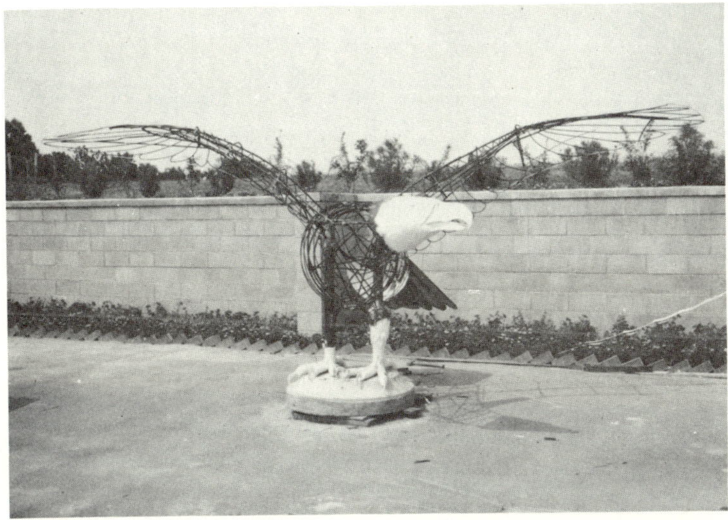

Fig. 11. Steel bars in place; tail and head already fabricated.

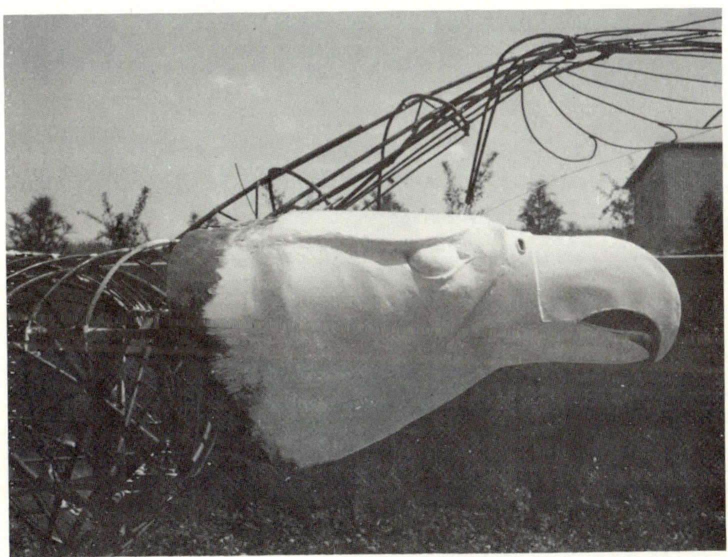

Fig. 12. Detail of head before feathers were attached.

reached. Then the feathering will proceed in a normal fashion. After the tail has been completed and painted with a white rustproof paint, it should appear as shown in Figs. 13 and 14.

Feather most of the under sides of the bird leaving sufficient space for the wings to be attached.

Design the head. Cut paper patterns before you cut the designs in sheet metal. To make the proper contours the metal has to be stretched in many places. Make the bill (or beak) first. Design this part of the head carefully. It is probably the most significant shape in the whole bird. After both sides of

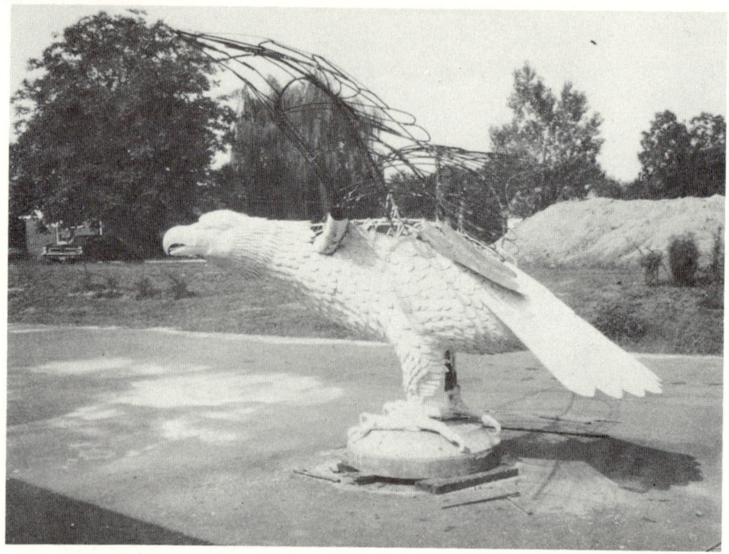

Fig. 13. Feathering completed on one side.

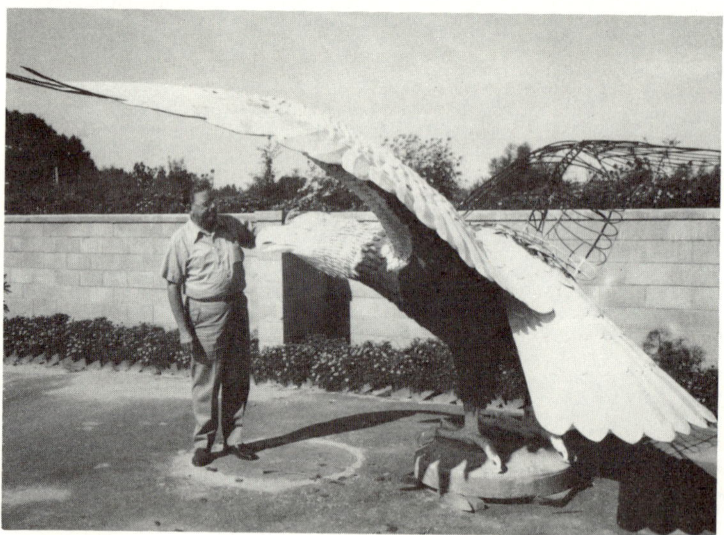

Fig. 14. Left wing installed.

the beak have been cut, hammer them in a concave shape over the open jaws of a machinist's vise. When the two sides are placed together, the beak should look natural. If the appearance pleases you, braze them together from the inside. Leave about a 6″ opening at the base of the upper mandible.

Design a piece of sheet metal to fit the opening and braze in place. Design the lower mandible and hammer it to shape as in the top part. It should fit inside of the upper mandible. If you are clever enough, you may fashion the sides and under part from one piece of metal. Otherwise the lower mandible must be fabricated of three pieces cut to the proper shape. Fabricate the tongue and braze it in place before attaching the lower mandible. The elevated section at the base of the beak in which the nostrils are formed is designed and the forward edge turned over 14 g. wire. Bend it in place and braze fast. Make the nostrils separately and braze to the beak.

The head proper should extend toward the tail to the first ¼″ hoop where the outline bars are welded together. Design the head pattern of paper first and be sure the paper pattern is correct before cutting the sheet metal. The seam should be on top of the head. Be careful of the beak end. Notice the pronounced "V" shape where the two mandibles come together. After the metal has been cut to its proper shape, bind the forward edge with wire and bend in position. Some hammering will be necessary to stretch the metal to cause the head to be shaped properly. Wooden mallets with peen heads like the ones body and fender workers use are ideal for stretching metal. Shape the head to beautiful and natural contours before brazing together. Be sure the tail end slips over the ¼″ hoop. Cut the holes for the eyes. The eyes are made like the caps for the toes by stretching sheet metal down a 2″ pipe with a male die. Braze the eyes in place and form the eye cavity. The fold over the eye is a specially designed sheet of metal brazed over the top of the head. Study the photograph in Fig. 12.

In stretching metal freehand, peened depressions will be left by the mallet or hammer. Again the body and fender-working techniques may be used. Fill in the depressions and make a smooth surface by spreading polyester filler or putty over the low spots. While the putty itself is not waterproof, the paint which covers the bird is. Give the completed head a coat of white rustproof paint. The surface should appear smooth and devoid of peen marks. Braze the head in place.

Wing Structure and Design

The main support for the wings is a fabricated strut (*see* Fig. 15). It originates at the leg pipes and extends to the primary feathers, tapering along the length to a single ½″ bar. It is located in the high curve of the wing. The strut should be welded very securely to the leg pipes for this section of the bird must carry all of the weight of the wings which are nearly 10′ long. The cross struts are shaped as the cutaway section indicates. There are three, evenly spaced—the first at the joint where the wings and the back of the bird come together. These cross struts carry the feather bars shown by dotted lines in the top view of Fig. 15. Install the longest two primary feathers. This location should be the starting point for a long No. 10 g. wire outlining the shape of the wing at the primary and secondary feathers. Temporarily tack

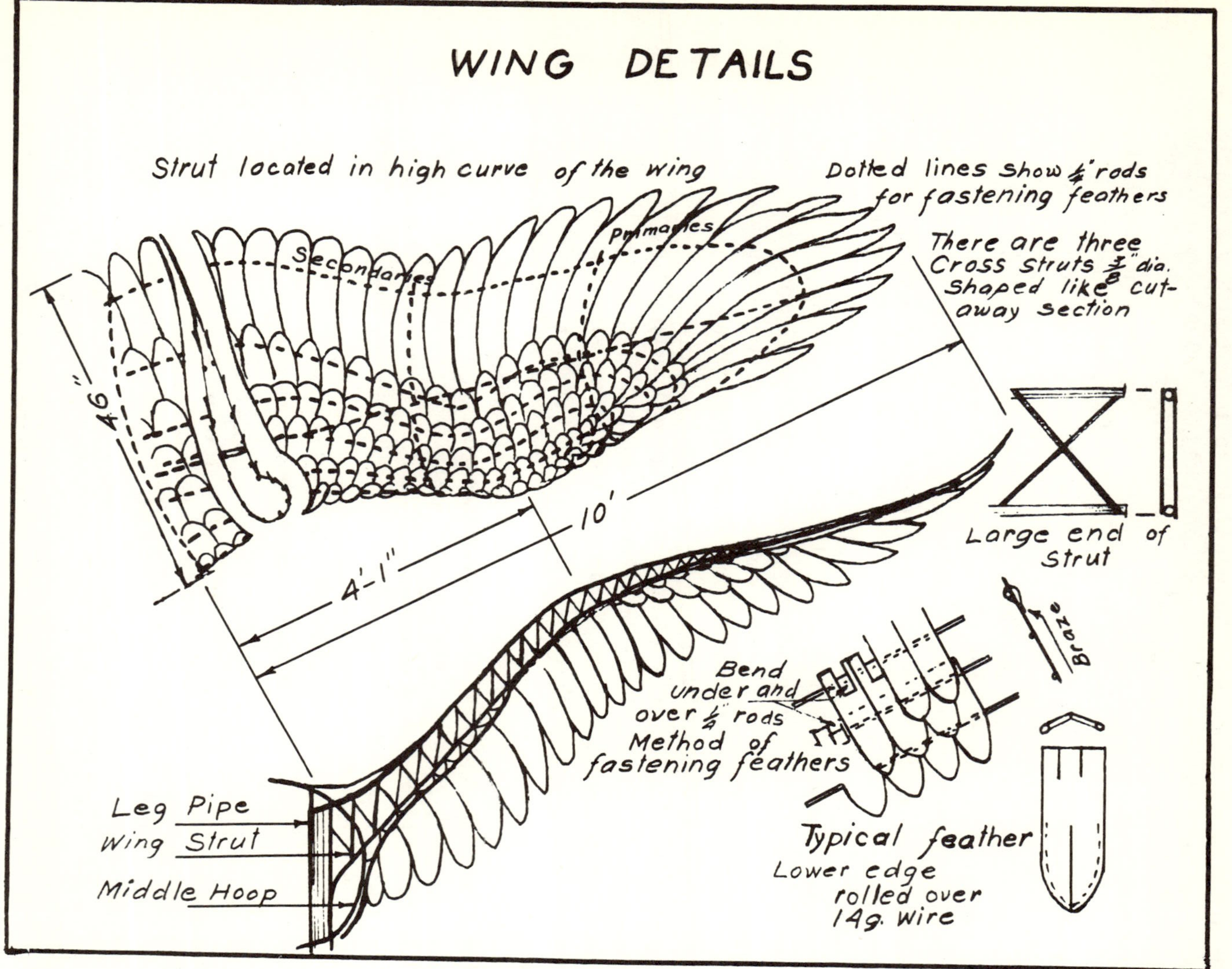
WING DETAILS
Strut located in high curve of the wing
Dotted lines show 1/4" rods for fastening feathers
There are three Cross struts 3/8" dia. Shaped like cut-away section
Primaries
Secondaries
46"
4'-1"
10'
Large end of Strut
Braze
Bend under and over 1/4" rods
Method of fastening feathers
Leg Pipe
Wing Strut
Middle Hoop
Typical feather
Lower edge rolled over 14g. wire

Figure 15.

the wire in a position to guide the location of the feathers while being installed. Start with the first secondary feather. (The body feathers at this place should have been installed.) Design it and cut it to shape. Bind the edge next to the body and the crescent end. The under part of the wing should be fabricated first. Leave the edge toward the wing tip plain. The No. 10 wire may be tacked to this feather after it is brazed in place. Remember the shaft elevation. The center of each feather, large or small, should be shaped as shown in the detail in Fig. 15. This elevation is simply done by placing the feather over the open jaws of a machinist's vice and hammering a ½″ rod over the center. In some of the long feathers this center elevation must be curved to follow the contour of the feather. The secondary feathers are fastened to the ¼″ bars by brazing them together. The ends of the feathers should be split and the middle section bent over the bar in a loop and brazed in place. The second feather should be designed like the first but the edge toward the body turned over 14 g. wire and brazed over the plain edge of the first feather. The guide wire should establish its main position on the wing. Design and fabricate all secondary feathers in the same manner as the first two. There are usually ten secondary and ten primary feathers on a wing; design your feathers accordingly. The primaries are shaped differently, and usually longer but are installed like the secondaries. After the last feather is installed, the trailing edge of the wing should closely resemble the design of the drawing. Make a number of metal loops with the edges turned over in a hem to braze over the bars to attach the feathers whenever and wherever necessary. Chalk the design of the small feathers on the large feathers already brazed in place. Proceed with the small feathers until they are all installed. The feathers are small near the advancing edge of the wing and around the circular edge. This is a tedious procedure but it must be done. Several ¼″ bars should be brazed on the round edge of the cross struts (parallel to each other) to which the feathers are to be brazed. After all of the feathers have been installed, the under feathers should be given a coat of rustproof paint on both top and under surfaces.

The top wing feathers are installed like the under side. First, start with the first secondary. Its edges should be left plain all around. Fold the edge toward the body over the under feather and braze lightly the entire length. Fold the crescent edge over the under secondary and braze it fast. Loop the split middle section of the other end around the ¼″ bar and start the second secondary. The body edge is bound with wire this time and brazed to the plain edge of the first. The crescent end is turned over the lower secondary and brazed fast, as in the first instance. Braze solid all joints where water might enter and tack securely to the bars and under feathers where necessary. Proceed along the wing until all of the secondaries and primaries have been brazed in place. (The No. 10 g. wire may be removed as the feathers are completed.) Chalk out the design of the small feathers and proceed to braze them in place as in the large feathers. Now, however, the exposed surface of each feather must be bound all around with wire to give it definition.

Throughout the construction of the eagle there will be times when you will have to use your imagination. Many techniques are inadvertently unmentioned. It is assumed that the individual attempting this project has considerable mechanical ability and some know-how in working metal. Such a person can fill in the gaps of instruction and do a masterful job. Cutting out the feathers, binding them, and otherwise shaping them is a tedious procedure. Double-action tin snips will make this job much easier. An anvil and sheet-metal worker's tools will be of great help too. The great reward will be brazing the feathers in place and observing the development of the eagle. You will have plenty of company. Many people will become interested in your bird, and when he is close to completion they will beat a path to your shop.

Before the back feathers are installed, the inside of the bird should be sprayed with several coats of rustproof paint. The procedure will greatly help to prevent condensation rust. Notice how the long slim head feathers are installed. If the head is not properly shaped, correction may be made with the head feathers.

Paint your bird a dark, dark brown. Of course, the head and tail feathers are white. Give the eagle several coats of lacquer and if any open places are discovered, fill them with polyester putty and paint over them. Three coats should be sufficient for the first year. Then the bird may be painted two more coats which should last indefinitely. Automotive lacquer should be used for satisfactory results.

Now you are ready to move your bird to its permanent location. Our bird faces down the long driveway toward Route 291. Bob Irwin, manager of the Delmarva Power and Light Company (in our community), seemed very happy to use his equipment to lift the bird over the concrete block wall—gratis. I mention this fact not only to suggest a method of moving your bird, but also to show that there is still some kindness left in this sordid world and that all service is not equated with a fast buck. Study the picture of the bald eagle which the Michigan Department of Natural Resources allowed us to use (see headpiece). Study all of the pictures and drawings before starting this project, especially the frontispiece. It is a big job but extremely rewarding.

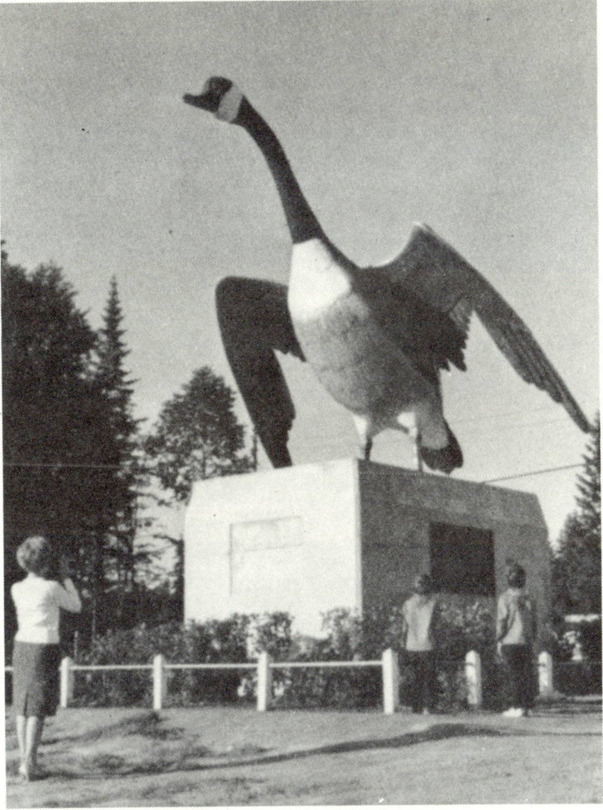

Fig. 16. A 24-foot, steel, 3,500-pound Canada goose welcomes visitors to Wawa, Ontario, Canada. Wawa is the Indian word for the Canada goose. *Courtesy:* Canadian Government Travel Bureau.

FABRICATED METAL SCULPTURE

David Caccia

David Caccia was fortunate enough to be born of artist parents. In such an inherited social environment there is little wonder that he is not only sensitive to the beauties of nature, but possesses outstanding talent in creating the likeness of birds and flowers with sheet metal and torch.

He took various courses, including sculpture, at the Graphic Sketch Club in Philadelphia, and a course in metal sculpture at the Tyler Art School, Temple University, also located in Philadelphia.

David believes a piece of sculpture succeeds or fails according to its artistic merits, regardless of subject matter. But the subjects an artist chooses reveal much about his artistic values. There is a wild smack in his work and we need artists to show us wildness. More than ever before, Thoreau's words ring true: "In wilderness is the preservation of the world."

David also sculpts plants with his torch. Currently he is working on a series of orchids and other wildflowers in stainless steel. One of these is in the collection of the Botanical Museum at Harvard. His work is represented in many private collections, including Prince Bernhard's, of the Netherlands. An osprey he made now graces the top of the new Wildlands Institute building at Stone Harbor, N.J.

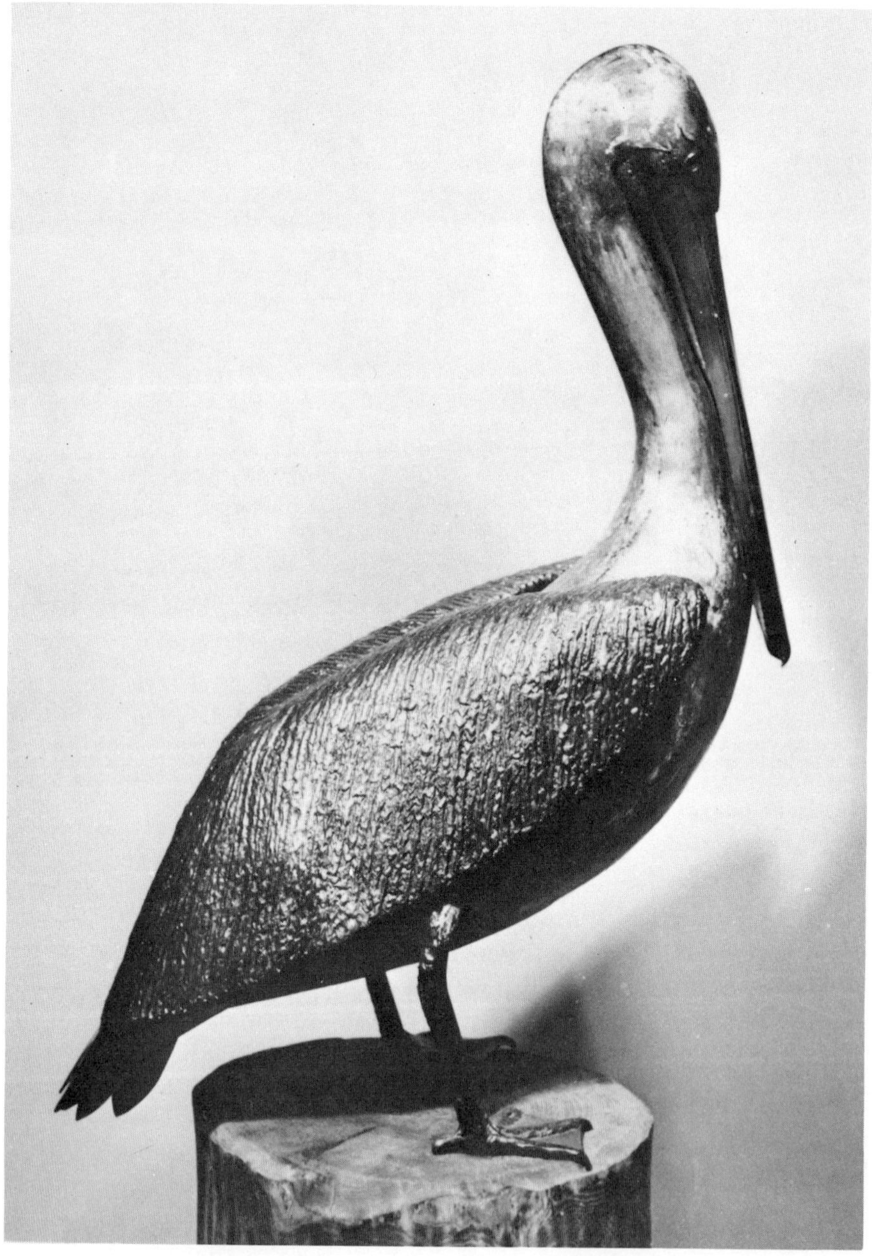

Fig. 17. Metal pelican, by David Caccia.

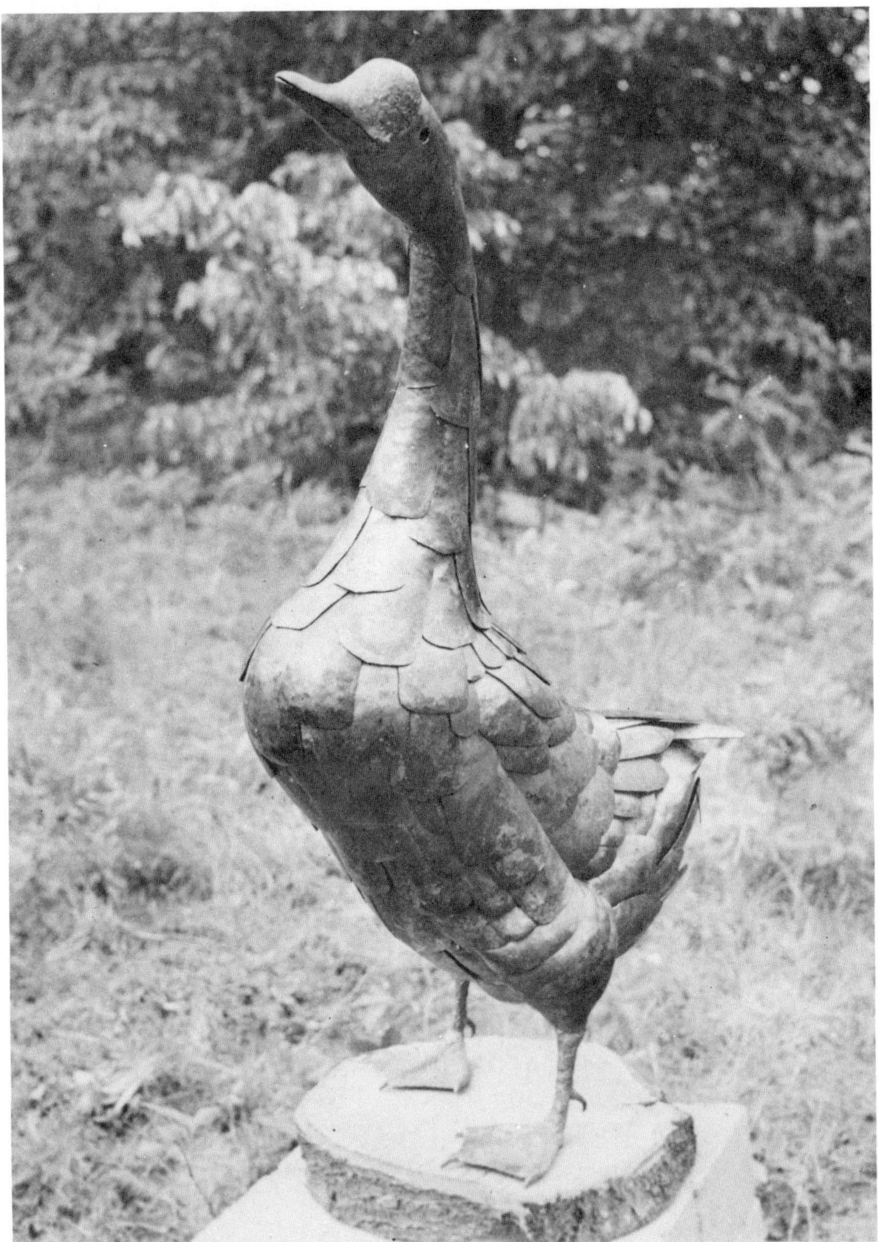

Fig. 18. Metal goose, by David Caccia.

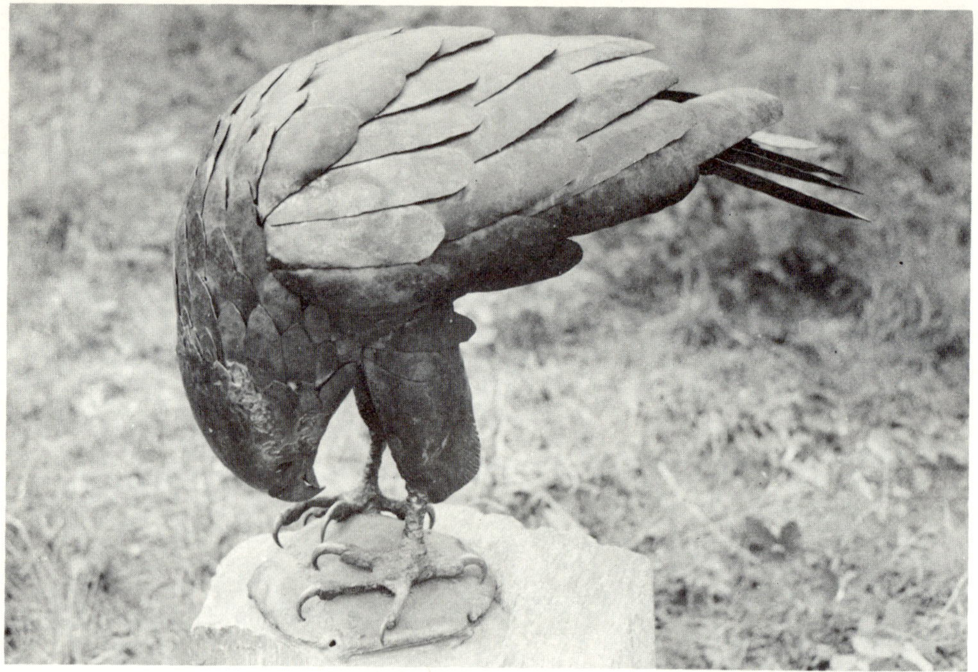

Fig. 19. Metal eagle, by David Caccia.

Alois A. Klein

Alois A. Klein of The Milestone Studio, East Concord, N.H., has acquired skills in many crafts through study at the Technical High School in Newark, N.J., Newark Academy of Art, Famous Artists School in Westport, Conn., and from many years of experience in a great variety of media. He has been a commercial illustrator, an industrial designer for various industries in New Jersey and in recent years has spent most of his time at metal sculpture and wood carvings of all sorts, but especially in the area of waterfowl and other birds. He has commissioned pieces in the Manchester National Bank, Concord National Bank, both in New Hampshire, the library in Elkton, Maryland, to list a few. He has exhibited and sold in New Jersey, Massachusetts, Maine, New York state, and the Wildlife and Waterfowl Show in Salisbury, Maryland. Mr. Klein is a member of the League of New Hampshire Craftsmen and has served on many of its committees, The New Hampshire Art Association in Manchester, and in order to keep up with the rest of the world, aside from enjoying it, teaches for the League of New Hampshire Craftsmen and the Manchester Institute of Arts and Sciences.

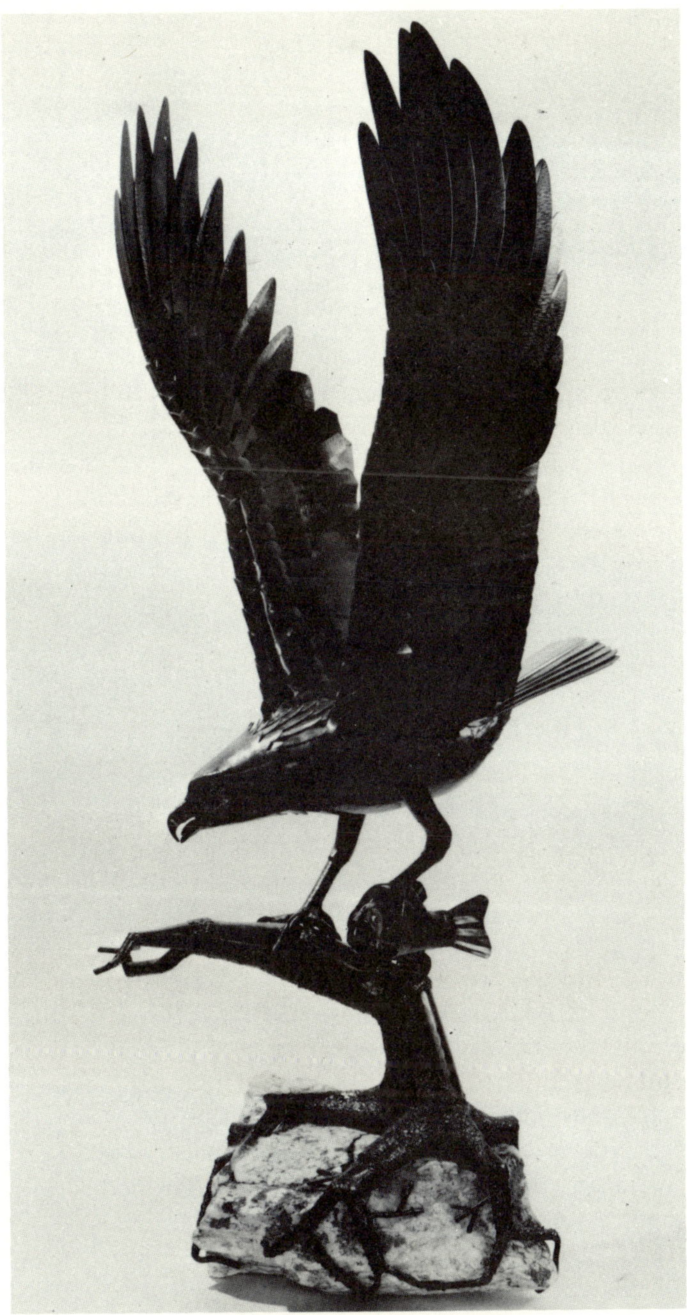

Fig. 20. Osprey. A steel sculpture, by Alois A. Klein. Overall height 48″; width 19″.

BLACKSMITHING

Samuel Yellin*

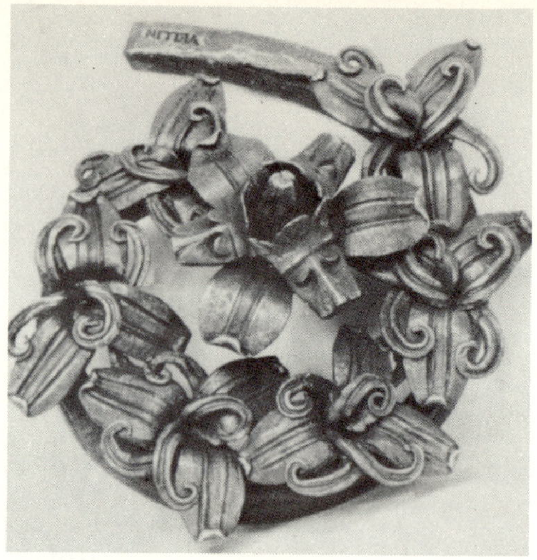

A smith cannot busy himself with iron alone, but must be on familiar terms with all of his brother crafts, at least so far as to understand their close affiliation.

Samuel Yellin

In 1906 a very talented young man, born in Galicia, Poland, emigrated to America and settled in Philadelphia. He was only 21 years old but he had already finished his apprenticeship under a Russian taskmaster in the blacksmith trade. His name was Samuel Yellin. He immediately applied for a job in a factory specializing in ornamental, wrought-iron bedposts.

"What can you do?" inquired the manager.

"A great many things," replied Samuel.

The manager pointed to a grotesque finial and told him to forge one. Samuel selected a piece of iron and in a few minutes had hammered out a replica.

"How did you do it so quickly?" asked the astonished manager.

"Such things have to be done quickly or better not at all."

Samuel was hired at $6.00 per week.

Fortunately, at the turn of the century a renaissance was occurring in the handcrafts in America, fortunately not only for the arts but for Samuel Yellin as well. The time was opportune for the exercise of his exceptional skill as a wrought-iron craftsman. He quickly won recognition and was engaged to organize and teach ironwork classes in the Philadelphia Museum and the School of Industrial Art. This phase of his work I have not researched, but in any event teaching did not appeal to him as much as owning his own shop. The "blacksmith," as he chose to call himself, rented a two-room garret where clients soon beat a path to his door.

In 1910 he built the present Spanish style, stucco building on Arch Street in west Philadelphia which now contains a museum of his work, and "my room" where he dreamed about his many projects.

In the early twenties his shop on Arch Street employed over 200 skilled craftsmen and his work was in demand all over the country. The architect of any monumental project thought that only Yellin could supplement his dream with suitable grills and light fixtures; the name Yellin became famous. Myriad awards and citations began to be presented by all kinds of organizations. Perhaps U.S. Senator George Pepper, in a speech concerning the Philadelphia

---

*The information for this brief sketch was gleaned from: "Sketches in Iron: Samuel Yellin," by Myra Tolmach Davis; The Dimock Gallery, George Washington University Auditorium, 21st. and H Sts. N.W., Washington, D.C.

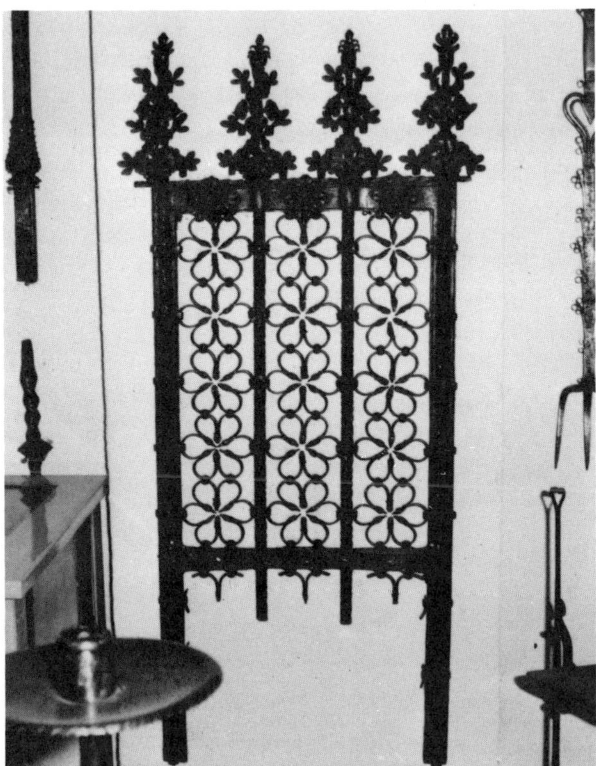

Fig. 21. Prototype of the children's gate, National Cathedral, Washington, D.C., by Samuel Yellin.

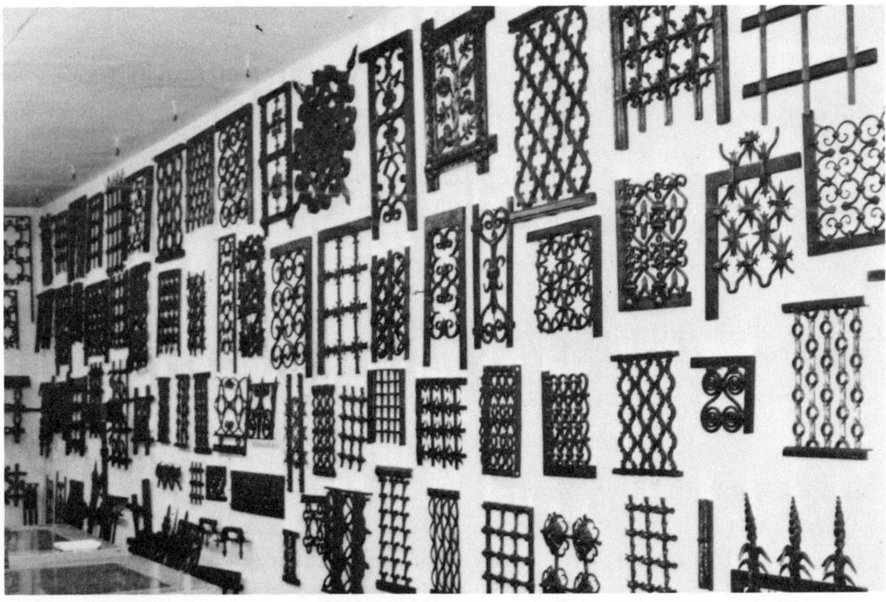

Fig. 22. Prototype forgings of famous work by Samuel Yellin, commissioned by various architects, institutions, and foundations. All eight walls of the two-room museum are covered with them.

Civic Award, summed up the reasons, in part, for all of them: Because of Samuel Yellin "the name of Philadelphia in iron craftsmanship stands for the very best in the artistic of all times. In honoring him we honor ourselves."

His authority in his chosen field was such that the Encyclopedia Britannica requested him to write the section "Modern Technique and Practice" on iron for its 14th edition. The Philadelphia Museum engaged him as a consultant. It was in this capacity while traveling abroad that he collected over 700 pieces of medieval English wood carving dating from the 13th to the 16th centuries. Yellin has been called the "poet in iron." Franklin Gordon gave him this distinction in *The American Hebrew* of September 11, 1925.

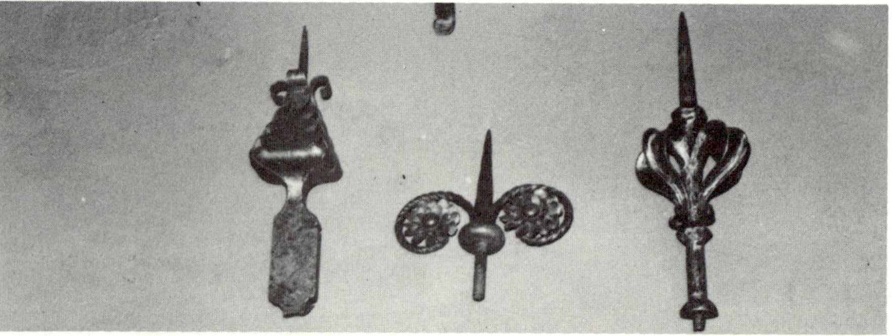

Fig. 23. Finials, by Samuel Yellin.

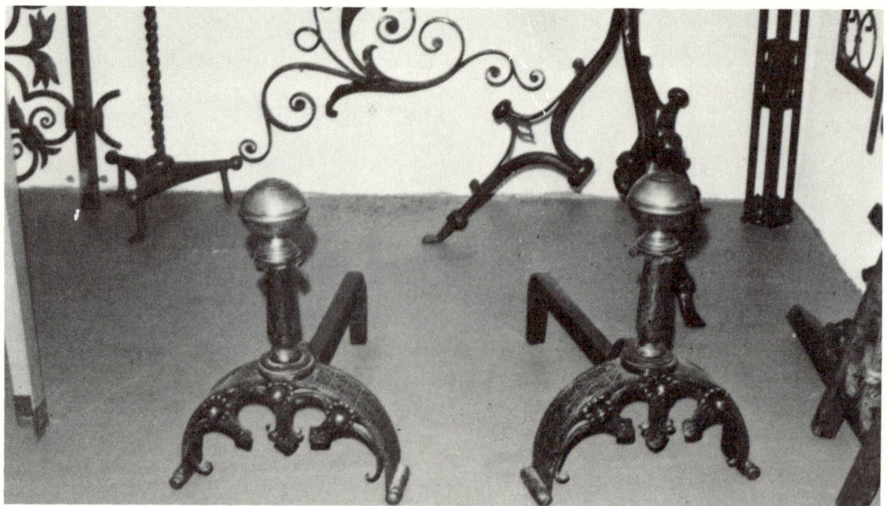

Fig. 24. Andirons and other forgings by Samuel Yellin.

In the early thirties I witnessed a demonstration by Yellin at his forge. It must have been during the period when he was "bowling over" the expert craftsmen of Delaware with his skills while doing the light fixtures, grillwork, and fences for the duPonts. Some years later, while visiting the Bok Carillon Tower at Mountain Lake, Florida, I again encountered the famous name, Yellin. He was the craftsman who designed and forged the light fixtures, hardware, and grillwork for this magnificent structure. The name became more relevant; so, when I decided to write a chapter on metal sculpture, the first craftsman I thought of was Samuel Yellin. I looked in the Philadelphia telephone directory and found the company was still in business. I wrote to the Yellin Metalworkers and received an immediate reply from his faithful son, Harvey; his father had passed away in 1940. Subsequently, I visited the museum of his prototype forgings with my camera. The accompanying pictures represent a very small cross section of the master's work.

Bailey's Forge

One evening in late March (1974) while listening to the CBS News Broadcast, Charles Kuralt featured Ivan Bailey in one of his "On the Road" series. I was impressed with the pictures showing the blacksmith at work and the skillful manner in which he used his blacksmith's hammer. After the broadcast I immediately wrote to Mr. Bailey and kindly requested him to make a contribution to my new book.

He answered by saying he would be happy to contribute and subsequently he sent me the material I requested and some information concerning himself. A brief thumbnail sketch of the artist follows.

Ivan Bailey was born in Portland, Oregon, 1945. In 1969, he graduated with a B.S. degree from Portland State University, where he majored in Art Metal work. After attending Penland School of Crafts, Penland, N.C., and the University of Georgia, M.F.A. (goldsmithing) in 1971, he studied on an Exchange Fellowship at Nordrhein-Westfalische Fachhochschule, Aachen, Germany.

This young man has now set up his forge in Savannah, Georgia, and has already won national recognition. He will go far in his trade if given proper support by the public and creative art authorities. He has been formally trained for his vocation and is very enthusiastic concerning his new venture. If given a ghost of a chance he could become the current prototype of Samuel Yellin of Philadelphia. In fact, some of his work already bears a striking resemblance to the work of the master blacksmith.

The plantation andirons (Fig. 25) are 44″ x 18″. They are not only functional but represent a rugged detail of art-metal craftsmanship of the period. While the design is simple, there is much skill indicated in the fabricated creation.

The four-branch candlestick (Fig. 26) is a more elaborate piece of craftsmanship. Notice the split standards to form the lattice work. He could have welded two thinner strips of wrought iron to the legs to achieve the same structural results, but with less artistic effect. The candle holders appear to be designed with a much-used motif, a rustic treatment which appears to be very effective.

The sunflower gate (Fig. 27) is a masterpiece of grill design. It represents a fine example of simple repoussé work. How did he hammer the intricate leaf designs? Did he have a form or an end-grain wood block for an anvil? Did he cleverly use the angle formed by the chipping surface where it drops from the face of the anvil to form the depressions? Did he form the extended stems of the leaves and their ribs over the open jaws of a machinist's vise, or

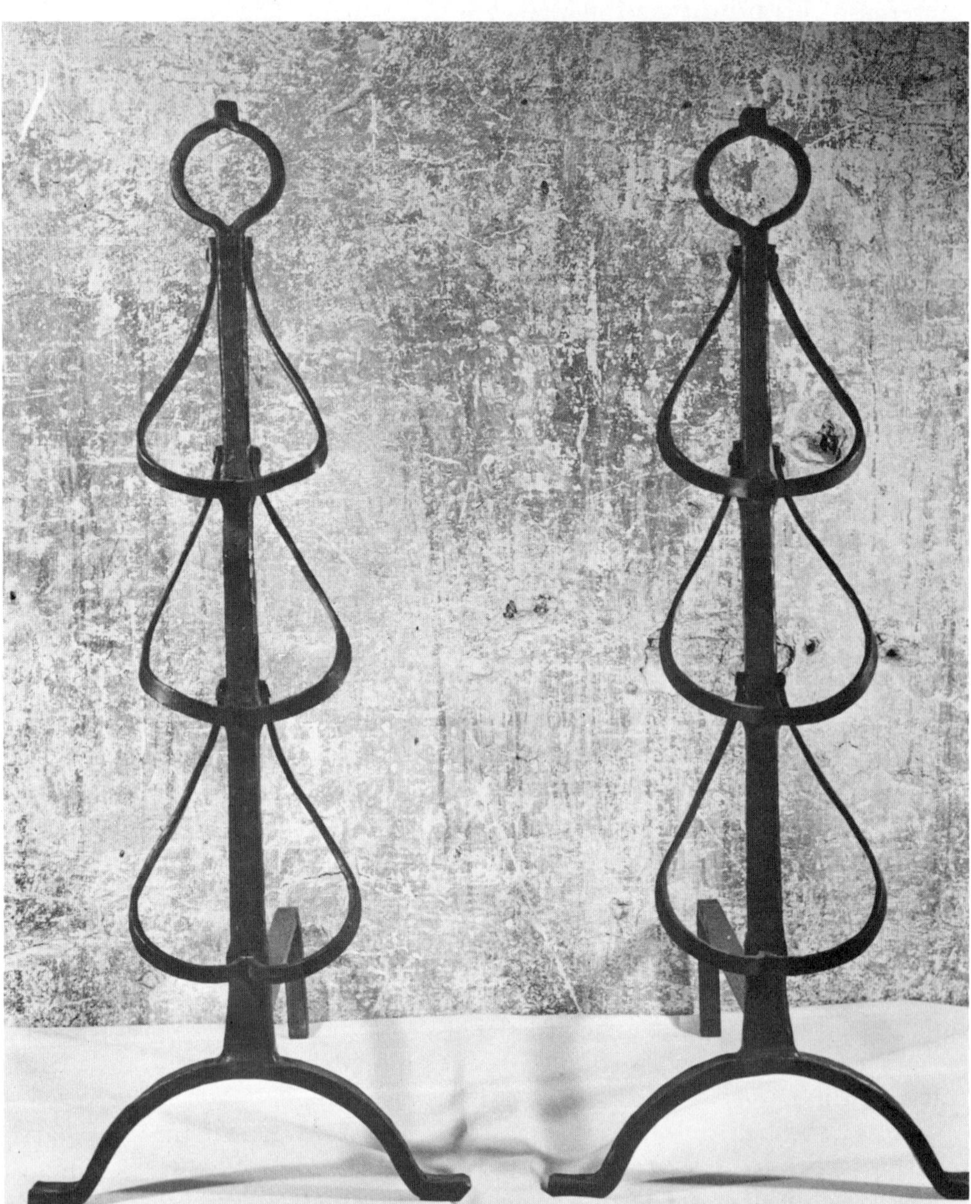

Fig. 25. Plantation andirons.

did he use dies? Who knows? The technical secrets of an artist are in his own keeping and not for publication.

The sunflower gate is a superb example of grillwork, and it sold for $2,150. We will, no doubt, hear more about the metal art work from Bailey's Forge.

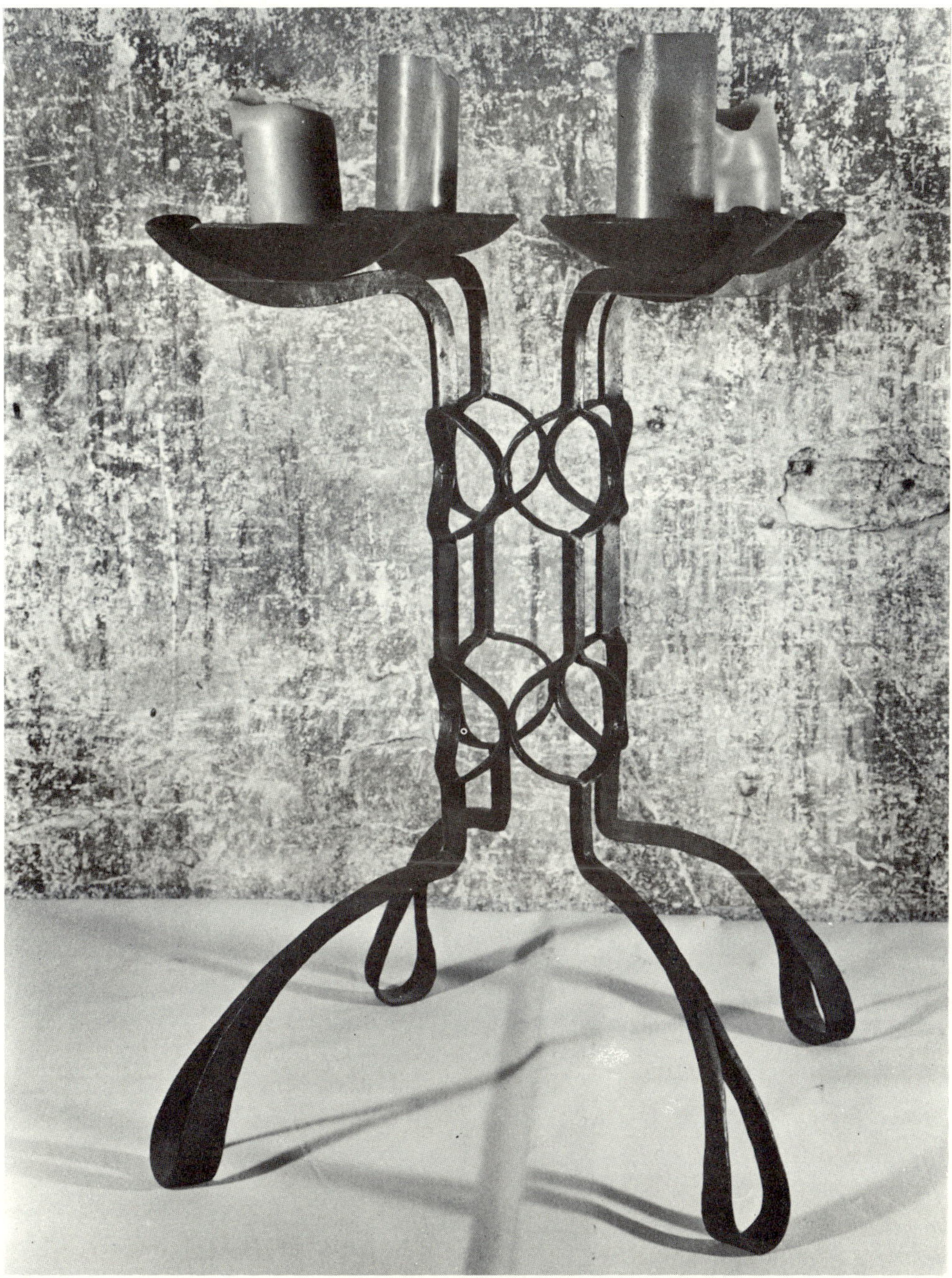

Fig. 26. Four-branch candlestick.

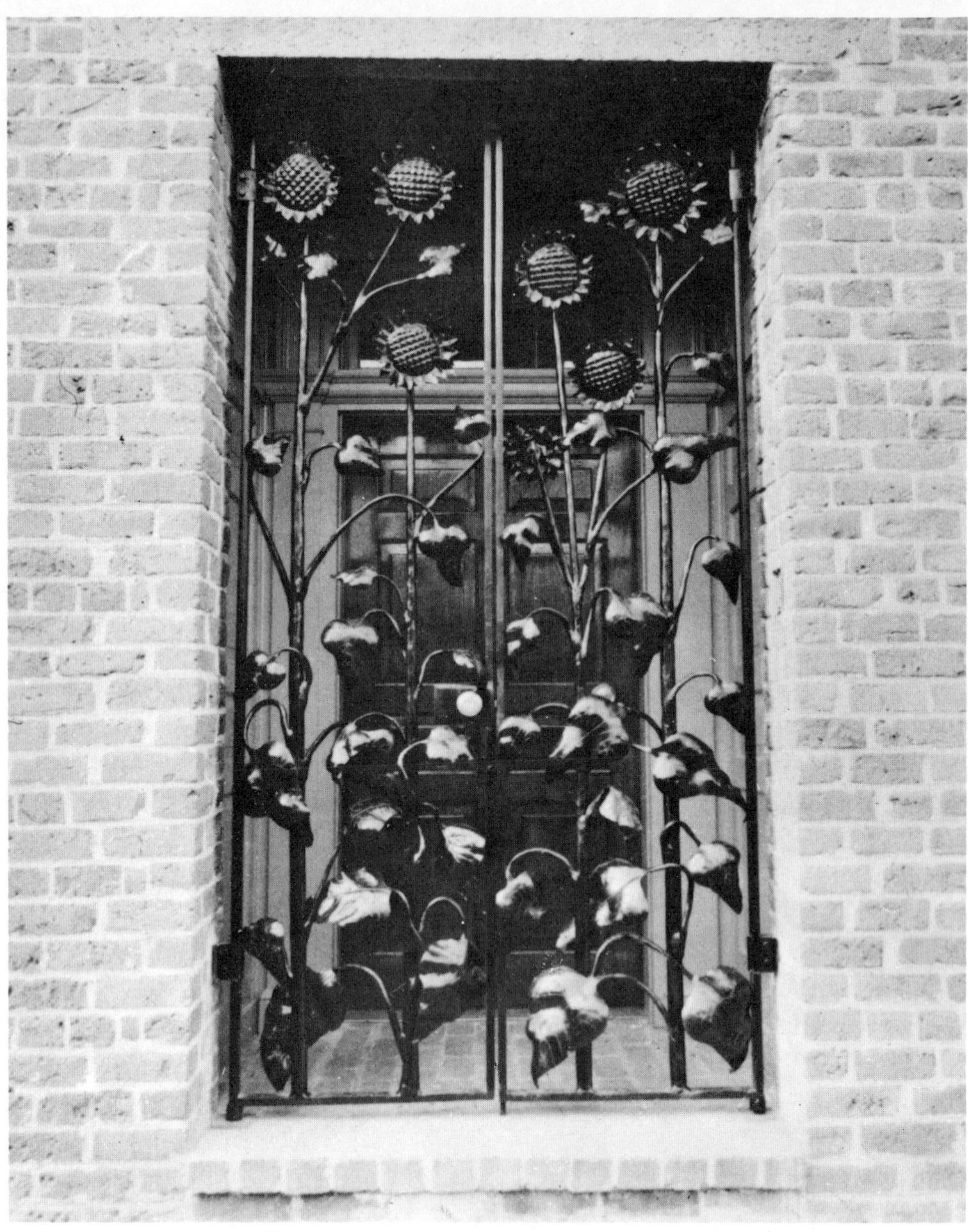

Fig. 27. Sunflower gate.

Thomas F. Googerty

Before the days of writing textbooks I placed little emphasis upon authors of this type of literature. I "picked their brains" to enrich my own efforts without a thought of the personal life or professional preparation of my benefactors. The number of these men is legion. Such a man was Thomas F. Googerty. His little paperback book: *Decorative Wrought Iron Work* (Manual Arts Press, Peoria, Illinois, 1937) was always a ready reference during those years when I taught General Metal Work on an Industrial Arts level. I leaned heavily on his book during the summer I taught Blacksmithing and General Metalwork at a teacher's college and still find it invaluable as an aid in some of my metal projects.

While I do not know anything about the creator of the metalwork illustrated in this section, I have reason to believe that Googerty was an expert blacksmith and fully informed about his subject. He indicates that he was a shop teacher; in any event, he was a creative educator.

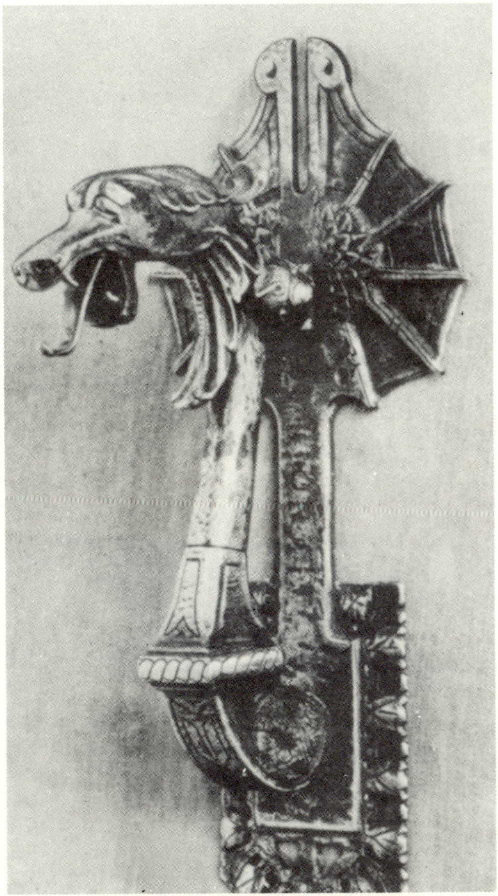

Fig. 28. Iron knocker, by Thomas F. Googerty.

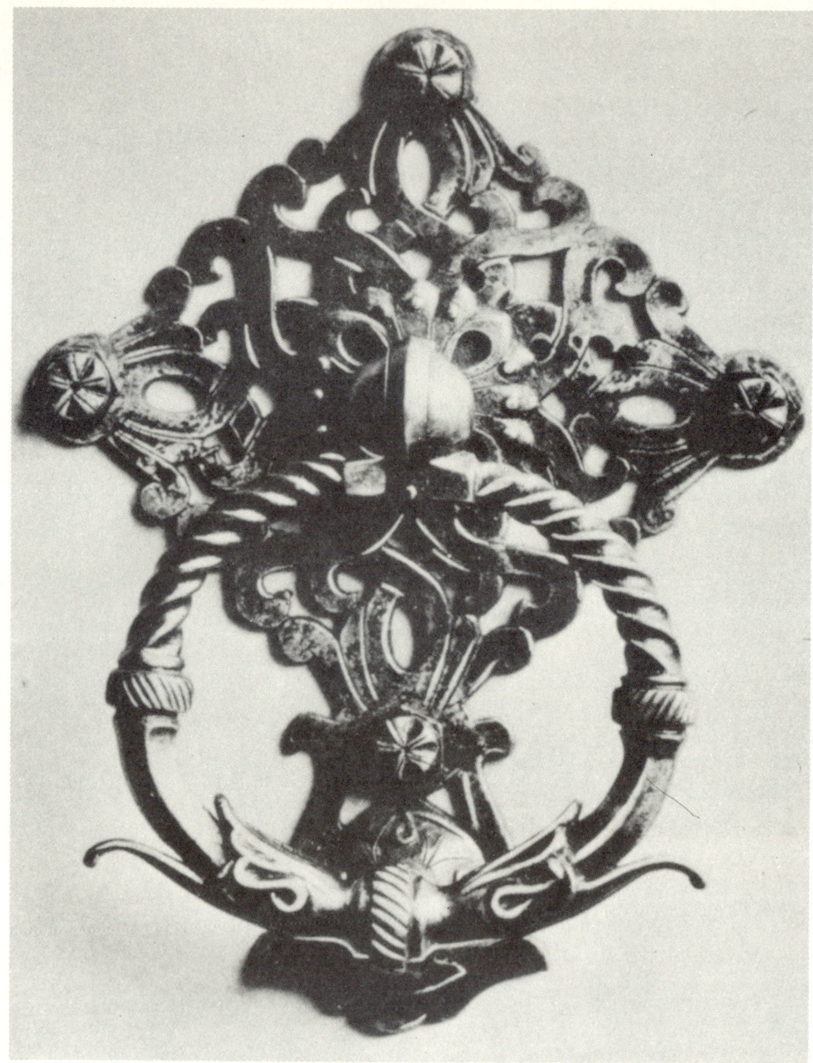

Fig. 29. Wrought iron knocker, by Thomas F. Googerty.

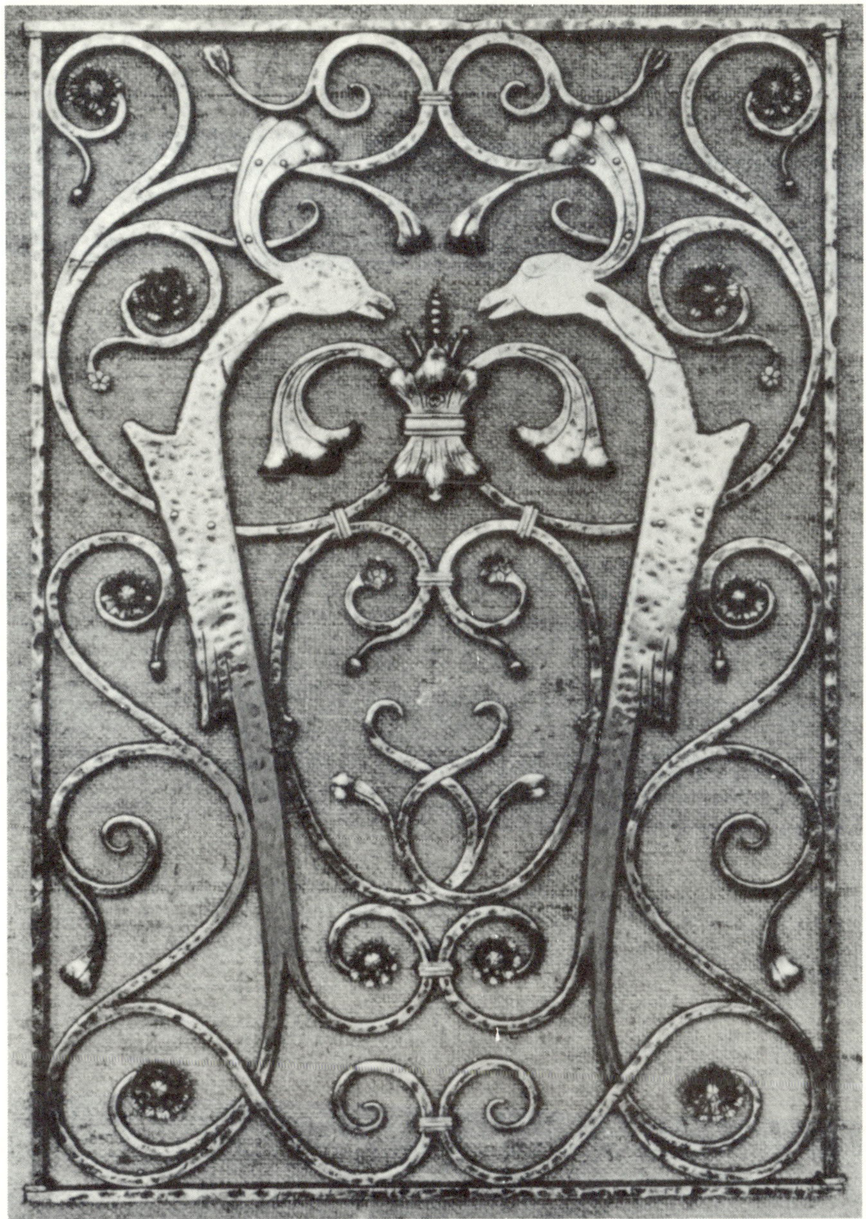

Fig. 30. Grill made by a group of students working under the instruction of Thomas F. Googerty.

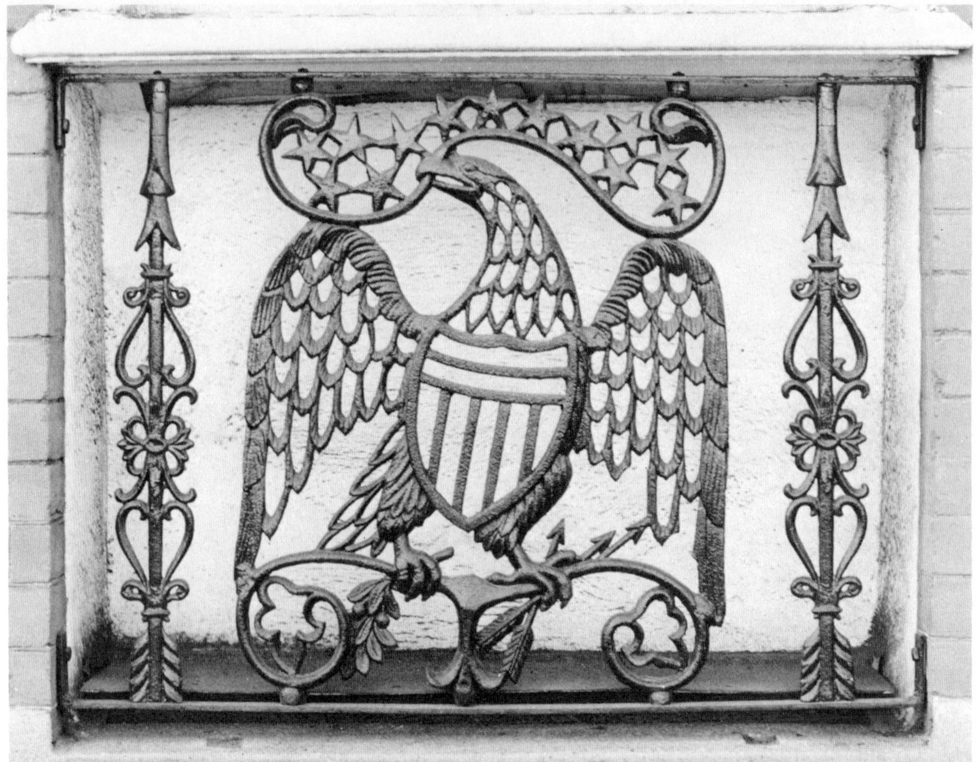

Fig. 31. The national symbol in a window grill. Metal artist unknown. *Courtesy:* U.S. Department of Interior, *Birds in Our Lives.*

FUNCTIONAL METAL SCULPTURE

Original projects designed for a specific purpose and machined to micrometric dimensions are not usually considered sculptural subjects. But an analysis of the basic creative procedures indicate a close kinship with any sculptural effort performed in any medium. When the work of a master designer and a skilled machinist are combined in the creation of an object, the result is not only a precise mechanism but a thing of beauty. It is an artistic work indicative of no mean ability. In the light of much current sculpture there is little comparison between it and the polished, precise product of a skilled machinist. The matter of classification and nomenclature is merely a case of semantics, for the work requires as much inspiration and imagination as does any other medium of creative art.

The illustrations of Jack D. Bailey (Figs. 32-36) are exceptional examples of graphic art. They not only have photographic qualities, but go beyond the medium to show Xray construction. At the time they were drawn, he was a recognized professional artist of national reputation. His illustrations of the machined mechanisms of Sgt. Victor N. Crone and T/3 Alex Zabor are accurate in every detail. One can imagine the sculptural quality of Bailey's models.

Behind these inventions and illustrations is a long story. It is probably typical of any exploratory work whether it be a reclamation project or a device to help place a man on the moon. Because the Oil Seal Reclamation project was a venture of creativity resulting in many original machined mechanisms of precise beauty, this aspect of the sculptural art has been included in this chapter.

I had the privilege to serve in the Ordnance Department during the early years of World War II. I was invited to join the Armed Forces for a specific work which required the qualifications of an educator and a skilled mechanic. True to Army tradition I never had the opportunity to serve in this capacity, but was assigned to another project which had high priority at the time. This particular work was of a research nature which required the skills of several talented men. Several of Walt Disney's artists were assigned to my project and one Sergeant Bailey. All were experts and served faithfully. They probably never received the praise and rewards which they rightfully deserved.

During the second year of the war, a critical shortage of oil seals for motor vehicles developed. Hundreds were "deadlined" at our camp and additional thousands throughout the various camps in the country. The oil seals were of the horseshoe analogy. Lacking them, the vehicle was lost and the challenge went out for relief; for a reclamation program to repair old damaged seals. I happened to be at a meeting in the Automotive Section when the problem was discussed. "Whoever develops a plan or method to reclaim oil seals will earn his full year's pay." This statement was more pretentious than it sounded, for few officers thought they were rightfully earning anything. After the meeting I talked to Captain Chirchyl, Chief of the Automotive Section, about the oil seal problem. After examining a damaged oil seal, I informed Captain Chirchyl that I thought the problem could be easily solved. "If you can," he said, "the Army will be eternally in your debt."

One of my duties at the time was as Commanding Officer of a small company of men who had been returned to the states and to our camp pending final discharge from the Army. These brave men had been caught in the trap at Kasserine Pass and had been shot to pieces. They were a part of the 2,624 men wounded in this fiasco. Most of them were held together with wires and could barely walk. I learned to know some of them very well. Two of them were skilled machinists and were not too badly hurt. When Captain Chirchyl loaned me the use of one of his shops and told me to give my idea a "whirl," I assigned the two machinists of my company to work with me. Retrieving several damaged oil seals from the dump and explaining to the men what I wanted them to do, they proceeded to make a tool according to my design. They were only too happy to escape the boredom of the barracks and both proved to be very able machinists. When they had their tool ready, they centered a damaged oil seal in a universal chuck of an engine lathe, adjusted their improvised tools in the tool holder and began to lift up the bead which held the oil seals together. In the twinkling of an eye, they both uncoiled the bead and the parts of the seal fell to the floor. Undamaged parts were taken from other scrapped seals and placed in the shells just opened. The bead was spun back easily, clamping the seal tightly together. The seals were polished, taken from the chuck and given a thin coat of grease like the unused one obtained from the Supply Depot. I took the reclaimed seal and the unused one to Captain Chirchyl's office and requested that he point out the reclaimed seal. He examined the seals carefully. "You cannot get away with this hoax, Lieutenant," he said. "Both are unused seals." He accompanied me over to the shop where the machinists were working and looked on with excitement as Sergeant Crone unspun a seal, replaced the damaged parts with good ones, and turned over the bead locking the seal together again. "I can hardly believe my eyes," he said, as he turned away to visit his chief to inform him of the good news.

The Commanding General soon learned about our work and I was summoned to his office. After listening to my story, he smiled and said: "Well done, Lieutenant! Congratulations!"

He directed that I have two seals ready the following morning for a two-ton truck. He called in his Executive Officer and directed him to have a two-ton truck and a driver ready for a desert test at 0900. He turned to me and said he wanted me to be present at the time to observe the installation of my seals and to be present when they were removed after the test run.

The following morning, two reclaimed seals were installed on one side of the truck and two unused seals on the other. The driver was directed to drive to the desert and test the vehicle over the course. When the driver returned in the afternoon, the seals were removed. Several automotive mechanics were present and none of them could discern any difference in the wear and tear of the seals. The General was satisfied and gave his Executive Officer directions to supply me with space, equipment, and men and get the reclamation project moving.

I was provided with a large shop and all of the necessary equipment. Sgt. Crone and T/3 Zabor were assigned to do all of the machine shop work; Sgt. Bailey, the illustrating; and Sgt. Leffler, the writing. Several enlisted men from my company were assigned to perform various tasks. Soon the work of reclaiming seals was progressing satisfactorily and experiments to streamline the work were in full swing.

Then when success was assured, the old, old story repeated itself. No great discovery had been made, after all. The art of spinning metal was known to every school kid; the impossible solution to a vital problem had become no problem at all; the whole project was given a downbeat and everybody knew how the job could be done from the very beginning.

The Commanding General had witnessed such developments before and he knew that his organization had broken the back of the seal problem. But as usual, there was interference all along the way when the whole camp became involved. The development of necessary tools and jigs necessary to speed up the work was impeded. The emphasis was placed on production and not on methods to increase it. Speed was vital if the Army was to profit from the work. Pressures from the top soon slowed down the incentive and the interest, and the whole project was headed for a classic "SNAFU-TARFU," if you know what I mean.* Very much discouraged, I felt that my tour in the Army should be terminated so I requested inactive duty. The General approved over the objections of several high-ranking officers.

Figure 32 is a beautiful air brush drawing of a chuck designed to hold the seals while they are being opened. The seals were slipped in and the ring tightened. The taper on the main part of the chuck and the tightening ring provided enough pressure to hold the seals securely.

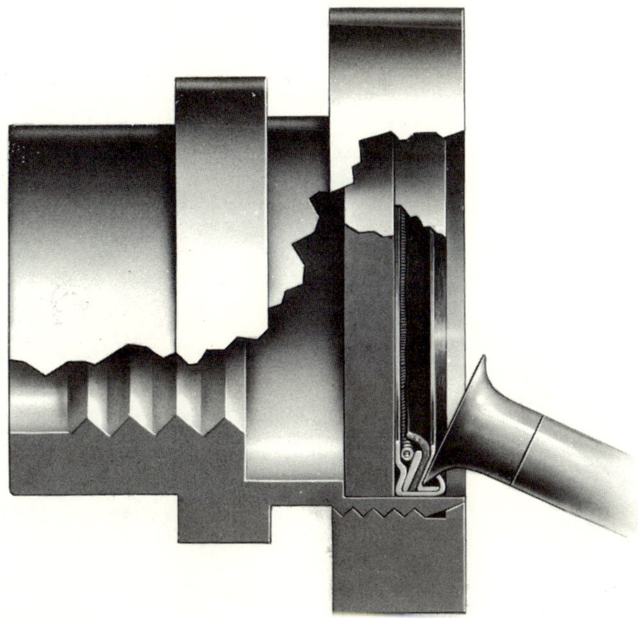

Fig. 32. Chuck for opening seals.

Figure 33 shows a multipurpose tool used to open and close the seals. It saved time and energy. Notice the clever shading in the illustration. The original model was just as beautifully formed.

Figure 34 is another chuck more refined in design. The seal is quickly clamped in place by a flip of the tightening ring. The taper is longer and the segments are more flexible because of the milled slots.

*After being washed clean of its vulgarity, SNAFU means Situation Normal, All Fouled Up. TARFU means Things Are Really Fouled Up. The alphabetical "SNAFU" is still used in current literature, but "TARFU" seems to have become obsolete.

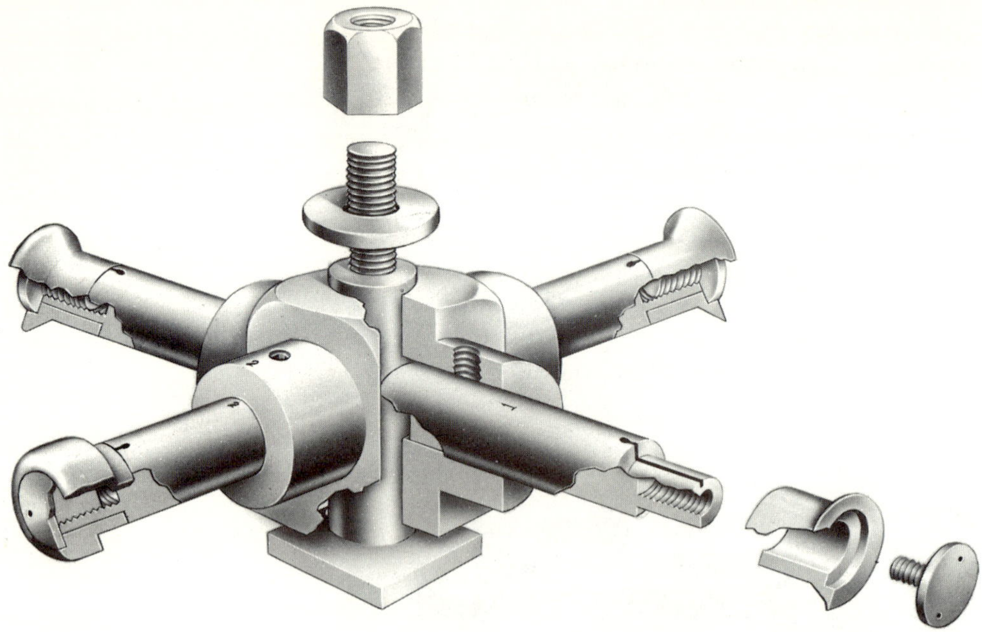

Fig. 33. Multipurpose tool.

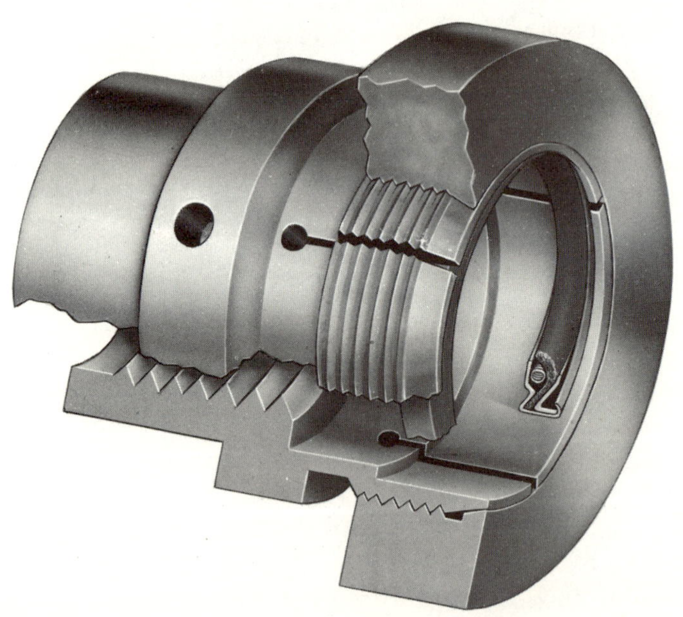

Fig. 34. A refined chuck for opening seals.

Figure 35 shows a device for rolling over the edge of a seal. This device was designed for mass production. What a beautiful piece of mechanism! With it a seal could be spun together in the twinkling of an eye.

Figure 36 is another device for rolling over the edge of a seal. It is smaller, and a tool post gadget is present in case of a stubborn seal with a contrary edge. Seals are of various sizes and shapes, so a number of tools of this type were necessary.

These beautiful illustrations, expertly drawn by Sgt. J.D. Bailey ('44), are faithful graphic reproductions of some of the tools designed and used to reclaim the seals.

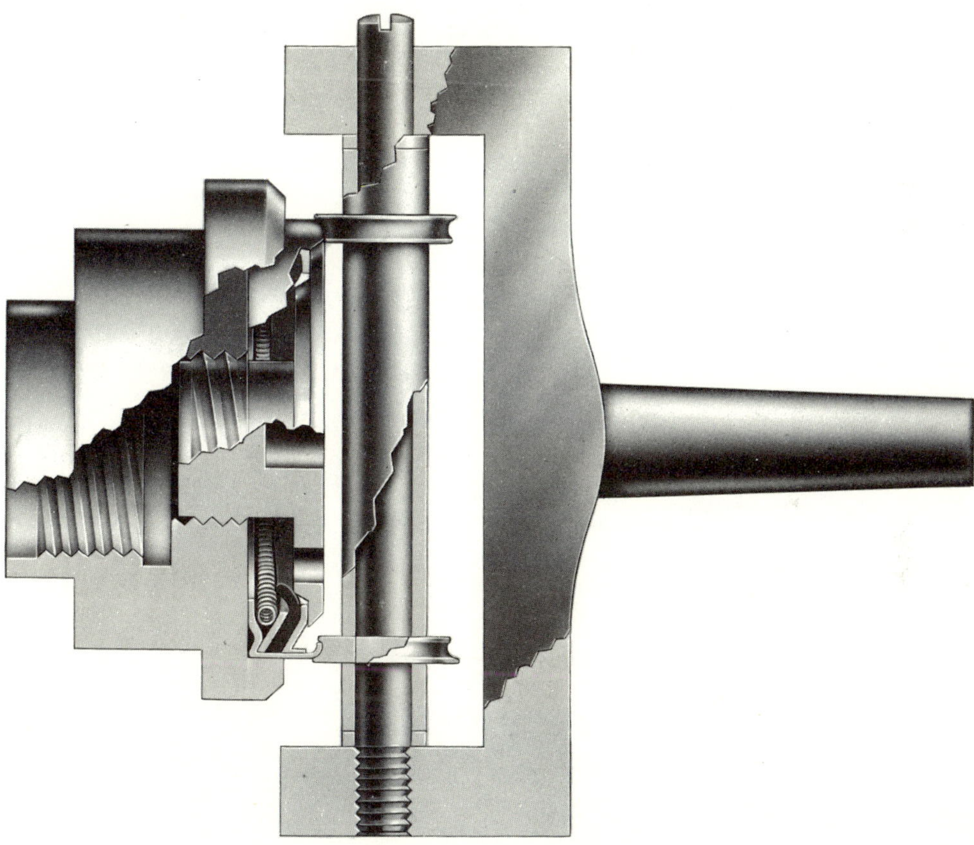

Fig. 35. Closing tool.

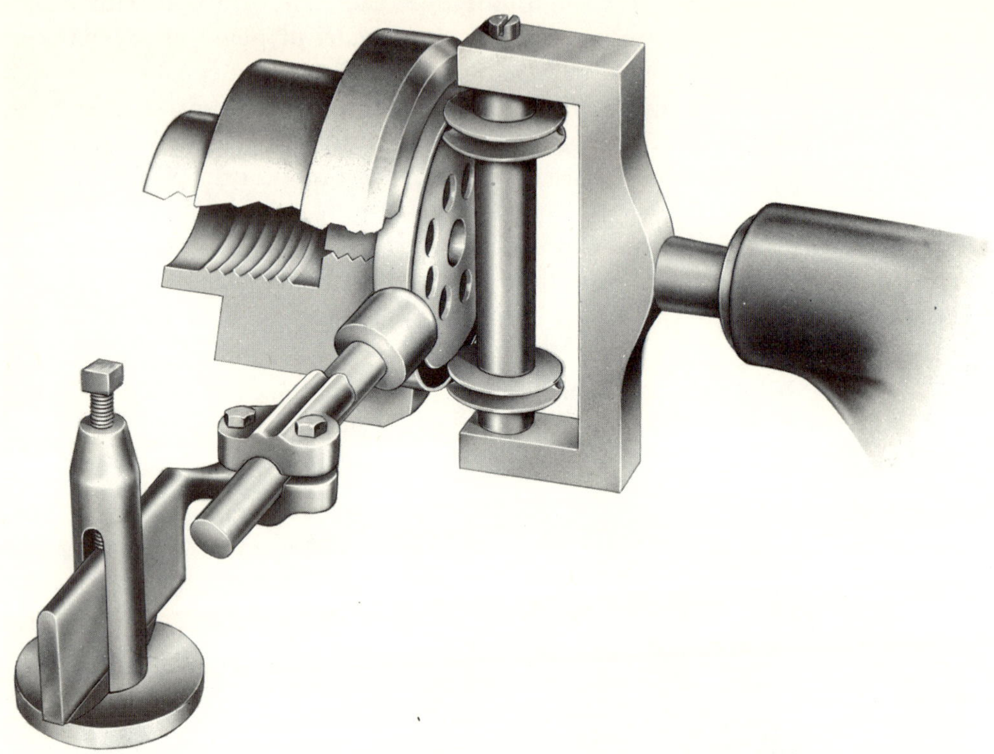

Fig. 36. Closing tool with attachment.

Chapter 16

A Formal Fish Pool

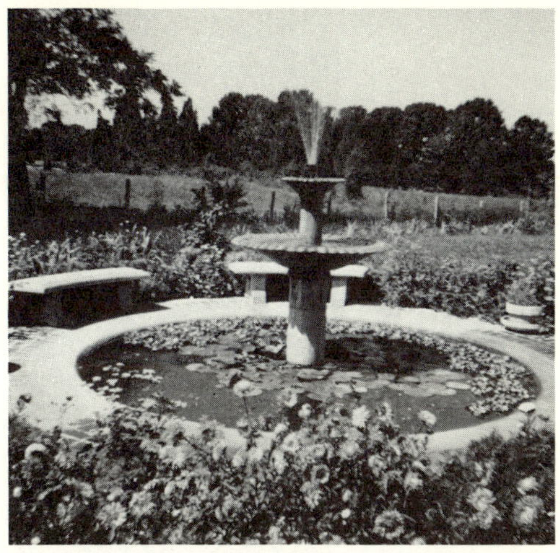

Pool stocked with fish, lilies, and landscaped around its apron.

During these days of ecological consciousness there is a trend to transform the garden into a refuge for birds and animals. Recently *National Wildlife Magazine,* in two consecutive issues, devoted several pages to landscaping the grounds to attract wildlife. One of the first ventures in such planning is a dependable source of water. Then, of course, there must be suitable cover to protect the birds and animals from their enemies. Our concern here is not so much with shrubbery and trees, but such natural environmental requisites are important to attract wildlife. There is no reason why the patch of real estate surrounding the pool should not only be designed for a suitable habitat for birds and animals, but as a thing of beauty of itself. An inconspicuous, bald, or just ordinary spot in the garden can be transformed to a restful place to spend many quiet hours in peaceful tranquility, an emotional release of which we may be unconscious, but which nevertheless, is real and satisfying. To rest by a pool, generously and thoughtfully landscaped, is to experience the peace of the gods. Surrounded by a profusion of flowers and shrubs, the pool can be a delight with waterlilies blooming along its surface and a hundred goldfish of various breeds flashing their radiant colors below. It's so nice to have a pool around the house!

Urban people living in crowded condominiums, apartments, or attached homes have the urge to take to the highways repeatedly to experience the sight of rural nature for which their souls hunger. The emotional uplift is indeed healthful therapy and will ameliorate much of the drudgery of routine living in the days ahead. An appointment with nature is an excellent "checkup."

A fish pool is not as expensive as one may imagine, especially if the work is done on a do-it-yourself basis. Cement, sand, and gravel are available in all localities—even the ready-mixed facilities. A simple arithmetical calculation determines the number of cubic yards of concrete required in either case. If the concrete is mixed by hand, it should be 1 part Portland cement, 2 parts sand, and 3 parts small gravel—a 1, 2, 3 mix. If ready-mixed, the mixture known as a 3-bag mix will have about the same strength. In the proposed project which will be discussed in this chapter, ready-mixed concrete has some limitations. It must be troweled in place immediately—all of it. There is

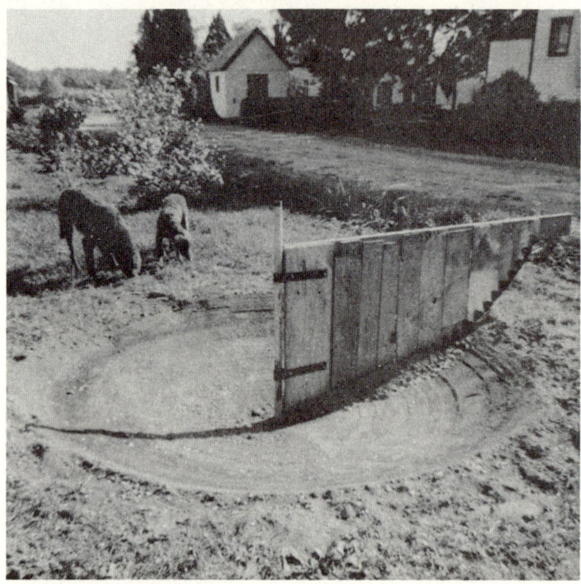

Fig. 1. Sweeping out the hole.

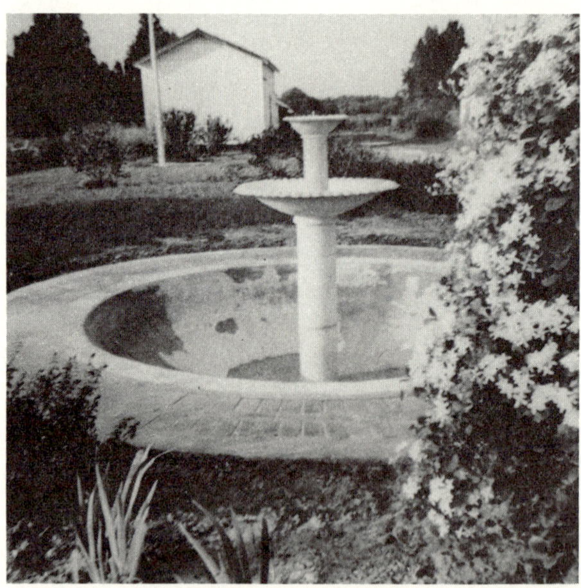

Fig. 2. Completed pool.

no time for one portion to set up before spreading the next batch. The incline should be less than 45° or it will slowly slide down. An expert cement finisher could probably use ready-mixed concrete, but the novice should mix his concrete by hand and take his time troweling it in place. By mixing the concrete by hand the work may progress around the walls of the pool in tiers which do not readily slip out of place for the tier below has had time to set up appreciably before the next tier is started. Only enough concrete is mixed at one time to go entirely around the pool. After the tier (about 1′ wide) is troweled in place, closing the gap, the next batch may be mixed and the work continued.

Concrete is sensitive to temperature changes. Even thick concrete roads have to be reinforced to keep them from buckling. So, every large surface of concrete, whatever the thickness might be, should be reinforced with a grid of steel sufficiently heavy to hold the surface in place.

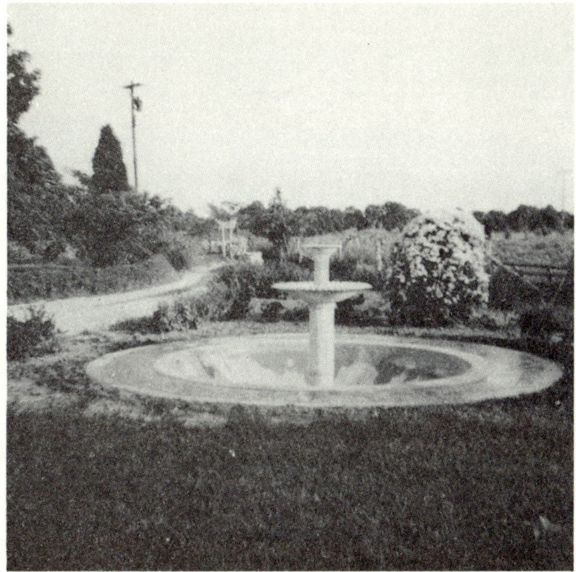

Fig. 3. Another view of the completed pool.

Study Figs. 1, 2, 3 and the chapter headpiece to get an idea of the overall construction of the pool before the actual work begins. Start with Fig. 2. The picture does not have an aesthetic background, but the construction details are evident. The darker area in the bottom is water collected after an April shower. Figure 1 shows the sweep in place and the hole scraped out about a foot deep. Notice that the cutting edge is made up of knife sections of a mower nailed in place, a good device if they are available. The headpiece shows the landscaped pool stocked with fish and waterlilies.

Digging the Hole

Foundrymen employ an operation in forming green sand molds known as "sweeping." Huge bells are cast this way without the use of patterns. The pool described in this chapter is not only dug in part by a sweep, but the concrete is smoothed in place by it also. The sweep is hinged to a 2″ pipe to

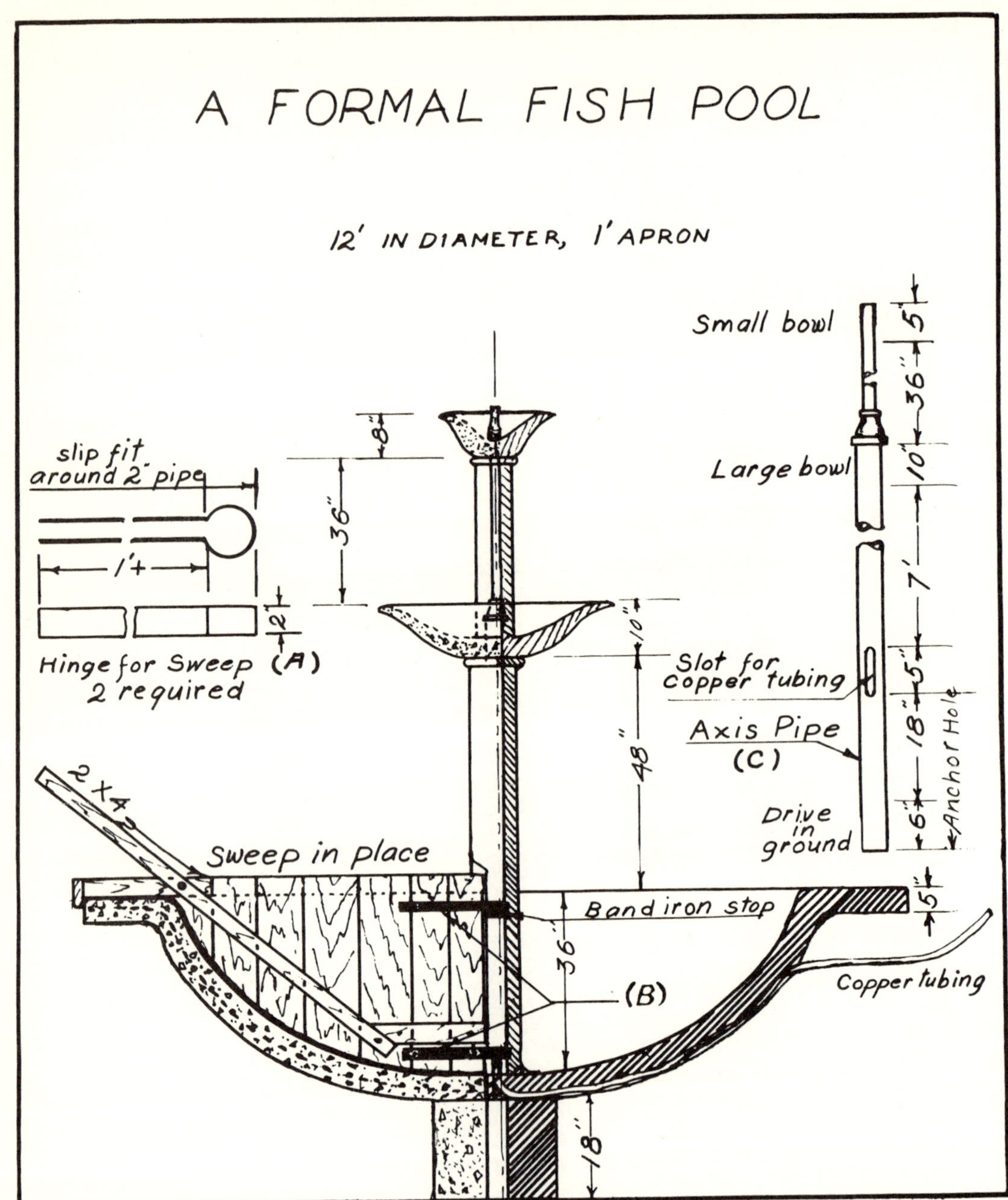
A FORMAL FISH POOL
12' IN DIAMETER, 1' APRON
slip fit around 2" pipe
1'+
2"
Hinge for Sweep (A)
2 required
8"
36"
10"
48"
2 X 4
Sweep in place
Band iron stop
36"
(B)
18"
Small bowl
5"
36"
Large bowl
10"
7'
Slot for copper tubing
5"
Axis Pipe
(C)
18"
Anchor Hole
Drive in ground
6"
5"
Copper tubing

Figure 4.

keep it revolving in concentric circles. In hard ground the dirt must be loosened ahead of the sweep and removed as the digging progresses. The hole should be dug about 41″ deep.

Installing the 2″ Pipe Axis

Locate the center of the planned pool. Study the drawings (Fig. 4) and understand them thoroughly. Some liberties have been taken with the rules of orthographic projection, but none that should be confusing. The right half is a cross section of the pool; the other half shows the shape of the finished pool with the sweep in place. The problem now is to install the 2″ axis pipe around which the sweep will rotate. Dig a large hole at least four or five feet in diameter and 41″ deep. Next, dig an 18″ hole 18″ x 18″ in the center of the hole just dug, for the concrete anchor. Prepare the axis pipe as shown in Fig. 4(C). The 2″ section of pipe should be 10′3″ long, threaded on one end, and a ½″ x 5″ slot cut 24″ up the other section. The slot should be long and wide enough to "snake" up the ½″ copper tubing easily. Drive the bottom end of the pipe 6″ down in the center of the 18″ hole. Be careful and do not damage the threads. Be sure the pipe is plumb; test with a spirit level. Mix a batch of lean concrete (1, 3, 3 mix) and pour in the hole. Allow the concrete to set at least two days. Before the concrete sets up, test again with a spirit level.

After it is loosened from the hole the spoil should be shoveled into a wheelbarrow or a pickup truck. This procedure will save considerable time in the long run.

Sweep Construction

The top of the sweep is a 2″ x 4″ piece of stock, 7′ long. Roofers (or any ¾″ boards) should be nailed to the 2 by 4's as shown in Fig. 4. The bottom contour of the pool's bottom should be drawn on the boards and sawn accordingly. Another 2″ x 4″ piece of stock should follow close to the contour and nailed to the boards on the opposite side as shown. Install the shorter piece of stock about 6″ from the bottom. Bolt the 2 by 4's together. Note the extension of the bottom 2 by 4. This extension will facilitate the sweeping operation.

Two hinges made of ¼″ x 2″ band iron are required (Fig. 4(A)). The bottom hinge should be bolted near the bottom of the sweep, as shown. Both hinges should be installed while the sweep is held in place (Fig. 4(B)). (The sweep is too heavy to lift over the axis pipe.) Be sure the hinge edge of the sweep is at right angles to the top and equidistant from the pipe. Position the hinges accordingly. The weight of the sweep does not matter. It must be built strong to take the punishment it will get before the pool is completed. The cutting edge of the sweep may be made from discarded mower teeth sections as stated before, or a piece of flat band iron (1/8″ x 2″) bent over the bottom of the sweep and fastened securely. Now the fun begins!

Although the author worked alone, the job should be done by two strong men. Digging most soil is hard labor. Dig the soil in front of the sweep with a mattock and shovel it into a wheelbarrow or pickup truck. Swing the sweep around the axis pipe with a steady forward motion; a backswing might be helpful at times. The primary purpose in this operation, however, is to act as a guide in shaping the hole and smoothing out the dirt. When the sweep has descended low enough to cut the apron form, the hole is completed. Remove the hinges and shorten the sweep 5″ before using it to smooth the concrete.

Flatten one end of the copper tubing to keep out the dirt, and snake it through the slot and up the 2″ pipe until it sticks out 1′ or more. Form the remainder of the tubing to conform with the bottom of the pool. About 18″ from the top (below the frost line) cut a trench long enough to go beyond the flagstone or brick apron. This trench should be cut in the direction of the water supply. Lay the copper tubing in the trench with the remainder of the coil on top of the ground. Fill in the trench and smooth the side of the hole as it was before.

Next, install the ½″ reinforcing bars (deformed bars especially rolled for concrete work). The radii bars are installed first. Place a foot on the end of the bar near the axis pipe and press down. About 18″ to 24″ from the foot, lift up the bar with your hands, bending it to fit flat on the bottom of the hole. Continue this operation up the side until the rim is reached; here the bar makes a sharp turn to pass through the apron. Do this operation with a 2″ pipe wrench with the tightened jaws held at right angles with the bar. With a hacksaw cut the bar 2″ beyond the apron and bend up with a piece of 1″ pipe passed over the end. Bend completely over to form a hook. The outside reinforcing hoop will pass through the hook, making a strong construction. Continue to bend the radii bars in place, allowing about 24″ space at the rim, until all of them have been formed. The circular, horizontal bars should be formed outside of the hole. Away from the hole drive two 2″ pieces of pipe about 4″ apart. By placing the bar between them, it may be bent in any required curve. Make the first hoop about 24″ in diameter. About 24″ beyond it install another hoop and so on up the side of the hole. Fasten each joint with a short piece of baling wire (14 g.). Be sure that the grid that has been formed is at least 1″ off the bottom of the hole (prop up where necessary with a rock), and not more than 4″ above the bottom. Pull down the high places with a hook driven in the bottom of the hole. No part of the grid should project out of the concrete after the pool has been formed. The wall of the pool should average 5″ thick.

Cut a piece of band iron ¼″ x 1½″ and long enough to bend around the axis pipe. Drill a ¼″ hole near each end and another between them. Countersink the holes for ¼″ flat-headed stove bolts. Bend the iron accurately around the axis pipe. (Form on the horn of an anvil or in a vise.) Replace the sweep, propping it 5″ above the bottom of the hole. Replace the hinges with the iron ring between them. Adjust the ring to fit tightly under the top hinge. Drill a 13/16″ hole in the center of each ring hole and tape with a ¼″

U.S. Std. tap. If you have never done this operation before, proceed with care. Do not twist the tap beyond its strength. Use pork fat on the tap and twist with a steady forward and backward motion. Be sure the tap is held perpendicularly to the pipe. Screw the stove bolts tightly in place. The stop ring should now control the height of the sweep around the pool. Have a triangular and oblong trowel handy before mixing the concrete.

Leave about 18″ of space around the axis pipe to anchor the column later on. Mix a batch of concrete—not juicy—and shovel near the center, leaving the space referred to above. Spread the concrete evenly in place with the sweep and trowel. The sweep should do an excellent job or something is wrong. The band iron on the edge might pull the concrete instead of smoothing it out. If this happens, the edges should be turned up slightly so that they slip over, smoothing out the mix. Mix up more concrete and continue the operation. As you near the top, the steep incline will not allow much concrete to be laid at one time. Plan to lay the concrete in tiers narrow enough to stay in place. While this tier is setting up, the next batch may be mixed. Little difficulty should be experienced in laying the concrete if the directions have been followed carefully. Stand on boards while working in the pool and be sure to have a smooth job before allowing the concrete to set up.

Installing the Columns

After the concrete has set for a day, the first half of the column may be poured. Secure three pieces of stovepipe (10″ in diameter) and push them together. Cut the resulting pipe 82″ long. Cut six bars of reinforcing steel, 8′6″ long and bend at right angles 18″ from one end. Wire these short ends in position for the column. Wire them to the radii bars so that the upright ends will be enclosed 1″ within the stovepipe form. Wire the top ends to the axis pipe and to each other equidistant apart. Mix up a batch of concrete and fill in the space in the bottom left for this purpose. (It is obvious that the sweep must have been removed in the meantime.) Adjust the stovepipe form in place, the lower seam below the waterline. Pour about 3″ of concrete in the pipe to hold it in place. If this operation is not done, the concrete will spill out under the pipe form. Be sure the pipe form is plumb. Allow the concrete to set for several hours and then mix a batch of concrete (no gravel) and pour into the form. The mix should be rather loose to ensure that the form will be filled tightly. Push a broom handle up and down in the form to remove any air pockets which may have been formed. While the concrete is setting up, make the form for the large basin or bowl and the 2″ thick plinth which is located between the column and the bowl.

Sweeping Out the Bowl

The bottom bowl is 4′ in diameter. Construct a square box with inside measurements 2″ more than the diameter of the bowl and 10″ deep. Screw fast a 1½″ pipe flange in the center and screw in it a pipe about 24″ long. Make the sweep out of sheet metal (about 20 or 22 gauge) to cut the form to the shape of the bottom of the bowl. Reinforce with wooden battens. Bend hinges as before, but the band iron may be 1/8″ x 1″ this time. The design of construction is left to your imagination, but be sure the sweep swings freely and at the same level around the axis pipe. Next, mix up a batch of lean cement, 1 part cement and 3 parts sand (masonry sand), and shovel into the box. The mix should be heavy—just enough water to hold it together. Form the *bottom* shape of the bowl with the sweep. After the cement has set up for a day or more, wax the form thoroughly with paste. This operation is to cause the forms to separate easily. Redesign the sweep to cut the *top* surface of the bowl. It will not be very different than the contour already formed. Fasten a stop ring under the top hinge as in the sweep for the pool. Fasten the ring so that the bottom of the bowl will be 3″ thick. Mix up a batch of cement and clean, fine masonry sand, a 1, 2 proportion will be about right.

Have a steel grid of reinforcing steel (3/16″) already made to cast in the bowl. Do not sweep the mix near the axis pipe as a large hole should be left there so that the bowl may be slipped easily over the 2″ x 1″ coupling on the column. Mix the cement heavy—just enough water to hold the particles together. Start with the center of the bowl and begin sweeping. Continue the work until the entire bowl has been completed. Be sure the concrete is packed firmly. Cut a ½″ hole 7″ from the center to allow the water to run out during the winter months. Next, divide the outside edge in as many parts as there are to be reversed flutes. Form these flutes by hand with sheet-metal slicks formed for this purpose. This is not a difficult task and the design greatly improves the appearance of the bowl.

Screw the 2″ x 1″ coupling tightly in place on the 2″ axis pipe. Enough of the copper tubing should be protruding to permit it to be lengthened after the large bowl has been set in place. If there is not enough of the pipe left over for this purpose, it should be lengthened next by sweating on a copper coupling and enough copper tubing to protrude through the top bowl.

Cast the 2″ x 12″ plinth. When the cement has set for a day or more, cement in place on the column.

After the fluted bowl has set for several days, carefully invert the whole form (unscrew and remove the axis pipe first) so that the corners of the box will rest on 1½″ blocks (when turned over completely). Meanwhile, place boards raised high enough to make the free fall of the bowl not more than ½″. If the free fall is greater than that, some damage might result to the bowl. Next, lift up one corner about an inch and drop sharply. Repeat this operation around the box until the bowl breaks loose from the form. Lift off the box and set aside for the top bowl. Have some help in turning over the bowl; the outer edge is fragile and might chip off if used as a fulcrum. Rub out any rough or deformed places with a carborundum block. Before trying to set the bowl in place, have several 2″ boards stretched across the pool.

Have at least three men to help lift the bowl in place over a soft pad of cement placed on the plinth. Level the bowl with a spirit level.

Prepare the box for the bottom form of the top bowl. Make the sweep in the particular shape shown, and use the same hinges used in making the first bowl. Sweep out the form as before and follow the same procedures. Allow the bowl to set up for several days. In the meantime, pour the top column.

The stovepipe for the top column is 8″ in diameter and 36″ long plus the depth of the bottom bowl. (The drawing shows 36″ above the rim of the bottom bowl.) If the copper tubing has not been lengthened, perform this operation next.* Cut a piece of 1″ pipe long enough to reach through the top bowl with an inch to spare. Insert the copper tubing through it and screw the pipe into the reducing coupling. (The pipe has to be threaded at both ends.) The copper tubing should project about 1″ above the steel pipe and the hole corked to keep out dirt. Place the 8″ stovepipe form in place and lock it concentric with the 1″ pipe by pouring in about three inches of cement. Allow the cement to set for several hours, then pour in enough cement to fill the form (use the same mix as for the first half of the column). After allowing the cement to set for several days, cement the plinth and the bowl in place. After the cement in the center of the bowl around the 1″ pipe has set, screw on a lock washer. Next, sweat on a fixture for the hose nozzle. This fixture has a sweat coupling on one end and is threaded for a hose nozzle on the other. Screw on a hose nozzle immediately as the tubing might get clogged.

After the pool has been completed, bail out any water which may have accumulated. Bathe the concrete sides with full strength vinegar with a large sponge. Concrete is very basic and it must be neutralized before the pool is filled with water. Goldfish cannot tolerate a strong basic condition in the pool, so the water must be neutralized as accurately as possible. Secure a testing kit which is available at most places where fish are sold. It will be helpful after the pool is filled with water. The reaction between the vinegar and the concrete will indicate the strong basic condition. Use as much vinegar as is necessary to neutralize the sides of the pool.

Now your pool is completed with the exception of the extended apron. This apron should be about 3′ wide and made of either bricks or flagstone. The contrast between the pool and the apron will be helpful in the overall appearance. Lacking an apron, your visitors will trample your shrubbery and grass. You will have visitors, so prepare for them.

---

*The author has presumed that the reader is acquainted with sweating copper tubing. If he is not, perhaps he should employ a plumber to do this work for him. But, with some experimentation he should easily perform the job efficiently himself. First, be sure the surfaces to be sweated together are clean (use emery cloth). A fluxing paste manufactured for this purpose is spread over the pertinent surfaces and the parts are pushed together. Heat the joint with a torch until solid core solder will melt when placed at the edge of the fitting. Capillary action pulls the liquid solder up into the space between the fittings. Do not use acid core solder.

Many construction variations may be made in this project at the beginning. For example, these instructions call for natural colored cement. Dry colors may be added to the mix, but just enough to give a tinted effect. (The dry colors weaken the cement to some extent.) Instead of the column and bowls, a molded cement ornament may be mounted on a column, especially designed for this purpose. A cherub holding a water jar is often used, and may be purchased at any large wayside garden supply mart. Have your plans firmly in mind before starting the project.

Consult the appendix for supply houses carrying pool and fish supplies and send for their catalogs. Stock your pool with several breeds of fish and at least three water lilies. Three lilies will almost cover the surface of your pool. Put in a dozen snails; they will help to keep your pool clean. Good luck!

You have made a good investment. The pool might even sell your property if you should ever want to move. Ours did.

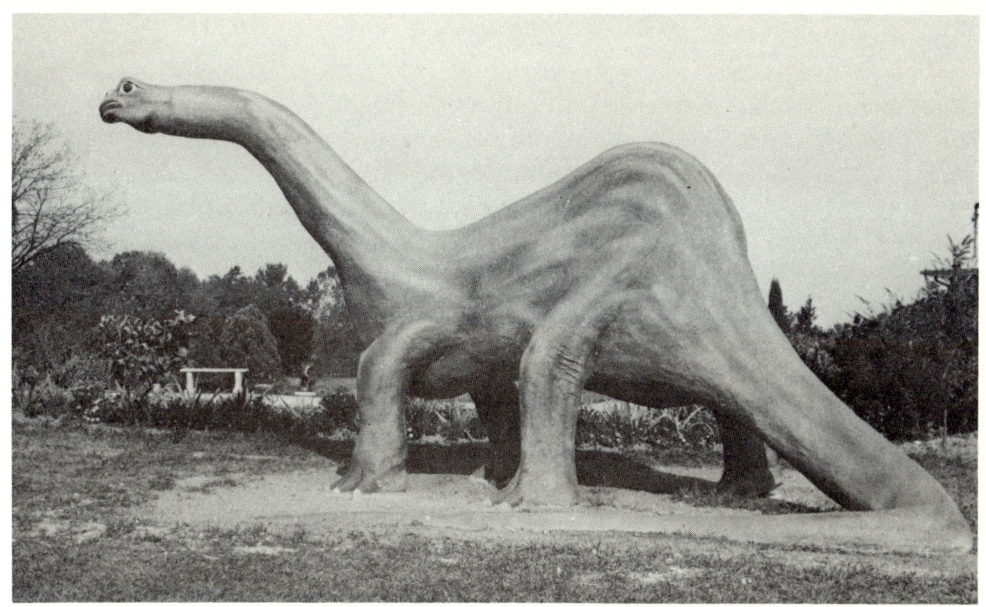

Completed Diplodocus. Sculptured by the ferro-cement process. It is 40′ long and weighs about three tons.

Chapter 17

Cement Sculpture

As this chapter is being written, considerable interest is being expressed in those prehistoric animals of the dinosaur family. They lived on our earth during the late Triassic period 140,000,000 years ago, and until the late Cretaceous period (60,000,000 years ago), when for some unknown reason they and all of their kin died out. The motion picture series, "Valley of the Dinosaurs," magazine articles, and other reading media have made "dino saur" a household word. The October 1974 issue of *Natural History Magazine* included an article by Adrian J. Desmond concerning Benjamin Waterhouse Hawkins who sculptured the dinosaurs for the London Great Exhibition (1851) which was to celebrate Great Britain's technological progress. Hawkins conceived the idea for sculpturing these immense creatures, full-size, after reading Richard Owens' articles concerning them. It was Owens who coined the word "dinosauria" (terrible lizard) in 1841. James A. Michener's book, *Centennial* narrates the life and death of a Diplodocus. This particular portion of the book was extracted and published by the *Reader's Digest* (November 1974). These and other writings have made the dinosaurs come to life again on the American scene.

When I had constructed the steel framework for my Diplodocus, everybody knew it was a dinosaur. They did not need to ask the name although a few did want to know the particular species. The idea of sculpturing one of these mammoth animals was conceived one night before going to sleep. A few days later most of the plans for a Diplodocus had been designed and drawn. I had the steelwork welded together and plastered before either of the aforementioned interesting articles was published. Soon traffic was stopping in front of our house and people began to beat a track to our lawn.

The Board of Commissioners of Central Park, New York City, aware of Hawkins' creations and the interest they aroused, employed him to sculpture similar reptiles for their zoo. It was a costly venture which vexed Boss Tweed and his "Ring" to such an extent that they conspired to destroy all of the sculptures. Tweed and his gang were stealing every cent of public money they could lay their hands on, so they smashed the huge sculptures in pieces so small that they could not be reassembled. Thus the Central Park venture came to an end. Subsequently, a retributive justice destroyed Boss Tweed and his gang, but the harm to Hawkins' sculptural creations had been done. The artist was so disillusioned that he discontinued his efforts.

Hawkins' models are now considered inaccurate by modern Paleontologists, but he put the dinosaurs in a prominent niche of the public's mind never to be forgotten.

His models had to deal with religious groups which were more conservative than they are today. Dinosaurs were not mentioned in the Bible; however, they once existed on our earth for there was little point in denying the proof of fossils. A compromise was reached which seemed to please all parties concerned. Even Archbishop Ussher, who calculated the dates of Bibical events, probably would have offered no objections. All authorities agreed that dinosaurs perished in the flood for they were too large to be included in Noah's Ark. Archbishop Ussher dates the flood as occurring 2348 B.C., with no plus or minus margin for mistakes; he believed in being precisely accurate!

Ferro-Cement Technique

My experience with ferro-cement was in the early thirties, long before the term had been coined. I was teaching Industrial Arts in a Public School in Northern Delaware when I decided to include a cement unit in my program of instruction. Forms were constructed for flowerpots, birdbaths, and other simple designs. The Art Department suggested a large Egyptian jar with a wide shoulder and a smaller bottom. The idea crystallized. An interior form made up of vertical sections, evenly spaced, was designed the shape of the jar (about 3′ tall). These sections were held in place by a center core which could be removed after the cement hardened. The whole form was fastened to a revolving platform which rotated in front of a stationary forming edge. This edge spread the cement evenly over the form and gave the outside its shape. Baby-chick wire was stretched over the form and fastened in place. Next, hoops of No. 10 g. wire were formed and spaced up the sides of the form about 5″ apart. Another layer of baby-chick wire mesh was stretched and fastened in place with No. 18 g. wire ties.

The cement mixture was one part Portland cement to two parts masonry sand. Just enough water was added to cause the cement to form over the surface. As the cement was plastered on, the form was revolved and the shaping and smoothing edge adjusted in place. The side walls were built up to about ¾″ and the rotation of the form continued until the cement would hold in place. In about a week the inside core was removed and the vertical sections loosened and pulled out. The Art Department used the jar for art models. When the vacation period arrived, the jar was put near the entrance of the building where it remained until some years later when vandals broke it in pieces.

The process was never used again and I thought no more about it until Naval Architects during World War II began to design seagoing craft made by the ferro-cement process. Now the process is quite common and small craft are being built of ferro-cement all over the country.

No detailed directions for sculpturing the Diplodocus are included in this chapter. The technique is merely providing a surface to which the cement will stick and hold fast. Of course, this surface must be made strong, especially in boatbuilding. The design for the Diplodocus includes a long neck stretching out and upward from the body. The steel in this part of the body should be designed like a bridge strut, strong and rigid. The cast head on the author's model weighed about 200 pounds. To balance this weight so far out from the body required very strong construction.

The Diplodocus shown here measures 40′ long and is only half-size. It was an immense animal in real life. The accompanying photographs (Figs. 1 and 2) should provide the necessary information concerning the method of construction. Some study should be given to the ferro-cement process if the technique is not already understood.* The cement is not only abrasive to the fingers, but caustic. The fingers are soon worn to the quick unless a pair of latex gloves (cut down to hand size) are used. One pair of gloves will be sufficient. A wheelbarrow may be used to mix the cement—three buckets at a time: 1 part Portland cement and 2 parts masonry sand. Use only enough water to make the mixture plastic and trowelable. Spread it on with a definite, steady pressure so that the cement will penetrate the inner two layers of mesh and "tongue over." If possible, another person should be on the inside to trowel out this surplus, forming a professional surface.

The top elevation of the Diplodocus should be laid out on the ground where the sculpture is to be located. Give it a reptilian curve which is gradually reversed toward the head. Swing the long tail around near the body and give it natural waves. To preserve this shape, the author used 2″ x 6″ x 12′ yellow pine boards set upright next to the central plane. The boards were set in concrete, but enough space was left in the holes so that they could be

*See Bibliography.

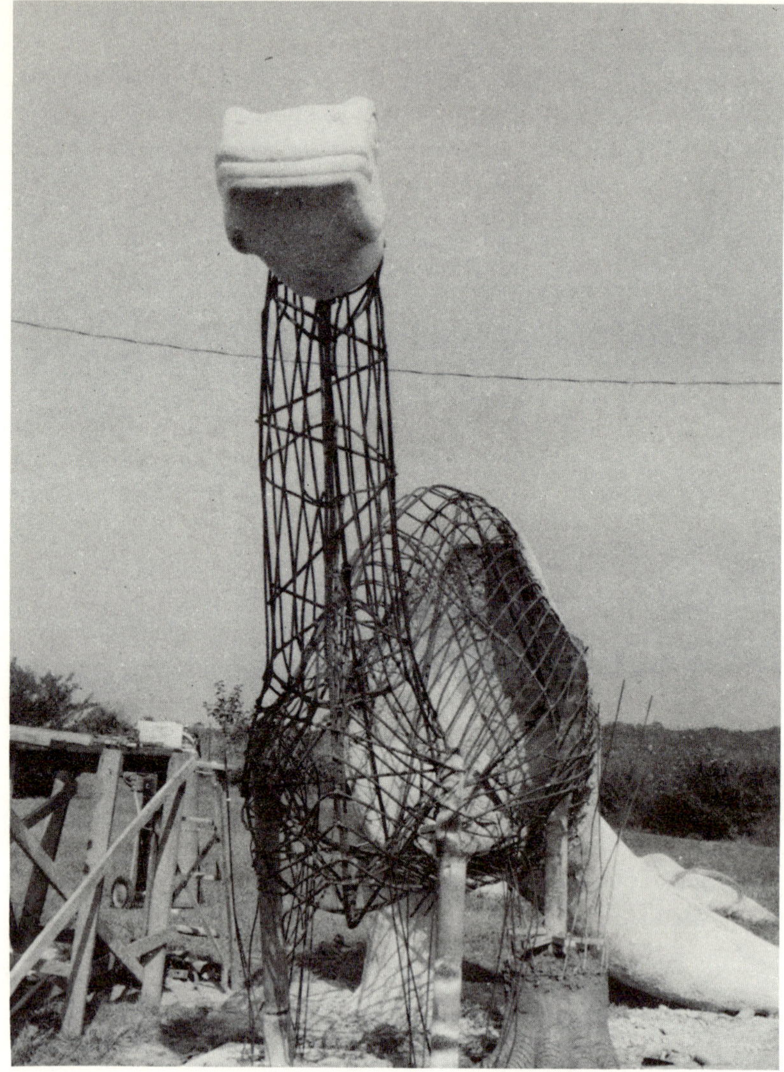

Fig. 1. Front view of Diplodocus showing cast head in place. Three-inch black pipe sections form the center of the legs. The hip section and tail have been plastered. The tail is not straight but is swung around the body in natural waves.

Bars forming the silhouette are 5/8″ in diameter. Other outline bars are 1/2″ in diameter. The bars on which the mesh is stretched and tied are 3/8″ in diameter, welded 4″ apart.

cut off later below the surface of the ground. This method will not only control the design, but provide a strong footing for the scaffolding and greatly assist in bending the heavy bars to shape.

The bars should be bent to shape and electrowelded in place by two individuals. The 5/8″ concrete reinforcing bars should be used to form the silhouette design. Be sure your curves are "clean" and natural. Of course, the frame sections should be designed and constructed first. Figure 3 shows the method of construction of the larger sections. Considerable care should be given to this operation so that when the bars are welded in place there will be no holes and hills in the surface. These sections should be located and fastened temporarily to the 2 x 6 uprights. The author found that leaving the bottom ends free to move in or out would provide convenient flexibility in the smaller sections of the neck and tail. (The vertical dimension has already been established.) When all of the sections have been formed and welded in place, the "skin" bars may be welded on, 4" apart.

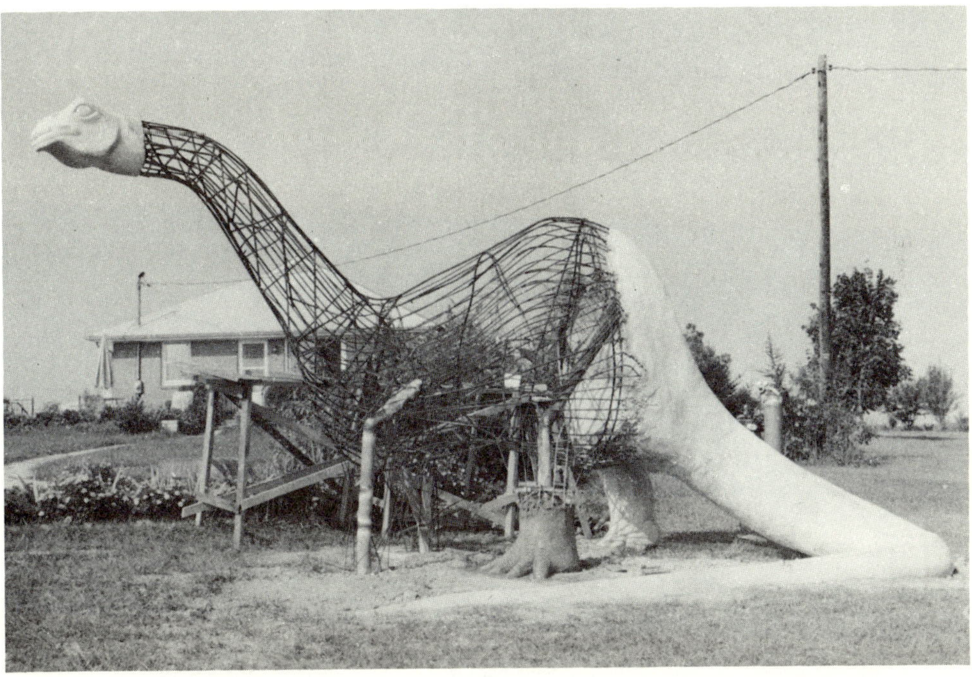

Fig. 2. Side view of Diplodocus showing steel skeleton of 5/8", 1/2", and 3/8" bars. Baby-chick wire mesh was stretched and tied to the 3/8" bars with 14 g. wire. Two layers of mesh were fastened to both the inside and outside of the 3/8" bars. The 3/8" bars were welded 4" apart.

The head of the author's model was first carved in white cedar and used as a pattern to mold the concrete form in which the head was cast in cement. As there are two areas of negative surfaces, one above the eyes and the other under the jaws, two cores were cast in these specific locations before the two halves of the form were poured. Floor wax was used to coat the surfaces to prevent the new cement from sticking. The two halves should pull free of pattern and cores after they have set for several days.

After the forms have been pulled free, their surfaces should be coated with a heavy layer of floor wax. Be sure the cores are in their proper locations before pouring the new cement to form the head. Four ½" bars should be properly bent to be cast in the walls of the head. A sheet-metal core should be constructed to prevent the cement from filling in the center and to provide a form to make the walls of the head uniform (they should average about 3″ in thickness). The ½″ bars should protrude from the neck of the head about 6″ so that the head may be welded strongly to the neck of the model. Of course, the head may be sculptured to the frame like the rest of the body, but there is less chance of satisfactory results. However, a good sculptor can do the trick and probably with better results.

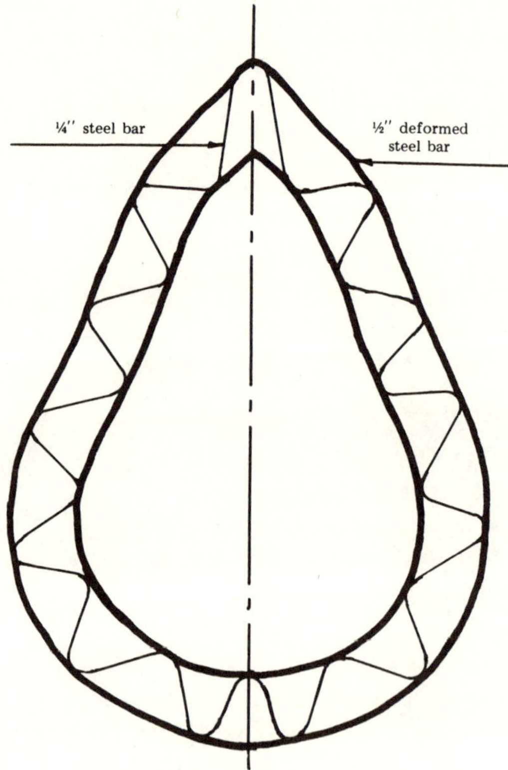

Fig. 3. Construction design of transverse mid-section of Diplodocus.

After the 3/8″ bars have been welded in place, two layers of baby-chick wire should be stretched and fastened in place on the inside. Then two more layers on the outside. Many, many 14 g. wire ties will be necessary for this operation. Be sure the tie ends do not project above the surface, and that the surface contours are flowing and smooth.

A manhole should be located in the belly, large enough to accommodate a man of average size. This manhole serves two purposes: (1) To allow the hot air to escape, and (2) to allow use of the inside of the sculpture for various purposes. With luck, a pair of owls may select the Diplodocus for their new home.

Portland cement No. 3, mixed with two parts masonry sand, was used to plaster the framework. The mixture should be plastic enough to trowel smoothly, but heavy enough to hold in place. As stated before, two persons should work together in this operation, one on the inside and the other on the outside. Curves which do not quite conform to the design may be plastered out or corrected. Locations like the neck should be plastered in a continuous operation so that the cement will have no parting surfaces.

The color of dinosaurs or the texture of their skin can only be conjectured. Hawkins conceived the skin to be bumpy as in some modern lizards, but most modern artists paint the skin comparatively smooth. A rule of the thumb should follow either of two lines of reasonings: (1) Paint them according to the color scheme of modern lizards; (2) paint them according to nature's way of protecting her creatures. Blend them in with their environment. As the Diplodocus was a vegetable-eating animal, its camouflage would be green, brown, and some other colors sympathetic to its environment. Rex Terraneous, a meat-eating monster with teeth six inches long, probably was unable to locate his prey too easily. If a bumpy skin is desired, a hardwood roller should be turned with the bumps gouged out in proper sequence so that when the roller is passed over the wet cement, a bumpy texture will result. If the plasterer is careful and skillful enough, a thin coat over the hexagonal-holed mesh will leave an imprint of the shape which is quite effective. The paint should be sprayed on and consist of a base compatible with the cement. A good latex paint will work nicely. A skillful painter with a spray outfit can blend the colors in a very interesting scheme. Several coats should be applied because the sculpture will be exposed to all sorts of weather conditions.

Sculpture a dinosaur. A Diplodocus is a good model but there are several others. The whole community will be interested in your project. Perhaps you can interest a Park Board, a Recreational Center, or some other organization in financing your model. A full-size animal will cost about $2,000.00—a lot of money, but well worth the investment. Remember the ferro-cement process—it is a good medium for large sculptures. The possibilities are unlimited.

Appendix

BIBLIOGRAPHY

Woodcarving and Sculpture

Acetylene Welding and Cutting. Order from Brookstone Co., Peterborough, N.H.

Austin, Oliver L., *Birds of the World;* Golden Press, New York (Illustrations by Arthur Singer).

Bingham, Bruce, *Ferro-Cement—Design, Techniques and Application;* Cornell Maritime Press, Inc., Cambridge, Md. 21613

Brunner, Frederick, *Manual of Wood Carving and Wood Sculpture;* Frederick Brunner, 369 High St., Westwood, Mass. 02090

Burk, Bruce, *Game Bird Carving;* Winchester Press, New York, N.Y. 10022

Fried, Frederick, *Artists in Wood;* Crown Publishers, New York 10016

Gilley, Wendell H., *The Art of Bird Carving;* Hillcrest Publications, Box 242, Heber City, Utah 84033

Graveney, Charles, *Wood Carving for Beginners;* Watson-Guptill, New York, N.Y.

Hoffman, Malvina, *Head and Tails.* Out of print.

——, *Sculpture Inside and Out.* Out of print.

Kortright, F.H., *The Ducks, Geese, and Swan of North America;* Wildlife Management Institute, Washington, D.C.

Pinkney, Pauline, *American Figureheads and Their Carvers;* Kennikat Press, Inc., 90 S. Bayles Ave., Box 270, Port Washington, New York 11050

Robbins, Chandler S., Bertel Bruun and Herbert S. Zim, *Birds of North America;* Golden Press, New York, N.Y.

Rood, John, *Sculpture in Wood;* University of Minnesota Press, Minneapolis, Minn.

Slobodkin, Louis, *Sculpture, Principles, and Practices;* World Publishing Co., Cleveland, Ohio, and New York, N.Y. Excellent! Discusses all techniques.

Tangerman, E.J., *Modern Book of Whittling and Woodcarving;* McGraw-Hill, New York, N.Y.

Tawes, William I., *Creative Bird Carving;* Tidewater Publishers, Cambridge, Maryland 21613

Metal Sculpture

Googerty, Thomas F., *Decorative Wrought Iron Work;* Manual Arts Press, Peoria, Ill.

Metal Sculpture (Continued)

Kronquist, Emil F., *Metalwork for Craftsmen;* Dover Publishing Co., Inc., 180 Varick St., New York, N.Y. 10014

Rood, John, *Sculpture with a Torch;* University of Minnesota Press, Minneapolis, Minn.

Catalogs

Albert Constantine and Sons, 2050 Eastchester Road, Bronx, N.Y. 10461

Art Mart, Inc., Clayton, Mo. (Large selection of supplies including jewelry findings.)

Arts and Crafts, 321 Park Ave., Baltimore, Md., or 9520 Baltimore Ave., College Park, Md. 20740

Brookstone Co., Dept C., 11 Brookstone Bldg., Peterborough, N.H. 03458

Buck Bros. Riverton Works, Millbury, Mass. (Tools.)

Craftsman Wood Service Co., 2727 S. Mary St., Chicago, Ill. (Tools, veneers, and wood.)

Foredom Electric Co., Bethel, Conn. 06801 (Flexible shaft tools.)

Frank Mittermeir, Inc., 3577 E. Tremont Ave., P.O. Box 2, Bronx, N.Y. (Excellent tools.)

Three Springs Fisheries, Lilypons, Md. 21717 (Fish pool supplies.)

U.S. General Supply Corp., 100 General Place, Jericho, N.Y. 11753 (Tools.)

Woodcraft Supply Corp., 71 Canal St., Boston, Mass. 02114

Glass Eyes

J.W. Elwood, 1202 Harney St., Omaha, Neb. 68102

M.J. Hoffmann Co., 963 Broadway, Brooklyn, N.Y. 11221

Jewelers' Supplies

Grieger's, Inc., 900 S. Arroyo Pky., Pasadena, Cal. 91109

Rock Haven Art Metal Co., Box 8, Whitefield, N.H. 03598

Sculpture Supplies

Ettl Studios, Inc., Ettl Art Center, Glenville, Conn. 06833

Sculpture Associates, 114 East 25th St., New York, N.Y.

Sculpture House, 38 East 30th St., New York, N.Y. 10016

Magazines

Chip Chats Magazine, of National Woodcarvers Association, Edward F. Gallenstein, Ed., 7424 Miami Ave., Cincinnati, Ohio 45234

Body Fillers

Martin-Senour Co., Chicago, Ill. 60608 Manufactures Pay Day, Blue Moon, and others.

Oatley Co., Cleveland, Chicago, San Jose, Cal. Manufactures White Diamond, White Tiger, Bondtight.

See local automotive supply stores.

Branding Irons

Norcraft, P.O. Box 277, 9 Short St., South Easton, Mass. 02375

Woodworking Tools

Frog Tool Co., 548 N. Wells St., Chicago, Ill. 60610

Woodcraft Supply Corp., 313 Montvale Ave., Woburn, Mass. 01801

Ferro-Cement Products

Aladdin Products, Inc., R.D. No. 2, Wiscasset, Maine 04578 manufactures a wire plank system composed of eight straight wire groups in continuous lengths. A composite produced with wire plank is FER-A-LITE. It is said to be superior to the Portland cement process.

Index